State Power

State Power
A Strategic-Relational Approach

BOB JESSOP

polity

First published in 2007 by Polity Press
Reprinted 2010, 2012

Polity Press
65 Bridge Street
Cambridge CB2 1UR, UK

Polity Press
350 Main Street
Malden, MA 02148, USA

ISBN-13: 978-07456-3320-6
ISBN-13: 978-07456-3321-3 (pb)

A catalogue record for this book is available from the British Library.

Typeset in 11.25/13 pt Dante
by Servis Filmsetting Ltd, Manchester
Printed and bound by the MPG Books Group

For further information on Polity, visit our website: www.politybooks.com

For my students, past, present, and future

Contents

List of Boxes, Figures, and Tables

List of Abbreviations

18B	*Eighteenth Brumaire of Louis Bonaparte*
CPE	cultural political economy
ISA	ideological state apparatus
KWNS	Keynesian Welfare National State
MLG	multi-level governance
OMC	open method of coordination
RSA	repressive state apparatus
SRA	strategic-relational approach
SWPR	Schumpeterian Workfare Post-national Regime

Acknowledgements

Many people have contributed, wittingly or otherwise, to the writing of this book. Because the strategic-relational agenda has been developed over some thirty years and has undergone a very uneven, zigzag development, it is difficult to recall all the intellectual debts incurred at different times over this period. The most important influence in the last few years has been Ngai-Ling Sum – especially regarding the arguments about time-space governance, the nature of post-disciplinarity, and cultural political economy. At the risk of neglecting those who have made significant contributions through their *ad hoc* informal comments and sustained written work, I would like to record inspirational conversations with Henrik Bang, Neil Brenner, Simon Clarke, Alex Demirović, Jupp Esser, Norman Fairclough, Jerzy Hausner, Colin Hay, Joachim Hirsch, Martin Jones, Michael Krätke, Gordon MacLeod, Jamie Peck, Moishe Postone, and Andrew Sayer. In addition, at different times, the following friends and colleagues have shaped some of the ideas in this book: Ash Amin, Jens Bartelson, Ulrich Beck, Robert Boyer, Gerda Falkner, Steve Fleetwood, Edgar Grande, Jamie Gough, Ray Hudson, Jane Jenson, Sven Kesselring, Rianne Mahon, Andrea Maihofer, David Marsh, Frank Moulaert, Yoshikazu Nakatani, Pun Ngai, Mark Neocleous, Claus Offe, Stijn Oosterlynck, Joe Painter, Ramon Ribera-Fumaz, Birgit Sauer, Alvin So, George Steinmetz, Rob Stones, Erik Swyngedouw, Gunther Teubner, Nik Theodore, Adam Tickell, Helmut Willke, Ruth Wodak, and Erik Olin Wright. I would like to acknowledge the support from Alvin So and his colleagues (especially Frida Ching) at Hong Kong University of Science and Technology for their friendly support over recent years and, in particular, for providing an excellent office with superb views over Clearwater Bay and an endless supply of green tea during the penultimate stages of writing. Bob Muir diverted me on our cycle rides. My editors at Polity Press, Emma Hutchinson and Louise Knight, displayed exemplary patience with the delays in submitting the typescript, and two anonymous referees (plus Ramon Ribera-Fumaz) made excellent recommendations on how to put the different chapters in their place. Justin Dyer provided excellent and eagle-eyed service and advice during the preparation of the typescript for publication and more than lived up to his reputation as one of Polity's best free-lance copy-editors. I dedicate this book to the changing group of scholars from whom I have drawn the most inspiration from day to day and from whom I have learnt so much through our joint intellectual endeavours: my graduate students.

Bob Jessop, Lancaster, 25 May 2007

General Introduction

The first and most difficult task confronting analysts of the state is to define it. For the state is a complex phenomenon and no single theory or theoretical perspective can fully capture and explain its complexities. States and the inter-state system provide a moving target because of their complex developmental logics and because continuing attempts to transform states and the state system leave their own traces in turn on their forms, functions, and activities. Theorizing the state is further complicated because, despite recurrent tendencies to reify it as standing outside and above society, there can be no adequate theory of the state without a theory of society. For the state and political system are parts of a broader ensemble of social relations and one cannot adequately describe or explain the state apparatus, state projects, and state power without referring to their differential articulation with this ensemble. This calls for a distinctive type of theoretical orientation that can take account not only of the state's historical and institutional specificity as a distinctive accomplishment of social development but also of its role as an important element within the overall structure and dynamic of social formations. It is just such an approach to the paradox of the state and state power that is elaborated in the present book, an approach that treats the state apparatus and state power in 'strategic-relational' terms.

The strategic-relational approach (hereafter SRA) starts from the proposition that the state is a social relation. This elliptical statement, first proclaimed by Nicos Poulantzas, requires extensive unpacking. Indeed, the strategic-relational approach in its state-theoretical application could be described as the meta-theoretical, theoretical, and empirically informed process of elaborating the implications of this initial proposition. Thus it is an ongoing project rather than a finished product, and the changing nature of the state and state power continues to generate new theoretical and empirical problems for strategic-relational analysts to address. However, while the SRA as presented below originated in critical engagement with debates about the state, it has a much wider field of application – one that is potentially co-extensive with social relations and, indeed, the increasingly complex interactions between the human and natural worlds. This book does not apply the strategic-relational approach so expansively – even though an adequate critique of political ecology (itself a small, if significant, part of this potential field) would certainly require serious examination of humankind's changing interactions with nature. Instead it explores the development of the SRA regarding state theory and critical political economy and its subsequent extension as a heuristic to social relations in general. It follows that the SRA is presented and elaborated below in a very uneven manner. Thus I present the overall *strategic-relational heuristic* in *relatively abstract-simple terms* through some basic ontological propositions with limited empirical content, with the result that the dialectical form of the argument takes precedence over the substantive content. In contrast, the *strategic-relational analysis* of the state, state power, and political economy more broadly is developed through a much richer set of increasingly substantive concepts as the argument moves towards more *concrete-complex* accounts (for the methodological principles informing this argument, see Jessop 1982: 211–20; 2002a: 91–101; see also M.J. Smith 2000).

What is the State?

No definition of the state is innocent because, as the strategic-relational approach itself implies, every attempt to define a complex phenomenon must be selective (for one review of attempts to define it, see Ferguson and Mansbach 1989). Moreover, as Bartelson remarks about attempts to define the state:

> If we accept that the state concept is foundational and constitutive of scientific political discourse, we should not be surprised to find that it cannot easily be subjected to the practices of definition [i.e., making stipulations about its meaning and reference within a given context of employment and according to given criteria], since the term state itself figures as a positive and primitive term in the definitions of other, equally central, concepts. This is what makes clarification both seem so urgent and yet so difficult to achieve. Hence, and as a consequence of its centrality, the concept of the state cannot be fully determined by the character of its semantic components or by its inferential connections to other concepts, since it is the concept of the state that draws these components together into a unity and gives theoretical significance to other concepts on the basis of their inferential and metaphorical connections to the concept of the state, rather than conversely. (2001: 11)

These problems of centrality and ambiguity, of the foundational nature of the state for political discourse and the constitutive nature of definitions of the state for political imaginaries and political practice, pose real difficulties for a rigorous analysis of the state. Indeed the variety of attempts to solve (or dissolve) them could be used to organize a critical review of state theory. They raise interesting questions about historical semantics as the concept of the state emerged hesitantly in the early modern period and was then selected and consolidated as an organizing concept of political practice in the high early modern period (cf. Luhmann 1990e; Skinner 1989). They also pose serious questions for historians, political geographers, and social scientists concerned with the process of state formation and transformation and with political practices oriented to the state both in Europe (where the 'modern state' first arose) and in other historical-geographical contexts. The same problems occur in more prosaic forms in everyday discourses, ordinary politics, and routine statal practices (cf. Bratsis 2006; Painter 2006). I consider these first.

Everyday language sometimes depicts the state as a subject – the state does, or must do, this or that. Sometimes it treats the state as a thing – this economic class, social stratum, political party, or official caste uses the state to pursue its projects or interests. But the state is neither a subject nor a thing. So how could the state act *as if* it were a unified subject, and what could constitute its unity as a 'thing'? And how do social actors come to act *as if* the state were a real subject or a simple instrument? Coherent answers are hard because the state's referents vary so much. It changes shape and appearance with the activities it undertakes, the scales on which it operates, the political forces acting towards it, the circumstances in which it and they act, and so forth. When pressed, a common response is to list the institutions that comprise the state, usually with a core set of institutions with increasingly vague outer boundaries. From the political executive, legislature, judiciary, army, police, and public administration, the list may extend to education, trade unions, mass media, religion, and even the family. Such lists typically fail to specify what lends these institutions the quality of statehood. This is hard to do because, as Max Weber famously noted, there is no activity that states always perform and none that they have never performed (1948: 77–8). Moreover, what if, as some theorists argue, states are inherently prone to fail in the tasks they undertake? Should the features of failing or failed states (ignoring for the moment the typically ideological construction of this term in contemporary political discourse) be included as part of the core definition of the state or treated as contingent, variable, and eliminable? Does a theory of the state require a theory of state failure? Finally, who are the principals and who are the agents in the activities that states undertake? Are the principals restricted to 'state managers', or do they include top advisers and other direct sources of policy inputs? Likewise, where does the boundary lie between (a) state managers as principals and (b) state employees as routine agents or executants of state programmes and policies? And do the agents include union leaders involved in policing incomes policies, for example, or media owners and media workers who circulate propaganda on the state's behalf?

An obvious escape route from these problems is to define the state in terms of its formal institutional features and/or the foundational instruments or mechanisms of state power. The *Allgemeine Staatslehre* (general state theory) tradition pursues the first approach. It focuses on the articulation of three key features of the state: state territory, state population, and state apparatus (e.g., Heller 1992; Jellinek 1921; Oppenheimer 1908; Schmitt 1928, 2001; Smend 1955; and for commentary, Kelly 2003; Stirk 2006). Max Weber largely follows the second approach. This is reflected in his celebrated definition of the *modern* state as the 'human community that (successfully) claims the *monopoly of the legitimate use of physical force* within a given territory' (Weber 1948: 78, parenthesis and italics in original; cf., more elaborately, 1978: 54–6). Yet other definitions highlight the modern (especially Westphalian) state's formal sovereignty *vis-à-vis* its own population and other states. This does not mean that modern states exercise power largely through direct and immediate coercion – a sure sign of crisis or state failure. For, where state power is regarded as legitimate, it can normally secure compliance without such recourse. Indeed, this is where the many state-theoretical traditions concerned with the bases of political legitimacy and/or social hegemony are so important in exploring the character of the state projects that endow the state with some institutional and operational unity as well as the nature of the societal projects that define the nature and purposes of government in relation to the social world beyond the state and/or inter-state systems. Nonetheless, organized coercion is a legitimate last resort in enforcing decisions. Even when blessed with political legitimacy, of course, all states reserve the right – or claim the need – to suspend the constitution or specific legal provisions and many also rely heavily on force, fraud, and corruption and their subjects' inability to organize effective resistance. Indeed, for theorists such as Carl Schmitt, it is the effective power to declare a state of emergency that defines the locus of sovereignty within the state system (Schmitt 1921, 1985; for a critique, see Agamben 2004).

Another solution is to regard the essence of the state (pre-modern as well as modern) as the territorialization of political authority. This involves the intersection of politically organized coercive and symbolic power, a clearly demarcated core territory, and a relatively fixed population on which political decisions are collectively binding. The key feature of the state would then become the historically variable ensemble of technologies and practices that produce, naturalize, and manage territorial space as a bounded container within which political power can be exercised to achieve various, more or less well-integrated, more or less changing policy objectives. Nonetheless a system of territorially exclusive, mutually recognizing, mutually legitimating national states exercising formally sovereign control over large and exclusive territorial areas is a relatively recent institutional expression of state power that is historically contingent rather than an inevitable and irreversible result of social development (Teschke 2003, 2006). The existence of such an inter-state system is also the source of the increasingly artificial division between domestic and international affairs (Rosenberg 1994; Walker 1993). This is reflected in recent debates about the future of the national territorial state and attempts to define emergent forms of political organization of a statal, semi-statal, or non-statal character. For other modes of territorializing political power have existed, some still co-exist with the so-called 'Westphalian system' (allegedly established by the Treaties of Westphalia in 1648 but realized, as Teschke notes, only stepwise during the nineteenth and twentieth centuries), new expressions are emerging, and yet others can be imagined. Earlier modes include city-states, empires, protectorates, enclaves, the medieval state system, absolutism, and modern imperial-colonial blocs. Emerging modes that have been identified, rightly or wrongly, include cross-border regional cooperation, a new medievalism, supranational blocs (e.g., the EU), a Western conglomerate state, and an embryonic world state. Nonetheless, while state forms shape politics as the 'art of the possible', struggles over state power also matter. State forms have been changed before through political activities and will be changed again.

While there are significant material and discursive lines of demarcation between the state *qua* institutional ensemble and other institutional orders and/or the lifeworld, the SRA emphasizes that its apparatuses and practices are materially interdependent with other institutional orders and social practices. In this sense it is socially embedded. Indeed, as Tim Mitchell argues,

> The state should be addressed as an effect of detailed processes of spatial organization, temporal arrangement, functional specification, and supervision and surveillance, which create the appearance of a world fundamentally divided into state and society. The essence of modern politics is not policies formed on one side of this division being applied to or shaped by the other, but the producing and reproducing of this line of difference. (1991: 95; on the construction of sovereignty, see also Bartelson 1995)

These detailed processes also divide the globe fundamentally into *different* states and societies and thereby create a more or less complex inter-state system within an emerging world society.

The manner in which these divisions are drawn, reproduced, and changed influences political processes and state capacities. These are always strategically selective. First, although the state apparatus has its own distinctive resources and powers, which underpin its relative autonomy, it also has distinctive liabilities or vulnerabilities and its operations depend on resources produced elsewhere in its environment. Second, state structures have a specific, differential impact on the ability of various political forces to pursue particular interests and strategies in specific contexts through their control over and/or (in)direct access to these state capacities – capacities whose effectiveness also depends on links to forces and powers that exist and operate beyond the state's formal boundaries. Third, the nature and extent of the realization of these capacities-liabilities – hence the nature and impact of state power – depend on the structural relations between the state and its encompassing political system, on the strategic ties among politicians and state officials and other political forces, and on the complex web of structural interdependencies and strategic networks that link the state system to its broader social environment. Together these considerations imply that, from a strategic-relational perspective, the state's structural powers or capacities, their structural and strategic biases, and their realization do not depend solely on the nature of the state as a juridico-political apparatus – even assuming its institutional boundaries could be precisely mapped and prove stable. They also depend on diverse capacities-liabilities and forces that lie beyond it. Putting states in their place like this does not exclude (indeed, it presupposes) specifically state-engendered and state-mediated processes. It does require, however, that they be related both to their broader social context and to the strategic choices and conduct of actors in and beyond states (Jessop 1990b, 2002d).

States do not exist in majestic isolation overseeing the rest of their respective societies but are embedded in a wider political system (or systems), articulated with other institutional orders, and linked to different forms of civil society. A key aspect of their transformation is the redrawing of the multiple 'lines of difference' between the state and its environment(s) as states (and the social forces they represent) redefine their priorities, expand or reduce their activities, recalibrate or rescale them in the light of new challenges, seek greater autonomy or promote power-sharing, and disembed or re-embed specific state institutions and practices within the social order. This holds for the international as well as national dimensions of state relations. The state's frontiers may display a variable geometry and its temporal horizons regarding the past, present, and future are also complex. There are also continuing attempts to redesign its institutional architecture and modes of working to enhance state capacities to achieve particular political objectives.

Two conclusions follow from this. First, we must recognize that the distinction between the state apparatus and the wider political system makes a real difference and is defined (and redefined) both materially and discursively. Thus analysing its constitution and its effects is an important task for the SRA. Second, it is important to accept the idea implicit in systems theory that the political system is self-substituting: that is, that a crisis in the political system leads normally not to its demise but to its reorganization. Clearly a fundamental part of such reorganization is the redefinition (or restructuring) of the forms of institutional separation between the economic and political systems and their relationship to the lifeworld, and, in this context, the redefinition of the 'line of difference' between the state and the political system. This is especially clear for the European Union insofar as it is a polity in the course of (trans)formation and this process is being contested by many different social forces. Indeed, as chapter 9 shows, the process of state formation in Europe provides a real-time experiment in the complexities and contingencies of state formation.

This suggests that an adequate theory of the state can only be produced as part of a wider theory of society, and that this wider theory must give due recognition to the constitutive role of semiosis in organizing social order. Even the neo-statists' principled rejection of a society-centred approach depends critically on arguments about the wider society both to reveal the state's distinctive logic and interests and to explore the conditions for its autonomy and effectiveness. Foucauldian, feminist, and discourse-analytic studies clearly have wider concerns too (see chapter 1). It is precisely in the articulation between state and society, however, that many of the unresolved problems of state theory are located. For the state involves a paradox. On the one hand, it is just one institutional ensemble among others within a social formation; on the other, it is peculiarly charged with overall responsibility for maintaining the cohesion of the social formation of which it is merely a part. Its paradoxical position as both part and whole of society means that it is continually called upon by diverse social forces to resolve society's problems and is equally continually doomed to generate 'state failure' since so many of society's problems lie well beyond its control and may even be aggravated by attempted intervention. Many of the differences between theories of the state considered above are rooted in contrary approaches to various structural and strategic moments of this paradox.

Trying to comprehend the overall logic (or, perhaps, 'illogic') of this paradox could be a fruitful route to resolving some of these differences as well as providing a more comprehensive analysis of the strategic-relational character of the state in a polycentric social formation.

In this context it should be noted that 'societies' (or, better, 'imagined human communities') can be dominated by different principles of societal organization (*Vergesellschaftung*) associated with different projects and priorities (e.g., economic, military, religious, political, social ranking, cultural). This will be reflected in the state as a key site where social power relations may be crystallized in different forms (Mann 1986) and, indeed, where struggles over these principles of societal organization are often conducted because of the part–whole paradox in which the state is so heavily implicated. Thus a state could operate principally as a capitalist state, a military power, a theocratic regime, a representative democratic regime answerable to civil society, an apartheid state, or an ethico-political state. There are competing principles of societalization linked to different functional systems and different identities and values anchored in civil society or the lifeworld, and, in principle, any of these could become dominant, at least for a while. There is no unconditional guarantee that the modern state will always (or ever) be essentially capitalist – although exploration of state forms may indicate certain strategically selective biases in this regard. Moreover, even where capital accumulation is the dominant axis of societalization by virtue of structural biases and/or successful political strategies, state managers typically have regard to the codes, programmes, and activities of other functional systems and the dynamic of the lifeworld in their efforts to maintain a modicum of institutional integration and social cohesion within the state's territorial boundaries and to reduce external threats. But such structural coherence and social cohesion is necessarily limited insofar as it depends on one or more spatio-temporal fixes to displace and/or defer the effects of certain contradictions and lines of conflict beyond its (or their) socially constituted spatio-temporal boundaries and action horizons. Different kinds of fix exist and they depend in various ways on specific forms of government, governance, and meta-governance ('governance of governance') (Jessop 2002d, 2004f, 2006b, 2006c).

Even these few preliminary remarks should have revealed the complexity of the state. They also imply that no definition can be given once-and-for-all; rather, the state will be redefined continually as the analysis unfolds. Moreover, as theoretical and empirical research on the state continues, whatever the initial starting point, as the analysis moves from the abstract-simple to the concrete-complex there could be an increasing overlap in concepts, arguments, and analysis in the case of progressive research paradigms or an increasing decomposition and incoherence as anomalies and exceptions emerge (on this distinction among research programmes, see Lakatos and Musgrave 1970). My previous work has been especially concerned to develop a coherent set of concepts with comparable ontological depth and complexity in order to facilitate a concrete-complex critique of political economy.

A Preliminary Definition of the State

Given the preceding remarks, I will now define the state in terms of a 'rational abstraction' that must be re-specified in different ways and for different purposes as a strategic-relational analysis proceeds. In short, in order to initiate the analysis rather than pre-empt further exploration, the *core of the state apparatus* can be defined as a distinct ensemble of institutions and organizations whose socially accepted function is to define and enforce collectively binding decisions on a given population in the name of their 'common interest' or 'general will' (cf. Jessop 1990b: 341). This broad definition identifies the state in terms of its generic features as a specific form of macro-political organization with a specific type of political orientation; it also indicates that there are important links between the state and the political sphere and, indeed, the wider society. Thus not all forms of macro-political organization can be classed as state-like nor can the state simply be equated with government, law, bureaucracy, a coercive apparatus, or another political institution. Indeed this definition puts the contradictions and dilemmas necessarily involved in political discourse at the heart of work on the state. This is because claims about the general will or common interest are a key feature of the state system and distinguish it from straightforward political domination or violent oppression (contrast Tilly 1973). This approach can also serve as a basis for describing specific states and political regimes and exploring the conditions in which states emerge, evolve, enter into crisis, and are transformed. A particular benefit of this initial cluster definition is its compatibility with diverse approaches to the analysis of the state and with recognition of what Mann (1986) terms the polymorphous crystallization of state power associated with alternative principles of societalization.[1]

This said, six qualifications are required if this multidimensional definition is to be useful in orienting a strategic-relational research agenda:

1 Above, around, and below the core of the state are found institutions and organizations whose relation to the core ensemble is uncertain. Indeed

the effective integration of the state as an institutional ensemble pursuing relatively coherent polices is deeply problematic and generates different governmental rationalities, administrative programmes, and political practices oriented to achieving such integration. Moreover, while statal operations are most concentrated and condensed in the core of the state, they depend on a wide range of micro-political practices dispersed throughout society. States never achieve full closure or complete separation from society, and the precise boundaries between the state and/or political system and other institutional orders and systems are generally in doubt and change over time. In many circumstances this ambiguity may even prove productive in pursuit of state policies. Similar problems emerge in relation to inter-state relations in the emerging world political system.

2 The nature of these institutions and organizations, their articulation to form the overall architecture of the state *qua* institutional ensemble, and its differential links with the wider society will depend on the nature of the social formation and its past history. The capitalist type of state differs from that characteristic of feudalism, for example;[2] and political regimes also differ across capitalist social formations.

3 Although the socially acknowledged character of its political functions for society is a defining feature of the normal state, the forms in which this legitimacy is institutionalized and expressed will also vary. Indeed the whole point of describing such political functions as 'socially acknowledged' is to stress that their precise content is constituted in and through politically relevant discourses. Here lies the significance of contested discourses about the nature and purposes of government for the wider society and the relationship of these discourses to alternative hegemonic projects and their translation into political practices.

4 Although coercion is the ultimate sanction available to states, they have other methods of enforcement to secure compliance. Violence is rarely the first resort of the state (especially in consolidated capitalist societies), and it would often prove counterproductive. A full account of the state must consider all the means of intervention at its disposal, their capacities and limitations, and their relative weight in different contexts. This is especially important, as chapter 9 shows, for evolving forms of statehood in an increasingly interdependent world society.

5 The society whose common interest and general will are administered by the state should no more be interpreted as an empirical given than should the state itself. The boundaries and identity of the society are often constituted in and through the same processes by which states are

built, reproduced, and transformed. Indeed it is one of the more obvious conclusions of the state-centred approach that state- and nation-building are strongly influenced by the emergent dynamic of the emergent international system formed through the interaction of sovereign states. An effect of globalization and its associated relativization of scale is the increasing difficulty of defining the boundaries of any given society – to the extent that some theorists claim that only one society now exists, namely, world society (Luhmann 1982b, 1997; Richter 1996; Stichweh 2000). Interestingly, the tendential emergence of world society reinforces the importance of national states in many areas of social life (Meyer et al., 1997).

6 Whatever the political rhetoric of the 'common interest' or 'general will' might suggest, these are always 'illusory' insofar as any attempt to define them occurs on a strategically selective terrain and involves the differential articulation and aggregation of interests, opinions, and values. Indeed, the common interest or general will is always asymmetrical, marginalizing or defining some interests at the same time as it privileges others. There is never a general interest that embraces all possible particular interests (Jessop 1983). Indeed, a key statal task is to aid the organization of spatio-temporal fixes that facilitate the deferral and displacement of contradictions, crisis-tendencies, and conflicts to the benefit of those fully included in the 'general interest' at the expense of those who are more or less excluded from it. This in turn suggests clear limits to the possibility of a world state governing world society because this would exclude a constitutive outside for the pursuit of a 'general interest' or require a fundamental shift in social relations to prevent social exclusion.

In listing these six preliminary qualifications, I hope to have indicated the limitations of starting analyses with a general definition of the state that is presented once-and-for-all and is never re-specified as the analysis unfolds. It is said that Marx was once asked why he did not begin *Capital* with a definition of the capitalist mode of production and that he replied that the whole of *Capital* was concerned with this topic. It would only be possible to provide such a definition at the conclusion of the work. Apocryphal or not, such a response would have been very apt for any request to define the state at the outset of this study. We will certainly return to this topic when we provide more detailed accounts of the state from different theoretical perspectives and, later still, present some strategic-relational analyses of contemporary states.

'Putting This Book in Its Place'

This is my fifth book directly concerned in one way or another with developing and applying a strategic-relational approach to the analysis of the state. My theoretical reflections on the state began in the mid-1970s as part of the revival of West European Marxist interest in the state in capitalist societies and have now provided the guiding thread of my intellectual project for more than three decades. I did not set out to develop a strategic-relational approach. Yet it has become an important heuristic perspective for my contributions to the critique of political economy and for addressing more general issues in the social sciences (for a well-informed and sympathetic account of this development, see M.J. Smith 2000). The driving force behind its development is a still incomplete project: to write a theoretically informed critical history of the changing political economy of post-war Britain and, in particular, to put the transformation of the British state into its broad economic, political, and socio-cultural context. This project provided the initial 'knowledge interest' for my work in state theory and, while the preparatory theoretical work often seems to have acquired an enchanted (and enchanting) life of its own, this continuing project has also prompted many of the twists and turns in my later theoretical investigations.

The first book in this strategic-relational series, *The Capitalist State: Marxist Theories and Methods*, was published in 1982. It reviewed the various approaches of Marx and Engels to the analysis of the state, how they were deployed, and their overall development, and then explored the three main methodological approaches to theory construction in subsequent Marxist analysis. *Subsumptionist essentialism* was illustrated from Marxist-Leninist theories of state monopoly capitalism that treated different cases as just so many empirical illustrations of the overall validity of a set of general propositions. *Logical derivation* was investigated via West German theories that sought to derive the necessary form and functions of the capitalist type of state from Marx's critique of the economic categories of capitalism. And the *method of articulation*, with its emphasis on contingent necessities and social practices, was analysed through the work of Gramsci and three of his post-war interpreters – Poulantzas, Laclau, and Mouffe – who explored the relative autonomy of the state in terms of expanded concepts of politics and the struggle to articulate a national-popular hegemonic project to secure the political, intellectual, and moral leadership of the dominant class(es). The book concluded by rejecting the idea of a general theory of the capitalist state (let alone of the state in general). Instead, it offered some methodological and substantive guidelines for the analysis of the state as a concrete-complex object of inquiry (1982: 211–59). These guidelines and their elaboration were based on a 'relational' approach (1982: 252) that has continued to inform my subsequent analyses. The core of this approach was its focus on 'the relations among relations', that is, 'an analysis of the relations among different relations comprising the social formation' (1982: 252). Accordingly, after presenting the guidelines for a relational approach to the state, the concluding chapter developed their implications for the more general analysis of structure, conjuncture, power, identity, subjective and objective interests, and strategic action. Chapter 1 discusses these guidelines and their implications in more detail and also comments on their initial reception.

My next major intervention in state theory was a monograph concerned with just one theorist. *Nicos Poulantzas: Marxist Theory and Political Strategy* (1985a) provided an exhaustive account of Poulantzas's intellectual biography in terms of successive steps in his theoretical development and political activities, and the impact on this development of often surprising shifts in the course of political events in his native Greece and adopted French homeland. After many years of study and at least three major shifts in theoretical orientation, Poulantzas claimed to have discovered the mystery of the Marxist theory of the state in his elliptical proposition that the state is a social relation. His last three books and associated outputs marked successive attempts to develop this intuition. However, while his insight and its subsequent elaboration are hugely significant (and not just for Marxist approaches to the state), Poulantzas's claim to have completed the Marxist theory of the state was certainly misleading. For his account was elaborated largely in and through a set of theoretical and historical reflections that covered many different topics rather than in a systematic movement from abstract-simple to concrete-complex. In this sense, his work was concerned to develop some core propositions in what I termed a distinctive 'relational theory' (in contradistinction to Poulantzas's earlier 'regional theory'[3]), and to apply these in some arguments about the state and politics in general, the capitalist type of state and bourgeois politics in particular, and the transformation of contemporary capitalism and the rise of authoritarian statism. Poulantzas never codified these propositions and arguments in one coherent statement and even the first principles of his 'strategic-theoretical approach' had to be reconstructed from a close symptomatic reading of his work. This probably reflected two facts. First, as he himself noted, no theorist is ever completely contemporary with his/her theoretical development with the effect that more time for reflection would have been required for him to have attempted a full systematization of its current stage of development – by which time, of course, the theory would already have been undergoing further changes. And, second, because actually existing states are so complex and changing (as the relational approach indicates in its rejection of any general theory of the state), any attempt at a rigorous, systematic, and complete analysis would be doomed to fail. This is why my critical exploration sought only to clarify some basic implications of Poulantzas's relational approach to the state and to introduce some additional middle-range concepts to facilitate the transition from abstract-simple to more concrete-complex analyses of the state apparatus and state power.

Some of these concepts were deployed in a co-authored book that falls outside the series under discussion – a set of interventions on the periodization of Thatcherism as a social movement, political project, accumulation strategy, state project, and hegemonic vision, and its implications for the economic transition from Fordism to post-Fordism, the restructuring of the British state, and the growing inequality in a society polarized into 'two nations' (Jessop et al., 1988, 1990; and Jessop 1980, 1989a, 1992a, 2002c). The critique of other positions and our own interpretation of Thatcherism were strongly informed by the strategic-theoretical approach (as it was then called). In particular, it applied some important middle-range concepts derived from Poulantzas's theoretical studies, his analyses of exceptional regimes (including Nazism, Italian fascism, and the Southern European military dictatorships), and his identification of increasing signs of exceptionalism in contemporary liberal democratic regimes. This work has continued with further explorations of the Major Government and the continued consolidation and extension of neo-liberalism under New Labour (cf. Jessop 2003a, 2004e, 2006a).

The third book in the SRA series proper was *State Theory: Putting the Capitalist State in Its Place* (1990b). As the subtitle indicates rather elliptically, this study sought to locate the form and functions of the state within capitalist social formations as a whole. Its various chapters developed the strategic-theoretical approach through (a) critical re-evaluations of recent contributions to Marxist state theory and the partly Marxist-inspired regulation approach in political economy; and (b) an exploration of structure–strategy dialectics in other types of state theory, including mainstream historical sociological and political scientific attempts to 'bring the state back in', recent work in systems theory, especially theories of self-organizing (or autopoietic) systems, and further developments in discourse analysis. In turn this book marked a departure from its precursors because it included, alongside critiques of other approaches, original studies directly concerned to develop some new strategic-theoretical arguments. In particular, it explored the implications of the argument that the state is a social relation that can be analysed as the site, the generator, and the product of strategies (1990b: 260). In short, this book marked an important transition in the movement from the critique of other contributions to state theory towards the elaboration of an original strategic-theoretical approach.

Following this work my attention turned towards a strategic-theoretical analysis of the profit-oriented, market-mediated economy typical of capitalist social formations. This adopted the same general heuristic as my work on the state but developed a different (but commensurable) set of substantive concepts suited to capital accumulation rather than political domination in analogous terms to those that had been developed for the state. This was partly a response to criticisms of 'politicism', that is, the one-sided concern with the political at the expense of the economic, in the critique of political economy, and partly an attempt to provide strong economic foundations for analysing the state's role in the crisis of Fordism and the transition to post-Fordism. These studies bore fruit in the fourth book in the series, *The Future of the Capitalist State* (2002d). This marked an even more radical move away from commentary on other theorists to provide my own strategic-relational (as it was finally called) analysis of recent and continuing economic and political restructuring in advanced capitalist social formations. The introduction to this book presented a relatively unified and minimum set of form-analytical, strategic-relational concepts for describing accumulation regimes, modes of regulation, and state projects and for analysing contemporary transformations in the state in terms of four key moments of state restructuring: economic and social policies broadly defined, re-scaling, and changing modes of governance. This monograph remains my most systematic presentation of a strategic-relational, form-analytical analysis to date but it is self-evidently more concerned with the structural than strategic dimensions of the transformation. This reflects the attempt to explore the formal and functional adequacy of the emerging state form rather than to explore its historical development on a case-by-case basis, for which serious engagement with the changing balance of forces would be required. Nonetheless, a key feature of *The Future of the Capitalist State* has been taken much further in current work in the field of cultural political economy, in which discursivity and agency acquire a far more central role (see Jessop and Oosterlynck 2007; Jessop and Sum 2001, 2006; Jessop 2004b; Sum 2002, 2003, 2005; Sum and Jessop 2006; Sum and Pun 2005).

It remains to explain what a fifth book might add to these studies in advancing the strategic-relational research agenda in state theory. The answer is found in five new contributions in *State Power*. Specifically, this book:

- reviews the development of the strategic-relational approach, beginning with reflections on state theory, generalizing the SRA to basic issues of structure and agency, growing concern with the spatio-temporal aspects of structure and agency, and increasing integration of the discursive (or, better, semiotic) moment of structure–agency dynamics;
- extends my critiques of basic trends and problems in Marxist state theory to other theoretical approaches and more recent emerging issues to show how strategic-relational themes seem to have arisen independently in quite different theoretical contexts, thereby indicating that the SRA may have a more general applicability grounded in basic ontological problems of social life rather than in the peculiar concerns of historical materialism;
- presents strategic-relational readings of 'classic' state-theoretical texts and/or bodies of work by Marx, Gramsci, Poulantzas, and Foucault with a view to developing further strategic-relational arguments and concepts;
- applies the strategic-relational approach to some familiar themes where it has not previously been applied: the gender selectivities of the state, the significance of globalization for the transformation of the state, its temporal sovereignty, and the changing nature of European statehood;
- grounds the SRA in complexity, complexity reduction, and semiosis, and also notes some of its implications for future research on the state.

These contributions are reflected in the overall organization of the book. Chapter 1 introduces the intellectual and political background to the strategic-relational approach (or SRA) and its principal intellectual and theoretical sources. This may provide useful context for readers to understand how and why it has been developed but it cannot, of course, establish the adequacy, let alone the validity, of the approach itself. Indeed, as the SRA has developed, its principal concepts and arguments have been disentangled from the immediate theoretical and historical contexts in which they were developed, and I and others have engaged in serious efforts to make them more generally applicable. Nonetheless my particular application still tends to combine the general approach with concepts drawn from geographical historical materialism (cf. Harvey 1982) and other concepts relevant to my specific areas of interest. The chapter then presents four partially overlapping phases in the development of the SRA in my own work as new theoretical problems were identified, either in general terms or in relation to my attempts to understand the development of Britain's post-war political economy from social democracy to Thatcherism and, most recently, New Labour. These problems emerged through variable combinations of criticism, self-reflection, and self-criticism.

Chapter 2 critically reviews some basic approaches to the state and thereby updates and extends analyses and arguments presented much earlier in *State Theory* (1990b). It is especially concerned to identify emerging issues that the strategic-relational approach is well equipped to address and/or that provide major challenges to be addressed in its subsequent development. In addition, for those unfamiliar with this complex field, this chapter serves as a general introduction to some key themes in post-war state theory and provides useful context for the more detailed, often strongly focused, analyses in later chapters.

Chapters 3 to 6 present re-readings of some major texts and approaches in political economy and state theory from a strategic-relational perspective in order to draw conclusions that are relevant to further development of the strategic-relational approach. These chapters are representative of a wider range of such strategic-relational readings that include other major theorists, such as Louis Althusser (Jessop 2007e), Manuel Castells (Jessop 2002d, 2003b), Anthony Giddens (Jessop 1989b, 2005), Stuart Hall (Jessop et al., 1988; Jessop 2002c, 2004e), Michael Hardt (Jessop 2003b), David Harvey (Jessop 2004g, 2006b), Ernesto Laclau (Jessop 2007b), Niklas Luhmann (Jessop 1990b, 1992b, 2001b, 2007a), Ralph Miliband (Jessop 2007c), Chantal Mouffe (Jessop 2007b), Tony Negri (Jessop 2003b), Karl Polanyi (Jessop 2001b, 2007d), and Saskia Sassen (Jessop 2003b). Each of these encounters has added something to the development of the strategic-relational approach and, I hope, has revealed something surprising and interesting about the work of those criticized. The four theorists chosen for inclusion in this book are those whose work has had the strongest positive impact on my development of the SRA and where the latter in turn reveals significant new aspects of the text or body of work concerned. Thus I explore Marx's famous text on *The Eighteenth Brumaire of Louis Bonaparte* (1852), the spatialization as well as historicization of political concepts in Gramsci's political writings and prison notebooks, the emergence of the strategic-relational approach and its increasing significance in the work of Nicos Poulantzas, and the concepts of governmentality and statecraft in the work of Michel Foucault. There is a risk of circularity in this procedure, of course, but I believe that the exercise has produced new results. Readers must judge whether or not this confidence is misplaced.

Chapters 7 to 9 illustrate in turn how the SRA can be applied to three topics that are somewhat removed from the theoretical issues through which it was originally developed and that will therefore provide interesting test cases of the value-added of the approach. Each of them originates in invitations from scholars who had not previously worked with the SRA and who, indeed, were not necessarily favourable to historical materialism. The chapter on gender selectivities, for example, originated in a challenge from feminist theorists in Germany to show that the strategic-relational approach was relevant to their concerns (see Jessop 1997a, 2001c). It has since been expanded in the light of further reading in the rich body of feminist and queer-theoretical scholarship but is not completely updated. The general strategic-relational line of argument should be valid (or not) regardless of the most recent studies. In addition, a textbook currently in preparation will review the most recent contributions to feminist and queer analyses of the state and politics as well as examine key contributions to other approaches to state theory (Jessop forthcoming). The chapter on globalization has its roots in an invitation to develop a strategic-relational critique of theories about the impact of globalization on the future of the national state. Finally, the chapter on the European Union was begun in response to several requests from political scientists interested in controversies about its nature as a type of state or political regime. In each case the challenge to apply the strategic-relational has been very productive for my own understanding of the world and the results also seem to have had some resonance outside the fields in which Marxist state theory is usually closely followed.

Chapter 10 concludes these reflections and explorations on the strategic-relational approach. It presents a strategic-relational research agenda that points beyond the preceding chapters and has been specially prepared for this book. It aims to bring the different lines of argument together. For the different entry points adopted to present and develop the SRA in the different parts of the present work illustrate the problems involved in addressing a complex phenomenon – thus each part reveals something about the approach and its development and, together, they reveal far more without, however, exhausting all of the possibilities. For this reason the concluding chapter is intended not as the final statement about the strategic-relational approach but as a further contribution to a continuing research programme.

Part I

Theorizing the State

1

The Development of the Strategic-Relational Approach

The primary focus of my work since 1975 has been the critique of political economy. This has involved both theoretically informed and theoretically informative studies of three interrelated themes: first, the dynamic of the profit-oriented, market-mediated economies associated with the capitalist mode of production; second, the capitalist type of state and, more generally, the nature of politics in societies dominated by capitalist relations of production; and, third, the path-dependent structural coupling between these economic and political orders and the limits to any and all efforts to coordinate them in order to shape the development of capitalist social formations. Although different themes have been pursued more intensely at different times, interest in the state and state power has been present from the beginning. Indeed my personal 'knowledge interest', to use Habermas's term (1987), in this long-term project is the origins, trajectory, crisis, and subsequent structural transformation and strategic reorientation of the type of state that was beginning to emerge in Britain during the immediate post-war years. Thus my original project, first envisaged over thirty years ago, was to write a critical political economy of post-war Britain. While this has been achieved only in part, I hope to complete it within the next ten years. There have been many detours on the way, some necessary, some accidental, as the problems involved in producing a theoretically and empirically adequate historical analysis became evident. While beginnings may well be hard in scientific development, so are conclusions. For it is always possible to re-specify the problem to be explained to make it more concrete and more complex, thereby requiring the introduction of additional concepts, assumptions, arguments, stylized facts, and empirical details (see Jessop 1982, 2002a). Moreover, given the inexhaustible complexity of the real world, there are many alternative starting points for such a movement. It follows that an adequate explanation is also one that is aware of some of its blind spots and what is at stake in choosing one or another starting point from those available.

The general line of attack that I have been developing to address such problems and to advance the longer-term project can be described with the benefit of hindsight as a critical realist, strategic-relational, form-analytical approach that is pre-disciplinary in inspiration and post-disciplinary in practice. It is premised on a critical realist philosophy of social science, adopts a dialectical approach to the material and discursive interdependence of structure and strategy and their co-evolution, and draws on the concepts, assumptions, and arguments of many disciplines in order to provide totalizing (or integrative) accounts of particular problems without being committed to the idea that social reality comprises a closed totality. This approach can be applied to many types of problem, but the present work focuses on its implications for the nature of the state and state power. Thus it aims to present the basic outlines of this approach, especially its strategic-relational dimensions, in successive steps. This chapter presents the general background to the SRA and distinguishes its four overlapping phases of development to date.

Three Sources of the Strategic-Relational State Approach

The strategic-relational approach as understood and presented in this work was first introduced in connection with debates in state theory and, somewhat later, analogous debates in critical political economy more broadly. It was then extended to issues of structure and agency in general and their spatio-temporal aspects. More recently still, it has informed a new theoretical orientation that Ngai-Ling Sum and I describe as 'cultural political economy', thereby returning to the SRA's initial field of application but in more complex terms (see Jessop and Sum 2001; Sum and Jessop 2008). The successive application of the strategic-relational approach to state theory, political economy, social theory, and cultural political economy can be said to emerge from my successive exposure to three different intellectual influences. But this reading depends on the benefit of hindsight because no theorist can be completely contemporary with his or her own theoretical development. Lenin claimed there were three major sources of Marxism: German philosophy, English economics, and French politics (Lenin 1913). Louis Althusser, a French structuralist Marxist, added many years later that Marx's ability to synthesize them was rooted in his commitment to proletarian revolution (Althusser 1976). My work takes Marx's critique of political economy as a primary reference point (without, however, reading it in either orthodox Marxist-Leninist or Althusserian structuralist terms) and is therefore imprinted in a path-dependent manner by his three sources too. But it also has its own set of secondary sources. These can be described, in the spirit of Lenin's remark and only half-jokingly, as post-war German politics, post-war French economics, and post-war Chilean biology (see below). Moreover, alongside the intellectual issues that drew me to these particular sources, the peculiarities of post-war British history have also played their own role. For much of my work, as noted above, has been driven by the attempt to understand issues such as Britain's flawed Fordism, its Keynesian Welfare National State, the rise, consolidation, and subsequent crisis of Thatcherism, and the rise and trajectory of New Labour (for a first account, see Jessop 1980; for later work, see, e.g., Jessop et al. 1988; Jessop 2002c, 2002d, 2003a, 2006a).

German politics refers in this context to post-war German state theory. This influence emerged indirectly in the mid-1970s through the Conference of Socialist Economists in the United Kingdom and, in particular, its introduction – through interested members – of the German state debate to Anglophone readers. I soon pursued this source more directly through German-language texts and contacts with German theorists. Their influence is especially clear in my work on the changing forms and functions of the capitalist state, but it co-existed with the influence of Antonio Gramsci, a pre-war Italian Communist, who is particularly associated with the concepts of 'integral state' and hegemony, and Nicos Poulantzas, a post-war Greek Marxist theorist who was closely identified with interest in the capitalist state (Jessop 1977, 1982, 1985a; see also chapter 5). It was Poulantzas's influence that prompted some Marxist critics, notably Bonefeld, Clarke, and Holloway, to accuse me of 'politicism'. For them, this deviation accords primacy in theory and practice to the state and politics without grounding these in the capital relation and/or its associated class struggle. Above all, politicism is said to derive from taking for granted the separation of the economic and political institutional orders of modern societies rather than seeing them as deeply interconnected surface forms of capitalist social formations and, in this context, from focusing one-sidedly on the political realm to the detriment of these interconnections and the determining role of the capital relation *vis-à-vis* its economic and political moments considered in isolation. This leads in turn, it is claimed, to voluntarism in theory and practice because it focuses on the power of political action to transform the world (cf. Bonefeld 1987; Clarke 1977; Holloway 1988).

These were important challenges and, whilst I did not accept that Bonefeld, Clarke, and Holloway had characterized my work accurately, I did wonder how to analyse the economy in a manner consistent with my emerging 'strategic-relational' approach to the state. Initially my ideas developed through reading contemporary debates on the significance of the commodity form (with its dialectically interrelated use-value and exchange-value aspects) in the Marxist critique of political economy (Marx 1867) and re-reading Gramsci's work on Americanism and Fordism (Gramsci 1971). This led to my account of accumulation strategies as means of imposing a provisional, partial, and unstable 'substantive unity' on the various interconnected formal manifestations of the capital relation and thereby securing the conditions for relatively stable periods of economic growth. These ideas originated in an analogy between Gramsci's analyses of *lo stato integrale* (the integral state) and what I termed *l'economia integrale* (the integral economy). While Gramsci defined 'the state in its inclusive sense' as 'political society + civil society' and saw state power in Western societies as based on 'hegemony armoured by coercion', my strategic-relational account defined the 'economy in its inclusive sense' as 'an accumulation regime + social mode of economic regulation' and analysed capital accumulation as 'the self-valorization of capital in and through regulation'. This analysis was combined with interest in state projects and hegemonic visions and an attempt to ensure the commensurability of all three concepts within a strategic-relational approach (Jessop 1983).

These self-evidently neo-Gramscian concepts were later refined through my encounter with post-war *French economics* in the guise of the Parisian regulation school in institutional economics. This interest was reinforced through my membership of the organizing committee of the first International Conference on Regulation, which was held in Barcelona in June 1988. This enabled me to meet leading regulation theorists from all the main approaches (for a review originating from this conference, see Jessop 1990a). A sustained theoretical engagement with the work of different regulationist schools followed. In general, this approach provides specific institutional answers to the old Marxist question of how, despite its structural contradictions and class conflicts, capitalism can continue to expand for relatively long periods. It stresses that economic activities are socially embedded and socially regularized and that stable economic expansion depends on specific social modes of economic regulation that complement the role of market forces in guiding capitalist development. Unsurprisingly, the state has a key role in the mode of regulation, and I am particularly interested in regulationist work that explores its changing role in securing the extra-economic as well as economic conditions for capital accumulation and in institutionalizing class compromises that facilitate accumulation. This is reflected in my work on the crisis of Atlantic Fordism and the transition to post-Fordism and the possibilities of delineating a post-Fordist form of state analogous to the Keynesian Welfare National State. More generally my concern with regulation has evolved in dialogue not only with French economics but also with some German state theorists whose work on the state's changing forms and functions has also been informed by regulationism (see, most recently, Jessop and Sum 2006). This engagement with another German debate once again provoked strong criticisms, this time for taking Marxist state theory in a reformist direction and for confirming rather than resisting the transition to post-Fordism (Bonefeld 1994; Holloway 1988).

At the time I thought these reflections could provide a neo-Gramscian perspective on the economy (or, better, capital accumulation) analogous to that generated by the earlier strategic-relational argument that the state (or, better, state power) is a social relation. With hindsight, however, these reflections were also politicist, albeit in a different way, because they focused on the national state's role in formulating accumulation strategies and regulating capitalism. In this sense, this new approach was guilty of 'methodological nationalism' (Taylor 1996), even though it had begun to take seriously the economic moment of political economy. Indeed, it ignored not only political scales other than the historically constituted national territorial state and its associated national economy and national society, but also the role of firms, fractions of capital, and other economic, political, and social forces in developing alternative accumulation strategies. These problems have been addressed in my work on the political economy of scale, interscalar articulation, and, in particular, the significance of spatio-temporal fixes for securing such improbable outcomes as relatively stable capital accumulation, relatively coherent state action, and social cohesion in class-divided societies marked by other sources of social division and friction too (see, e.g., chapters 4, 8, and 9; see also Jessop 1999, 2003d, 2004g, 2007a).

Whilst working on regulation, I continued to reflect on the relative autonomy of the state and the problem of 'politicism' and began to consider their relation to the apparently autonomous logic of profit-oriented market forces. This posed interesting issues about how the economic and political orders, despite their formal institutional separation and their organization under different types of social logic, may come to be structurally coupled to produce a relatively unified 'historical bloc'. This is Gramsci's term for the mutually reinforcing correspondence between what classical Marxism conventionally describes as the economic base and its politico-ideological superstructure. At the same time I became interested in the conditions, if any, under which economic and political structures and operations can be coordinated strategically by a power bloc (comprising dominant class fractions and political elites) to guide economic and political development. These are important questions from a strategic-relational viewpoint and lend themselves to a strategic-relational inquiry.

Finally, as I was attempting to combine relevant concepts from German politics and French economics I came across *Chilean biology*, if not directly, at least through German social theorists, especially Niklas Luhmann, Gunther Teubner, and Helmut Willke (Luhmann 1982a, 1982b, 1986, 1989,1990b, 1990c, 1995; Teubner 1993; Willke 1983, 1986). From them I took the concept of 'autopoiesis' or 'self-production' and several related notions. Transposed (some would say illegitimately) from cell biology to sociology, autopoietic theory suggests that major societal subsystems (such as the economy, law, politics, and science) can be studied as self-referential, self-reproducing, and self-regulating. A close analogy can be found in Marx's analysis of the apparent self-closure and self-valorization of the circuit of capital that is enabled by the generalization of the commodity form to labour power (Marx 1867). Marx and Engels also described the modern legal system in similar terms (see especially Engels 1886). A key conclusion of autopoiesis theorists is that such systems function according to their own operational codes and programmes rather than obeying an external logic or being readily steered from outside. Despite the *operational autonomy* of these functional systems, however, they are *materially interdependent*. One consequence of this, which is especially important for a materialist-discursive strategic-relational approach, even though almost completely absent in the source theory, is the scope it creates for the logic of one system to dominate the overall development of what could be described as the self-organizing ecology of self-organizing systems (cf. Jessop 1990a: 327–33; 2007b, 2007f; and Schimank 2005).

Drawing on these ideas suggests that the 'historical blocs' formed through the reciprocal consolidation of economic, legal, political, and certain cultural institutions could be understood in autopoieticist terms. Thus they would derive from the interactions among (a) the path-dependent 'structural coupling' of several *operationally autonomous* but *substantively interdependent* subsystems, (b) the path-shaping efforts of economic, political, and other social forces to influence (or govern) the nature and direction of this co-evolution, and (c) the 'ecological dominance' of the market-mediated, self-valorizing capitalist economy. These arguments prompted me to propose that the orthodox Marxist concept of economic determination in the last instance can be fruitfully replaced by 'ecological dominance'. This refers to the capacity of one system in a self-organizing ecology of self-organizing systems to cause more problems for other systems than they can cause for it. Recontextualized in geographical historical materialism, it can provide a more rigorously strategic-relational concept that can resolve many of the problems associated with economic determinism (Jessop 1990b, 1992b, 2000a, 2002d, 2007b, 2007f). In contrast with the influence of German state theory and the French regulation approach, however, which provided concepts that were easily integrated into the strategic-relational approach to political economy, my engagement with autopoietic systems theory has been more problematic. For the effective integration of concepts from the theory of self-organizing systems into a critical realist, strategic-relational framework required far more work than was needed for the influence of German politics and French economics. Thus my work with this source might be dismissed from some perspectives as flirtatious, analogous to the mature Marx's identification with Hegel and his coquetting 'here and there . . . with the modes of expression peculiar to him' (Marx 1873: 29). But it actually goes beyond mere playfulness. For my autopoietic theories have 'irritated' me, as Luhmann might have put it, into a radical rethinking of some key concepts for a critique of political economy. This has required the disembedding of the source ideas from their autopoietic systems context and an effort to break with their autopoietic mode of expression so that they can be more adequately integrated in the strategic-relational approach.

It has also been claimed that Marx's ability to produce a creative synthesis from German philosophy, French politics, and English economics involved more than his capacity to develop boils on the backside by spending long days in the British Museum Library. It was due to his identification with the class struggle of the proletariat (Althusser 1976). In a more modest (and, for orthodox Marxist critics, reformist) context, my interest in combining arguments from German politics, French economics, and Chilean biology (or, more accurately, modern systems theory) to produce a new theoretical synthesis is grounded in commitment to the ideological and political contestation of Thatcherism and its neo-liberal New Labour successor. For it is this commitment that has shaped my continuing personal 'knowledge interest' in understanding the specificity of the multiple crises of post-war British political economy, the changing significance of the Thatcherite response, and its legacies in New Labour's neo-liberal policies and attempts to sustain them through additional flanking and supporting measures. Rather than reflect on the successive steps in the development of British politics, however, let me now outline instead the successive steps in the development of the SRA under their indirect influence.

The First Phase in the Strategic-Relational Approach

The first steps in the first phase of the development of the SRA long predate the interaction between these three sources and the related work of theoretical synthesis. They began with my initial engagement with the question of the state in the Essex State Theory Group (1975–8), for which I prepared a critical review of recent Marxist theories (Jessop 1977; reprinted in 1990b: 24–47). This concluded that

> their overall effect has been to redefine the problem of the state in capitalist society in a way that makes theoretical and political progress possible once more. They have dissolved the orthodox approaches in terms of the state as a thing or a subject that is external to the capitalist mode of production. In their place, they have focused attention on the social nature of capitalist production and its complex economic, political and ideological preconditions. This means that the state and state power must assume a central role in capital accumulation, even in those apparently counterfactual cases characterized by a neutral, laissez-faire state, as well as those where the state is massively involved in the organization of production. Moreover, because the state is seen as a complex institutional system and the influence of classes is seen to depend on their forms of organization, alliances, etc., it is also necessary to reject a crude instrumentalist approach. It is no longer a question of how pre-existing classes use the state (or the state itself acts) in defence of capitalism defined at an economic level. Henceforth it is a question of the adequacy of state power as a necessary element in the overall reproduction of the capital relation in different societies and situations. And state power in turn must be considered as a complex, contradictory effect of class (and popular-democratic) struggles, mediated through and conditioned by the institutional system of the state. In short, the effect of these studies is to reinstate and elaborate the idea that the state is a system of political domination. (1977: 371; 1990b: 45)

The Capitalist State (1982) elaborated this preliminary conclusion through an expanded critique of the substantive arguments associated with three methodological approaches to Marxist state theorizing: subsumption, derivation, and articulation. It also offered methodological remarks on each approach and concluded with an extended set of ontological, epistemological, methodological, and substantive remarks for a research agenda. In particular, it rejected attempts to develop a general theory of the capitalist state (let alone of the state in general) and, instead, offered four guidelines for analysing the state as a concrete-complex object of inquiry. The guidelines comprise the following: (1) the state is a set of institutions that cannot, *qua* institutional ensemble, exercise power; (2) political forces do not exist independently of the state: they are shaped in part through its forms of representation, its internal structure, and its forms of intervention; (3) state power is a complex social relation that reflects the changing balance of social forces in a determinate conjuncture; and (4) state power is capitalist to the extent that it creates, maintains, or restores the conditions required for capital accumulation in a given situation and it is non-capitalist to the extent that these conditions are not realized (1982: 221). Some fundamental substantive concepts for analysing the state's institutional architecture, its social bases, state projects, and the organization of hegemony were then elaborated on the basis of these guidelines.

This analysis was based on a 'relational' approach that focuses on 'the relations among relations', that is, 'an analysis of the relations among different relations comprising the social formation' (1982: 252). This approach had some fundamental implications, which I then presented, for the analysis of structure and conjuncture, structural constraints and conjunctural opportunities, the complex, overdetermined nature of power relations, the vital role of specific mechanisms and discourses of attribution in identifying the agents responsible for the production of specific effects within a particular conjuncture, the significance of specific capacities and modes of calculation in framing individual and collective identities, the relational and relative nature of interests, and the dialectical relation between subjective and objective interests (1982: 252–8). These concepts, principles of explanation, and general arguments also inform the SRA research agenda in the current concluding chapter.

These arguments imply that what is conventionally called 'power' is a complex, overdetermined phenomenon and can serve at best to identify the production of significant effects (i.e., significant or pertinent at the level of abstraction and degree of complexity in terms of which the explanandum is defined) through the interaction of specific social forces within the limits implied in the prevailing set of structural constraints. This means in turn that the 'contingency' of power compared to the 'determinacy' of structure rests on the fact that the conduct of the agents in question and, *a fortiori*, its effects in a given set of circumstances cannot be predicted from knowledge of the circumstances themselves. But it does not mean that power is indeterminate in terms of factors peculiar to the agents themselves and/or indeterminate in terms of the pattern of their interaction. In this sense the analysis of power is closely connected with the analysis of the organization, modes of calculation, resources, strategies, tactics, and so forth, of different agents (unions, parties, departments of state, pressure groups, police, etc.) and the relations among these agents (including the differential composition of the 'structural constraints' and 'conjunctural opportunities' that they confront) which determines the overall balance of forces.

It follows that the analysis of 'interests' must be concerned with comparative advantage rather than some notion of absolute interests posited in isolation from specific conjunctures. A situation, action, or event can be said to be in an agent's interest if it secures a greater net increase (or smaller net decrease) in the realization of that agent's conditions of existence than do any feasible alternatives in a given conjuncture. This implies that an agent's interests must be assessed in relation to the structural constraints and conjunctural opportunities obtaining in a given period. It implies that agents can face conflicts of interest such that a given situation, action, or event undermines at least some conditions of existence in at least some respects at the same time as it advances these and/or other preconditions in other respects. So we must always specify which aspects of an agent's interests are being (dis)advantaged rather than engage in blanket assertions about such matters. Moreover, insofar as an agent is involved in different relational systems and/or has been interpellated with different subjectivities or identities, there may be conflicts among the conditions of existence relevant to these systems and/or subjectivities with the result that the agent has no unitary and non-contradictory set of interests capable of realization. Indeed, the net balance of advantages for a given agent can change in parallel with variations in conjunctural opportunities and structural constraints and the same conjuncture can have different implications for interests if the manner in which the agent is interpellated is changed. Indeed a key area of ideological struggle consists in the redefinition and/or recombination of subjectivities and hence the interests that agents may have in various situations. This argument should help to clarify the manner in which a given 'hegemonic project' privileges certain particular interests compatible with its conception of the general interest and derogates other competing or contradictory particular interests.

There is a dialectical relation between subjective and objective interests. Objective interests must always be related to a particular subjectivity occupying a particular position in a given conjuncture; a particular subject can nonetheless miscalculate these interests since they are defined in terms of the conditions actually necessary for its reproduction rather than the subject's own views on these conditions. This dialectic also defines the limits within which one can legitimately attribute interests to other agents. For, whilst external 'interpretation' without regard to an agent's various subjectivities is unacceptable, we can argue 'interdiscursively' that commitment to a given subjectivity contradicts the realization of interests in another of the agent's identities. Examples of these oppositions might include Soviet man and democrat, housewife and woman, patriot and proletarian. Whereas the former approach is inherently authoritarian, the latter is at least potentially democratic.

These guidelines proved controversial in some quarters because they rejected the view that there is a fundamental ontological distinction between state power and class power. I was careful to note that the 'third guideline implies a firm rejection of all attempts to distinguish between "state power" and "class power" (whether as descriptive concepts or principles of explanation) insofar as they establish this distinction by constituting the state itself as a power subject and/or deny the continuing class struggle within the state as well as beyond it' (1982: 224–5). This guideline was based on the sound strategic-relational arguments that (a) the state is neither a unified subject nor a neutral instrument but an asymmetrical institutional terrain on which various political forces (including state managers) contest control over the state apparatus and its distinctive capacities; and (b) class power depends less on the class background of those nominally in charge of the state or their subjective class identities and projects than on the differential class relevance of the effects of the exercise of state capacities in a complex and changing conjuncture. This does not reduce state power to class power. Nor does it exclude the influence of the core executive, the military, parliamentary deputies, or other political categories in all their complexity in the exercise of state power or the determination of its effects. Nor again does it exclude that the state's role as a system of political class domination could sometimes be secondary to its role as a system of official domination over 'popular-democratic forces' or, indeed, secondary to its institutional mediation of the relative dominance of another principle of societalization (such as theocracy, 'racial' apartheid, or genocide). But such issues can only be adequately explored by refusing a radical distinction between state power and class power.

The hostility to this argument was (and remains) a measure of the continuing influence of the instrumentalist and subjectivist views of the state and the fetishistic treatment of the state as a separate entity that I had taken such pains to reject in *The Capitalist State*, and of the problems faced in persuading mainstream scholars of the virtues of treating the state as a social relation. I claimed no credit for developing this relational argument – it goes back at least to the arguments of Marx himself and it was also clearly elaborated by Gramsci and Poulantzas, and it is compatible with a long tradition of methodological relationalism in the social sciences. But much work was still needed to make the case for methodological relationalism in the field of state theory when this was being combined with historical materialist arguments about class power. In fact, my preparatory work for *The Capitalist State* involved work on the structural selectivity of bourgeois democracy (1978), corporatist arrangements (1979; see also 1985b, 1986), and the development of the British state, its structural biases, and its crises in the post-war period (1980). I also embarked on a detailed intellectual biography of Nicos Poulantzas, the Greek theorist who, on the basis of his own theoretical, historical, and contemporary analyses of the capitalist type of state, had first explicitly proposed that the state is a social relation. This played a crucial role in the next step from a 'relational orientation' to the strategic-relational approach.

This step involved a close examination of Poulantzas's theoretical progression from a structuralist framing of the question of the relative autonomy of the state and political region within capitalism (which, in Poulantzasian terminology, can be called a 'regional theory') to an analysis of the position of the state and the role of state power within the expanded reproduction of class relations (which, following Poulantzas's own claim to distinctiveness, I termed his 'relational theory') (Jessop 1985a: 53–146). These conclusions were strengthened by a critical exegesis of Poulantzas's changing ideas about social classes, ideology, exceptional regimes, and the changing nature of the normal form of the capitalist type of state (especially the rise of authoritarian statism) (Jessop 1985a: 149–283). On this basis it was possible to reconstruct the key principles of Poulantzas's relational theory and to begin the task of codifying them and drawing out their main implications for future work on the form and functions of the state in capitalist social formations (see chapter 5 below).

The most significant general conclusion from this study built on earlier statements of the relational approach but also shifted its focus from structural to strategic questions. This refocusing aimed to escape the false choices posed in West German debates over capital- and class-theoretical analyses and in Anglophone debates about structuralism and instrumentalism. Poulantzas had been engaged in the second of these debates on the side of structuralism through his critique of Miliband's cathartic analysis of the state in capitalist society (Miliband 1968, 1973; Poulantzas 1969, 1976d; see also Jessop 2007c). But Poulantzas seriously misrepresented his own position in round one and the next round was largely irrelevant to his emerging relational analysis of the capitalist type of state and the expanded reproduction of class domination. Accordingly I focused less on the outcome of this debate than on the new relational approach and its implications for both sets of debates. This is reflected in my conclusion that

> [f]or too long in Marxist state theory there has been a dichotomy between 'capital-theoretical' and 'class-theoretical' approaches. For the 'capital-theoretical' or 'capital logic' theorists, the *capitalist state* is the political support of the imperatives of capital accumulation. The form of the state

corresponds to the current stage in the development of the relations of production and its functions correspond to the current needs of bourgeois class domination. In addition the 'capital-theoretical' approach tends to work on the unstated assumption that there is only one logic of capital at any given stage of capitalist development. This means that there is only one set of imperatives. For the 'class-theoretical' analysts of *the state in capitalist society*, its form and functions reflect the changing balance of class forces in struggle. But class struggles themselves are analysed in more or less mechanical fashion with little regard for the distinction between economic-corporate or particular interests and the interests of capital (or the working class) in general. In turn this means that the 'class-theoretical' approach lacks any concern for the dialectical relation among these interests. Its proponents focus on specific struggles without regard to their implications for the overall reproduction of the social formation and/or take such reproduction for granted in focusing on questions of class hegemony at the most abstract levels of analysis.

Thus we are confronted with a false dilemma. Either we emphasize the abstract logic of capital with its iron laws of motion, that is, its structurally-inscribed tendencies and counter-tendencies. Or we concentrate on the concrete modalities of a class struggle considered in a purely empiricist manner and have no way of explaining how this class struggle tends to reproduce capitalism rather than produce a collapse into barbarism or a transition to socialism. Between the two approaches there is little attempt at mediation. Yet the notion of strategy seems ideally suited to this purpose.

'Strategic-theoretical' concepts can be employed to link these two modes of analysis. They can be used to dissolve the abstract, unitary, and essentialized laws of motion and needs of capital constructed by the capital logicians into a series of more concrete, competing, and contingent logics of capital. And they can be used to overcome the 'class-theoretical' tendency to focus on the concrete modalities of socio-economic struggles in such a way that *form* is neglected in favour of *content*. Yet the restriction of class struggles to specific forms (such as trade union struggle within the limits of market rationality or party political competition within the limits of bourgeois parliamentarism) is an important element in securing their compatibility with the expanded reproduction of bourgeois class domination. [Indeed,] these forms themselves represent, inter alia, the crystallisation of different class strategies and must be reproduced in and through class struggle. At the same time attention must be paid to how particular class-conscious and/or class-relevant struggles are related to more general problems of maintaining social cohesion under bourgeois hegemony. This requires one to go beyond particular struggles to see how different particular interests and concerns are coerced and/or hegemonies into conformity with a viable national-popular outlook and programme. In this context it must be realised that, just as there are alternative capital logics, so there can be alternative hegemonic projects. And, as Poulantzas indicated (if never fully explicated), hegemony must be seen in terms of its dual determination by structures and strategies.

Thus we could say that strategic concepts provide the 'middle-range' concepts needed to bridge the gap between the 'capital-theoretical' and 'class-theoretical' approaches. First, they provide the means to examine alternative *logics of capital*; and, secondly, they help to understand why the interplay among particular class struggles does not produce a collapse into 'barbarism'. In this context I would like to suggest that the alternative logics of capital should be examined in terms of competing *accumulation strategies* and that the field of class struggles should be examined in terms of competing *hegemonic projects*. In both cases it is essential to consider these phenomena from the dual perspective of *structural determination* and *class position*. In turn the moment of structural determination should be considered as the crystallisation or material condensation of past strategies (both successful and unsuccessful). Likewise the elaboration of class strategies (class positions) should be related to the constraints imposed by existing forms of class domination as well as the prevailing balance of forces. In the absence of this it would be impossible to distinguish adequately between strategies that are 'arbitrary, rationalistic, and willed' and those that stand some chance of becoming 'organic'. (Jessop 1985a: 343–5)

This extended conclusion aimed not only to highlight the one-sidedness of the respective poles in these debates but also to show that such unilateralism could not be overcome by oscillating between these positions to reveal their respective blind spots or by combining them mechanically to produce 'the complete picture'. It suggested instead that that the key to resolving the impasse was to emphasize not just that structure and agency were dialectically related but also that each moment in this dialectical relation contained elements from its 'other'. This had already been emphasized in the relational conclusions of *The Capitalist State* (1982) but was now elaborated in explicitly 'strategic-theoretical' terms inspired by Poulantzas's own 'strategic turn' (Jessop 1985a: 340–3). Indeed he was well aware of the need for strategic concepts to mediate between the abstract level of structural determination and the concrete modalities of the class struggle in specific conjunctures and had already begun to introduce concepts for the analysis of the strategically selective spatio-temporal matrices entailed in specific structural forms and for the analysis of the spatio-temporal horizons of different social forces. He also explored the implications of these issues for class polarization and class alliances, the formation of power blocs and popular mobilization, wars of manoeuvre and wars of position, and the appropriate balance between parliamentary and direct democratic mobilization.

The methodological conclusions to this study therefore focused on more strategically oriented analyses of economic, political, and ideological class domination, on class hegemonies and class strategies, and on the significance of strategic dilemmas for the action of class forces, parties, and social movements. But I also argued that this approach had been identified as 'strategic-theoretical' only in contrast to the 'capital-' and 'class-theoretical' approaches. It was certainly not exhausted by concepts of strategy and emphasized instead how a concern with strategy fundamentally transformed the other concepts in his analysis. And, just as the call for a general theory of the state was rejected in the conclusions of *The Capitalist State* (1982: 211–13), this new study argued equally that a general theory of strategy was unnecessary for a strategic-theoretical analysis (1985a: 354). These and other recommendations for moving beyond Poulantzas's theoretical approach are integrated into the research agenda in the conclusions to the present monograph.

The first phase in the development of the strategic-relational approach ended with the publication of *State Theory* (1990b). This consolidated the relational and strategic-theoretical arguments from earlier theoretical studies and from my work on the strategic selectivity of state forms in the transition from Fordism to post-Fordism. The major theoretical change in this work was its elaboration of arguments about the inherently strategic nature of the state into the claim that it was theoretically productive to regard the state as political strategy. For the state could be seen as the site, the generator, and the product of strategies (1990b: 248–72; see below). This argument was elaborated on the basis of critical exegeses of various non-Marxist as well as Marxist theoretical approaches, of work concerned not just with the state but also with middle-range studies of capital accumulation and its regulation, and of studies concerned with semiosis and historical semantics as well as with the specific features of modern (as opposed to capitalist) societies and their tendency towards increasing polycentrism due to the consolidation of many operationally autonomous functional systems with their own codes and programmes. There was also a minor change in the presentation of the approach insofar as it was now called the 'strategic-relational approach'. This label, which combined the relational orientation and the strategic-theoretical approach, had been suggested during informal discussions by René Bertramsen, who took my state theory course at Essex University in the late 1980s. He also codified some of the main method-ological guidelines for its application in a work co-authored with two other Danish students (Bertramsen 1991; more generally, see Bertramsen et al. 1991). I was pleased to adopt this new label and, for good or ill, it is now accepted by interested scholars to describe, endorse, or criticize this approach.

At this stage, the SRA was still primarily concerned with the state and politics and it combined general strategic-relational propositions with specific concepts for the analysis of state power as the material condensa-tion of a changing balance of forces. The two crucial concepts of this approach had become the structurally inscribed strategic selectivities of the state and the capacity of social forces to engage in strategic context analysis and pursue strategies that are more or less well adapted to these selectivities – including strategies oriented to circumventing and/or modifying their associated constraints. Specifically, three main arguments were advanced:

> First, the state system is the site of strategy. It can be analysed as a system of *strategic selectivity*, i.e., as a system whose structure and *modus operandi* are more open to some types of political strategy than others. Thus a given type of state, a given state form, a given form of regime, will be more accessible to some forces than others according to the strategies they adopt to gain state power; and it will be more suited to the pursuit of some types of economic or political strategy than others because of the modes of intervention and resources which characterize that system. . . . this notion of strategic selectivity is more fruitful than that of structural selectivity because it brings out more clearly the *relational* character of this selectivity. For the differential impact of the state system on the capacity of different class(-relevant) forces to pursue their interests in different strategies over a given time horizon is not inscribed in the state system as such but in the relation between state structures and the strategies which different forces adopt towards it. . . .
>
> Second, the state is also a site where strategies are elaborated. Indeed one cannot understand the unity of the state system without referring to political strategies; nor can one understand the activities of the state without referring to political strategies. Marxists often argue that the cap-italist state has an essential institutional and/or class unity but none of the reasons put forward for this are convincing. At best they establish the *formal* unity of the state system (e.g., as a sovereign state with a central-ized hierarchy of command) but this cannot guarantee its *substantive* operational unity. For the state is the site of class(-relevant) struggles and

contradictions as well as the site of struggles and rivalries among its different branches. This poses the problem of how the state comes to act, if at all, as a unified political force. It is here that the role of state managers (both politicians and career officials) is crucial for understanding how a relative unity is imposed on the various (in)activities of the state and how these activities acquire a relative autonomy from the conflicting pressures emanating from civil society. Thus we must examine the different strategies and tactics that state managers develop to impose a measure of coherence on the activities of the state. . . .

Third, the structure and *modus operandi* of the state system can be understood in terms of their production in and through past political strategies and struggles. These strategies and struggles could have been developed within that system and/or at a distance from that system; and they could have been concerned to maintain it and/or to transform it. In this sense the current *strategic selectivity* of the state is in part the emergent effect of the interaction between its past patterns of *strategic selectivity* and the strategies adopted for its transformation.[1] In turn the calculating subjects that operate on the strategic terrain constituted by the state are in part constituted by the *strategic selectivity* of the state system and its past interventions. (Jessop 1990b: 260–2)

It also follows that, as an institutional ensemble, the state does not (and cannot) exercise power; it is not a real subject (cf. 1977: 371; 1982: 221, 224–5). Indeed, rather than speaking about *the* power of the state, one should speak about the various potential structural powers (or state capacities), in the plural, that are inscribed in the state as an institutional ensemble. The state is an ensemble of power centres that offer unequal chances to different forces within and outside the state to act for different political purposes. How far and in what ways their powers (and any associated liabilities or weak points) are actualized depends on the action, reaction, and interaction of specific social forces located both within and beyond this complex ensemble. In short, the state does not exercise power: its powers (always in the plural) are activated through the agency of definite political forces in specific conjunctures. It is not the state that acts; it is always specific sets of politicians and state officials located in specific parts and levels of the state system. It is they who activate specific powers and state capacities inscribed in particular institutions and agencies. In doing so, they may well take account of the prevailing and, perhaps, future balance of forces within and beyond the state (including beyond its territorial borders as well as its domestic juridico-political boundaries). Moreover, as in all social action, unacknowledged conditions influence the success or failure of their actions and there are always unanticipated effects.

The Second Phase in the Strategic-Relational Approach

The first steps in the second phase of the SRA began during the first phase as I attempted to generalize its arguments from state theory to critical political economy more generally. Crucial intermediate steps were my growing interest in a relatively concrete-complex ('middle range') neo-Gramscian analysis of the economy in its inclusive sense and, soon afterwards, my growing engagement with the regulation approach and the scope for developing a strategic-relational analysis not only of the state but also of the capital relation itself. These efforts initially remained at a middle-range level but I returned over several years to Marx's analysis of the value form in order to re-ground the regulation approach in Marx's critique of political economy.

Marx was, of course, the first to emphasize that capital is not a thing but a social relation, that is, a relationship between people mediated through the instrumentality of things. It would be interesting at some future stage to reinterpret this critique of capital in strategic-relational terms. One aspect of this would be to revisit the fundamental contradiction in the commodity form between exchange- and use-value. This was the starting point for Marx to unfold the complexity of the capitalist mode of production and its dynamic and to show the necessity of periodic crises *and* their role in re-integrating the circuit of capital as a basis for renewed expansion. Building on these arguments, I suggested that all forms of the capital relation embody different but interconnected versions of this contradiction and that they impact differentially on (different fractions of) capital and (different strata of) labour at different times and places (Jessop 1983, 1999, 2000a, 2002d, 2004a). These contradictions are reproduced along with capitalism but do not keep the same weight or significance. In addition, as Poulantzas noted, 'the reproduction of these contradictions with their contradictory effects and their impact on the historical tendency of capitalist development depends on the *class struggle*' (1975: 40–1, italics in original). These claims have informed my efforts from the mid-1990s onwards to address the problem of politicism and, in particular, to reintegrate the analysis of economics and politics without conflating them or subsuming them under a generic logic of accumulation (see especially Jessop 2002d; and Jessop and Sum 2006).

Partly overlapping these regulation- and value-theoretical developments was an attempt to generalize the SRA to more general issues of structure and agency. This relationship is one of the long-standing and defining controversies of social inquiry and many attempts have been made to solve it.

I had already been reflecting on these issues, especially in relation to the multidimensional nature of power (e.g., Lukes 1974), to debates about power in Marxist theory (e.g., Isaac 1987), and what I regarded as the unwarranted popularity of Giddens's solution to the problem of structure and agency in his theory of structuration (Giddens 1984; for a useful introduction, see Parker 2000). But the attempt to generalize the SRA explicitly was occasioned by an invitation to review a book by Holmwood and Stewart on *Explanation and Social Theory* (1991). This work was a trenchant critique of the recurrent attempts of neo-Weberian theories of social action to transcend the inhuman positivism of the dominant schools of social thought through the development of a distinctive interpretivist methodology inspired by Max Weber. Holmwood and Stewart claimed that such efforts invariably culminated in a rediscovery of the pathos of human action trapped in the 'iron cage' of more encompassing social systems. They argued that the basic reason for this recurrent failure is the 'social scientific fallacy', that is, the belief that social scientists have privileged knowledge about the social world compared to lay actors. They illustrated this claim in a series of chapters that focus on recurrent dualities in abstract theories of social action: the distinction between rational and non-rational action; the alleged mutual entailment of action and structure; the antinomy of power as an antagonistic and coercive relation of domination and as a collectively produced normative order; the contradiction between the independence of different functional systems and their interdependence within the overall social order; and the status of (false) consciousness and ontological alienation.

For present purposes, their most important criticisms concern the structure–agency duality and the relation between structure and function. Regarding the former, Holmwood and Stewart argued that action theorists either tend to absorb agency and structure into each other with the result that it is unclear what each category includes or excludes; or else they assign these categories to different theoretical or empirical sites – which thereby justifies retaining the dualism rather than prompting efforts to transcend it. And, regarding the latter distinction, they suggest that it typically rests on a hierarchy of concepts that privileges the atemporal, abstract potentialities of reproducible structures that must provide the reference point for judging functionality over concrete behaviours marked by contingent strains and disturbances that then dysfunctionally disrupt the reproduction of these structures. This inevitably leads, they continue, to debilitating conflicts between general analyses of structure and context-specific analysis of (dys)functions. This problem is allegedly compounded when action theorists attempt to reconcile claims about the existence of a plurality of independent functional systems and recognition of their substantive interdependence.

My review endorsed this critique of neo-Weberian interpretivism but rejected its conclusion that abstract analyses of structure and agency should be abandoned in favour of concrete studies of how lay actors identified and sought to solve problems in everyday life. Specifically, I tried to show that the SRA provided the theoretical means to transcend these various antinomies and that the proposed strategic-relational solution should even elicit the approval of Holmwood and Stewart. For, in rejecting Lukes's self-styled 'dialectical' analysis of power as undialectical, they argued that a truly dialectical account must not only recognize the contradictoriness of its categories but also 'go on to consider how this affects their meaningfulness singly and together' (Holmwood and Stewart 1991: 115). So I tried to show that the SRA account of structure and agency adopted the self-same dialectical method that they had called for and that it could demonstrate 'how abstract theorizing has the potential to resolve even this basic dualism *in the abstract*' (Jessop 1996: 123).

> This possibly hubristic exercise involves a radical departure from sociological convention in dealing with the problem in so far as both categories [structure and agency] will be thoroughly relativized. Sociologists are wont to condemn the irreconcilable, and thus theoretically inadmissible, *dualistic dichotomy* of unconditional, absolute, external constraints and unconditional, wholly free-willed subjective action. They propose replacing it with the dualized conceptual couplet of an emergent, contingent, but still determining, social structure and the actions selected by more or less well socialized agents. In this theoretical agenda, external constraints are said to be produced in and through meaningful social action; and meaningful social action is said in turn to be oriented in and through socially shared and communicated values, norms, and modes of calculation. This is the stuff of sociology textbooks. At best it provides only a partial solution to the structure–agency dichotomy or dualism, however, because it has not yet been theoretically relativized to take account of specific agents and actions. It still inclines to treat social structure (now emergent) as constraining and determining regardless of the agents and actions subject to constraint; and, with its emphasis on the socialization of competent actors, it treats social action as being essentially rule-governed, repetitive and reproductive of structures, regardless of strategic contexts and orientations. In this sense, even if there is no longer a dichotomy that divides the social world into mind (free will) and matter (social facts), there is still a dualism in which structure and agency are supposed to be mutually reproductive and consistent. It is in criticizing this

dualism masquerading as a duality that Holmwood and Stewart are at their most effective.

This false duality links the two categories by counterposing structure (as rules and resources) to action (as concrete conduct) and / or regarding them as recursively reproductive of each other. Despite its counterposition of structure to action, this approach is still abstract; and, despite its ritual reference to recursivity, it remains atemporal. Yet a genuine duality can be created by dialectically relativizing (as opposed to mechanically relating) both analytical categories (see Figure 1.1). In this context, social structure can be studied in 'strategic-relational' terms as involving structurally inscribed strategic selectivity; and action can likewise be analysed in terms of its performance by agents with strategically calculating structural orientation. The former term signifies that structural constraints always operate selectively; they are not absolute and unconditional but are always temporally, spatially, agency- and strategy-specific. The latter term implies that agents are reflexive, capable of reformulating within limits their own identities and interests, and able to engage in strategic calculation about their current situation. A number of significant theoretical consequences flow from such a redefinition of the structure–agency relationship.

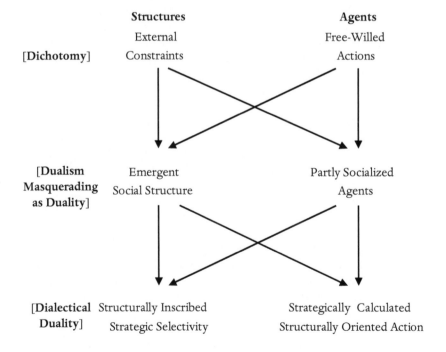

Figure 1.1 Structure–agency beyond structuration theory

First, the 'structural' moment in social relations is now seen to comprise those elements in a given temporal-spatial context that cannot be altered by a given agent (or set of agents) pursuing a given strategy during a given time period. The 'conjunctural' moment in turn will comprise those elements in a given temporal-spatial strategic context that can be modified.

Second, once such a 'strategic-relational' approach to the dual 'structural-conjunctural' character of strategic action contexts is adopted, conventional views of the structure–agency duality must be rejected. For this new approach implies that the self-same element(s) can operate as a structural constraint for one agent (or set of agents) and as a conjunctural opportunity liable to transformation by another agent (or set of agents). It also implies that a short-term structural constraint for a given agent (or set of agents) could become a conjunctural opportunity over a longer time horizon or even within the same time horizon if there is a shift in strategy. This in turn implies that agents may be able to pursue different types of alliance strategy and so modify the selective impact upon themselves and others of social structural constraints and opportunities. Likewise, regarding the spatial dimension of strategic contexts, this approach implies that, since agents may be able to operate across variable spatial scales as they also do across changing time horizons, spatial structural constraints and conjunctural opportunities will also be determined in a 'strategic-relational' manner. Thus, notwithstanding Holmwood and Stewart's generalized strictures against social action theory, it is possible to transcend an abstract, atemporal and unlocated account of structures and develop a context-specific conjunctural account that refers to determinate time-space horizons of action as well as to particular agents and actions. But this creative and resourceful solution requires an adequate account of the dialectic of structure and agency, i.e., serious consideration of how a strategic-relational approach to these twin phenomena 'affects their meaningfulness singly and together' (Holmwood and Stewart 1991: 115).

Third, in regarding actors as reflexive, strategically-calculating subjects oriented to the structural-conjunctural complexities of action contexts, the SRA implies that they reflect on their identities and interests, are able to learn from experience and, by acting in contexts that involve strategically selective constraints and opportunities, can and do transform social structures. If they consistently adopt such an approach, social action theorists will be readily sensitized to the potential creation of new resources, new rules and new knowledge with all that this implies for the rearticulation of constraints and opportunities. They will also be aware that actors might (re)formulate their strategies in the light of changing experience and knowledge about the strategic contexts in which they perform.

Fourth, if structures are seen as relativized and relational complexes of social constraints/opportunities, then the analysis of power will involve the attribution of responsibility to specific acts by specific agents for the realization of a specific range of effects in specific temporal and spatial horizons. If power involves an agent's production of effects that would not otherwise occur, it is essential both to identify the structural constraints and conjunctural opportunities confronting these agents and the actions that they performed which, by realizing certain opportunities rather than others, 'made a difference'. A strategic-relational approach nonetheless challenges orthodox accounts of power in two respects. It not only sees the exercise of power as an *explanandum* rather than as a *principle of explanation* but also radically relativizes it by treating it as an issue of attribution. For the scope of the explanandum will vary with the relative tightness of the spatial and temporal definition of the conjuncture in which particular agents 'made a difference' and of the field of possible effects and repercussions rippling out over social time and space. Moreover, if analysing power relations poses issues of attribution, i.e., identification of those social forces or actions allegedly responsible for realizing a specific set of effects, it also means absolving other forces of responsibility. But such analyses can be overturned by redefining the conjuncture in which an alleged exercise of power occurred (widening or further tightening its scope) and/or by focusing on the prior formation of the agents whose actions are alleged to have made a difference. This does not mean that individual actions do not 'make a difference' but it does undermine unqualified, non-contextualized talk about power. Nor does a strategic-relational approach mean that social forces cannot realize intended effects to a significant extent. For they may do so within a circumscribed context in which they can shape conjunctures and so constrain the actions of others. It goes without saying, of course, that the resulting repercussions will sooner or later escape not only the control but also the cognizance of the actors who set the scene for their initial realization (cf. Luhmann 1995; Matzner 1994).

In short, structures do not exist outside of specific spatial and temporal horizons of action pursued by specific actors acting alone or together and in the face of opposition from others. Likewise, actors always act in specific action contexts that depend on the coupling between specific institutional materialities and the interaction of other social actors. Strategic analysis can be taken still further if we allow for a measure of self-reflection on the part of some actors regarding the identities and interests that orient their strategies. For actors can and do reflexively remake their identities and the interests that follow therefrom in specific conjunctures. In turn, structural analysis can be taken further by investigating the path-dependent structural coupling and co-evolution of different operationally closed (or autopoietic) systems (cf. Luhmann 1995).

Does this approach avoid the problems identified by Holmwood and Stewart? I would claim that it does. First, it does not posit abstract, atemporal and unlocated structures or wholly routinized activities performed by 'cultural dupes'. Structures are irredeemably concrete, temporalized and spatialized; and they have no meaning outside the context of specific agents pursuing specific strategies. In this sense there is no abstract theory to be rendered inconsistent with concrete data about lay behaviour. Rather than seeking to resolve concrete-complex issues of practical action in specific conjunctures through abstract epistemological or methodological fiat, the 'strategic-relational approach' leaves these issues underdetermined on an abstract-simple level and permits their resolution through appropriately detailed conjunctural analysis. It is impossible to conceptualize structural constraints outside specific time horizons and spatial scales of action because any constraint could be rendered inoperable through competent actors' choice of longer-term and/or spatially more appropriate strategies. This very fact excludes any possibility of a general theory of social action of the kind so trenchantly criticized by Holmwood and Stewart. But, contrary to their own prescriptions in the guise of conclusions, it does not preclude worthwhile abstract theoretical reflections on the nature of the dialectical relationship between structure and agency. (Jessop 1996: 123–7)

These criticisms and arguments developed the general conclusions from the earlier works in the SRA series. Overall, they imply that, whether one looks at concepts such as 'structural constraint', 'power', or 'interests', it is always necessary to situate them in terms of the relations among social relations. Their meaning in specific conjunctures derives from the overall articulation of elements. Structural constraints comprise those elements in a situation that cannot be altered by agent(s) in a given time period and will vary according to the strategic location of agents in the overall matrix of the formation. This matrix involves a complex hierarchy of potential powers determined by the range and determinacy of opportunities for influencing elements that constitute constraints for other agents. This potential for power depends not only on the relations among different positions in the social formation but also on the organization, modes of calculation, and resources of social forces. In turn the actual balance of power is determined *post hoc* through the interaction of the strategies or actions pursued by these forces within the limits imposed through the differential composition of structural constraints. The interests advanced or harmed through the exercise of power must also be assessed relationally. For interests depend on the conjunctural opportunities in a given period and hence on the potential balance of power. All this has major implications for calculating political strategies over different time periods and also highlights the importance of a conjunctural, relational approach to such issues as the nature of state power (cf. Jessop 1982: 258).

This generalized strategic-relational heuristic has since been applied and extended in four contexts. First, it informed a critique and elaboration of the institutional turn and issues of spatio-temporal selectivity (Jessop 2001a). Second, it was used to critique Bourdieu's 'methodological relationalism', with its concern for the potential convergence of objective history and embodied history, habitat and habitus, position and disposition (Bourdieu 1981; Bourdieu and Wacquant 1992) as well as 'actor-network theory' as developed within science studies and subsequently applied to the analysis of the institution and reproduction of markets (Callon 1998a, 1998b, 1999; Callon and Latour 1981; Jessop 2004c).

Third, it has been critically compared and contrasted with other positions on structure and agency from the critical realist tradition within which the SRA itself is located. Critical realism is a philosophy of science (natural and social) that distinguishes between real structures (mechanisms, capacities, vulnerabilities), actual processes or events (the actualization of certain potentials), and empirical evidence (traces of these events) (Archer et al. 1998; Bhaskar 1978; Sayer 2000). In this context, the SRA is similar to Bhaskar's 'transactional mode of social analysis' (1989) and Archer's morphogenetic approach (1995). But it takes their analyses one or two stages further because of its emphasis on the double relativization of structure and agency (discussed above) and the scope it allows for structured coherence (and historical blocs) based on the recursive adaptation of strategically selective structures and structurally oriented reflexive action (Jessop 2001a, 2005a). This may explain why other social scientists have sometimes adopted the SRA in preference to its critical realist alternatives (cf. Hay 2002; Hay et al. 2005; Marsh et al. 1999). Moreover, while the generalized version of SRA is consistent with other critical realist approaches, its Marxist provenance means that it has normally been applied to particular problems in critical political economy for which its additional concepts are especially suited.

Fourth, the SRA was extended through an explicit concern with the spatio-temporality of social structures, agents, and agency and their articulation from a political-ecological perspective with the spatio-temporality of nature and transformed nature. Structures emerge in specific places and at specific times, operate on one or more particular scales and with specific temporal horizons of action, have their own specific ways of articulating and interweaving their various spatial and temporal horizons of action, develop their own specific capacities to stretch social relations and/to compress events in space and time, and, in consequence, have their own specific spatial and temporal rhythms. Such features are not accidental or secondary but are constitutive properties that help to distinguish one organization, institution, institutional order, or structural configuration from another. All structures privilege the adoption, as a condition for success, of certain spatial and temporal horizons of action by those seeking to control, resist, reproduce, or transform them. Thus the spatio-temporal selectivity of an organization, institution, institutional ensemble, or structural configuration involves the diverse modalities in and through which spatial and temporal horizons of action in different fields are produced, spatial and temporal rhythms created, and some practices and strategies privileged and others hindered according to how they 'match' the temporal and spatial patterns inscribed in the relevant structures. Spatio-temporal matrices are always differentially distantiated and compressed; and strategies and tactics are often concerned with the most appropriate spatio-temporal horizons, forms of spatio-temporal governance, the reflexive narration of past and present to change the future, and so forth. And, finally, a short-term constraint for a given agent or set of agents could become a conjunctural opportunity if there is a shift to a longer-term strategy. This implies that agents could pursue different types of alliance strategy and so modify the selective impact upon themselves and others of social and institutional constraints and opportunities. Spatial structural constraints and conjunctural opportunities are also determined in a 'strategic-relational' manner because agents may be able to operate across variable spatial scales as well as across several time horizons. In short, another advantage of the strategic-relational approach is that it can integrate spatio-temporality from the outset and, indeed, insists on the spatio-temporal selectivity of structures and the importance of the spatio-temporal dimensions of strategic calculation and action.

A further conclusion of the strategic-relational approach in this phase of its development was that the reciprocal interaction between structurally inscribed strategic selectivity and structurally oriented strategic calculation could lead through the usual evolutionary mechanisms of variation, selection, and retention to the formation of a configuration characterized by 'structured coherence'. One form that such structured coherence can take is the formation of a 'historical bloc', that is, the mutually implicated, structurally coupled, and historically co-evolving ensemble of economic, political, and socio-cultural relations, the construction of which depends on the activities of organic intellectuals and collective projects as well as on the gradual and emergent co-adaptation of institutions and conduct. This conclusion would be extended to include the analysis of spatio-temporal fixes, that is, social arrangements that facilitate the deferral and displacement of contradictions, crisis-tendencies, and conflicts and thereby help to produce zones of relative stability at the expense of future problems, other spaces, territories, or places, and social forces excluded from these relatively stable zones (see Jessop 2001a, 2002d, 2006b; and chapter 8).

A final preliminary conclusion in this phase of strategic-relational theorization was that structured coherence is always multiply tendential. There are three reasons for this. First, the reproduction of structures is only ever tendential; so too are their strategic selectivities. Second, because structures are strategically rather than structurally selective, there is always scope for actions to overflow or circumvent structural constraints. And, third, because subjects are never unitary, never fully aware of the conditions of strategic action, never fully equipped to realize their preferred strategies, and always face possible opposition from actors pursuing other strategies or tactics, failure is an ever-present possibility.

The Third Phase in the Strategic-Relational Approach

Arguments in favour of 'cultural political economy' (CPE) seem to have emerged in several contexts during the 1990s as part of and/or in response to the cultural turn. The present version was developed by scholars at Lancaster University drawing on a far wider range of sources. The Lancaster approach was prefigured in my neo-Gramscian approaches to the state and regulation theory; and in Sum's work on the discursive and material dimensions of the 1997 transfer of Hong Kong to mainland China (Sum 1994) and East Asian economic strategies (Sum 1996, 2000). Sum initiated cultural political economy *avant le concept* in the early 1990s, outside an explicitly strategic-relational framework, and, indeed, gave more weight to agency and mechanisms of subjectivation (for further examples, see the bibliography). Through our continuing joint discussions and collaborative research, a bilateral convergence has occurred as she has integrated strategic-relational concepts and I have given more – and more explicit – weight to semiosis. The roots of my interest in CPE go back many years but, for a long time, it took second place to my interest in state theory and the regulation approach. It should also be noted, of course, that CPE has been anticipated in some major versions of critical political economy (including aspects of the work of the founding fathers of Marxism) as well as in some 'old institutionalisms'. It also has significant parallels in various contemporary disciplinary and trans-disciplinary endeavours.[2]

The first state theorist working explicitly with the SRA to recognize that it can be applied to discourse was Colin Hay, formerly at Lancaster and Birmingham and now at Sheffield University. He adopted it to explore how discursive paradigms privilege some interlocutors, discursive identities/ positionings, discursive strategies and tactics, and discursive statements over others (e.g., Hay 1995a, 1995b, 1996, 1998; Jenson 1995; Jessop 2004b). Marx had already explored this theme in relation to alternative discourses about the material causes and social responsibility for poverty and their implications for political struggle between conservative and progressive forces (Marx 1844); and, some years later, in relation to the inadequacy of available political discourses to the mobilization of subaltern forces behind a genuine revolutionary strategy suited to contemporary capitalism (Marx 1850, 1852; see also chapter 3). Gramsci's analysis of passive revolution and hegemony could also be re-read in similar discourse-theoretical terms to show his sensitivity to the changing scope for articulating hegemonic projects (Gramsci 1971). Hay's early work in this area focused on the ways in which ideas, narratives, and discourse more generally play a crucial role in mediating social structuration. In particular, he argued that, in periods of moral panic or social crisis, which are often associated with moral or social disorientation, struggles to interpret an uncertain conjuncture could shape subsequent developments. More importantly, in the present context, the ability to win such struggles depended not only on structural factors (strategic selectivity) but also on discursive factors (discursive selectivity). For the resonance of particular discourses and their associated imaginaries and projects is a function of the discursive field more generally (see especially Hay 1995a, 1996). In subsequent work, Hay has developed this crucial strategic-relational insight further into a broad-ranging argument about the role of the cognitive framing of action and, *a fortiori*, of the importance of strategies and struggles over such framing. Thus he argues:

> If it is controversial to insist that the distinction between structure and agency is an analytical rather than a real one, then at least equally controversial is the second ontological premise of the strategic-relational approach (as developed here [by Colin Hay]). That is that the distinction between the material and the ideational is also purely analytical. Just as structures and agents do not exist in isolation, so too the material and the ideational are complexly interwoven and mutually interdependent. What is likely to make this ontological insistence yet more controversial is the popular idea that the material itself circumscribes the realm of the real.

Whilst this may well be a convenient assumption to make for those keen to retain their access to a positivist methodology, it is somewhat difficult to reconcile with our own experiences. For, whether we come to reject them at some subsequent date, the ideas we hold about our environment (about what is feasible, possible and desirable, for instance) have substantive effects. Moreover, they do not do so independently of that environment itself – both the effects themselves and the ideas we fashion in the first place are mediated by the context in which we find ourselves. Consequently, as with the question of structure and agency, whilst it may be useful to distinguish analytically between the material and the ideational, it is important that an analytical strategy does not set into an ontological dualism. . . .

Once again, access to the context itself is discursively mediated. How actors behave – the strategies they consider in the first place, the strategies they deploy in the final instance and the policies they formulate – reflects their understanding of the context in which they find themselves. Moreover, that understanding may eliminate a whole range of realistic alternatives and may, in fact, prove over time to be a systematic misrepresentation of the context in question. Nonetheless, for particular ideas, narratives and paradigms to continue to provide cognitive templates through which actors interpret the world, they must retain a certain resonance with those actors' direct and mediated experiences. In this sense the discursive or ideational is only ever relatively autonomous of the material. . . . What the above discussion hopefully demonstrates, is the centrality of ideas to any adequate understanding of the relationship between agent and structure, conduct and context. It also suggests the power of those able to provide the cognitive filters, such as policy paradigms, through which actors interpret the strategic environment. In sum, in the same way that a given context is *strategically-selective* – selecting for, but never determining, certain strategies over others – it is also *discursively-selective* – selecting for, but never determining, the discourses through which it might be appropriated. (Hay 2001)

These ideas are fully compatible with, and, indeed, mark an advance within, the strategic-relational approach as it existed in the mid-1990s. Their significance does not really consist in the substantive argument, which, like many other aspects of the strategic-relational approach, is implicit in much social scientific analysis even when it is not explicit. Indeed, one might argue that, just as Monsieur Jourdain discovered with wonderment that he had been speaking prose all his life, strategic-relational theorizing is also a prosaic feature of everyday social action and social analysis that gets close to everyday life in all its concrete-complex contingency and variety. Rather, the significance of this discursive turn in the SRA lies in its ontological, epistemological, and methodological implications for the development of the strategic-relational approach as a whole. For it highlights the ontological significance of semiosis for the social world and, *a fortiori*, for an adequate analysis of selectivity and strategic action. The challenge for the SRA then becomes that of how best to integrate social imaginaries into its overall theoretical framework and its empirical analyses. In other words, how can the strategic-relational approach combine material and discursive concerns in the description and explanation of selectivity and strategic action and their implications for social integration and social cohesion, their tensions and crises, and their reproduction and transformation?

While Hay had been developing these ideas in his doctoral research and later theoretical and empirical studies, my own work in the strategic-relational approach arrived at similar conclusions by a different route. This began with the influence of Gramsci on my propositions about accumulation strategies, state projects, and hegemonic visions (Jessop 1983); and it continued with my involvement in debates on the importance of the ideological for the analysis of Thatcherism (Hall 1985; Hall et al. 1978; Jessop et al. 1984, 1988). Additional influences were critical discourse analysis (especially Fairclough 1992), studies in narratology and narrative policy analysis (especially Somers 1994; Sum 1995, 1996), Foucauldian arguments about power and knowledge (Foucault 1980b), studies of changing economic discourses about competitiveness and flexibility (Jessop 1992c; Jessop et al. 1991, 1993), and interest in the influence of spatial imaginaries in economic and political restructuring (especially Lefebvre 1974). These different trajectories converged in a joint paper prepared for a research project funded by the Economic and Social Research Council on local governance in England that sought to combine the ideas of structural selectivity and discursive selectivity in a general account of the strategic-relational approach (Hay and Jessop 1995).

This led on my part to further strategic-relational work on changing discourses of competitiveness, narratives of enterprise, and entrepreneurial cities (Jessop 1997c, 1998b; Jessop and Sum 2000). Collaboration with Ngai-Ling Sum reinforced this cultural turn in the SRA and, indeed, she was the first of us to introduce the term 'cultural political economy' to describe this step in the development of the strategic-relational approach. She had previously worked with her own 'discursive-material' approach, which combined an emphasis on the interaction of discursivity and materiality within the field of political economy. While this did not explicitly adopt the SRA, it did pay equal attention to issues of structure and strategy as well as the material and discursive (see, e.g., Sum 1994, 1995, 1996, 1999a, 1999b, 2000, 2001, 2002, 2004). We have since worked closely in developing CPE.

The decisive advance in this new phase of development of the strategic-relational approach came, however, with work on new economic imaginaries surrounding the emergence of the knowledge-based economy. It was then that I realized that the evolutionary mechanisms of variation, selection, and retention could be applied to the notion of discursive selectivity. In other words, in order to explain why some discourses rather than others became hegemonic, it was necessary to explore how specific material and discursive mechanisms combined in different ways with different weights at different times to select some discourses (imaginaries) from others (especially during periods of crisis when there was a massive proliferation of competing narratives offering interpretations of the origins of the crisis, its significance, and the way forward) and in a next round retained (embrained, embodied, and institutionalized) some of the previously selected discourses. This was the basis for the development of 'cultural political economy', that is, a strategic-relational analysis of political economic dynamics and transformation based on taking the cultural turn seriously without losing sight of the material specificity of economic and political categories in a Jourdainian fascination with their semiotic dimensions (cf. Fairclough et al. 2004; Jessop 2004b; Jessop and Oosterlynck 2007; Jessop and Sum 2001, 2006; Sum and Jessop 2008).

An indication of what is at stake in this third phase of the strategic-relational approach can be gleaned from the following statement about cultural political economy:

> CPE is not only concerned with how texts produce meaning and thereby help to generate social structure but also how such production is constrained by emergent, non-semiotic features of social structure as well as by inherently semiotic factors. Although every social practice is semiotic (insofar as practices entail meaning), no social practice is reducible to semiosis. Semiosis is never a purely intra-semiotic matter without external reference and involves more than the play of differences among networks of signs. It cannot be understood without identifying and exploring the extra-semiotic conditions that make semiosis possible and secure its effectivity – this includes both the overall configuration of specific semiotic action contexts and the complexities of the natural and social world in which any and all semiosis occurs. This is the basis for the concept of the 'economic imaginary' outlined above. For not only do economic imaginaries provide a semiotic frame for *construing* economic 'events', they also help to *construct* such events and their economic contexts. (Jessop 2004b: 163–4)

Combining critical semiosis with critical political economy enables a strate-gic-relational analysis to avoid two complementary errors in political economy. First, if semiosis is studied apart from its extra-semiotic context, accounts of social causation will be incomplete, leading to semiotic reduc-tionism and/or imperialism. But, second, if material transformation is studied apart from its semiotic dimensions and mediations, explanations of stability and change risk oscillating between objective necessity and sheer contingency. In offering a 'third way', CPE emphasizes that capitalism involves a series of specific economic forms (the commodity form, money, wages, prices, property, etc.) associated with generalized commodity pro-duction. These forms have their own effects that must be analysed as such and that therefore shape the selection and retention of competing eco-nomic imaginaries. Thus a Marxist CPE would robustly reject the confla-tion of discourses and material practices and the more general 'discourse imperialism' that has plagued social theory for two decades. It would also provide a powerful means both to critique and to contextualize recent claims about the 'culturalization' of economic life in the new economy – seeing these claims as elements within a new economic imaginary with a potentially performative impact as well as a belated (mis)recognition of the semiotic dimensions of all economic activities (for sometimes contrasting views, see du Gay and Pryke 2002; Ray and Sayer 1999). And, in addition, as many theorists have noted in various contexts (and orthodox Marxists sometimes forget), the reproduction of the basic forms of the capital rela-tion and their particular instantiation in different social formations cannot be secured purely through the objective logic of the market or a domina-tion that operates 'behind the backs of the producers'. For capital's laws of motion are doubly tendential and depend on contingent social practices that extend well beyond what is from time to time construed and/or con-structed as economic. CPE provides a corrective to these problems too. In part this comes from its emphasis on the constitutive material role of the extra-economic supports of market forces. But it also emphasizes how different economic imaginaries serve to demarcate economic from extra-economic activities, institutions, and orders and, hence, how semiosis is also constitutive in securing the conditions for accumulation.

Interim Strategic-Relational Conclusions

It is premature to draw conclusions about the strategic-relational approach so early in this monograph. The remaining chapters are also concerned with its development and implications and the concluding chapter will present a future research agenda. So this chapter can close with three summary propositions. First, then, the SRA is a heuristic based on a general social ontology. As such it cannot validate a particular set of concepts for analysing a particular theoretical and/or empirical problem. Indeed, the SRA as a general heuristic is compatible with a range of particular strategic-relational theories, which must be derived from other forms of theoretical reflection, empirical observation, or practical intervention. In this sense, regardless of the specific application of the SRA to state theory below, its meta-theoretical arguments might survive and be developed in other ways. Second, for the same reasons, the SRA can be used to interrogate other theoretical approaches, emerging concepts, and empirical analyses, to highlight their interrelated structural and strategic dimensions, and to explore their implications. And, third, if the SRA is to be a comprehensive heuristic, it should also be applied to itself. In other words, it should be possible to provide a strategic-relational account of the development of the strategic-relational approach both as a general heuristic and in its particular variants. This would involve an analysis of the material and discursive factors behind the emergence, selection, retention, contestation, and replacement of one particular strategic-relational paradigm by another or, indeed, the replacement of the general strategic-relational heuristic by another that is at least as powerful. In this sense, the present work can be seen as an attempt to promote the selection and retention of the strategic-relational approach.

2

Bringing the State Back in (Yet Again)

Chapter 1 has shown how the strategic-relational approach developed on the basis of critical engagement with particular debates in Marxism and the philosophy of social science. This chapter provides a more coherent account of Marxist state-theoretical debates and examines other approaches that, despite their limited role in developing the SRA, illustrate how analogous arguments have been developed in response to similar problems. This suggests that the SRA is not an arbitrary theoretical *construal* of social relations but a more or less adequate depiction of how social relations actually get constructed and reproduced and how lay actors who are neither 'structural' nor 'cultural' dupes engage in strategic action. Indeed, applying the evolutionary mechanisms of variation, selection, retention, and contestation to the field of scientific development and its embedding in the wider social environment, one might argue that the SRA and its equivalents tend to get selected in different fields of inquiry because they are theoretically and substantively better at describing and explaining structure–agency dialectics than the alternatives. Thus different theorists should tend to adopt something like the SRA as they move from more abstract, one-sided analyses to more concrete-complex issues. But there are many material and discursive obstacles to such a smooth process of scientific development and to ignore them would be inconsistent with the strategic-relational approach itself. Indeed, applying the strategic-relational approach to the SRA would suggest that it is itself path-dependent as well as path-shaping – that it is not only generated by specific problems but also shaped by the available material and discursive resources to resolve them. This emphasizes the material-discursive mechanisms of variation, selection, retention, and contestation and argues that these apply in all social fields, including the scientific field and its embedding in a wider nexus of social relations. Thus the present chapter is less concerned to

This is a heavily revised and updated version of 'Bringing the state back in (yet again): reviews, revisions, rejections, and redirections', *International Review of Sociology*, 11 (2), 2001, 149–73.

present a triumphalist account of eventual convergence around an emerging strategic-relational agenda in state theory than it is to show the continuing variation in paradigms and to assess their significance for recent and future studies of the state and state power and their general significance for the nature and development of social formations.

I will review two major waves of post-war interest in the state. The first emerged in the mid-1960s and was mainly led by West European Marxists and American radicals interested in the general form and functions of the capitalist state; a key supporting role was played by Marxist-feminists who extended such ideas to the patriarchal capitalist state (for useful reviews of such Marxist theorizing, see Altvater and Hoffman 1990; Barrow 1993; Carnoy 1984; Chandhoke 1995; Clarke 1990; Jessop 1977; Thomas 1994; and, on Marxist-feminism, Burstyn 1982; Mahon 1991). The trajectory of this Marxist debate reveals that theoretical paradigms can be selected and developed for some time, lose momentum and get displaced, and yet survive in marginal forms to be resurrected (or not) in new rounds of theoretical and empirical inquiry. The second revival in the late 1970s involved more theoretical currents and substantive concerns and was also more institutionalist in approach. The self-declared movement to 'bring the state back in' originated in the United States and has also undergone phases of expansion, consolidation, and eventual displacement. Some of the most innovative work in this period was rooted in less overtly state-centred approaches from Western Europe and, indeed, some of these argue that the state as such should be dethroned from its central position in analyses of political power and domination. This contributed in part to the withering of interest in state theory in the 1990s, but it has nonetheless re-emerged by default in less explicitly state-theoretical analyses that have moved inquiries about the state in new directions with interesting implications for more orthodox work on the state and state power. Bartelson has suggested that, whenever scholars seek to deny the existence of the state or to displace it from the centre of political analysis, it re-emerges in another nominal, conceptual, or theoretical form. For, even when explicitly removed from the research agenda, the state concept is tacitly presupposed by research practices. It therefore remains foundational to large and important parts of modern political discourse. Indeed, however much it has been wished away, the state concept remains a convenient shorthand whenever the pressure of semantic precision is relaxed or ignored (Bartelson 2001: 4–5, 10–11). Thus this chapter can be seen as a preliminary and partial strategic-relational exploration of social scientific engagement with the state and politics as theoretical and empirical objects.

The Marxist Revival and the Strategic-Relational Approach

The legacy of Marx and Engels does not include an adequate theory of the state. Their work comprises a loose and often irreconcilable series of philosophical, theoretical, journalistic, partisan, *ad hominem*, and purely *ad hoc* comments (for serious reviews of their contributions to state theory, see Althusser 2006; Artous 1999; Draper 1977, 1978; Fine 1984; Frerichs and Kraiker 1975; Hennig 1974; and Teeple 1983). Their work nonetheless contained an *implicit* account of *the state as a social relation* – an account, as noted in chapter 1, first *explicitly* identified by Nicos Poulantzas (1978b). This is quite consistent with Marx's overall approach to social analysis and is best expressed in his foundational claim that capital is a social relation:

> property in money, means of subsistence, machines and other means of production, does not as yet stamp a man as a capitalist if there be wanting the correlative – the wage-worker, the other man who is compelled to sell himself of his own free-will. . . . capital is not a thing, but a social relation between persons, established by the instrumentality of things. (1867: 717)

The same argument runs through his and Engels's reflections on the state and can be paraphrased to read that state power is a social relation between political forces mediated through the instrumentality of juridico-political institutions, state capacities, and political organizations (cf. Marx 1843, 1850, 1852, 1871a; and chapter 3). Poulantzas expressed this intuition in his thesis that state power is an institutionally mediated condensation of the balance of forces in political class struggle (chapter 6). Because Marx and Engels did not present this account in a systematic movement from abstract-simple to concrete-complex arguments, however, it was easy for subsequent Marxist state theorizing to read their work on the state in highly selective and often simplistic ways.

Both the broadly social democratic Second International and the narrowly Marxist-Leninist Comintern (or Third International) developed various one-sided accounts based on partial interpretations of the more accessible key Marxian and Engelsian texts on the state. The Second International primarily advanced instrumentalist and/or epiphenomenalist views of the state, modified on occasion to recognize the changing balance of political forces, stages of capitalism, and the relative (in)stability of capitalism. Instrumentalism sees the state primarily as a juridico-political apparatus deployable for any purpose by whichever forces happen to control it; and epiphenomenalism regards the state's form, functions, and purposes as reflections of the economic base (forces and relations of production) and the changing balance of economic forces. In neither case was the state apparatus accorded much autonomy. The relationality of state power is thereby limited to changes in the balance of forces and/or base–superstructure relations, and the state's specific form and capacities are generally considered irrelevant. The main exception is support for the parliamentary road to socialism based on electoral victories and the nationalization and/or state planning of the economy's commanding heights. This assumes that bourgeois democratic regimes provide relatively favourable conditions for political gradualism and that the growing concentration and centralization of economic and political power associated with organized capitalism will facilitate the socialist takeover. This strategy suggests in turn that state power is partly a function of the structures and forces over which (or in and through which) it is exercised.

The Comintern, formed after the Bolshevik revolution, also inclined to instrumentalist and epiphenomenalist views. It was particularly associated with Lenin's argument, advanced during the Great War with its tendencies towards the consolidation of finance capitalism and 'war socialism', that the state and monopolies had fused into a single mechanism of economic exploitation and political oppression. Another line of argument developed the Marxian claim (as modified by Lenin) that the bourgeois democratic republic was essentially capitalist in nature because of its disorganizing effects on the economic and political struggles of the subordinate classes and its tendential containment of such struggles within the limits of market rationality and electoral majorities, respectively (for a general review of arguments pertaining to Lenin's claim that the bourgeois democratic republic is the best possible political shell for capital, see Jessop 1978). This strategic bias in bourgeois democracy excluded a parliamentary road to socialism and called for an entirely new state form to replace bourgeois democracy based on direct democracy through workers' councils, prefigured in the Paris Commune. There was an obvious tension between the commitments to direct democracy and the vanguard role of the Communist Party. Indeed, in strategic-relational terms, the dominance of the vanguard party promoted authoritarianism rather than grass-roots democracy.

The other main interwar contributions came from first-generation Frankfurt School 'Critical Theorists' concerned with trends towards a strong, bureaucratic state – either authoritarian or totalitarian in form.[1] They suggested that this state form corresponded to the rise of organized or state capitalism, relied increasingly on the mass media for its ideological power, and had integrated the trade union movement as a political support or else smashed it as part of the consolidation of totalitarian rule. Gramsci also lived (and died) in this period, but his most important state-theoretical work, found in his prison notebooks (written during his incarceration under Italian fascism in 1926–34), was not published in Italian until the 1950s and only became widely known and influential in the 1960s (see chapter 4).

A serious revival of Marxist interest in the state, going well beyond the main pre-war approaches and arguments, occurred in the late 1960s and 1970s. It was stimulated by the apparent success of the Keynesian welfare state in managing the post-war economy and the desire nonetheless to show that this state form was still essentially capitalist. Marxist theorists initially tried to derive the necessary form and functions of the capitalist state from the fundamental categories of Marx's critique of political economy and prove that contemporary states could not suspend the crisis-tendencies and contradictions of capitalism. The interventionist welfare state's apparent autonomy to act against the interests of capital was illusory because it corresponded to a particular phase of capitalist development and a particular balance of class forces. It could at best displace or defer capital's contradictions and, when crisis-tendencies re-surfaced in economic or extra-economic forms, state efforts at crisis-management would reveal the post-war state's capitalist character. This approach began to implode in the late 1970s under the weight of a multitude of theoretical starting points and highly abstract theorizations that blithely disregarded the historical variability of political regimes and the diverse forms taken by capitalism. Indeed, with rare exceptions, individual contributions to this debate have been lost in the mists of time (for specific contributions, see Jessop 1982: 78–141).

Nonetheless several of the better analysts did formulate two key strategic-relational insights that are relevant to a far wider theoretical circle and/or that concern more specific historical and comparative issues. Although these insights were not always expressed in the same words, they did converge in their core underlying arguments.

First, in turning from functional to form analysis, Marxist theorists discovered that form threatens function. Much early work sought to derive the necessary form of the state from the functions it was supposedly required to perform for capital. Seen in such terms, form follows function. This argument is consistent with relative autonomy provided that this is limited to the state's ability to meet the overall interests of capital. Later work explored how the typical form of the capitalist state problematized its overall functionality for capital accumulation and political class domination. Thus viewed, dysfunction may follow from form, for the institutional separation of the state and the market economy, a separation regarded as a necessary and defining feature of capitalist societies, means they are dominated by different (and potentially contradictory) institutional logics and modes of calculation (e.g., Hirsch 1976, 2005; Offe 1984; Poulantzas 1978b; Reuten and Williams 1989; Wood 1981). Thus political outcomes that serve the needs of capital cannot be guaranteed – even if (and, indeed, precisely because) the state is operationally autonomous. This conclusion fuelled work on the structural contradictions, strategic dilemmas, and path-dependent (i.e., historically conditioned) development of specific state forms. It also prompted a decline in highly abstract and often essentialist theorization in favour of more detailed accounts of the complex interplay of social struggles and institutions.

Second, gradually abandoning views of the state apparatus as a simple thing or a unitary political subject, Marxist theorists began to analyse state power as a complex social relation. Some early works saw the state as little more than a neutral instrument of class domination; some adopted a more structuralist view according to which the state was institutionally destined to serve capitalist interests regardless of who controlled it; and yet others viewed the state as a kind of rational calculating subject, an ideal collective capitalist, able to discern and pursue the real interests of capital in general against the particular or perceived interests of individual capitals. None of these views proved satisfactory. (For criticisms of these positions, see Carnoy 1984; Jessop 1977, 1982, 1990b; Offe 1972; Poulantzas 1967, 1978b.) What gradually (and partially) replaced them were implicitly strategic-relational studies of different states' *structural selectivity* and *strategic capacities*. Thus they explored the ways in which the state as an ensemble of institutions had a specific, differential impact on the ability of various political forces to pursue particular interests and strategies through access to and control over given state capacities – themselves dependent for their effects on links to forces and powers beyond the state (on this concept see, especially, Offe 1972; Poulantzas 1978b). They also studied variations in these capacities, their organization, and exercise. This prompted greater emphasis on the relational nature of state power and on states' capacities to project their power into social realms well beyond their own institutional boundaries. And, as with the first set of insights, it led to more complex studies of struggles, institutions, and political capacities. The SRA as presented in this book emerged from my reflections on these two themes in the light of Poulantzas's contributions to state theory and, in this sense, originated as a codification and elaboration of these themes.

Of the Marxist state theorists whose work attracted sustained attention in this first post-war revival, Gramsci was almost alone in still enjoying widespread critical acclaim in the 1990s. It is surely no accident that Gramsci studied the concrete modalities of state power rather than theorizing the capitalist state in general. He investigated the 'state in its inclusive sense' (i.e., 'political society + civil society') and showed how state power in bourgeois societies rested on 'hegemony armoured by coercion' (Gramsci 1971). Moreover, rather than treating specific institutions and apparatuses as essentially technical instruments of government, Gramsci was concerned with their social bases and stressed how their functions and effects are shaped by their links to the economic system and civil society. An excessively literal reading of Gramsci's aphorisms and other notes on the state led Perry Anderson (1978) to argue that the Italian was confused about the state, suggesting that Gramsci variously defined it as political society, political society + civil society, or civil society. But Gramsci was less concerned with defining the state apparatus than with elaborating the modalities of state power in an implicitly strategic-relational manner (see chapter 4). Together with its incomplete and tentative character, this makes his approach compatible with several other theoretical currents. Among these are discourse theory, feminism, Foucauldian analyses, and post-modernism (e.g., Golding 1992; Holub 1992; Lester 2000; Sassoon 1987; Smart 1986). The open-ended, polyvalent texture of Gramsci's work has helped to maintain this vitality because it is a site of often productive misunderstandings and theoretical alliances.

A more recent source of continued interest in Marxist state theory is much less direct: the regulation approach to political economy. This emerged in the late 1970s and flourished in the 1980s, making it part of the second wave of interest in state theory. For present purposes its essential (re-)discovery was that capitalist economies are socially embedded and socially regularized, and this led some regulationists to study the state's key role in the reproduction-*régulation* (or governance) of accumulation. This opened the way for more complex and concrete analyses of the state's various contributions to shaping, sustaining, and undermining specific accumulation regimes and modes of growth. This is one of the main themes of second- and third-generation regulation theory in its three main variants, namely, the Parisian *régulation* school, the West German state-theoretical approach, and the Amsterdam school of transnational historical materialism (see, respectively, Boyer and Saillard 2002; Häusler and Hirsch 1989; Overbeek 2004; and, for reviews, Jessop 1990a, 1997d, 1997e; Jessop and Sum 2006). Interestingly, the leading contributors to the Parisian *régulation* approach, despite its recognition of the importance of the state to the reproduction-*régulation* (or economic and extra-economic regularization of capital accumulation despite its inherent contradictions, crisis-tendencies, and conflictuality), rarely applied their own critical realist, relational approach to the nature of the state itself (cf. Jessop 1990b: 311–20; Jessop and Sum 2006: 90–103). Important exceptions were Théret's social topological approach, which explored the matrix produced by the necessary presence of economic *and* political relations inside the institutionally differentiated economic and political regimes of capitalist social formations (Théret 1992, 1994); and, more recently, work by Palombarini (1999), developing the Parisian claim that the state institutionalizes class compromises as a condition of effective economic management. West German theorists were more consistent in this regard, and some have produced major contributions to a more or less explicitly strategic-relational analysis of the role of the state and hegemony accumulation regimes (e.g., on Fordism in the European Union, Ziltener 1999; and on the neo-liberal variant of post-Fordism organized under American hegemony, Candeias 2005).

Strategic-Relational Tendencies in the Second Wave

Possibly the most important single theoretical current in the second revival of interest in the state was the movement (most popular in the USA) to 'bring the state back in' as a critical explanatory variable in social analysis. But this did not go unchallenged. Besides the continuing influence of Gramsci and the variable impact of other neo-Marxist currents, additional competition came from several other rival approaches. Among these are, first, the work of Foucault and his followers on the disciplinary organization of society, the micro-physics of power, and changing forms of governmentality – an approach that ran counter to neo-statism in tending to remove the state from theoretical view once again (chapter 6); second, the development of a broad-based feminist critique of malestream state theory – an approach that asked, among other questions, whether feminists (and others) really need a theory of the state; and, third, growing interest in the discourses and practices that constitute the state – an approach that moves rather unsteadily between deconstructing and reconstructing the state as a theoretical object. This list is incomplete but does serve to illustrate the range of positions in the second revival.

State-Centred Approaches

Demands to 'bring the state back' in came from social scientists who claimed that the dominant post-war analyses of politics were too 'society-centred'.

The latter tried mistakenly to explain the *state's* form, functions, and impact through factors rooted in the organization, needs, or interests of *society*. Marxism was accused of economic reductionism for its focus on base–superstructure relations and the class struggle; pluralism was charged with limiting its account of competition for state power to interest groups and movements rooted in civil society and thus ignoring the distinctive role and interests of state managers; and structural-functionalism was criticized for assuming that the development and subsequent operations of the state or political system were determined by the functional requirements of society as a whole. For 'state-centred' theorists, such approaches put the cart before the horse. Instead, they argued, the state's activities and impact are easily explained in terms of its distinctive properties as an administrative or repressive organ and/or the equally distinctive properties of the wider political order encompassing the state. Societal factors, when not actually deemed wholly irrelevant, were certainly secondary; and their impact on state affairs was always filtered through the political system and the state.

In its more programmatic guise the statist approach often advocated a return to classic theorists such as Machiavelli, Clausewitz, de Tocqueville, Weber, or Hintze.[2] In practice, however, those working in the statist paradigm showed little interest in (let alone any real familiarity with) such thinkers, with the partial exception of Weber.[3] Indeed it seems that they are cited chiefly to legitimate neo-statism by linking it to a long tradition of state-centred thought. In any event, the real focus of state-centred work is detailed case studies of state-building, policy-making, and implementation.

In this context, six themes are emphasized: (1) the geo-political positions of states in the international system of nation-states and their implications for the logic of state action; (2) the dynamic of military organization and warfare's impact on state formation; (3) the modern state's distinctive extractive, legislative, and penetrative powers and its strategic reach into other institutional orders (including the economy), organizations (including capitalist enterprises), and forces (including classes) in its domain; (4) the state's distinctive contribution to shaping institutions, group formation, interest articulation, political capacities, ideas, and demands beyond the state; (5) the distinctive pathologies of government and the political system – such as bureaucratism, political corruption, government overload, or state failure; and (6) the distinctive interests and capacities of 'state managers' (career officials, elected politicians, etc.) *vis-à-vis* other social forces. Different 'state-centred' theorists emphasize different (combinations of) factors. But the main conclusions remain that there are distinctive political pressures and processes that (a) shape the state's form and functions, (b) give it a real and important autonomy when faced with pressures and forces emerging from the wider society, and, thereby, (c) give it a unique and irreplaceable centrality in national life and the international order. In short, the state is a force in its own right rather than subordinate to economy or civil society (e.g., Krasner 1978; Nordlinger 1981; Skocpol 1979; Stepan 1985).

This leads 'state-centred' theorists to a very different approach to state autonomy from that considered in the preceding section. Whereas Marxist theorists understood autonomy primarily in terms of the state's capacity to promote the long-term, collective interests of capital even when faced with opposition from particular capitals, neo-statists reject this class- or capital-theoretical account and argue that the state can exercise autonomy in its own right and in pursuit of its own, quite distinctive, interests. They emphasize: (a) state managers' ability to exercise power independently of (and even against resistance from) non-state forces – especially where a pluralistic universe of social forces provides them with broad room for manoeuvre; and (b) the grounding of this ability in state capacities or 'infrastructural' power, that is, the state's ability to penetrate, control, supervise, police, and discipline modern societies through its own specialized capacities. Neo-statists also argue that state autonomy differs across states, by policy area, and over time. This is due partly to external limits on autonomous state action and partly to variations in the capacity and readiness of state managers to pursue a strategy independent of non-state actors (e.g., Atkinson and Coleman 1989; Brødsgaard and Young 2000; Dandeker 1990; Fukuyama 2005; Giddens 1989; Mann 1984, 1986; Nordlinger 1981; Skocpol 1985; Tilly 1973; Weiss 1998, 1999, 2003).

War-centred state theory is a distinctive variant of state-centred theorizing. A growing band of theorists have re-instated the military dimension of state theory and complained about its neglect by other schools – something they attribute to Marxists' exaggerated interest in class struggle and to sociologists' false belief in the inherently pacific logic of industrialism. These theorists regard the state as an apparatus for war-making and repression that is obliged to defend its territorial integrity against external enemies and maintain internal social cohesion by maintaining military preparedness and resorting to coercion as and when necessary. It is seen in the first instance as the bearer of military power in a world of nation-states rather than as a political community in which citizenship rights may be realized (cf. Giddens 1989). Indeed, for some war-centred theorists, not only is the fully formed state a military-repressive apparatus, but state formation is itself closely tied to war. For, as Tilly (1973) pithily notes, wars make states and states make wars. This goes beyond the trite remark that states are often forged in the heat of war (either in victory or defeat); it also involves the idea that war-making can induce political centralization, encourage the development of a modern taxation system, encourage the extension of citizenship rights where mass conscription is required, and produce other distinctive features of a modern state. Moreover, once the state emerges (through war or preparation for war), many key aspects of the state's form and functions are determined primarily by concerns with external defence and internal paci-fication (e.g., Bobbitt 2002; Dandeker 1990; Mann 1986, 1987, 1988; Porter 1994; Shaw 1991; Tilly 1973, 1992; for an accessible review of war's impact on state formation and the wider society, see Hirst 2001; for a critical eval-uation of Mann's historical sociology, see Hall and Schroeder 2006; Teschke 2003 also criticizes neo-liberal realist approaches to modern state formation as well as Mann's organizational materialism).

Five main lines of criticism have been advanced against neo-statism. First, the approach is hardly novel and all its core themes can be found in the so-called 'society-centred' approaches (e.g., Almond 1988; Domhoff 1987, 1996). Second, neo-statism is allegedly one-sided because it focuses on state and party politics at the expense of political forces outside and beyond the state. In particular, it substitutes 'politicians for social formations (such as class or gender or race), elite for mass politics, political conflict for social struggle' (Gordon 1990: 181). Third, some critics claim to have identified empirical inadequacies in several key statist studies as well as incomplete and misleading accounts of other studies cited to lend some credence to the statist approach (e.g., Cammack 1989, 1990; Mitchell 1991). Fourth, there are charges of political bad faith. For example, Binder (1986) argued that neo-statism implies that politically autonomous state managers can act as effective agents of economic modernization and social reform and should be encouraged to do so; in support of this charge, he notes that no neo-statist case studies exist revealing the harmful effects of their authoritarian or autocratic rule.

Finally, and most seriously, neo-statism is held to rest upon a fundamen-tal theoretical fallacy. It assumes there are clear and unambiguous bound-aries between state apparatus and society, state managers and social forces, and state power and societal power. It implies that the state (or the political system) and society are mutually exclusive and self-determining, each can be studied in isolation, and the resulting analyses added together to provide a complete account. This reifies and renders absolute what are really emer-gent, partial, unstable, and variable distinctions. It rules out hybrid logics such as corporatism or policy networks; divisions among state managers due to ties between state organs and other social spheres; and many other forms of overlap between state and society (e.g., Atkinson and Coleman 1989; Jessop 1990b; Poulantzas 1975). If this assumption is rejected, however, the distinction between state- and society-centred approaches dissolves. This invalidates the extreme claim that the state apparatus should be treated as the independent variable in explaining political and social events; and it reveals the limits of lesser neo-statist proposals, such as combining state-centred and society-centred accounts to produce the complete picture. Given the need to reduce complexity by making simplifying assumptions, it may not invalidate the heuristic value of bending the stick in the other direction within a longer-term research programme on state formation and the dynamics of state power. But the state-centred approach should then treat the demarcation of the state from other institutional orders as socially constructed and variable rather than natural, and be prepared to explore the functions of such demarcations as means of connecting institutional orders and social forces as well as means of containing and insulating state power from external pressures. The key conclusion here is that theoretical analyses of the state can be important and productive on condition that they do not take the state for granted. For the very existence of the state and its operational unity are problematic. Thus Mitchell concludes his own critique of neo-statism with a plea to study 'the detailed processes of spatial organization, temporal arrangement, functional specification, and supervision and surveillance, which create the *appearance of a world fundamentally divided into state and society*' (1991: 95, italics mine; cf. Bartelson 2001). This division is conceptually prior to any possible influence of state on society, or society on the state; and it is one that is always produced in and through practices on both sides of the state–society divide. This leads us to Foucault's work.

Foucauldian Approaches

If state-centred theorists hoped to bring the state back in from the cold, putting it out for the garbage collector could well describe Foucault's ultimate goal in his concern with the micro-physics of power. He linked his historical investigations into power, knowledge, and discipline to sustained theoretical rejection of liberal and Marxist views of sovereignty, law, and the state. More generally his work has major implications for all state theorists because it questions their preoccupation with the state – whether as an independent, intervening, or dependent variable. Indeed he rejected efforts to develop any kind of general theory about the state and developed instead a heuristic 'analytics of power' to be applied to power relations wherever they emerge (see also chapter 6).

Foucault's rejection of state theory was grounded in three key arguments. First, he alleged that state theory is essentialist: it tries to explain the state and state power in terms of their own inherent, pre-given properties. Instead it should be trying to explain the development and functioning of the state as the contingent outcome of specific practices that are not necessarily (if at all) located within, or openly oriented to, the state. Second, state theory retains medieval notions of a centralized, monarchical sovereignty and/or a unified, juridico-political power. In contrast, Foucault stressed the tremendous dispersion and multiplicity of the institutions and practices involved in the exercise of state power and insisted that many were extra-juridical in nature. And, third, state theorists were allegedly preoccupied with the forms of sovereign political and legal power at the summits of the state apparatus, with the discourses that legitimated power at the centre, and with the extent of the sovereign state's reach into society. Conversely, Foucault advocated an ascending, bottom-up approach that proceeds from the diffuse forms of power relations in the many and varied local and regional sites where the identity and conduct of social agents were actually determined. He was concerned with what he described as the micro-physics of power, the actual practices of subjugation, rather than the macro-political strategies that guide attempts at domination. For state power does not stem from control over some substantive, material resource peculiar to the state. It is actually the provisional, emergent result of the complex strategic interplay of diverse social forces within and beyond the state. It is dispersed and involves the active mobilization of individuals and not just their passive targeting, and can be colonized and articulated into quite different discourses, strategies, and institutions. In short, power is not concentrated in the state; it is ubiquitous, immanent in every social relation (see notably Foucault 1980a, 1980b).

Nonetheless, while Foucault rejected the identification of the state with the sovereign state described in juridical-political discourse, he developed a powerful set of arguments about states as sites of statecraft. Thus he studied how different political regimes emerged through shifts in 'governmentality' (or governmental rationality). What came to interest the later Foucault more and more was the art of government, a skilled discursive practice in which state capacities were used reflexively to monitor the population and, with all due prudence, to make it conform to specific state projects. At the origins of the Foucauldian state was *raison d'état*, an autonomous political rationality, set apart from religion and morality (Gordon 1990: 9). This in turn could be linked to different modes of political calculation or state projects, such as those coupled to the 'police state'

(*Polizeistaat*), social government, or the welfare state (Gordon 1991: 26–7). It was through these governmental rationalities or state projects that more local or regional sites of power were colonized, articulated into ever more general mechanisms and forms of global domination, and then maintained by the entire state system. Foucault also insisted on the need to explore the connections between these forms of micro-power and mechanisms for producing knowledge – whether for surveillance, the formation and accumulation of knowledge about individuals, or their constitution as specific types of subject.

Foucault's work has inspired many studies of the state and state power. A few have tried to develop a general account of the state based on Foucauldian perspectives. For example, Dandeker elaborated some insights from Giddens' treatment of surveillance as one of four institutional clusterings in modern societies (alongside industrialism, capitalism, and militarism) to generate a typology of states based on their surveillance mechanisms and the interests they serve (Dandeker 1990; Giddens 1989). Far more productive have been studies that focus on specific policies and policy apparatuses and/or specific political discourses and strategies in the contested process of state formation and reformation (e.g., Barry 2001; Barry et al. 1996; Burchell et al. 1991; Chatterjee 2004; Cooper 1998; Dean and Hindess 1998; Ferguson and Gupta 2005; Hannah 2000; Meyet et al. 2006; Miller and Rose 1990; Mitchell 1988, 2001; Neocleous 1996; Rose 1999; Rose and Miller 1992). Foucault's work has gained influence because of the growing construction of 'security' as a problem and site of state intervention and their implications for new forms of power/knowledge around such issues as environmental security, bio-security, or the 'war on terror' (e.g., Agrawal 2006; Dillon and Reid 2001; Feldman 2004; Lemke 2000).

It is hard to assess Foucault's *oeuvre* because he deliberately never codified his work and his views tended to change with each monograph. Taking together his ideas on the ubiquity of power relations, the coupling of power-knowledge, and governmentality, however, he offers a useful theoretical and empirical corrective to the more one-sided and/or essentialist analyses of Marxist state theory and the taken-for-grantedness of the state that infuses neo-statism. But his work can be charged with tending to reduce power to a universal technique (whether panoptic surveillance or disciplinary normalization) and ignoring how class and patriarchal relations shape the state and the more general exercise of power (e.g., Kerr 1999; Ramazanoglu 1993). It also neglects the continued importance of law, constitutionalized violence, and bureaucracy for the modern state (cf. Poulantzas 1978b).

Moreover, whatever the merits of highlighting the ubiquity of power, Foucault's work provided little account of the bases of resistance (bar an alleged plebeian spirit of revolt). In consequence, early studies based on his critique of conventional state theory and sovereign power showed little interest in the organizational conditions that make it even half-way possible for a state to engage in effective action or, again, in the various limitations on the capacities of even the most well-endowed state. Both issues require a concern with institutional and organizational factors that go beyond the typical concepts and assumptions of Foucault's work on the general analytics of power. Moreover, even though he later studied the state and statecraft and more macro-structural and macro-strategic questions, Anglophone Foucauldian studies lagged behind because many of his crucial contributions to the study of statecraft were translated with considerable delay, if at all. This problem has been partially overcome since the mid-1990s and a growing body of work is now engaging directly with Foucauldian arguments about statecraft and governmentality (e.g., Corbridge et al. 2005; Walters and Larner 2004; see also chapter 6).

Feminist State Theory

State theory is a relatively neglected topic in feminism (Connell 1990; Genetti 2003; Knuttila and Kubik 2001; Kuwalik and Sauer 1996; MacKinnon 1982). For, while feminists have developed distinctive theories of gender and the gendering of social relations, even where they have been interested in the state, their ideas on its general nature and form have often been imported from outside. This observation is not intended to belittle the many powerful feminist critiques of political (as opposed to state) theory or to denigrate the many important feminist accounts of particular, gender-relevant aspects of the operation and impact of states (see chapter 7). Instead I want to highlight the difficulties involved in developing distinctively feminist accounts of the general form and functions of the state.

Not all feminists would agree that feminism needs such a theory – either intellectually or politically. Allen argued that feminists should concentrate on developing concepts appropriate to a feminist theoretical and political agenda and reject existing state theories 'with [their] definitions, parameters and analytic tasks forged for political positions other than feminism' (1990: 21). She urged feminists to focus on categories such as policing, law, medical culture, bureaucratic culture, organized crime, fraternalism, paternalism, misogyny, subjectivity, the body, sexuality, men, masculinity, violence, power, pleasure, and so forth, which bear directly on feminist political concerns (1990: 28). In other cases it is not so much their purported irrelevance that prompts rejection of existing theories as their malign 'malestream' or, worse yet, phallocratic character and their resulting debilitating impact on feminist thought and mobilization (e.g., MacKinnon 1982, 1983). But other feminists call on their sisters to theorize the complexities of state power precisely because of its pervasive impact on gender relations. Thus Brown argued that feminists should analyse the state because it is so central to many women's issues and so many women are state dependants (Brown 1992: 7; cf. Franzway et al. 1989: 12–13). But, rather than a single, all-purpose theory that fails to register the real strategic complexity of the state, its discourses, and technologies of power, Brown suggested developing insights from different state theories relevant to the different faces that the state presents to women.[4]

Feminists first began to tackle the state as such in the attempted marriage of feminism and Marxism (cf. Mahon 1991; Pringle and Watson 1992). This was an important current in the 1970s state theory revival and typically involved attempts to graft theories of reproduction and patriarchy onto Marxist analyses of production in order to show how patriarchy served capitalism and how the latter depended in turn on specific social forms that reproduced labour power and gender relations as well as specific social relations of production (e.g., Eisenstein 1981; McIntosh 1978). Indeed Marxism-feminism dominated feminist state theories for some time, and this is reflected in the main methods in feminist theorizing during the 1970s: subsumption, derivation, and articulation (cf. the methods adopted in Marxist theory, Jessop 1982).

Some radical feminist theories simply subsumed each and every state under the overarching category of patriarchal domination: whatever their apparent differences, all states are expressions of patriarchy or phallocracy and so must be opposed. Such arguments either assimilate the state to patriarchy in general or identify specific gendering mechanisms of the state itself. For some, patriarchy is diffused throughout society, with the state as one more institution that treats men and women unequally, adopts the male viewpoint, and serves and consolidates the interests of men as a sex. Thus the state is just another site of male domination over women; at best (or worst) it serves as the 'patriarch general' (Mies 1986: 26). More complex versions of this approach view the state as a specific form of patriarchal or phallocratic domination with its own determinate (and distinctive) effects on gender relations. It engenders power relations in specific ways, through its own patriarchal strategic selectivity, capacities, and needs.[5] However, insofar as patriarchy defines the core of the state and all else is treated as secondary, these views remain subsumptionist (for critiques of early feminist state theories, see Allen 1990: 26–7; Anthias and Yuval-Davis 1989; Connell 1990: 516–17; Pringle and Watson 1992: 62–3).

Other feminists tried to derive the necessary form and/or functions of the patriarchal state from the imperatives of reproduction (rather than production), from the changing forms of patriarchal domination, or from the 'domestic' mode of production, and so forth. Such work suffers from similar theoretical problems to the Marxist derivation debate, namely, the assumption that form necessarily follows function and the consequent denial of any real autonomy or contingency to the state. In some cases this simply provides a feminist variation on economism; in others we find a more elaborate version of subsumptionism which defines all too well the mechanisms guaranteeing the state's patriarchal character (cf. criticisms in Jenson 1986; Walby 1990).

Others again try to analyse the contingent articulation of patriarchal and capitalist forms of domination as crystallized in the state. The best work shows that patriarchal and gender relations make a difference to the state at the same time as refusing to prejudge the form and effects of this difference. In other words, 'acknowledging that gender inequality exists does not automatically imply that every capitalist state is involved in the reproduction of that inequality in the same ways or to the same extent' (Jenson 1986: 10; cf. Brenner and Laslett 1991). The same sort of approach highlights differences among women as well as between gender groups, and this is an important corrective to extreme forms of gender essentialism. Indeed there is now an extensive literature on the complex and variable forms of articulation of class, gender, and ethnicity in specific state structures and policy areas (e.g., Boris 1995; Sainsbury 1994; Williams 1995). This 'intersectional' approach has been elaborated by third wave feminists and queer theorists, who emphasize the instability and socially constructed arbitrariness of dominant views of sexual and gender identities and show the wide variability of masculine as well as feminine identities and interests (on third wave feminism, see Butler 1990; Ferree et al. 1999; Fraser 1997; Mann and Huffman 2005; Randall and Waylen 1998; Yuval-Davis 1997; for a useful introduction to queer theory, Duggan 1994; and for critiques of this approach from a materialist position, see Ebert 1996, 2005, and Hennessy 2000). This has created the theoretical space for a recent revival of explicit interest in gender and the state, which has contributed much across a broad range of issues – including how specific constructions of masculinity and femininity, their associated gender identities, interests, roles, and bodily forms come to be privileged in the state's own discourses, institutions, and material practices (for a review of increasingly nuanced feminist state-theoretical studies in jurisprudence, criminology, and welfare state policies and practices, see Haney 2000). Such studies rule out any analysis of the state as a simple expression of patriarchal domination and also cast doubt on the very utility of 'patriarchy' as an analytical category (see chapter 7).

The best feminist scholarship on state theory casts doubt on key malestream assumptions. First, it is widely argued that the modern state claims a legitimate monopoly over the means of coercion. Feminists often attack this view because men can get away with violence (not to say murder) against women in the confines of the family and, through the reality, threat, or fear of rape, also oppress women in public spaces. The orthodoxy relates to the separation of coercion from the organization of production in market economies and to the associated centralization of publicly organized power rather than to the exercise of parental or patriarchal coercion in the family (interestingly, Weber makes the same point: 1978: 56–8). Even so feminists might add that this rational-legal legitimation of state coercion is just the public form assumed by masculine violence and is actually used to support its private expression within the family and civil society.

Such arguments were taken further in work on different forms of masculinity and the state (Connell 1995, 1996). This last point bears on a second crucial contribution of feminist theorizing: its critique of the juridical distinction between 'public' and 'private'. This not only serves to obfuscate class relations (as Marxists have argued) but also, and perhaps even more fundamentally, hides a key mechanism of male domination. Thus, while Marxists suggest that the rise of the liberal bourgeois state and its attendant split between public citizen and private individual is grounded in capitalist development, feminists would interpret it as the product of the patriarchal ordering of the bourgeois state (Eisenstein 1981). While Marxists tend to equate the public sphere with the state and the private sphere with private property, exchange, and individual rights, feminists tend to equate the former with both the state and civil society, the latter with the domestic sphere and women's alleged place in the 'natural' order of reproduction. Men and women are differentially located in the public and private spheres; indeed, historically, women have been excluded from the public sphere and subordinated to men in the private. Yet men's independence as citizens and as workers is premised on women's role in caring for them at home (Pateman 1988: 120, 123, 203). Moreover, even where women have won full citizenship rights, their continuing oppression and subjugation in the private sphere hinders their exercise and enjoyment of these rights (Siim 1988: 163).[6] Not only is the distinction between 'public' and 'private' political, then, but the very organization of the 'private' sphere has major implications for the strategic selectivity of the state.

A third area of feminist criticism focuses on the links between warfare, masculinity, and the state. In brief, as Connell notes, 'the state arms men and disarms women' (1987: 126; cf. Elshtain 1987). At its most extreme, this criticism involves concepts such as the 'sado-state' (Daly 1984), the suggestion that the military apparatus is a simple expression of male aggression and destructiveness, or the view that militarism and imperialism are expressions of a cult of violent masculinity (Fernbach 1981). Thus Lloyd notes that 'the masculinity of citizenship and the masculinity of war have been conceptually connected in Western thought' (1986: 64). More nuanced historical accounts have shown how state legitimacy is structured in terms of masculinity: whilst the *Ancien Régime* was organized around notions of personal and family honour, patronage, and military prowess, for example, the modern state rests on ideas of rationality, calculation, orderliness, hierarchy, and informal masculine codes and networks (Connell 1990: 521; Landes 1988; on modern bureaucracies, whether public or private, Ferguson 1984; and, more generally on different forms of masculinity, Connell 1995, 1996).

Three broad positions could be adopted by non-feminist and/or non-queer theorists to such work: (a) dismiss it as irrelevant; (b) accept it as an important supplement to the core contributions of another account; or (c) welcome it as a fundamental challenge to the received wisdom. The first position is untenable, for, as the second view suggests, feminist research shows that other theories have missed or marginalized key aspects of the state's form and functions and has also provided new examples of how form problematizes function and creates specific contradictions, dilemmas, and conflicts. This holds for conventional Marxist and neo-statist accounts and the study of international relations (e.g., Enloe 1983, 2000; Peterson 1992; Sylvester 1994, 2002) and interest in Foucauldian analyses (for critical feminist appropriations of the latter, see, e.g., Cooper 1995; Fraser 1988; McNay 1992; Martin 1982; Ramazanoglu 1993; Sawacki 1991). Moreover, supporting the third view, feminist research shows basic flaws in malestream theorizing. Thus an adequate account of the strategic complexity of the state must include the key feminist insights into the gendered nature of the state's structural selectivity and capacities for action as well as its key role in reproducing specific patterns of gender relations (see chapter 7).

Discourse Analysis and Stateless State Theory

To read some discourse-analytic work might lead one to believe that the best kept of all official secrets is that the state does not exist (e.g., Abrams 1988: 77). Instead it is an illusion: a product of the political imaginary. Its emergence depends on the prevalence of state discourses (cf. Neocleous 2003). The state appears on the political scene because political forces orient their actions towards the 'state', acting as if it existed. But, since there is no common discourse of the state (at most there is a dominant or hegemonic discourse) and different political forces orient their action at different times to different ideas of the state, the state is at best a polyvalent, polycontextual phenomenon and its institutional architecture, *modus operandi*, and specific activities change along with the dominant political imaginaries and state projects. Various theoretical or analytical approaches support this argument.

First, following a review of Marxist and other attempts to define the state as a distinct material entity, agent, function, or political relation, Abrams noted that such attempts only create difficulties. He recommended abandoning the state as a material object of study. For the institutional ensemble that comprises government can be studied without resorting to the concept of the state; and the 'idea of the state' can be studied in turn as the distinctive collective (mis-)representation of capitalist societies that serves to mask the true nature of political practice (Abrams 1988). Political systems theorists have condemned the conceptual morass and vapid debates that accompany state theorizing (e.g., Easton 1981). But Abrams is both more positive and more negative because he ascribes a constitutive role to the 'state idea' in both shaping and disguising political domination. In turn this calls for a historical analysis of the 'cultural revolution' (or ideological shifts) involved when state systems are transformed (cf. Corrigan and Sayer 1985). This approach has become much more significant in recent years with the development of post-structural, post-modern, and Foucauldian accounts of the constitutive role of political imaginaries, geo-political imaginaries, and risk and security discourses.

Second, Melossi urged a 'stateless theory of the state', that is, recognition that the state is just a juridical concept, an idea that enables people to 'do the state', to furnish themselves and others with reasons and grounds for their own actions. As such, it can be used reflexively by different types of official to provide a vocabulary of motives for their (in)actions and to account for the state's unity in a divided and unequal civil society (Melossi 1990: 2, 6, 150). Thus state autonomy should not be seen as a reified property of a reified state. Instead it varies with the degree of autonomy with which governmental elites see themselves endowed in specific places at particular times (Melossi 1990: 128; cf. Watson 1990: 7). This argument connects with a growing body of work in the field of political performativity, practices of statecraft, and the involvement of everyday practices and habitus in reproducing political order (e.g., Bratsis 2006; Goswani 2004; Hood 1998; Neocleous 2003; Painter 2006; Scott 1998).

Third, in addition to general ideological demystification and an emphasis on the self-reflexive use of the state idea, we find a growing interest in specific narrative, rhetorical, or argumentative features of state power. This is reflected in various case studies of policy-making that suggest that state policies do not objectively represent the interests located in or beyond the state or objectively reflect 'real' problems in the internal or external environments of the political system. For they are discursively mediated, if not wholly discursively constituted, products of struggles to define and narrate 'problems' that can be addressed through state action. It follows that the effectiveness of policy-making is closely tied to its rhetorical and argumentative framing – especially as effectiveness, like beauty, often exists only in the eyes (or ears) of the beholder (see, e.g., Bevir and Rhodes 2003; Fischer and Forester 1993; Hajer and Wagenaar 2003; Roe 1994; Schram and Neisser 1997). In addition to detailed domestic policy studies along these lines, 'critical geo-politics' has made important contributions on key international dimensions of the state – notably discourses of sovereignty, the changing nature of 'security' and threats thereto, and the remaking of states' territorial boundaries (e.g., Bartelson 1995; Campbell 1992; Dillon and Reid 2001; Kunz 2005; Luke 1994; O Tuathail 1996; Walker 1993).

Fourth, theorists of the increasing functional differentiation of modern societies have advanced the idea that the 'state' is simply a self-description or internal model of the political system. The key feature of contemporary functional systems is their radical operational autonomy or autopoiesis (on autopoiesis, see Jessop 1990b; Luhmann 1989, 1990b, 1990c, 1995, 2000). This derives from their power to determine their own operational codes and programmes and to reproduce (or transform) themselves despite attempts at control from outside and/or other perturbing influences in their environment. One such system is the modern economy as a self-organizing system of payments (cf. Marxists on the self-valorization of capital). Two others are the legal system (a self-contained and self-modifying system of legally binding legal decisions) and the political system (a circuit of power passing among governors and governed and producing decisions that are binding on all participants). Since power continually circulates through the political system, it is wrong to reify the state by treating it as a distinct entity with its own power and resources. Certainly the centrifugal dynamic of functionally differentiated modern societies means that the state is no longer able to play the superordinate role attributed to it in early modern political theory (Willke 1986). It is best understood as the means whereby participants simplify problems of political action by polarizing them around the issue of government and opposition. And the polity in turn should be seen as one system among others in a polycentric, fundamentally anarchic society. Neither it nor the 'state' is superordinate or sovereign. Instead they are the means that supplies society with legitimate and binding decisions about collective goods. These include internal and external security (with the infrastructural power to secure this collective good being based on organized violence); economic and social security (with a key role for government-controlled fiscal and financial resources); and, most recently, technological and ecological security (where infrastructural capacities are based on collectively organized knowledge). Each of these forms of security corresponds to distinctive political projects and forms of intervention. Thus the contemporary polity is particularly concerned with how best to 'guide' other functional systems without attempting direct (and fruitless) intervention into their operations. This is said to be best achieved by defining the parameters within which they operate, generating knowledge about the unintended external consequences of their activities, and seeking to build consensus on social projects (see Luhmann 1990c; Teubner 1993; and, most importantly in this context, Willke 1992, 1996; on changing state capacities and knowledge, see also Wagner 1989 and Wittrock 1989).

In all four cases, rejection of state reification is linked to efforts to theorize the critical role of the idea of the state and its associated narrative and rhetorical practices in the operation of the political system and/or wider society. This role is variously defined as mystification, self-motivation, pure narrativity, or self-description, but, regardless of standpoint, discourses about the state have a key constitutive role in shaping the state as a complex ensemble of political relations linked to society as a whole. This approach contrasts markedly with the reification of the state–society distinction in state-centred theorizing. It also offers a different slant on the Foucauldian rejection of orthodox accounts of the state by highlighting the functions of such accounts within the political system. And, for autopoietic theorizing at least, it gives further, systems-theoretical reasons for disputing that the modern state could ever be a superordinate, sovereign authority standing above society and controlling it from outside.

New Directions of Research

Despite declining interest in the more esoteric and abstract modes of theorizing about the state, substantive research on states and state power has exploded in recent years so that the literature can no longer be reviewed in a comprehensive manner. But we can mention five themes that have attracted serious attention from various perspectives and offer a useful point of confrontation among the theoretical approaches outlined above. These are: the historical variability of statehood (or stateness); the relative strength or weakness of states; the future of the national state in an era of globalization and regionalization; issues of scale, space, territoriality, and the state; and the rise of governance mechanisms and their articulation with government. None of these issues can be adequately addressed without turning from the abstract theorizing that marked early stages in the rediscovery of the state and all five pose theoretical and empirical problems that only well-developed and sophisticated theoretical frameworks could ever hope to decipher.

First, interest in stateness has been prompted both by growing disquiet about the abstract nature of much state theory (especially its assumption of a ubiquitous, unified, sovereign state) and increasing interest in the historical variability of actual states. This has led some theorists to focus on the state as a conceptual variable and to examine the varied presence of the idea of the state (Dyson 1980; Melossi 1990; Nettl 1968). Others have examined the state's differential presence as a distinctive political form. Thus Badie and Birnbaum usefully distinguish between the political centre required in any complex social division of labour and the state as but one possible institutional locus of this centre. For them, the defining features of the state are its structural differentiation, autonomy, universalism, and institutional solidity. They see France as having the archetypal state in a centralized society; Britain has a political centre but no state; Germany has a state but no centre; and the Helvetian Confederation (Switzerland) has no state and no centre (Badie and Birnbaum 1983). Such approaches are important because they historicize the state idea and stress the wide variety of its institutional forms. A growing number of studies have explored these issues on all scales from the local to the international with considerable concern for meso-level variation.

Second, while stateness as a variable concerns the institutionalization of the state, interest in strong and weak states concerns the factors that make for state strength. This can be interpreted in two ways: internally it refers to a state's capacities to exercise authority over society; externally it refers to the state's power in the international community of states (on the latter, see especially Handel 1990). This concern is often linked with interest in the state's capacity to penetrate and organize the rest of society. It is especially marked in recent theoretical and empirical work on predatory and/or developmental states. Whereas the predatory state is essentially parasitic upon its economy and civil society, the developmental state has been able to develop one or both of them. Whereas predatory states have a significant measure of despotic power, developmental states enjoy a balance of despotic power and infrastructural power and wield it in market-conforming ways (e.g., Castells 1992; Evans 1989, 1995; Johnson 1987; Levi 1988; Weiss 1998; Weiss and Hobson 1995). One problem with much of this literature is its blanket contrast between strong and weak states. The wide range of interpretations of strength (and weakness) also undermines coherent analysis.[7] Most seriously, much work risks tautology insofar as strength is defined purely in terms of outcomes (for reviews, see Clark and Lemco 1988; Lauridsen 1991; Migdal 1988; Önis 1991; Waldner 1999). A possible solution is to adopt a strategic-relational approach to the variability of state capacities by policy area, over time, and in specific conjunctures.

Third, work on globalization has increasingly questioned the survival of the national state. This issue was already posed during earlier debates on the internationalization of finance and the activities of multinational firms. It has become more pressing with the emergence of the triadic economic blocs (North America, Europe, and East Asia), development of cross-border regional cooperation, and the re-emergence or rediscovery of cities, regions, and industrial districts as major bases of (international) competitiveness. Fourth, and closely linked to the previous issue, is the changing scale of politics. While some theorists tend to see the crisis of the national state as displacing the primary scale of political organization and action to either the global or the regional scale, others suggest that there has been a relativization of scale. For, whereas the national state provided the primary scale of political organization in the economic space of Atlantic Fordism, the current after-Fordist period is marked by the dispersion of political and policy issues across all scales of organization, with none of them primary. This poses particularly difficult problems about securing the coherence of action across different scales (for different approaches to both issues, see Beck and Grande 2004; Brenner 1999; Caporaso 1996; Evers 1994; Hirst and Thompson 1995; Jessop 1999; Mann 1993; Scharpf 1999; Schmitter 1992; Taylor 1995; Ziebura 1996; Zürn 1992).

Finally, if Atlantic Fordism was largely dominated by concerns about the relationship between state and market, the current theoretical and empirical agenda is much concerned with 'governance' and networks. This involves forms of coordination or concertation that rely neither on governmental hierarchies nor on market anarchy but are based on self-organization. Governance is emerging on different scales of organization (ranging from international and supranational regimes through national and regional public–private partnerships to more localized networks of power and decision-making). Although this trend is often taken to imply a diminution in state capacities, it has also been seen as enhancing its power to secure its interests and, indeed, as providing states with a new (or expanded) role in the metagovernance (or overall coordination) of different governance regimes and mechanisms (on governance, see Jessop 1995, 1998b, 2003c; Kitschelt 1991; Kooiman 1993; Messner 1998; Pierre 1999; Scharpf 1999; Streeck and Schmitter 1985).

Conclusions

This review reveals some interesting convergences among the approaches examined here. First, all seem to agree in dethroning the state from its superordinate position within society and analysing it simply as one institutional order among others. Marxists no longer treat it as the ideal collective capitalist; neo-statists no longer treat it as a sovereign legal subject; it has been deconstructed by Foucauldians; feminists no longer view it simply as the patriarch general; and discourse analysts and autopoieticists alike see it as constituted, ironically or otherwise, through contingent discursive or communicative practices. In short, the state is seen as an emergent, partial, and unstable system that is interdependent with other systems in a complex social order. This has vastly expanded the realm of contingency in the state and its operations and this implies the need for more concrete, historically specific, institutionally sensitive, and action-oriented research. All schools attempt in their different ways to provide such analyses and the same concerns can be found in the growing body of substantive research into stateness and the relative strength (and weakness) of particular political regimes. All of this marks an important general advance on the loose talk that equates the state to a simple thing or subject and/or neglects its variability as a complex social relation within and across given societies.

Second, these structural powers and capacities cannot be understood by focusing on the state alone but must be located in their broader 'strategic-relational' context. For, by virtue of its structural selectivity and always specific strategic capacities, state powers are always conditional or relational. Their realization depends on the structural ties between the state and its encompassing political system, the strategic links among state managers and other political forces, and the complex web of interdependencies and social networks linking the state and political system to its broader environment. It is here that neo-statism often proves weak due to its tendency to reify the state–society distinction and that discourse-analytic work often misses the deep-rooted, extra-discursive structural conditions that shape the effectiveness of state power. The other approaches considered above would find few difficulties in accepting this conclusion.

This suggests, finally, that an adequate state theory can only be produced as part of a wider theory of society. Even the neo-statists' principled rejection of a society-centred approach draws on arguments about the wider society both to reveal the state's distinctive logic and interests and to explore the conditions for its autonomy and effectiveness. Foucauldian, feminist, and discourse-analytic studies are even more clearly oriented to wider concerns: Foucault starts from a socially dispersed micro-physics of power, feminism is concerned with gender relations, and stateless state theory begins from the discursive constitution of the state. Recent Marxist work also continues, of course, to relate the state to capitalism and the anatomy of civil society. This involves an important redirection of work on the state and state power. But it is precisely on this terrain that many of the unresolved problems of state theory are located. For the state is the site of a paradox. On the one hand, it is just one institutional ensemble among others within a social formation; on the other, it is peculiarly charged with overall responsibility for maintaining the cohesion of the social formation of which it is a part. Its paradoxical position as both part and whole of society means that it is continually called upon by diverse social forces to resolve society's problems and is equally continually doomed to generate 'state failure' since so many of society's problems lie well beyond its control and can even be aggravated by attempted intervention. Many of the differences between theories of the state considered above are rooted in contrary approaches to various structural and strategic moments of this paradox. Trying to comprehend the overall logic (or, perhaps, 'illogic') of this paradox may well be the best route to resolving some of these differences as well as providing a more comprehensive analysis of the strategic-relational character of the state in a polycentric social formation.

Part II

Sources of the Strategic-Relational Approach

3

Marx on Political Representation and the State

The Eighteenth Brumaire of Louis Bonaparte has a key place in debates over Marx's approach to the state and political representation. According to some critics, this text embodies two potentially complementary theories of the state. Thus, whereas Marx normally saw the state as the executive committee or direct instrument of the ruling class, in some contexts he regarded it as relatively autonomous from all classes even as it continued to perform a class function (e.g., Miliband 1965). For others, this same text reveals devastating inconsistencies in Marx's class-based account of the state, because it allows for an executive (apparatus) that wins autonomy for itself *against* the dominant class(es). This inconsistency is said to be especially clear in Marx's subsequent remarks on the tendential rise of a *pretorian state*, in which the army, led by Bonaparte III, starts to represent itself against society rather than acting on behalf of one part of society against others. This emerges especially clearly in a one-off statement that

> the rule of the naked sword is proclaimed in most unmistakable terms, and Bonaparte wants France to clearly understand that the imperial rule does rest not on her will but on 600,000 bayonets. . . . Under the second Empire the interest of the army itself is to predominate. The army is no longer to maintain the rule of one part of the people over another part of the people. The army is to maintain its own rule, personated by its own dynasty, over the French people in general. . . . It is to represent the *State* in antagonism to the *society*. It must not be imagined that Bonaparte is not aware of the dangerous character of the experiment he tries. In proclaiming himself the chief of the Pretorians, he declares every Pretorian chief his competitor. (1858: 465)

According to Mehlman, for example, 'the piquancy of Bonapartism lies entirely in the emergence of a State which has been emptied of its class

This is a lightly revised and expanded version of 'The politics of representation and the Eighteenth Brumaire', in M. Cowling and J. Martin, eds, *The Eighteenth Brumaire Today*, London: Pluto Press, 2002, 179–94.

contents' (1977: 15; cf. Hunt 1974: 47–56). Others suggest that Marx resolves these alleged inconsistencies 'by analysing the Bonapartist regime, if not as the organized rule of a class bloc, nevertheless as the determined product of the class struggle' (Fernbach 1973: 15; cf. Berberoglu 1986). For others again, the same text confirms the generic (rather than exceptional) tendency of the capitalist state to acquire relative autonomy in order better to organize the interests of the dominant class(es) and to win the support of subordinate classes (e.g., Poulantzas 1973). The exceptional nature of state autonomy in the Bonapartist case merely indicates the exceptional nature of the circumstances in which this role has to be played (see also Draper 1977).

The Eighteenth Brumaire poses similar problems for the nature and significance of representation in the wider political system, for the complexity of the ideological and organizational forms in which Marx claims to discern class interests at work undermines any attempt to show a one-to-one correlation between economic classes and political forces. Some commentators suggest that this indicates the need to take political identities, political discourses, and political forms of representation seriously in theoretical analysis and to explore the practical problems this poses in advancing economic interests (Katz 1992; LaCapra 1987; Lefort 1978; McLennan 1981). According to others this simply confirms the radical disjunction between the economic and political such that no unilateral translation or relay mechanism can ensure that politics reflects economic class interests (e.g., Hindess 1978, Hirst 1977). This highlights the problem of economic class reductionism that allegedly plagues Marxism and leads to the twin conclusions that political representation has its own dynamic and that it is invalid to look behind the political stage to discover hidden economic forces. Yet others argue that this text illustrates how much Marx anticipated later discourse-theoretical insights into the performative nature of language, the discursive constitution of identities and interests, and their role in shaping the forms and terms of political struggle. For Marx regarded politics in *The Eighteenth Brumaire* as formative rather than superstructural, performative rather than reflective (Petrey 1988; Stallybrass 1990).

For these and other reasons, *The Eighteenth Brumaire* appears as a key text for any interpretation of Marx's state and political theory. Its implications for state theory and class analysis are typically contrasted with a 'standard' Marxian position derived variously (and with quite different results) from *The Communist Manifesto* (1848), the 1859 *Preface to the Contribution to the Critique of Political Economy* (1859), or the three volumes of *Capital*. This is a highly dubious procedure because the *Manifesto* is a programmatic text that serves as a prophetic call to arms rather than providing a detailed analysis of class formation and political representation; because the status of the *Preface* as a canonical text is highly questionable given that it was written under the financial pressure of a publisher's deadline and the political pressure to divert the Prussian censor's gaze from the revolutionary implications of Marx's critique of political economy so that *A Contribution to the Critique of Political Economy* could be published (cf. Prinz 1969); and because Marx's analysis of class in *Capital* is incomplete even in economic, let alone political or ideological, terms (cf. Krätke 2002, 2003; Lebowitz 2003). There can be no innocent reading of *The Eighteenth Brumaire* but it might be useful to read it initially without adopting preconceived views about Marx's theory of the state and class politics that have been derived from other studies that were not concerned with specific political conjunctures. So the first question to ask is: what does Marx aim to achieve in his history of *The Eighteenth Brumaire*? (All quotations from this text, Marx 1852, are from Terrell Carver's 2001 translation and are indicated in this chapter by the abbreviation *18B*.)

What Does *The Eighteenth Brumaire* Accomplish?

First, as a substantive exercise in historiography, *The Eighteenth Brumaire* describes the background to Louis Bonaparte's *coup d'état* on 2 December 1851 and treats it as the farcical repetition of the tragic *coup d'état* made by Napoleon Bonaparte on 9 November 1799 (or, as it was identified in the new revolutionary calendar, the 18th Brumaire VIII). It presents the run-up to this *coup d'état* in terms of a periodization of political developments that is analysed in terms of four closely interwoven objects of inquiry. These comprise the following:

1 The *political scene*, that is, the visible but nonetheless 'imaginary' world of everyday politics as acted out before the general public through the open and declared action of more or less well-organized social forces (Poulantzas 1973: 246–7). Marx employs a wide range of theoretical metaphors and allusions to describe and map the political stage and to critically assess how the resulting political theatre is played out by actors who assume different characters, masks, and roles according to changing material circumstances, strategies, and moods.
2 The *social content* of the politics acted out on this stage. This involves a closer inspection of 'the rude external world' (Marx *18B*: 90) based on looking 'behind the scenes' (*18B*: 57) of 'the situation and the parties,

this superficial appearance, which veils the *class struggle*' (*18B*: 55). This class struggle is nonetheless related to the present situation and its various strategic and tactical possibilities rather than to abstract, eternal, and idealized interests that are attached to pre-given classes defined purely in terms of their position in the social relations of production. Thus Marx emphasizes the concrete-complex articulation of the economic and *extra*-economic conditions for the 'expanded reproduction'[1] of specific class relations and what this implies for the reordering of what are always relative advantages in the class struggle. In this sense he also describes *avant la lettre* the stakes, strategies, and tactics involved in what Gramsci (1971) would later term 'wars of position' and 'wars of manoeuvre'.

3 The transformation of the *institutional architecture of the state* and wider political system insofar as this entails a structural framework that differentially constrains and facilitates the pursuit of particular strategies and tactics in wars of position and/or manoeuvre, provides a target of strategic action in its own right as diverse political forces struggle to maintain or transform it, and, indeed, itself derives from the results of past class (or, at least, class-relevant) struggles in the ideological, political, and economic realms.

4 The interconnected movements of the *local, national, and international economy* over different time scales insofar as these shape the political positions that could feasibly have been adopted in given conjunctures. Here too, although Marx strongly asserts his belief (and, indeed, even protests too much in this regard) that the ultimate victory of the proletarian social revolution is guaranteed, he also emphasizes the need to relate political action to the present situation.

Note that these four moments imply a strategic-relational approach to periodization that is deeply sensitive to spatio-temporality and to the different ways in which strategic-relationality operates.

Second, Marx also poses questions throughout this text about the *language and other symbols* in and through which the class content of politics comes to be represented or, more commonly, misrepresented. This reflects an interest in discourse in its various forms that was present in his work from the beginning but is rarely given full recognition (for an exception see Fairclough and Graham 2002; for an early illustration, see Marx 1844; and, more generally, see Cook 1982; Erckebrecht 1972; Lecercle 2004; Ruschinski and Retzleff-Kresse 1974). Thus *The Eighteenth Brumaire* develops a strategic-relational approach to semiosis. Marx explores the semiotic forms, genres, and tropes through which political forces articulate their identities, interests, and beliefs and reflects on the appropriate political language in which the proletariat might formulate its demands. He argues that the social revolution of the nineteenth century must develop its own, novel political language rather than draw, as did earlier revolutions, on the 'poetry of the past' (*18B*: 34). Thus *The Eighteenth Brumaire* is more concerned with the discursive limitations on the representation of class interests ('tradition from all the dead generations', 'the superstition of the past', 'an entire superstructure of different and peculiarly formed sentiments, delusions, modes of thought and outlooks on life': *18B*: 32, 34, 56) than it is with the organizational forms through which they might be advanced. This need to develop an appropriate political language holds particularly for the proletariat and its potential allies. Indeed, one could well interpret this text as a contribution to the critique of *semiotic* economy, that is, to an account of the imaginary (*mis*)recognition and (*mis*)representation of class interests, rather than to the political economy of capital accumulation. The most extreme illustration of this is found in the floating signifier himself, Louis Bonaparte. For, as Marx argued in *The Class Struggles in France*, although Bonaparte was 'the most simple-minded [*einfältig*] man in France', he had 'acquired the most multiplex [*vielfältig*] significance. Just because he was nothing, he could signify everything save himself' (1850: 81). So different class forces could project their own hopes and fears onto Bonaparte; and he in turn skilfully manipulated and exploited this polyvalence for his own purposes.

Third, as a serious and self-consciously literary work in its own right, *The Eighteenth Brumaire* adopts a highly distinctive and powerful set of literary techniques to narrate the historical background of the *coup d'état*. Above all it adopts the form of parody to unfold this narrative, portray the ironies in French history, express the problems of class representation, and resolve the relative importance of external circumstances and willed action in shaping the course of history. In this regard Marx's use of language is itself performative at several levels. Indeed, as he puts it in his preface to the second edition, he intended to submit the cult of the first Napoleon to 'the weapons of historical research, of criticism, of satire and of wit' (*18B*: 8). Thus Marx's withering descriptions of Louis Bonaparte also serve to belittle the stature of his uncle, Napoleon Bonaparte. As an intervention intended to influence the subsequent course of French politics, Marx's use of a specific literary genre and his choice of language have specific pedagogical and political purposes. Far from being arbitrary, then, his mode of emplotting the historical background to the 18th Brumaire is organically related to the intended political effects of this narrative.

On Periodization

Marx's text presents a complex periodization of contemporary history rather than a simple chronology. As such it has inspired many subsequent Marxist analyses and also won the respect of many orthodox historians for its theoretical power and empirical insight. In the first instance Marx relates key turning points in the class struggle to the unfolding of actions and events on the political stage. He distinguishes three successive periods, the first of brief duration, the second and third having three phases each, and the third phase of the third period having four steps (*18B*: 110–11).[2] His periodization is mainly based on movements in parliamentary and party politics as these are influenced by actions and events occurring at a distance from the state (e.g., in the press, petitions, salons and saloon bars, the streets of Paris, the countryside, etc.: *18B*: 50, 59, 70, 71). Marx identifies the three periods as follows: (a) the 'February' period from 24 February to 4 May 1848 in which, after the overthrow of Louis Philippe, the stage was prepared for the republic – the period of improvised or provisional government; (b) the period of constituting the republic or the constituent assembly for the nation; and (c) the constitutional republic or legislative national assembly (*18B*: 36–7). It is worth noting here that Marx offers three interpretations of each period. First, he refers to its immediate conjunctural significance. Second, he discusses the primary institutional site in and around which the political drama unfolds. And, third, he examines each period (and its phases, where these are distinguished) in terms of its past, present, and, as far as it was already on the public record or Marx deemed it knowable, future significance.

Periodizations and chronologies differ in three ways. First, whereas a chronology orders actions, events, or periods on a single unilinear time scale, a periodization operates with several time scales. Thus *The Eighteenth Brumaire* is replete with references to intersecting and overlapping time horizons, to unintended as well as self-conscious repetitions, to dramatic reversals and forced retreats as well as to surprising turnarounds and forward advances, and to actions and events whose true significance would emerge only in the later course of history. Second, while a chronology recounts simple temporal coincidence or succession, a periodization focuses on more complex conjunctures. It classifies actions, events, and periods into stages according to their conjunctural implications (as specific combinations of constraints and opportunities on the pursuit of different projects) for the actions of different social forces on different sites of action over different time horizons. For each period, Marx identifies the possibilities it offers for different actors, identities, interests, horizons of action, strategies, and tactics. He also interprets periods from diverse perspectives (e.g., from a long-term democratic viewpoint as opposed to the immediate stakes declared by protagonists); emphasizes how the balance of forces comes to be transformed over time (e.g., the neutralization of democratic elements in the army through a series of deliberate manoeuvres); and identifies decisive turning points (e.g., the Party of Order's loss of the lever of executive power when it was excluded from the Cabinet) (*18B*: 55, 64, 67). Third, whereas a chronology typically provides a simple narrative explanation for what occurs by identifying a single temporal series of actions and events, a periodization rests on an explanatory framework oriented to the contingent, overdetermined interaction of more than one such series. In this regard there can be no doubt about the complex emplotment of *The Eighteenth Brumaire*. For it presents a story marked by repetition and deferral, tragedy and farce, high politics and low cunning, political theatre and mob violence – set against a background in which a modern French national capitalism is gradually being consolidated in city and countryside alike in the broader context of an increasingly integrated world market. This provides the basis for a complex narrative.

The Political Stage

Marx is especially concerned with the language and impact of political action on the political stage and explores this in terms of a wide range of theatrical metaphors. This could well reflect both real changes in the nature of politics following the French Revolution and Marx's own interest in literary forms, styles, and tropes along with his extensive knowledge of specific plays and novels. For, on the one hand, the French Revolution coincided with major changes in the actors' art in the literary theatre and in the official politics of representation. As Friedland has shown, based on detailed analyses of French theatre and politics from 1789 to 1794, the theatre and acting were politicized and French politics was theatricalized. Given our concern with *The Eighteenth Brumaire*, it is important to note that French revolutionary politics did, indeed, adopt old political languages, old character masks, and old roles as its protagonists sought to develop a new politics of representation in which the national assembly now claimed to actively 'represent' the nation rather than, as occurred in the Estates system of the *Ancien Régime*, serving as its corporate embodiment (Friedland 1999, 2002). Marx, too, stresses the theatricality of politics not only as metaphor but also as a self-conscious political practice on the part of political actors as they sought to persuade and impress their audience by adopting character masks and roles from the historical past and/or from a dramatic repertoire. And, on the other hand, Marx had a solid grounding in ancient and modern philosophies of literature and drama, their theory and history, and an immense range of what he and Engels described in the *Communist Manifesto* as 'world literature' (see, in general, Prawer 1978; and, on *The Eighteenth Brumaire* in particular, Petrey 1988; Riquelme 1980; Rose 1978; Stallybrass 1998; White 1973). This is reflected in his passionate use of parody as a mode of emplotment to ridicule the two Bonapartes.

Marx takes great pains to emphasize how the political stage has its own effectivity. Far from being a simple political reflection of economic interests, it has its own logic and its own influence on class relations. This is quite consistent, of course, with *The Communist Manifesto*'s claim that every class struggle is a political struggle. This is almost painfully evident in Marx's initial attempts in the first instalment of *The Eighteenth Brumaire*, written, it should be recalled, in separate parts over several months and intended for serial publication,[3] to establish correspondences between different political parties and different classes or class fractions. But even at this stage Marx recognizes that there is no one-to-one fit between party and economic class interests (see, e.g., his analysis of the pure republican faction which, as he stresses, is little more than a political-intellectual coterie unified by shared political antipathies and nationalist sentiments: *18B*: 41). And, over the course of writing *The Eighteenth Brumaire*, Marx moves towards an account of the logic of political struggle in the modern (and capitalist type of) state and the manner in which specific conjunctures and distinctive institutional ensembles shape the forms and content of political struggle. Here he builds on the *institutional separation* and *potential antagonism* between state and civil society that he had already identified in his critique of Hegel's *Philosophy of Right* (Marx 1843); and he explores how the institutional terrain of the state apparatus and its articulation to the wider public sphere shapes the forms of politics. He notes many distinctive features of the state's organization and articulation to the public sphere – electoral, parliamentary, presidential, bureaucratic, administrative, military, state-orchestrated mob violence, etc. – that directly condition *not only* the diverse struggles on the political stage *but also* struggles that aim to modify the political balance of forces discursively, organizationally, and institutionally.

Among the many effects of the forms of politics on the course of political struggle we can note, first, the (inevitably constrained) choice of political genre and language in and through which different political forces express their aspirations. For, implicitly conceding that there is no neutral language in and through which social identities, interests, and desires can be truly and unambiguously expressed, Marx emphasizes that every political movement needs to find appropriate discourses and symbolism as the means of political expression to advance its interests. Second, Marx refers to the political space that this creates for the *literary representatives* of a class (*18B:* 59). Thus he notes the emergence of a parliamentary republican faction organized around political sentiments rather than common material interests or position in the relations of production. He describes this pure republican faction as no more than a 'coterie of republican-minded business, writers, lawyers, officers and officials whose influence rested on the personal antipathy of the country to Louis Philippe, on recollections of the old republic [of 1789–99], on the republican faith of a number of enthusiasts, above all on *French nationalism*' (*18B:* 41). Third, there is the phenomenon of '*parliamentary* cretinism, which confines its victims to an imaginary world and robs them of their senses, their recollection, all knowledge of the rude external world' (*18B:* 90). A fourth (but far from final) example is the emergence of a self-interested military and bureaucratic caste (see below).

The Social Content of Politics

Marx's account of the superficial (but nonetheless significant and causally effective) movements on the political stage is combined with an analysis of the 'social content of politics' (*18B:* 57). The economic 'base' figures in these analyses in two main ways. First, the necessary institutional separation and potential antagonism between state and civil society (and hence the existence of a specific type of political scene and its possible dissociation from the economy) depend on a particular form of economic organization. Second, and, for present purposes, more important, the economic 'base' is treated, rightly or wrongly, as the ultimate source of the *social* or *material* conditioning of political struggles. Here Marx refers both to the changing economic conjunctures and successive modes of growth in which political struggles occur and to the more general, underlying connection between these struggles and basic economic interests in a fundamentally capitalist social formation. Nonetheless the social content of politics is related mainly to the economic interests of the contending classes and class fractions in specific conjunctures and/or periods in a particular social formation rather than to abstract interests identified at the level of a mode of production. This approach is particularly important, of course, for intermediate classes (e.g., the petty bourgeoisie), classes with no immediate role in production (e.g., the surplus population), or *declassé* elements (e.g., the lumpenprole-tariat). But it also holds for other classes. For example, in writing about the central role of the peasantry in French politics, Marx noted how industrial-ization and the increasing power of financial capital had transformed its class position. Whereas it had been a major beneficiary of land redistribu-tion under Napoleon I, parcellization and debt had undermined the viabil-ity of many smallholdings and prompted a growing division between a revolutionary and a conservative peasantry. It was the latter whose propri-etorial identity and traditional aspirations Bonaparte claimed to represent (whilst doing little to help them in practice) and whom he also mobilized as a crucial *supporting class* in his political manoeuvres against other social forces. Likewise, over the course of successive analyses of the relations between the financial aristocracy and the industrial bourgeoisie, Marx would come to emphasize how their original antagonism was moderated through the emergence of a modern form of finance capital (for details, see Bologna 1993a, 1993b; Draper 1977).

In addition, Marx is careful to emphasize the scope for disjunction between the surface (but nonetheless effective) movement and the deeper social content of political struggle. Thus he writes that '[j]ust as in private life, one distinguishes between what a man thinks and says, and what he really is and does, so one must all the more in historical conflicts distinguish between the fine words and aspirations of the parties and their real organ-isation and their real interests, their image from their reality' (18B: 56). It is important, for example, to distinguish the ' "so-called" people's party' from a real people's party (18B: 55). Likewise, writing about the Orléanist and Legitimist factions of the bourgeoisie, Marx argues that,

> on the public stage, in high politics and matters of state, as a grand parlia-mentary party, they pawned off their royal houses with token acts of rev-erence, and adjourned the restoration of the monarchy *ad infinitum*, and did their real business as the *party of order*, i.e., under a *social* rather than a *political* banner, as a representative of the bourgeois world order, . . . as the bourgeois class against other classes, not as royalists against republicans. (18B: 57)

Interestingly and significantly, Marx also indicates that, the more critical the economic situation, the less significant becomes the disjunction between the political and the social. For divisions in the political field are then realigned, if possible, around more basic social conflicts. Divisions within the bourgeoisie are overcome, for example, when the bourgeoisie as a whole is threatened. Political crisis may also prompt a realignment of state and society when their separation risks becoming too antagonistic and con-flictual. Thus, some years after the 18th Brumaire, when a more or less completely autonomized Bonapartist 'rule of the sword' over society is threatened by social unrest, Napoleon III recognizes the need to retreat and rebuild his links to bourgeois civil society (on the Bonapartist 'rule of the pretorians', its specificity, and its limitations, see especially Marx 1858; and, for a conspectus and critical interpretation of Marx's writings on this issue, Draper 1977: 459–63).

The State Apparatus and Its Trajectory

Another dimension of Marx's analysis concerns the increasing centraliza-tion of state power in France and its implications for the antagonism between state and society. Two brief points are worth making here. One concerns how changes in the overall architecture of the state shape the terrain of political struggle and affect the political balance of forces. Strategic and tactical possibilities altered as the articulation among parlia-ment, Cabinet, and presidential authority was modified; or, again, as the state gained increasing control over every aspect of social life throughout the land. This claim was taken further in Marx's later remarks on the pre-torian state; and was even more carefully elaborated in *The Civil War in France* (Marx 1871a, 1871b). It reinforces the point that the existence of an institutionally separate state (and wider political system) excludes any pos-sibility that the political field can be a simple reflection of economic class interests. Instead the general form of the state and the particular form of political regimes modify the balance of forces and thereby become stakes in the class struggle itself. Marx develops this point most forcefully in exploring the implications of the transition from a monarchical regime to a parliamentary republic for the capacity of the two main fractions of the bourgeoisie to defend their common interests. Thus he writes:

> The *parliamentary republic* was more than the neutral territory where the two factions of the French bourgeoisie, legitimists and orléanists, large-scale landed property and industry, could take up residence with an equal right. It was the inescapable condition of their *joint* rule, the sole form of state in which the claims of their particular factions and those of all other classes of society were subjected to the general interest of the bourgeois class. As royalists, they lapsed into their old antagonism, a battle for supremacy between landed property and money, and the highest expres-sion of this antagonism, the personification of it, were their kings, their dynasties. (*18B*: 94)

Second, and as Marx takes pains to demonstrate, such state transformations are far from innocent; they are partly the result of political actions consciously directed at securing modifications in the balance of forces. The clearest example of this in *The Eighteenth Brumaire* is Louis Bonaparte's conduct of a war of position to centralize power in the hands of the president and then, through a final war of manoeuvre, to venture the *coup d'état* that serves as the denouement of this particular Bonapartist farce. But it does not follow that all such transformations are deliberate and their consequences intended (even if they are anticipated). For Marx also notes the double bind in which the French bourgeoisie found itself in the same conjuncture. Indeed, it 'was compelled by its class position both to negate the conditions of existence for any parliamentary power, including its own, and to make the power of the executive, its adversary, irresistible' (*18B*: 68).

More on Political Representation

The preceding analysis draws primarily from *The Eighteenth Brumaire* (1852). Examining this text in conjunction with his analysis of the preceding two years in *The Class Struggles in France* (1850), it becomes clear that Marx had a sophisticated approach not only to periodization but also to the nature and dynamics of political representation and its articulation with political class domination. Marx rarely implied a one-to-one correlation between class position, class identity, and partisan affiliation and usually took great pains to explore their contingent articulation and, indeed, frequent disarticulation. This is partly a reflection of his rigorous distinction between the political scene, the institutional architecture of the state, and the embedding of the state within a broader ensemble of economic and political forms and relations that engendered strategically selective constraints/opportunities on different economic, political, social, and intellectual forces. Moreover, in rejecting such a one-to-one correspondence, Marx and Engels also seem to have worked with a clear distinction between class position, class identity, and class politics based on their calculation of the *class relevance* of specific forms of economic, political, social, and intellectual action (and inaction) almost independently of the *class identity* proclaimed by a given social force and of the underlying *class position* of its participants and supporters (see also Jessop 1982: 212–25). In particular, they prioritized class relevance over class identity and therefore examined the significance of party programmes, party politics, and party organizations in this regard. It should be recalled here that the 1848 *Manifesto* was intended for a relatively disorganized political current rather than an organized political party. Marx and Engels continued to see communists simply as the most class-conscious, theoretically advanced, and resolute activists whose task was to assist workers in struggle and to deepen and broaden working-class organization (Debrizzi 1982). In short, class is the key concept in their approach to politics, not party (cf. von Beyme 1995).

They nonetheless emphasized that political parties had a key role to play in class politics. Indeed, following the emergence of the period of mass politics with the revolutions in 1848, the political project of Marx and Engels depended strongly on the success of party forms of organization. Thereafter they emphasized that revolutionary theory must be de-militarized – even from a military viewpoint, the insurrectionary approach was out of date – and there must be a shift from conspiratorial societies to propaganda organizations (Marx and Engels 1850; see also Nimtz 2000: 83–112, 141–67).[4] Moreover, in arguing for the necessity of party political organization, they rejected other political forms such as secret leagues and conspiratorial groups and called for open forms of political organization insofar as these were permitted by the authorities.

Johnstone (1967) has explored this issue in terms of the different types of party that Marx and Engels joined and/or attempted at different times to promote. He notes five types: (1) small international communist cadres organized in and through the Communist League from 1847 to 1852 and largely concerned with propaganda and entering other parties to develop a mass line; (2) the 'Marx party', which Marx and Engels tried to develop as an intellectual centre with no definite organizational form following the decline of the working-class movement after the period of revolutionary ferment; (3) the First International, which they used to promote a broad, international federation of working-class organizations and mass parties based on internal democracy; (4) national Marxist mass parties, to which they gave broad support and encouragement to adopt a radical, communist programme; and, in the absence of such mass parties and significant numbers of socialist intellectuals, they backed (5) broad working-class parties organized independently of middle-class parties, encouraging them to work on Chartist lines (Johnstone 1967).

This analysis is quite consistent with Cunliffe's (1981) suggestion that Marx and Engels saw particular 'parties' as just temporary expressions of the 'class' as it matured towards self-emancipation. Thus their most general use of the term referred to working-class political organization in general and did not privilege any particular form of party organization. Taken in the 'great historical sense', then, party referred to the gradual, spontaneous, historical development of the working-class movement, including each and every manifestation of its political organization. This view was opposed to all sectarian organizations that sought to liberate the working class through conspiratorial *coups d'état* and/or through utopian-messianic propaganda addressed to the downtrodden masses. Regardless of their specific type, each instance of the 'party' would be large-scale and have a democratic internal structure. Second, within this framework, Marx and Engels also applied the term 'party' to formally organized groups which had a programmatic commitment to the conquest of power for the working class. Third, since this left a measure of ambiguity about organizations such as the Communist League or the First International, Marx and Engels also offered a more restrictive definition that applied only to parties which also had a national organization, a national programme, and were oriented to a national framework of state power. The 'Chartists' and the German Socialist Party (SPD) exemplified this third type of party. Finally, Marx sometimes used 'party' to refer to a group aspiring to understand and propagate Marxian theory, whether or not it was organized, national, programmatic, as long as it rejected sectarianism and ceded place to the historical party as and when it grew in power. Cunliffe (1981) concludes that the common element in each definition is the distinction between 'party' and 'sect' and that Marx and Engels were committed in all their own political struggles to an open and spontaneous organization of the working class. This analysis is quite consistent with a strategic-relational approach to state power insofar as it both assesses the significance of different forms of party organization and mobilization in relation to the prevailing state form and political conjuncture and calculates the appropriate political strategy to be followed in the light of a strategic context analysis of what could reasonably be achieved within a given time horizon and on the basis of more or less extensive alliances within and across national boundaries.

Turning from his reflections on the organization of the working class to his more general analysis of political parties as forms of political representation, a certain consistency emerges in Marx's approach. His work was especially concerned with alternative forms of political organization that transcended the formal institutional separation of economic and political, representatives and represented typical of the liberal democratic state (see especially his critique of Hegel's *Philosophy of Right* and his comments on the Paris Commune). Parties had a key role in this context once we see party as involving more than electoral strategies or the relations among voters, parties, and leaders. For political parties should provide the organic connection among different social forces that links forms of representation and the institutional architecture of the state system and the exercise of power. But, as Marx's historical analyses demonstrate again and again and as his own political battles were to prove likewise, this organic link cannot be taken for granted. The disjunction between democratic rhetoric and undemocratic practice was so clear in the 1830s and 1840s that Marx hardly needed to elaborate on it (Doveton 1994; cf. Nimtz 1999, 2000). Subsequently, as *The Eighteenth Brumaire* and *The Civil War in France* demonstrate, Marx was able to distinguish between appearance and reality – between the language and the imaginary aspirations of parties and their real character and interests, between the historical functions of republican discourse in providing a crucial ideological support for the institutions of capitalist society and the potential of republican institutions once the material bases of class exploitation have been eliminated (cf. Isaac 1990). Indeed, Marx is acutely aware of the frequent disjunction between classes-in-themselves and their organization through discussion circles, clubs, cooperative organizations, trade unions, professional bodies, newspapers, political parties, and so forth, as classes-for-themselves. Serious attention to such forms of organization is essential for the otherwise unbridgeable gap between class-in-itself and class-for-itself to be explored and explained (cf. Balibar 1978; Gramsci 1971; Poulantzas 1967, 1978b).

In this regard Katz (1992) suggests that Marx distinguishes two axes of class conflict: the first concerns the conflict among various social forces to shape the contours and the stakes of such conflict in particular ways and the second involves conflicts between classes as they emerge (and to the extent that they do) from struggle to define them and their interests (cf. Przeworski 1977). Katz further suggests that the complexities of *The Eighteenth Brumaire* are due to Marx's attempts to grapple with both axes. This is especially clear in his analysis of the different fractions of the nineteenth-century French peasantry. The structural definition of this class refers to its private property in small land parcels; but one cannot understand its differential capacity for class struggle against aristocratic proprietors and modern capital without taking account of the legacies of earlier struggles, the relative importance in different conditions of internal divisions among the peasantry, and issues of political culture. Thus Marx's concern was to understand the different forms that peasant resistance could take and the reasons why they were incapable of independent class action on a national basis. On this basis, Katz (1992) concludes that class action cannot be derived exclusively from the structural coordinates of a class (even if these are broadly defined), but also depends on how culture and politics affect capacities for resistance and struggle and on the changing social conjuncture.

This poses major problems of a strategic-relational character concerning the structurally inscribed selectivity of particular forms of state and its insertion into the broader political system and the capacities for political reflexion and self-organization of social forces over different spatio-temporal horizons of action (see chapters 1 and 9). Once we treat the state apparatus as a strategically selective terrain with its own institutional dynamic and treat state power as the resultant of the action of social forces pursuing strategies on this terrain, it is clear that the state cannot be reduced to institutions inside the formal part of the state. In addition to its formal institutional features (forms of representation, internal articulation, forms of intervention), there are crucial substantive aspects to the state. In earlier work I have mentioned three of these: the social basis of the state, the 'state project', and the hegemonic project of the state (Jessop 1990b: 7–9, 345–7). In loose terms these correspond to the forms of representation, internal articulation, and interventionist role of the state. We can analyse the relations between these elements in terms of the party system and the role of intellectuals and the strategies they pursue. It is vital to bring strate-gies into the account since the alternative is likely to be an overemphasis on structural factors. In this context, for example, the natural governing party in the constitutional bourgeois democratic state is the party that can mobilize electoral support behind a feasible accumulation strategy and national-popular project. For the unity of political power does not flow automatically from the constitutional guarantee of a sovereign authority, nor is it the magical result of a parallelogram of forces operating on the biased terrain of the state. Instead it is the result of political leadership, the active constitution and cohering of the state. Moreover, for the continued reproduction of capitalist class domination, this requires the continued reproduction of the institutional separation of a profit-oriented, market-mediated economic order and a law-based, majoritarian political order. For, as long as economic class struggles are confined within the limits of the market and political class struggles operate under the constraints of elec-toral majorities, there is a structurally inscribed strategic bias towards the reproduction of capitalist domination in the economic and political orders alike (cf. Gramsci 1971; Moore 1957; Portelli 1973; Poulantzas 1973, 1978b).

Conclusions

Building on these remarks, I conclude with five brief comments about the problematic dialectic of historical circumstances and social action from this (re-)reading of *The Eighteenth Brumaire*. First, rather than denying it, Marx clearly recognizes the 'problem of representation'. From the outset he inquires into the semiotic resources available to political forces to express their identities, interests, and aspirations. If men do make their own history but not just as they please in circumstances they choose for themselves, then one key feature of the present circumstances, given and inherited, is the semiotic repertoire that they inherit from the past (*18B*: 32). Engels makes much the same point in his commentary on *The Peasant War in Germany* when he writes that all revolutionary social and political doctrines directed against German feudalism were necessarily theological heresies because of the dominance of religion in feudal legitimation (1850: 412–13, cf. 421, 451). This is why it is so important for the proletariat to seek a 'new poetry' to express its identities, interests, and aspirations (cf. Löwy 1989).

Second, another key feature of these circumstances is the topography of the political stage on which leading political forces appeal for support from multiple audiences and the problems this produces for political choreography. Marx regards the political scene as the site of an experimental theatre as political actors adopt different character masks, roles, and styles of political action. A third key feature of these circumstances is the political conjuncture. This makes it imperative for different political forces to read the present situation correctly in order to identify the horizons of possibility (i.e., the scope of possible actions in specific, but moving, fields of political action) and the appropriate strategies and tactics to maximize gains in an unfolding, open, and indeterminate field. Marx indicates the importance of reading the general line (ascending, descending, etc.) of political development and choosing one's actions accordingly. In the conditions facing them from June 1848 up to Louis Bonaparte's *coup d'état*, for example, it was quite right for the defeated revolutionary proletariat to remain passive before the advance of Bonapartism. Indeed, as a far from neutral observer who was nonetheless confined to the sidelines, Marx hoped this would serve to crystallize the gulf between state and society and thereby clarify what was at stake for the revolutionary movement.

A fourth dimension of the circumstances confronting political actors is the class-biased structure of the state and the need to overcome this bias through actions to transform the state. Bonaparte proved a skilled practitioner of 'the art of the possible' in this regard. In *The Civil War in France* Marx would finally identify the commune as the most appropriate political form for a revolutionary political regime. And fifth, these other dimensions must be seen against the background of the nature of the economic base and the dynamic of class struggles that provide frameworks of possibilities. Two fine examples are Marx's accounts of the changing economic conditions of the peasantry (see above) and the increasing fusion of financial and industrial capital associated with the rise of a modern fisco-financial system in the 1840s and 1850s and the novel Bonapartist institution of the *Crédit Mobilier* (on this, see Bologna 1993a, 1993b). Indeed this aspect will play an increasing role in Marx's analysis of Bonapartism and its role in the development of a modern capitalist economy – and hence in further modifying his analysis of its significance as a form of capitalist state.

4

Gramsci on the Geography of
State Power

This chapter argues that Gramsci's philosophy of praxis involves not only the *historicization* but also the *spatialization* of its analytical categories. These theoretical practices are deeply intertwined in his 'absolute historicism'. This argument is useful not only because Gramsci regularly explores geographical themes but also because 'bending the stick in the other direction' enriches our understanding of his overall approach. I do not claim that Gramsci was a geographer *manqué* or was more a geographer than historian. These are disciplinary questions inappropriate to the pre-disciplinary traditions of Italian philosophy and historical materialism and to the political agenda of Italian state formation. Conversely, while it is certainly appropriate to consider, like Said (2001),[1] the import of Gramsci's familiar spatial metaphors, it would be misleading to focus exclusively on these here, for this would divert attention from Gramsci's less obvious but more significant analyses of the inherent spatiality as well as temporality of social relations. This approach had significant practical as well as theoretical implications and is my primary focus here.

Spatializing the Philosophy of Praxis

Gramsci writes that, while everyone is an intellectual, not everyone is an intellectual by social function (1971: 9). One might add that, while everyone has a practical sense of place, space, and scale, not everyone is a geographer by social function. This certainly holds for Gramsci. He was a deeply spatial thinker but he did not explicitly prioritize spatial thinking. This may explain both why Gramsci 'did not fully and explicitly develop his geographical insights' (Morera 1990: 89) and why the inherently spatial nature of his thought has been neglected. But he did take geography seriously. He studied it alongside his major subject of philology at Turin University (passing his

This is a lightly revised and expanded version of 'Gramsci as a spatial theorist', *Critical Review of International Social and Political Philosophy*, 8 (4), 2005, 421–37.

geography exam in 1912). He called for its teaching in primary schools as part of 'reading, writing, sums, geography, history' (1971: 30); and proposed that a potential party textbook contain a 'critical-historical-bibliographical examination of the regional situations (meaning by region a differentiated geo-economic organism)' (Gramsci 1985: 415). He continued to explore geology, geography, and geo-politics after leaving university and also taught history and geography in prison following his arrest (Gramsci 1971: 30; 1995: 195–217; Hoare and Nowell-Smith 1971: lxxxix). He noted the popularity of geographical novels (1985: 360); and recommended that touring clubs promote national culture by combining geography with sport (1995: 153). He reflected on the geo-political and geo-economic implications of the International Conferences in the 1920s for Italy, Europe, internationalism, and future world politics (1995: 195–215). And he regularly approached political problems not only in terms of 'structural' (economic and class) factors but also in regional terms (cf. Morera 1990: 149).

These interests reflect Gramsci's experiences as a Sardinian in the most exploited and oppressed part of the *Mezzogiorno* (Southern Italy) and his movement to Turin, the capital city of Piedmont and the North's industrial centre. They also derive from his reflections on more general influences in Italian economic, political, and cultural development. These include the Vatican's role as a cosmopolitan mini-state situated at the heart of Italy supported by a traditional intellectual elite with a long-established supranational orientation serving the leaders of Europe; the long-running debate on the Southern Question (especially from the 1870s); the spatiality of the Risorgimento and the flawed Italian unification process dominated by the Piedmontese state; the continuing economic and social problems posed by uneven development, dependent development, and, indeed, internal colonialism in Italy; the communists' political problems in breaking the class alliance between northern capital and the southern agricultural landowning class and in building an alliance between the northern workers and southern peasants; the changing nature and forms of imperialism (including the obstacles, challenges, and opportunities involved in the diffusion of Americanism and Fordism in Europe); and the problems for the wider communist movement posed by the Soviet Union's international isolation.

Gramsci's university training in philology under Matteo Bartoli also stimulated his spatial sensibilities. He followed the latter's new approach to linguistics as a historical science concerned with the social regularities of language (Gramsci 1985: 174, 551). Bartoli developed a 'spatial' analysis of language that sought to trace 'how a dominant speech community exerted prestige over contiguous, subordinate communities: the city over the surrounding countryside, the "standard" language over the dialect, the dominant socio-cultural group over the subordinate one' (Forgacs and Nowell-Smith 1985: 164). He also charted the continuing flow of *innovations* from the prestigious *langue* to the receiving one, such that earlier linguistic forms would be found in a peripheral rather than central area, isolated rather than accessible areas, larger rather than smaller areas (Brandist 1996: 94–5). Gramsci inflected Bartoli's analysis in a strongly materialist direction and highlighted its practical implications. For he saw the problem of revolution as closely tied to the unification of the people – a task that had to pass through the medium of language if a coherent collective will was to emerge that could unify different classes, strata, and groups (Helsloot 1989; Ives 2004a, 2004b; Lo Piparo 1979). The resulting complexities are evident in his analyses of how language use is stratified. Among many examples is his comment on how country folk ape urban manners, how subaltern groups imitate the upper classes, how peasants speak when they move to the cities, and so forth (1985: 180–1). In short, Gramsci's work on language as a medium of hegemony is not just historical but also highly sensitive spatially.

These influences suggest, as remarked earlier, that there is more to Gramsci as a spatial theorist than his famous use of several spatial metaphors (on which, see box 4.1). These have certainly been influential in the reception of his work, but we should also consider his interest in the actual rather than metaphorical spatiality of social relations and practices, in their spatial conditioning, and in the relevance of social relations and practices to spatial issues. For Gramsci was sensitive not only to the *historical*

East/West morphology of the state
North/South popular cosmology
War of position
War of manoeuvre
Base and superstructure
Historical bloc
Hegemonic bloc
Molecular transformation
Passive revolution
United front
Vanguard
Trenches, fortifications, bulwarks, outer perimeter

Box 4.1 Some spatial metaphors in Gramsci

specificity of all social relations (Morera 1990: 85) but also to their distinctive *location in place, space, and scale.* Indeed these two are clearly interconnected in any ensemble of social relations. Thus I now consider how Gramsci integrates place, space, and scale in his philosophy of praxis. However, because he does this in a largely 'pre-theoretical' manner, I will define these concepts before illustrating their significance for his theory and practice.

Place (or locale) refers to a more or less bounded site of face-to-face relationships and/or other direct interactions among social forces. It is generally closely tied to everyday life, has temporal depth, and is bound up with collective memory and social identity. Its boundaries serve both to contain and to connect: they provide a strategically selective social and institutional setting for direct interactions that privileges some identities and interests over others and also structure possible connections to other places and spaces on a range of scales. For this and other reasons, the naming, delimitation, and meaning of places are always contested and changeable and the coordinates of any given physical space can be connected to a multiplicity of places with different identities, spatio-temporal boundaries, and social significance (cf. Massey 1995). Gramsci was sensitive to all of these aspects. He stresses the importance of place or locale in his comments on how common sense, popular culture, and everyday practices are shaped by life in different types of cities and in the countryside, the design of locales (e.g., school architecture), or built forms (e.g., street lay-out and street names) (1971: 30–3, 40, 90–2, 282–3; 1995: 155). He discusses the struggle for control over places (factories, public buildings, streets, neighbourhoods, etc.) (1977, 1978). He famously emphasized that hegemony in the USA is grounded in the factory (1971: 285). He contrasts the secure meeting places of the industrial and landowning bourgeoisie with the vulnerability of working-class premises and the problems of protecting the streets ('the natural place where the proletariat can assemble without cost') (1978: 35, 268–9). In addition to exploring the contestability of places and their intertwining with other places, he also comments on their links to memory, identity, and temporality (1971: 93–5; 1978: 446). This is especially clear in his comments on the folklore of the subaltern and provincial classes and in his discussion of the social origins of intellectuals in spatially specific rather than a-spatial class terms and their implications for building different types of hegemony. And, of course, it pervades his analysis of the Southern Question with its emphasis on the rootedness (or otherwise) of social classes and political and intellectual forces in specific places, spaces, and scales of economic and social life.

Space comprises the socially produced grids and horizons of social life. It offers a whole series of strategically selective possibilities to develop social relations that stretch over space and time. Gramsci considers space from several viewpoints: (a) the spatial division of labour between town and countryside, between north and south, between different regional, national, and even continental economies; (b) the territorialization of political power, processes of state formation, and the dialectic of domestic and external influences on political life; and (c) different spatial and scalar imaginaries and different representations of space. Gramsci did not believe that space exists in itself, independently of the specific social relations that construct it, reproduce it, and occur within it. As a profoundly relational and practical thinker, he was never tempted by such spatial fetishism.[2] Nor did he accept the geographical determinism common in the nineteenth-century 'scientific' field and still reflected in folklore and common sense – a determinism that regards the physical and/or human environment as the most important determinant of social relations and their historical development. This would have been equally anathema to Gramsci's philosophy of praxis.[3] Instead he treated space like history, that is, in relational terms. For example, he regarded historical grammar (philology) comparatively, arguing that 'the linguistic fact, like any other historical fact, cannot have strictly defined national boundaries' (1985: 181). This is reflected in his exploration of local linguistic usages and particularisms, tendencies to territorial unity and fragmentation, and external influences on national languages. He concluded 'that history is always "world history" and that particular histories exist only within the frame of world history' (1985: 181; cf. 1971: 182). This is directly comparable to his view that national states are not self-closed 'power containers' but should be studied in terms of their complex interconnections with states and political forces on other scales. Indeed he combines temporal and spatial perspectives in an early form of 'geographical historical materialism' (cf. Harvey 1982).

Scale comprises the nested (and sometimes not so nested) hierarchy of bounded spaces of differing size: for example, local, regional, national, continental, and global. Scale is typically the product of social struggles for power and control. Gramsci was extremely sensitive to issues of scale, scalar hierarchies of economic, political, intellectual, and moral power, and their territorial and non-territorial expressions. He was not a 'methodological nationalist' who took the national scale for granted but typically analysed any particular scale in terms of its connection with other scales. Thus he examined relations of hegemony and domination at the local level (e.g., the Parisian urban bloc's domination of other French cities), regional level (e.g., Piedmontese domination of Italy's flawed and incomplete unification or the Giolittian strategy of passive revolution based on an alliance between a dominant northern urban bloc and a southern rural bloc), national level (e.g., the influence of the French bourgeoisie as the leading, dominant class throughout the Continent), the Transatlantic level (e.g., Americanism and Fordism), and the hemispheric level (e.g., the probable transfer of economic and political domination from America to Asia). The general methodological principles involved here are evident in his insistence on interpreting the organic connection of internal and international forces in Italian nation-formation as a problem of 'coordination and subordination' (1985: 199) and in his spatialized as well as historical analyses of the development, consolidation, and crises of coherent historical blocs formed through reciprocal linkages between structure and superstructure.

Finally, far from affirming that there is a simple 'nested hierarchy' of scales from the local to the global with distinct sets of economic, political, and social relations on each scale, Gramsci was especially sensitive to the ways in which tangled hierarchies of scale acted as a source of economic, political, and socio-economic instability. This can be seen, for example, in his comment that '[i]n the period after 1870, with the colonial expansion of Europe, all these elements change: the internal and international organizational relations of the State become more complex and massive, and the Forty-Eightist formula of the "Permanent Revolution" is expanded and transcended in political science by the formula of "civil hegemony" ' (1971: 243).

A crucial issue in the analysis of scale is the relative dominance of different scales of economic, political, intellectual, and moral life. Scale dominance is 'the power which organizations at certain spatial scales are able to exercise over organizations at other, higher or lower scales' (Collinge 1999: 568). It can derive from the general relationship among different scales considered as strategically selective terrains of power and domination and/or from the features, characteristics, capacities, and activities of organizations located at different scales. One or more scales can gain special socio-political significance by playing the dominant role in the scale division of labour within and across different fields of social practice. In turn, nodal scales are non-dominant overall but nonetheless serve as the primary loci for delivering certain activities in a given spatio-temporal order or matrix (Collinge 1999: 569). Finally, subaltern scales are marginal or peripheral but may also become sites of resistance.

Gramsci operates implicitly with these distinctions in analysing historical and contemporary patterns of domination. For example, he can be interpreted as arguing that the national level was nodal rather than dominant in Italian state- and nation-building. For he lived in a conjuncture when *Italia fatta, bisogna fare gli Italiani* (Italy being made, we must make the Italians) and could not have presumed the primacy of the national scale – especially politically – that appeared to characterize the dominant powers in Continental Europe, namely, France and Germany. He argued that Italy was weakly integrated domestically, the national scale had not yet become dominant over local and regional scales, and that this posed problems both for the completion of the bourgeois revolution and for revolutionary communist strategy. Gramsci was also acutely aware of the international weakness of the Italian state and the influence of external factors on its development.

On the other hand, he saw that 'Italian Catholicism was felt not only as a surrogate for the spirit of the nation and the state but also as a worldwide hegemonic institution, an imperialistic spirit' (1985: 220–1). He also recognized the distinction between dominant and nodal scales on a continental as opposed to the world scale. Concerning European and world politics, for example, he wrote: 'These two are not the same thing. In a duel between Berlin and Paris or between Paris and Rome, the winner is not master of the world. Europe has lost its importance and world politics depends more on London, Washington, Moscow, Tokyo than it does on the Continent' (1995: 195). And, more generally, he remarked on the need to examine

> the organic relations between the domestic and foreign policies of a State. Is it domestic policies which determine foreign policy, or vice versa? In this case too, it will be necessary to distinguish: between great powers, with relative international autonomy, and other powers; also, between different forms of government (a government like that of Napoleon III had two policies, apparently – reactionary internally, and liberal abroad). (1971: 264)

In short, for Gramsci, the international order should not be studied in terms of the mechanical interaction among formally sovereign nation-states but as a concrete, emergent international order, based on an informal hierarchy of states[4] and other international forces (such as Catholicism) that were characterized by complex and tangled internal and external relations. Thus his analyses of struggles for national hegemony were not confined to the national but closely examined the articulation and, indeed, interpenetration of the local, regional, national, and supranational scales. He commented on the respective opportunities and constraints involved for different social forces in the dissociation of scales across different institutional orders – notably the disjunction between the increasing formation of the world market and the continued survival of national states (1995: 220). He discussed the different scalar horizons of action and influence associated with such dissociations. The best known example of this, of course, is the cosmopolitanism and external orientation of traditional intellectuals in Italy from Imperial Rome to the contemporary Catholic Church based in Rome and their impact on Italian and European politics. And, just as he remarked on the implications of dissociation and the possibilities of scale jumping available to some social forces but not others, he also identified and elaborated the need for new forms of interscalar articulation to mobilize multiple social forces behind specific projects and / or to form new historical blocs. This is especially clear in his comments on the Southern Question (see below) and on the appropriate political strategies to enable the Soviet Union to break out of the isolation produced by Stalin's policy of 'socialism in one country'.

Arguments about different scales of economic, political, intellectual, and cultural organization were also central to Gramsci's analyses of individual identity formation and the creation of collective wills. For example, noting that Pirandello identified himself as local, national, and European, Gramsci argued that he could only become an Italian and national writer because he had de-provincialized himself and become European (1985: 139, 141–2). This observation may reflect Gramsci's own indecision regarding whether he was Albanian, Sardinian, Italian, or, perhaps, an internationalist starting out from a local, regional, and national viewpoint. More generally, Gramsci distinguished between the social functions of *northern* (industrial, technical) and *southern* (rural, organic) intellectuals in building different types of hegemony (1971: 11–12, 93–4). He also observed that the cosmopolitan role of traditional Italian intellectuals contributed to the continued territorial disintegration of the peninsula (1971: 18–19). And, in another example of scalar dissociation, he noted that intellectuals, because of their disembedding from national life, might fail to develop a specific national-popular project and draw instead on other national complexes or present abstract and cosmopolitan philosophies and worldviews (1985: 118).

Gramsci and the Southern Question

The Southern Question was posed in many ways as a central problem in Italian state- and nation-building. Gramsci analysed these twin processes in terms of the 'passive revolution' that occurred as the Italian northern bourgeoisie sought to unify the peninsula in the face of a heterogeneous and divided population and vast regional disparities (Davis 1979). Italy's weak economic, political, and social integration and the lack of dominance of the national scale inform Gramsci's early political writings, the 'Lyons Theses' (co-authored in 1926 with Togliatti), and his incomplete essay on 'Some Aspects of the Southern Question' (1926). These discuss three issues: (a) the complex, multi-layered economic and political subordination of secondary centres of accumulation to the northern industrial and financial centres and its implications for class alliances; (b) the resulting complexities of class formation, regional disparities, and fragmented forms of intellectual and moral life that block a Jacobin road to national unification; and (c) the problems this poses for the leading role of the proletariat, which is 'a minority of the working population and geographically distributed in such a manner, that it cannot presume to lead a victorious struggle for power unless it has previously resolved very precisely the problem of its relations with the peasant class' (1978: 316, cf. 233–4, 299). Thus, in their 'Lyons Theses', Gramsci and Togliatti write:

> Industrialism, which is the essential part of capitalism, is very weak in Italy. Its possibilities for development are limited, both because of the geographical situation and because of the lack of raw materials. It therefore does not succeed in absorbing the majority of the Italian population (4 million industrial workers exist side by side with 3½ million agricultural workers and 4 million peasants). To industrialism, there is counterposed an agriculture which naturally presents itself as the basis of the country's economy. The extremely varied conditions of the terrain, and the resulting differences in cultivation and in systems of tenancy, however, cause a high degree of differentiation among the rural strata, with a prevalence of poor strata, nearer to the conditions of the proletariat and more liable to be influenced by it and accept its leadership. Between the industrial and agrarian classes, there lies a fairly extensive urban petty bourgeoisie, which is of very great significance. It consists mainly of artisans, professional men and State employees. (Gramsci and Togliatti 1978: 343)

Gramsci takes this theme up again in his essay on the Southern Question. He claims that the Italian proletariat was too small relative to other subaltern classes and too concentrated in the north to become the leading (*dirigente*) and dominant class without forming class alliances. The key was to mobilize the real consent and active support of the broad peasant masses (Gramsci 1978: 79–82, 129–31, 449–50; Gramsci and Togliatti 1978: 347). But the peasant question is always historically determined: it is not the 'peasant and agrarian question in general'. In Italy the peasant question, through the specific Italian tradition, and the specific development of Italian history, has taken two typical and particular forms – the Vatican and Southern Questions (Gramsci 1978: 443).

This argument, his earlier analyses, and his *Prison Notebooks* all involve a deeply spatialized rather than a-spatial analysis of classes, social categories, and political forces. Thus Gramsci identified five crucial forces in Italy based on the relation between city and countryside: '1. the Northern urban force; 2. the Southern rural force; 3. the Northern-Central rural force; 4. the rural force of Sicily; 5. that of Sardinia' (1971: 98). On this basis, he analysed inter-urban and inter-regional relations using the analogy of a train whose locomotive would be the northern urban force. The key question then becomes which other forces should be mobilized by this locomotive to effect a rapid and successful path to communism. Accordingly he recommended that the Communist Party promote a hegemonic alliance of the proletariat with the peasantry and petty-bourgeois intellectuals and lead them in a war of position before the final military-political resolution of the conflict. This would dissolve the defensive alliance between northern industrialists and southern landowners, which also benefited from rural and urban petty-bourgeois support.

Gramsci on Americanism and Fordism

Gramsci's analyses of economic relations are spatial as well as historical – indeed, it would be better to write that they are spatial because they are historical or, better still, that they are inherently spatio-temporal. Rejecting classical and vulgar political economy as well as economic liberalism and economistic Marxism, he emphasized the broad historical location and specific spatio-temporal specificities of economic organization and economic regularities. This is why he substituted the notion of *mercato determinato* (definite forms of organizing and regulating market relations with their associated laws of tendency) for transhistorical economic analysis based on the actions of rational economic man. Thus he explored dependent development in the *Mezzogiorno* and the general tendency towards internal colonialism in Italy; the interrelations between different economic places and spaces, including geographical variations in relationships between town and country and how different parties aimed to remodel this relationship (Gramsci 1971: 90–102); and the interconnection, articulation, and real or potential tensions between local, regional, national, international and transnational economies. He was well attuned to the spatial division of labour, issues of the differential integration of rural, urban, and regional economies both within a national territory and in relation to foreign markets, the importance of scale in an emerging world market, and the conflict between place and space. And he paid special attention theoretically and practically to the class relations that follow from the placing, spacing, and scaling of economic organization. In short, as argued by Morera, an acute interpreter of Gramsci's 'absolute historicism', 'Gramsci not only rejected sociology for abstracting from time conditions, but also from space. That is, from the geographical conditions of social processes' (Morera 1990: 89).

Turning to international economic relations, Gramsci attacked liberalism for taking the nation-state as its horizon of economic policy-making and assuming that the world economy could safely be left to market regulation (Vacca 1999: 160). In the same context, he argued that *laissez-faire, laissez-passer* could not be rooted in agriculture but only in commerce and strong industry – suggesting that different economic and political strategies and policies were grounded in specific relations to place and space. He also remarked upon the growing contradiction between cosmopolitanism in the world market and the nationalism of political life – which, he claimed, had to be the starting point for any move to internationalism in the revolution-ary socialist movement (1995: 220). Gramsci was interested in the dynamics of uneven and combined development in an emerging global capitalism. His notes on Americanism and Fordism explored how the centre of economic dynamism was moving from old Europe to the United States and was prompting Europe to adapt. He did not adopt a narrowly economically determinist view of American economic progress here – let alone a simplis-tic technological determinism. Instead he examined the specific historical and material conditions that had enabled a new techno-economic paradigm to develop there, including the establishment of an *economia programmatica* at the level of the enterprise, the factory town, and the wider society. The originality and significance of Fordism as accumulation regime, mode of regulation, and way of life hindered its diffusion to Europe because this required more than the export of technical means of production and a tech-nical division of labour. Nonetheless, to the extent that it did spread to Europe, it also facilitated the hegemony of American imperialism.

In contrast to the Comintern, Gramsci emphasized the shift in the centre of economic gravity from Europe to the USA, which had developed a more rationally organized economy. If workers could take the lead in adopting this model, it could become the basis for the working class to guide world historical development (Baratta 1997; Vacca 1999: 9). But he also asked prophetically whether the centre of gravity might shift again, this time from the Atlantic to the Pacific.

> The largest masses of the world's population are in the Pacific. If China and India were to become modern nations with great volumes of indus-trial production, their consequent detachment from a dependency on

Europe would in fact rupture the current equilibrium: transformation of the American continent, shift in the axis of American life from the Atlantic to the Pacific seaboard, etc. (1995: 196)

Gramsci on Territoriality and State Power

Gramsci did not naturalize or fetishize national territory as the pre-given or pre-destined basis of state formation – and could not have done, indeed, given the historical problems of nation formation that he recognized and also struggled to overcome. The territorialization of political power is a crucial first material step in national state formation and nation-building.[5] It is unsurprising, then, that Gramsci studied the problems of the transition from medieval communes to absolutism and thence to a bourgeois liberal democratic state (e.g., Italy vs the Netherlands) and the need to break out of the economic-corporate phase of medieval urban relations with their political fragmentation. Thus he noted that class consciousness depends on a clear understanding of the state (1971: 272–5, especially 275) and that Italy still suffered from weak class formation and a negative rather than positive class awareness because of the fact that 'in Italy political, territorial and national unity enjoy a scanty tradition (or perhaps no tradition at all)' (1971: 274).

Gramsci was also aware that territorial unity did not itself ensure political unity. This is apparent in his contrast between Bodin and Machiavelli:

> Bodin lays the foundations of political science in France on a terrain which is far more advanced and complex than that which Italy offered to Machiavelli. For Bodin the question is not that of founding the territorially united (national) State – i.e., of going back to the time of Louis XI – but of balancing the conflicting social forces within this already strong and well-implanted State. Bodin is interested in the moment of consent, not in the moment of force. (1971: 142)

Securing political unity also requires the institutional integration of the state through appropriate state forms, its embedding in the wider ensemble of social relations, and its capacity to engage in relatively unified action through appropriate state and national-popular projects. As symptoms of a failed national unification project in Italy, Gramsci regularly cited the Vatican and Southern Questions and the passive revolution that occurred under the domination of Piedmont and the Moderate Party. And, in one of his most famous comparisons in state theory, he claims that '[i]n the East the state was everything, civil society was primordial and gelatinous; in the West, there was a proper relation between state and civil society, and when the state trembled a sturdy structure of civil society was at once revealed' (1971: 238).

This approach raised crucial issues concerning passive revolution, hegemony, and the historical bloc. Gramsci provides many other examples of problems in the mechanisms in and through which political unity is created and identifies enormous variability in its forms – ranging from sheer coercion through force-fraud-corruption and passive revolution to inclusive hegemony. Nor did he see this mainly as a technical question of public administration, political reform of the state apparatus, or constitutional design. Instead it was deeply related to the social bases of the state in class, religious-secular, and territorial terms and to the concomitant articulation between political and civil society to form the state in its integral sense. This is reflected in the rich conceptual vocabulary Gramsci developed for analysing class relations and the different moments in the balance of forces in economic, political, military, intellectual, and moral terms (1971: *passim*). And, for present purposes, it is especially important to note how much attention he paid to the local, regional and urban–rural origins and the cosmopolitan–national orientations of intellectuals, functionaries, bureaucrats, soldiers, the clergy, and so forth (1971: 79, 203–4, 214–17; 1995: 12). For, far from being a neutral instrument with wide-ranging capacities, the state had to be analysed theoretically and addressed politically in terms of its embedding in the wider ensemble of social relations in all their spatio-temporal specificity. This in turn implies the spatiality as well as the historicity of the state as a social relation.

> The chief defect of Italian intellectuals was not that they formed a powerful and resilient 'cultural hegemony', but that, because they were cosmopolitan rather than national, no authentic hegemony had ever been realised. Like the artificial or perverted state hegemony of Piedmont, the cultural tradition deriving from the Renaissance humanists could provide only a weak and eccentric form of hegemony, because it was not national. (Ghosh 2001: 36)

Gramsci and International Relations

Although Gramsci regrets the failure of the Italian nation-state compared with France's successful Jacobin state-building project, he recognizes that even this took decades to accomplish and that contemporary nation-states were being forged in a much changed and deeply contested international context. For example, he suggests that, whereas Versailles re-established the prerogatives of nation-states, the Bolshevik world revolution project aimed at an eventual society of nations. After Versailles, the nation could no longer remain, if it ever had fully been, the dominant horizon of state life. Thus it was crucial to analyse how the internal balance of forces was overdetermined by international forces and a country's geo-political position and to assess whether and how the latter balance modifies domestic forces, reinforcing or breaking progressive and revolutionary movements (Gramsci 1971: 116). Gramsci therefore deemed it 'necessary to take into account the fact that international relations intertwine with these internal relations of nation-states, creating new, unique and historically concrete combinations' (1971: 182). He also noted that winning international hegemony was partly an educational relationship, affecting complexes of national and continental civilizations (1971: 350; cf. 1995: 207–8). This applied not only to Americanism and Fordism but also to the role of the international communist movement and its involvement in united front activities.

When exploring the international dimensions of economic, political, and socio-cultural relations, Gramsci did not assume that the basic units of international relations were national economies, national states, or nationally constituted civil societies. Instead, he explored the mutual implications of economic and political organization, their social and cultural presuppositions, and the consequences of the dissociation of the dominant scales of economic, political, intellectual, and moral life. This made him sensitive to the complexities of interscalar relations and he never assumed that they were ordered in a simple nested hierarchy.[6]

Gramsci's approach to international relations was never presented in systematic form. But it is nonetheless worth drawing out some of its implications because of the very widespread tendency to try to reconstruct it on the basis of a simple generalization of his arguments from a presumed national scale to the transatlantic or wider transnational scale. But a simplistic 're-scaling' of concepts such as passive revolution, historical bloc, hegemony, power bloc, and so forth, fails to capture the complexities of Gramsci's engagement with questions of place, space, and scale. His philosophy of praxis and vernacular materialism (Ives 2004b) made him very sensitive to the social construction of social relations, institutions, and identities, including their international dimensions. Indeed he was careful to emphasize the social constitution of categories such as 'North' and 'South' and 'East' and 'West', their reflection of the viewpoint of European cultured classes, their ideological representation of differences between civilizations, and their material significance in practical life (Gramsci 1971: 447). This also meant that he was interested in the material and intellectual struggles to reconstruct place, space, and scale in response to the crisis of liberalism, dependent development, and internal colonialism in Italy and to analogous crises in the international order with its imperialist rivalries and clash between capitalism and a fledgeling socialism.

First, whereas Marx mainly developed an abstract-simple analysis of the capitalist mode of production, Gramsci took this for granted and focused on concrete conjunctures in emerging and developed capitalist social formations in a world shaped by imperialism and the Bolshevik Revolution. Second, Gramsci integrated his analysis of structure and superstructure with concrete political analyses. This was a key element in his concept of historical bloc and his systematic concern with the role of intellectuals in mediating these relations (see, e.g., Portelli 1973). This analysis began beneath the national scale and extended beyond it (e.g., his analyses of Italian intellectuals, Americanism and Fordism, and the failure of the Bolshevik Revolution to spread from the 'East' to the 'West'). Third, in opposing economism both theoretically and politically, Gramsci showed the role of political and civil society in constituting and reproducing economic relations on diverse scales up to and including the international. Fourth, in contrast to (neo-)realism in more recent international relations theory, Gramsci did not fetishize the nation-state as the basic unit or scale of analysis. Indeed his work could be interpreted as a protracted reflection on 'the failure of the Italian state to constitute itself as a national state – a failure that reflects the laborious emergence of a modern Italian nation, impeded by a balance of internal and international forces' (1985: 199). Fifth, writing during and after the Great War with its inter-imperialist rivalries and open hostility between the capitalist bloc and the fledgeling Soviet Union, Gramsci was especially concerned with two issues: (a) the international as well as national and regional context of the defeat of the working-class movement and the rise of fascism; and (b) the spread of Americanism and Fordism as the basis for modernization in Italy and Europe more generally. And, sixth, he was strongly interested in international relations and studied work on geo-politics and demo-politics (which would now be called bio-politics) to better understand the political implications of the international balance of forces.

In this context, and in contrast to the methodological nationalism that still affects much thinking on international relations, Gramsci did not draw a rigid distinction between the national and the international but explored issues of interscalar articulation and reciprocal influence in a more complex and dialectical manner.

> Do international relations precede or follow (logically) fundamental
> social relations? There can be no doubt that they follow. Any organic
> innovation in the social structure, through its technical-military expres-
> sions, modifies organically absolute and relative relations in the interna-
> tional field too. Even the geographical position of a national State does
> not precede but follows (logically) structural changes, although it also
> reacts back upon them to a certain extent (to the extent precisely to which
> superstructures react upon the structure, politics on economics, etc.).
> However, international relations react both passively and actively on
> political relations (of hegemony among the parties). (1971: 176)

Gramsci explores the links between economic, political, and international strategy in his analysis of the inter-linkage between domestic class
alliances and foreign economic policy. Italy's ruling class had to choose
between rural democracy based on 'an alliance with the Southern peasants,
a policy of free trade, universal suffrage, administrative decentralization
and low prices for industrial products'; or 'a capitalist/worker industrial
bloc, without universal suffrage, with tariff barriers, with the maintenance
of a highly centralized State (the expression of bourgeois dominion over
the peasants, especially in the South and the Islands), and with a reformist
policy on wages and trade-union freedoms' (1978: 449–50). As Gramsci
then immediately added, it was no accident that the ruling class chose the
latter solution.

Conclusions

Gramsci not only emphasized the *historical specificity* of all social relations
but was also attuned, less explicitly, to their distinctive *location in place, space,
and scale*. Thus almost all of his crucial concepts are sensitive to issues of
place, space, and scale as well as to issues of periodization, historical structures, specific conjunctures, and social dynamics. Whether we consider the
relations of production, the determined market (*mercato determinato*), the
contrast between the dynamism of Americanism and Fordism and the relative stagnation of European and Soviet planned economies, the forms of
class relations (economically, politically, intellectually), the territoriality of
state formation and the relative strengths or weakness of specific states
(considered both in terms of political and civil society), the spatial roots of
intellectuals and their different functions in economic, political, and moral
organization, the nature of political alliances, the appropriate forms of economic-corporate, political, and military strategy, and so forth, Gramsci
emerges as a spatial thinker as much as he does as a historical thinker. This

is rooted in his profoundly historicist concern with the spatio-temporality of all social relations. In addition, Gramsci's analysis of strategy was objectively as well as metaphorically sensitive to temporality and spatiality. Not only did Gramsci emphasize the interweaving of different temporalities into complex conjunctures and situations and search for the openings between a path-dependent present and possible futures, but he also regarded strategy as inherently spatial. He was always aware of the need to mobilize in and across specific places, spaces, and scales, each with their own distinctive determinations and strategic selectivities. At stake in both cases is the transformation of spatio-temporal horizons of action and the interweaving of different temporalities and spatialities. It is only in this context that Gramsci's notions of war of position and war of manoeuvre make sense. For his interest in place, space, and scale was not merely academic but had to do with his analysis of revolutionary conjunctures. Thus he argues that a collective will must be formed 'with the degree necessary and sufficient to achieve an action which is coordinated and simultaneous in the time and the geographical space in which the historical event takes place' (1971: 194). In short, his comments on the political failures of left strategy are also spatially as well as historically attuned.

5

Poulantzas on the State as a Social Relation

> [*State, Power, Socialism*] takes a distance from a certain conception that I
> held earlier, i.e., the relative autonomy of the state, which considered
> social reality in terms of instances or levels. This was, in sum, the
> Althusserian conception. Here I offer a series of criticisms, because it was
> a conception that did not succeed in exactly situating the specificity of the
> state, which did not succeed in grasping the relations between state,
> society, and economy in a sufficiently precise fashion. ... For example, it
> is true that for some time, I tended to consider the state (even in its broad
> sense, including ideological apparatuses) as the (almost) exclusive site of
> the institutions of power. This was an error: there are a whole series of
> other power centres that are extremely important in society. ... In this
> book I have tried to break with both a conception that considers the state
> as the totality of power and another conception which neglects entirely,
> or almost entirely, the state's role: that of Foucault or, ultimately, that of
> the *Revue Libre* [edited by Castoriadis, Lefort and Gauchet].
>
> (Poulantzas 1978a: 27–8, my translation)

Poulantzas often surprises us with his ability to develop new insights
into the state and his political shifts on major issues whilst still adhering
to historical materialism as a research programme and guide to political
action. Theoretically, he was initially inspired by Sartrean existentialism,
then Althusserian structuralism, and, later, Foucault's views on the relational nature and ubiquitous dispersion of power. Politically, he was
successively committed to democratic politics, Marxism-Leninism, left
Eurocommunism, and, eventually, a radical democratic politics that was
pluri-partite and committed to cross-class alliances and an independent role
for social movements (cf. Jessop 1985a; 1991). His concern to understand
Greek and French politics eventually led to his insight that *the state is a social*

This chapter is a much shortened version of 'The strategic selectivity of the state: Reflections
on a theme of Poulantzas', *Journal of the Hellenic Diaspora*, 25 (1–2), 1999, 1–37. It also incor-
porates elements of my *Nicos Poulantzas: Marxist Theory and Political Strategy*, New York:
St Martin's Press, 1985.

relation – an insight that he presented as the long-awaited realization of the Marxist theory of the state (cf. Poulantzas 1976c, 1977, and 1980b).

Marxist Theory and Political Strategy

Poulantzas's work, for all its alleged 'hyper-abstractionism' and theoretical obscurities (Miliband 1970, 1973), was primarily motivated by deep-felt commitments to contemporary working-class and popular-democratic struggles (Jessop 1985a). Thus he criticized theories of state monopoly capitalism, the view that an ultra-imperialism had now been organized under the hegemony of a US superstate or the domination of stateless monopoly capital, and the view that the European Economic Community was becoming a supranational political apparatus to serve European capital in its struggle against the hegemony of American capital. Poulantzas's concern with political strategy is especially notable in his analyses of changes in imperialism and their implications for national states and class struggles in Europe; his concerns about a democratic transition to democratic societies after the crisis of the Greek, Portuguese, and Spanish dictatorships in the mid-1970s; his reflections on the emerging crisis of state socialism; and his interest in the prospects of radical democracy despite a trend towards authoritarian statism. It was in grappling with these issues that Poulantzas integrated his long-standing interests in state theory and political strategy more closely and more coherently with traditional Marxist economic themes. Economic themes first became prominent in his work on the internationalization of capital (Poulantzas 1975) and they were then integrated even more closely with his state theory in *State, Power, Socialism* (1978b).

Poulantzas also brought new insights to the traditional Marxist critique of political economy. In particular, he analysed the labour process in terms of a complex economic, political, and intellectual division of labour in which the constitutive effects and actions of the state were always present; and, in similar vein, he studied social classes in terms of their '*extended reproduction*' rather than a 'narrow' economic concern with their place in production, distribution, and consumption. The idea of extended reproduction refers to the role of economic, political, and ideological relations within the circuit of capital and non-capitalist relations of production – including not only the technical division of labour but also changing forms of managerial control and ideological relations. Marx had already indicated this, as Poulantzas notes, in his discussions of factory despotism and the role of science in the capitalist production process (1978b: 55). But

Poulantzas developed this analysis in terms of (a) the changing articulation between economic, political, and ideological relations within capitalist production (1975: 109–38); and (b) the changing forms of capitalist state and mental–manual division and their role in reproducing the social relations of production as a whole (1975: 165–8; and 1978b: 26–7, 55–7, 80–2, 166–94). Overall his approach rests on the central claims that 'politico-ideological relations are already present in the actual constitution of the relations of production'; and that 'the process of production and exploitation involves reproduction of the relations of politico-ideological domination and subordination' (1978b: 26, 27). Thus Poulantzas put the social relations of production *in this expanded, or integral, sense*[1] at the heart of his analysis of class struggle and examined their social reproduction in terms of the interrelated economic, political, and ideological conditions bearing on accumulation within and beyond the circuits of capital (see 1975, 1978b).

New Methodological Considerations

Poulantzas set out a broad agenda in his last major work. His concerns ranged from changes in contemporary capitalism and the rise of a new form of capitalist state through actually existing socialism to political strategy and radical democracy. But he first offered some basic theoretical guidelines and arguments. Many are found in his earlier work but some are presented for the first time in *State, Power, Socialism*. In particular, he elaborated his relational approach to the 'institutional materiality' of the state and undertook a partial, albeit critical, rapprochement with Foucault's analytics of power (chapter 6 below). The key ideas are presented in the 'Introduction'. After rejecting yet again both instrumentalist and voluntarist approaches to state power, he elaborated his own approach in more detail than previously. In particular, he argued that political class domination is inscribed in the material organization and institutions of the state system; and that this 'institutional materiality' is grounded in turn in the relations of production and the social division of labour (1978b: 14).

In discussing the relations of production and the social division of labour, Poulantzas drew more heavily on *Classes in Contemporary Capitalism* (1975) than his earlier, more structuralist work, *Political Power and Social Classes* (1973). For he focused on the interpenetration of the more or less distinct economic, political, and ideological moments of the social division of labour rather than the structural matrix constituted by the economic, political, and ideological regions of the capitalist mode of production. He argued that the production process is based on the *unity* of the labour process and relations of production organized under the dominance of the latter. These relations are not purely economic (let alone merely technical) but also involve specific political and ideological moments. Power has precise bases in economic exploitation, the place of different classes in the various power apparatuses and mechanisms outside the state, and the state system itself. Class power is first determined by the contrasting positions occupied by different classes in the social division of labour. But it is further determined by their different modes of organization and their respective strategies in the different fields of class struggle (1978b:147; cf. 1973: 95, 105–7). For production and exploitation also embody and reproduce relations of politico-ideological domination and subordination (1978b: 26–7). In other words, politics and ideology are not limited to reproducing the general, external conditions in which production occurs; they are also present in the heart of the labour process as constitutive moments of the social relations of production. Thus the relations of production are expressed in specific *class powers* organically articulated to the more general political and ideological relations that concretize and legitimize them (1978b: 26–7).

In presenting his new, relational approach, Poulantzas argues that the economic and political regions 'are *from the very beginning* constituted by their mutual relation and articulation – a process that is effected in each mode of production through the determining role of relations of production' (1978b: 17, italics in original). This excludes any general theory of economics or the state and indicates the need for particular theoretical analyses of specific types of economy or state. Poulantzas also reiterates that the relative institutional separation of the state in the capitalist mode of production provides a distinct object for analysis. This is no longer, as it was in *Political Power and Social Classes*, the political as a distinct, relatively autonomous region within the overall articulation of the capitalist mode of production. Instead it is now redefined as 'nothing other than the capitalist form of the presence of the political in the constitution and reproduction of the relations of production' (1978b: 19). Accordingly this distinctive presence is the new focus for Poulantzas's regional theory of the capitalist state and its relation to social classes and class struggle (1978b: 14–22, 25–7; cf. 1973: 13, 17–18, 22).

After these, and other, brief methodological remarks, Poulantzas discussed the general nature of the capitalist state. This involves more than repression and/or ideological deception. It does more than negatively delimit and protect the rules of the economic game and/or inculcate 'false consciousness' among subordinate classes. For it is actively involved in constituting and maintaining the relations of production and the social division of labour; in organizing hegemonic class unity for the power bloc; and in managing the material bases of consent among the popular masses. In short, the state's role in reproducing class domination is a positive one and by no means reducible to the simple couplet of repression–ideology.

Poulantzas emphasized that the cornerstone of power in class-divided formations is class power. This is grounded in economic power and the relations of production rather than the state. However, given the ultimately determining role of the relations of production, Poulantzas also argued that political power is primordial. For changes in state power condition all other essential transformations in class and non-class relations. Thus, in a manner reminiscent of Foucault (see chapter 6), Poulantzas continually stressed the state's positivity and ubiquity in constituting and reproducing the relations of production. He regarded the state as 'the factor which concentrates, condenses, materializes and incarnates politico-ideological relations in a form specific to the given mode of production' (1978b: 27). Hence the state is everywhere. Indeed, Poulantzas argued that 'we cannot imagine any social phenomenon (any knowledge, power, language or writing) as posed in a state prior to the State: for all social reality must stand in relation to the state and to class divisions' (1978b: 39). Every social reality must be conceived as maintaining constitutive relations to the state. This involves class and non-class relations alike as the state intervenes in all relations of power and assigns them class pertinence and enmeshes them in the web of economic, political, and ideological powers of the dominant class (1978b: 40, 43). Since class relations are always and necessarily relations of struggle, however, they resist integration into apparatuses and tend to escape all institutional control. In this sense, indeed, the mechanisms of power are self-limiting. For they always incorporate and condense the struggles of the dominated classes without necessarily fully integrating and absorbing them. The class struggle always has primacy over the institutions-apparatuses of power (1978b: 149–52). And, because both class and non-class struggles escape state control, state power is always provisional, fragile, and limited (1978b: 43–5).

The State and Political Class Struggle

Poulantzas argued that the nature of the state is closely related to the social division of labour and that, *a fortiori*, the capitalist type of state is closely related to the specifically capitalist form of this division (especially between mental and manual labour). But he added immediately that a theory of the capitalist state involved more than relating it to the social division of labour and class struggle in general. This would risk subsuming all its forms under an indifferent 'dictatorship of the bourgeoisie' (1978b: 158). Instead the capitalist state must be considered as a *sui generis* political phenomenon and related to the specificities of political class struggle in different conjunctures (1978b: 123–6). This requires attention to how political class struggle is reproduced and transformed within the state apparatus so that bourgeois political domination is secured.

In this context, Poulantzas repeated arguments first extensively developed in *Political Power and Social Classes*. There he defined the capitalist state's principal political roles as organizing the power bloc and disorganizing the popular masses. But he now went beyond this in both respects and qualified his comments on the role of the state personnel. In particular, he gave more weight to class conflicts and contradictions and the particular strategies pursued by different classes, fractions, and categories in contesting political class domination. In this sense Poulantzas stressed that the state is neither a monolithic bloc nor simply a sovereign legal subject. Instead its different apparatuses, sections, and levels serve as power centres for different fractions or fractional alliances in the power bloc and/or as centres of resistance for different elements among the popular masses. Thus the state must be understood as a strategic field formed through intersecting power networks that constitutes a favourable terrain for political manoeuvre by the hegemonic fraction (1978b: 136, 138). It is in constituting this terrain that the state helps to organize the power bloc.

The state also gets involved in disorganizing the masses. It obstructs a unified front against the state and links different sections severally to the power bloc through its management of material concessions. In particular, he suggests, it mobilizes the petty bourgeoisie and rural classes in support for the power bloc (either directly or through their support for the state itself) so that they are unavailable to ally with the proletariat (cf. Marx's *Eighteenth Brumaire*, as analysed in chapter 3). Different fractions in the power bloc adopt different strategies towards the masses. This explains their preference for different state forms with different social bases and/or their attempts to rally the popular masses behind their own fractional struggles (1978b: 140–2). However, even if the masses are physically excluded from certain state apparatuses, popular struggles still affect their operation in two ways. First, they can be mediated through state personnel, who have different class affiliations at different levels of the state system. Discontent inside the police, judiciary, and state administration in contemporary France is cited in this regard (1976b, 1977, 1978a). Second, popular struggles at a distance from the state may also affect the strategic calculations of fractions within the power bloc. This is shown in the eventual collapse of the military dictatorships in Greece, Spain, and Portugal (1978b: 143–4).

Overall this entails that popular struggles traverse the state system from top to bottom. This does not mean that their bridgeheads inside the state operate in the same way as the *power centres* occupied by different fractions of the power bloc. For this would suggest that there was a permanent situation of 'dual power' *within* the capitalist state such that it represented the political class power of labour as well as that of capital. Instead Poulantzas claimed that the popular masses merely have *centres of resistance* inside the state. These may oppose the real power of the dominant class but cannot advance the long-term political interests of popular forces. Lastly, he noted that the latter can also pressurize the capitalist state by establishing movements for rank-and-file democracy, self-management networks, and so forth, that challenge normal liberal democratic forms of representation (1978b: 144–5).

Finally, Poulantzas also considered the distinctive role of the state personnel. He noted that the dominant ideology could help to unify the functions of the state system. But he also argued that it could not eliminate the internal quarrels and divisions that occur within the state owing to the differential class affiliation of the state personnel. Nonetheless, since state personnel allegedly live their revolt through the dominant ideology, they rarely question the social division of labour between rulers and ruled or between mental and manual labour. They are therefore disinclined to support rank-and-file initiatives and self-management and would try to maintain the continuity of the state apparatus during any transition to democratic socialism – not simply to defend their 'economic-corporate' interests but also because of their more general statolatry, views on the national interest, and so forth. So the socialist movement must deal 'gently' with the state personnel during the transitional period when state structures must be radically reorganized (1978b: 154–8).

The reproduction of class struggles in internal divisions, fractures, and contradictions among and within each and every branch of the state system is reflected, according to Poulantzas, in the prodigious incoherence and chaotic character of state policies when seen in terms of what Foucault calls the 'microphysics of power' (Poulantzas 1978b: 132, 135–6, 229; cf. 1974: 329–30; 1976a: 49–50, 84). Yet Poulantzas also argued that the state's organization as a strategic terrain ensures that a general line is imposed on these diversified micro-policies (1978b: 135, 136). This general line emerges in a complex fashion from the institutional matrix of the state and the clash of specific strategies and tactics. It is not reducible solely to the effects of the state as an institutional ensemble, because this is always cross-cut by class contradictions and conflicts. Hence, in contrast to the term *'structural selectivity'*, which he took from Offe (1972) and which implies invariant constraints, Poulantzas's approach is better described as concerned with *'strategic selectivity'*. Nor is the emergent general line reducible to the more or less successful application of a coherent, global[2] strategy established at the apex of the entire state system (1978b: 135–6). For it is only the interaction of the state's structural matrix and the specific strategies pursued by different forces that accounts for the general line.

In short, Poulantzas emphasized that political domination is inscribed in the state's institutional materiality, that is, its institutional matrix. Only this approach could clarify the conjoint impact on the state produced, 'on the one hand, by changes in the relations of production and social division of labour and, on the other hand, by changes in class struggles, especially political struggles' (1978b: 158). This relational perspective illuminates: (a) how each national state system develops in a distinctive way according to the material condensation of the specific political relations that have developed in a given nation-state; and (b) how the state changes according to each stage and phase of capitalism, according to normal and exceptional periods, and across diverse forms of regime (1978b: 158–60).

The Relational Approach and Strategic Selectivity

Poulantzas argued that the state is a social relation. This excludes any treatment of the state either as a simple instrument or as a subject. Thus, although Poulantzas obviously stressed the importance of the changing balance of class forces in his approach to state power, he equally emphatically disputed that the state is somehow neutral as between classes. Instead it is a *material* condensation of the balance among class forces insofar as the state actually helps to constitute that balance rather than simply reflecting it. Poulantzas also treats the state as an *institutional ensemble* rather than a unitary political subject. It is shot through with contradictions and has no political power of its own. While the diacritical value of this argument is clear, its positive theoretical content is less obvious.

The simplest explication is Poulantzas's claim that the capitalist state should not be regarded as an intrinsic entity: 'like "capital", *it is rather a relationship of forces, or more precisely the material condensation of such a relationship among classes and class fractions, such as this is expressed within the State in a necessarily specific form*' (1978b: 128–9, italics in original). By analogy with Marx's analysis of capital as a social relation, this can be reformulated as follows: state *power* (not the state apparatus as such) should be seen as a *form-determined* condensation of the balance of forces in political and politically relevant struggle. This reformulation combines the themes of a necessarily specific form, material condensation, and balance of forces. Exploring this theme involves two issues. We need first to examine the state form as a complex institutional ensemble with a specific pattern of 'strategic selectivity' that reflects and modifies the balance of class forces; and, second, to consider the constitution of these class forces and their strategies themselves, including their capacity to reflect on, and respond to, the strategic selectivities inscribed in the state as a whole. In short, from a strategic-relational viewpoint, the state's effectiveness is always shaped by capacities and forces that lie beyond it. Indeed, as Poulantzas notes, class struggles have primacy over, and stretch far beyond, the state; and, in addition, far from being exhausted by class relations, power relations may also go beyond them (1978b: 43).

Re-Reading Poulantzas

I now re-examine Poulantzas's views on the state's 'structural selectivity' (*sic*), strategy, and tactics in the light of more recent work on the strategic-relational approach (see chapter 1). In exploring his ideas on the institutional materiality of the state, I proceed from more abstract to more specific determinations. Likewise, in exploring his ideas on strategy, I begin with general comments on the constitution of the power bloc and hegemony and move to more specific, conjunctural analyses.

Poulantzas grounded the distinctive form of the capitalist state in capitalist relations of production, that is, the articulation of production, distribution, and exchange under the dominance of the social relations of production. This requires looking at the division between mental and manual labour – which extends far beyond the economic region and penetrates the state and ideological region too. In this context, Poulantzas argued that the state is directly involved in constituting and reproducing the mental–manual division. Indeed the state is the distinctive material embodiment of intellectual labour in its separation from manual labour (1978b: 55–6). This can be seen in the relation between *knowledge* and *power* within the capitalist state. Thus the state establishes a distinctive national language and forms of writing and is also involved in reproducing the mental–manual division through such institutions as education. These links occur in the state's core (so-called 'repressive') apparatus and its associated ideological state apparatuses (hereafter ISAs), whether inside or outside the socially constructed distinction between the public and private spheres, or political society and civil society. They serve to exclude the popular masses from full and effective participation in political power (1978b: 56). Particular intellectual skills are required for participation, especially as official discourse and bureaucratic secrecy obscure the realities of political power. These links also shape the institutional and ideological matrix in which state-enrolled intellectuals and functionaries seek to unify the power bloc and secure its popular hegemony (1978b: 57–62).

In this framework, the structural selectivity of the state consists in a complex set of institutional mechanisms and political practices that serve to advance (or obstruct) particular fractional or class interests. Included here are: selective filtering of information; systematic lack of action on certain issues; definition of mutually contradictory priorities and counter-priorities; the uneven implementation of measures originating elsewhere in the state system; and the pursuit of *ad hoc* and uncoordinated policies concerned with specific conjunctural problems affecting particular branches or sections of the state system (1978b: 132–4; cf. 1976b: 40). Thus the state system involves complex, cross-cutting, decentralized, non-hierarchical, and antagonistic relations among the different branches of the state ensemble. Yet Poulantzas also insisted that 'the state does not constitute a mere assembly of detachable parts: it exhibits an *apparatus unity* which is normally designated by the term centralization or *centralism*, and which is related to the fissiparous *unity of state power*' (1978b: 136, italics in original). This clearly poses problems in explaining the institutional and class unity of the state. For how does such micro-diversity culminate in a unified system of bourgeois domination?

Unity cannot be explained in terms of constitutional and administrative law. Even if spheres of competence were strictly delimited and a precise hierarchy of formal authority had been defined, this would not affect the real structures of power (1978b: 134). Rather it was the dominance of the branch or apparatus that represents the interests of the hegemonic fraction that secured any institutional unity. This occurs in two ways. For the hegemonic fraction can establish the dominance of the state apparatus that already crystallizes its interests; and any apparatus that is already dominant can be transformed into a privileged centre of its interests (1978b: 137). This argument is supplemented by reference to strategic practices. For Poulantzas also accounted for the class unity of the state in terms of the political practices pursued by the dominant apparatus. It is not due to any formal, juridical unity that might be established through legal codes. It depends instead on the capacity of the dominant apparatus to shift real power around without undue regard for constitutional formalities. Thus the dominant apparatus will duplicate subordinate branches, establish its own 'parallel power networks', penetrate the personnel of other apparatuses, short-circuit decision-making elsewhere in the state system, reorganize the traditional hierarchies of power when appropriate, and switch the relays and circuits of power to suit the global interests of the hegemonic fraction (1978b: 137; cf. 1976b: 41–2). This can be accomplished in various ways and the dominant 'mass' party (sic) plays a crucial role here in authoritarian statism (1978b: 232–40).

But these mechanisms must be examined in relation to state strategies and tactics. Sometimes the strategies and tactics required for political class domination are openly formulated and expressed by the state (albeit through an opaque and diversified official discourse). But the most appropriate strategy more often emerges only *ex post* through collision among mutually contradictory micro-policies and political projects formulated in different parts of the state system. Thus, in phraseology that is strikingly reminiscent of the contemporary Foucault, Poulantzas writes that, although the general line of the state's policy is 'certainly decipherable in terms of strategic calculation', it is 'often not known in advance within (and by) the state itself' (1978b: 136, 33). It should not be seen as 'the rational formulation of a coherent and global project' (1978b: 136) and, indeed, 'it is not always susceptible to rational formulation' (1978b: 33, corrected translation). In short, Poulantzas resorted, not to a purely *structural* causality à la Althusser, but to a *strategic* causality. This explains state policy in terms of a process of strategic calculation without a calculating subject.

Thus, in language that appears once more to flirt with Foucault's mode of expression, Poulantzas argued that the unity of political class domination must be explained through the strategic codification of power relations. The state is

> a strategic field and process of intersecting power networks . . . traversed by tactics which are often highly explicit at the restricted level of their inscription in the state: they intersect and conflict with one another, finding their targets in some apparatuses or being short-circuited by others, and eventually map out that general line of force, the state's policy, which traverses confrontations within the state. (1978b: 136)

No power can be exercised on this field without a series of aims and objectives. Yet no individual, group, or class subject can be said to have chosen or decided the final outcome of conflicting micro-power plays. Thus political class domination is both intentional and non-subjective.

This argument is developed at several levels. For Poulantzas did not develop a general theory of the capitalist type of state that could then be applied unmodified to any and all of its various instantiations. Instead he offered a series of methodological guidelines for state theory starting from the first principles of the Marxist critique of political economy (1978b: 18–20; cf. 1973: 123–56). This explains the wide range of concepts that Poulantzas deployed in exploring the structural (or strategic) selectivity of the state. Among them are: (a) the capitalist type of state; (b) the stages of the capitalist type of state – transitional, liberal, interventionist, authoritarian statist; (c) the normal and exceptional form of the capitalist type of state – distinguished in terms of the presence–absence of an institutionalized mechanism for national-popular representation within a bourgeois democratic framework; (d) a range of 'normal' political regimes, differentiated in terms of the relative dominance of different representative apparatuses – the legislature, the executive, the authoritarian mass party – and a range of 'exceptional' political regimes, differentiated in terms of the relative dominance of other state apparatuses – the military, the bureaucracy, the political police, the fascist party, and so forth; (e) a further differentiation of political regimes in terms of the specific mechanisms of political representation – parliamentary vs presidential, types of party system, relationship between different tiers of government, and so forth – and/or different forms of articulation between parts of the state apparatus; and (f) specific conjunctural analyses and moments of crisis. Such analyses aim to specify the strategic selectivities of the state's institutional materiality in increasingly fine-grained accounts.

Exceptional Elements in the Contemporary State

Poulantzas's analysis of the intensification of exceptional elements in the contemporary state is an excellent illustration of his overall strategic-relational approach. In line with classical Marxist arguments, he regarded the two key features of the normal form of the capitalist state as democratic institutions and hegemonic class leadership. Representative democratic institutions facilitate the organic circulation and reorganization of hegemony because they offer a space for open class and fractional conflicts. This inhibits major ruptures or breaks in social cohesion and, *a fortiori*, in the system of political class domination. However, if political and ideological crises cannot be resolved through the normal, democratic play of class forces, democratic institutions must be suspended or eliminated and the crises resolved through an open 'war of manoeuvre' that ignores constitutional niceties. But the very act of abolishing democratic institutions tends to congeal the balance of forces prevailing when the exceptional state is stabilized. This makes it harder to resolve new crises and contradictions through routine and gradual policy adjustments and to establish a new equilibrium of compromise. Indeed the apparent strength of the exceptional state actually hides its real brittleness. This makes exceptional states vulnerable to sudden collapse as contradictions and pressures accumulate. Conversely, apparently weak democratic states bend under the strain and therefore provide more flexible means to organize political class domination (1976a: 30, 38, 48–50, 90–3, 106, 124).

In short, whereas normal states correspond to conjunctures in which bourgeois hegemony is stable and secure, exceptional states are responses to a crisis of hegemony. This basic contrast is reflected in four sets of institutional and operational differences between the two forms of state. First, whereas the normal state has representative democratic institutions with universal suffrage and competing political parties, exceptional states suspend the electoral principle (apart from plebiscites and/or referenda closely controlled from above) and end the plural party system (1974: 123, 230; 1973: 324–7; 1976a: 42, 91, 114). Second, whereas the transfer of power in normal states follows constitutional and legal rules and occurs in stable and predictable ways, exceptional states suspend the rule of law to facilitate constitutional and administrative changes allegedly required to help solve the hegemonic crisis (1974: 226–7, 311; 1973: 320–4; 1978b: 87–92). Third, ISAs in normal states typically have 'private' legal status and enjoy significant autonomy from official government control. In contrast, ISAs in exceptional states are generally subordinated to the repressive state apparatus (RSA) and lack real independence. This subordination serves to legitimate the increased resort to coercion and helps overcome the ideological crisis that accompanies a crisis of hegemony (1973: 314–18; 1976a: 113–14). And, fourth, the formal separation of powers within the RSA is further reduced through the infiltration of subordinate branches and power centres by the dominant branch and/or through the expansion of parallel power networks and transmission belts cutting across and linking different branches and centres. This produces greater centralization of political control and multiplies its points of application in the state. This serves to reorganize hegemony, to counteract internal divisions and short-circuit internal resistances, and to secure flexibility in the face of bureaucratic inertia (1973: 315–16, 327–30; 1976a: 50, 92, 100–1; 1978b: 87–92).

Poulantzas identified important differences among exceptional forms of state. The most flexible and manoeuvrable regime is fascism, then comes Bonapartism, and military dictatorship is the most brittle regime (Jessop 1985a: 96–7). But Poulantzas also insisted that no exceptional regime can secure the sort of flexible, organic regulation of social forces and the smooth circulation of hegemony that occurs in bourgeois liberal democracies (1976a: 124). Accordingly, just as the movement from a normal to an exceptional state involves political crises and ruptures rather than taking a continuous, linear path, so the transition from an exceptional to a normal form will also involve a series of breaks and crises rather than a simple process of self-transformation. This places a premium on the political class struggle to achieve hegemony over the democratization process. Indeed Poulantzas insisted that the class character of the normal state will vary significantly with the outcome of this struggle (1976a: 90–7, 124, and *passim*; see also 1976b: 20–4, 30–8).

Drawing on the analysis, Poulantzas argued that a new form of state was emerging in advanced capitalist societies. He called this 'authoritarian statism' and identified its basic developmental tendency as 'intensified state control over every sphere of socio-economic life combined with radical decline of the institutions of political democracy and with draconian and multi-form curtailment of so-called "formal" liberties' (1978b: 203–4). This involves enhanced roles for the executive branch, its dominant 'state party' (whose function is to act as a transmission belt from the state to the people rather than from the people to the state), and a new, anti-democratic ideology. This undermines the already limited involvement of the masses in political decision-making, severely weakens the organic functioning of the party system (even where a plurality of parties survives intact), and saps the vitality of democratic forms of political discourse. Accordingly there are fewer obstacles to the continuing penetration of authoritarian-statist forms into all areas of social life. While one should neither over-estimate the capacities of the state and its technologies of power nor under-estimate capacities for resistance, the tendencies that Poulantzas identified are even more marked now than they were thirty years ago.

Poulantzas identified nine such tendencies:

1　Power shifts from the legislature to the executive and is even concentrated within the latter – typically within the office of prime minister or executive president, giving the impression of personalistic rule.
2　Fusion between the legislature, executive, and judiciary branches accelerates and a decline in the rule of law occurs in favour of particularistic, discretionary regulation.
3　As their ties to the power bloc and the popular masses weaken, political parties decline as privileged interlocutors of the administration and leading forces in organizing hegemony.

4 The political significance of parties correspondingly shifts away from their traditional functions of elaborating policy through compromise and alliances around a party programme and of legitimating state power through electoral competition towards a more restricted role as the transmission belts for executive decisions as the administration assumes the parties' legitimation functions.

5 Dominance within the ISAs is displaced from the school, university, and publishing house to the mass media, which now play a key role in political legitimation and mobilization and, indeed, increasingly draw both their agenda and symbolism from the administration and also experience a growing and multiform control at its hands.

6 Linked to these shifts is the growth of new plebiscitary and populist forms of consent alongside new technocratic and/or neo-liberal forms of legitimation.

7 Parallel power networks have also grown – networks that exercise a decisive share in its activities, promote a growing material and ideological community of interest between key civil servants and the dominant mass party, and consolidate policy communities that cement dominant interests outside the state apparatus with forces inside at the expense of popular forces.

8 A reserve repressive para-state apparatus has grown too, parallel to the main organs of the state and serving in a pre-emptive capacity to police popular struggles and other threats to bourgeois hegemony.

9 The dominant ideology has been reorganized by integrating certain liberal and libertarian themes from the 1960s as well as displacement of notions such as the general will and democracy in favour of instrumental rationality and technocratic logic (cf. Poulantzas 1978b, 1979a, 1979b, 1979c, 1979d, 1980a).

We should recall that Poulantzas operated with multiple levels of analysis. He treated authoritarian statism as a new form of the capitalist type of state in the current period of capitalism that characterized metropolitan and dependent capitalist states alike. It could be associated with different forms of regime: more neo-liberal in France, for example, more authoritarian in Germany (cf. Poulantzas 1979b). Thus, whilst drawing attention to these general tendencies, he was also well aware that their realization and impact could vary and that how far authoritarian statism was consolidated depended on measures taken to combat and resist it as much as to further it. Both the theoretical arguments and the political implications would merit further study.

Periodizing the Class Struggle

Such analyses of the strategically inscribed strategic selectivity in state forms are complemented by the periodization of state power in terms of conjunctures in the class struggle. These ideas are most fully developed in Poulantzas's accounts of fascism in pre-war Italy and Germany and of the evolving crisis of the military dictatorships in Southern Europe during the 1970s. He emphasized in both cases how the significance of state structures changes along with the class struggle. He rejected blanket generalizations about fascism's role in the class struggle and insisted on a careful retrospective periodization according to the successive steps of a complex war of position and manoeuvre. Likewise his analysis of the transition to democracy in Southern Europe attempted a real-time periodization in order to identify feasible horizons of political action (on the relevance of such horizons in calculating interests, see 1973: 60–2, 110–12).

Two issues are at stake here. First, given that the state power is a form-determined condensation of forces in struggle, the significance of particular strategies pursued by particular agents varies with the nature of the state. Different types of state and political regime selectively reward different types of actors and strategies. Second, given again that state power is a form-determined condensation of forces in struggle, the state apparatus and its capacity to act depend heavily on the capacities and aims of forces represented within the state, struggling to transform it (or prevent its transformation), and operating at a distance from it. Social forces are not mere *Träger* (bearers) of pre-constituted class identities and interests but active agents, reflecting on their identities and interests in specific conjunctures, with all that this implies for changing horizons of action. Thus different types of state and political regime will be more or less vulnerable to different types of strategy pursued by different blocs or alliances and this vulnerability will change with the overall balance of forces in a complex war of manoeuvre and tactics.

Two brief illustrations must suffice here. First, during the step of the working-class offensive in the rise of Italian fascism, the fascist movement primarily consisted in armed bands that were financed by big capital, large landowners, and rich peasants to wage their counter-attack. During the phase of relative stabilization, the fascist bands were abandoned by the power bloc and fascism attempted to transform itself into a mass party. With the launch of the bourgeois offensive, the fascist movement increasingly turned into a mass party and was once more openly maintained by big capitalist circles. Initially the fascist party genuinely represented the short-term political interests of the petty bourgeoisie and established organizational and ideological ties with this class at all levels from voters to higher party cadres. Subsequently fascism won the support of monopoly capital as a whole and tried to build organizational ties with other elements in the dominant classes. Poulantzas identified this crucial step in the rise of fascism as the '*point of no return*', when it would be difficult to reverse the tide of events. This coincided with a conjunctural coincidence of the interests of the power bloc and the petty bourgeoisie, mediated through the fascist party, which juggled concessions in securing compromises among their demands. When fascism came to power, there was an initial period of instability as the fascist party pursued policies favourable to big capital whilst seeking to consolidate popular support. Finally, there was a period of fascist stabilization. This arrived when the fascist party was subordinated to the state apparatus, the petty-bourgeois members of the state apparatus broke their representational ties with their class of origin, and monopoly capital combined the position of hegemonic fraction and ruling class (see 1974 *passim*).

Second, in analysing the political conjuncture after the crisis of the dictatorships in Southern Europe, Poulantzas insisted that the horizon of action was limited in that period to the form of democratization. It did not extend to an immediate transition to socialism. It was therefore important strategically to stabilize forces committed to bourgeois democracy (understood in terms of the current authoritarian statist form of state, not in terms of nineteenth-century liberal parliamentarism) rather than adopt a more radical socialist programme that might polarize the balance of forces in an antidemocratic, conservative reaction (see 1976a, 1976c, 1977, 1979a, 1979b).

The Spatio-Temporal Matrix of the State

Poulantzas also commented on the spatio-temporal selectivity of the state. His comments focused on the nation-state, which he saw as the typical form of the capitalist type of state. His analysis of the state's role in constituting and reproducing the capitalist forms of nationhood and nationalism owes much to the arguments of Henri Lefebvre (1974) and, regarding national identity, Otto Bauer (1924). Nationhood is a crucial element in the institutional matrix of the capitalist state. Historically the latter tends to encompass a single, constant nation; and modern nations have a corresponding tendency to establish their own states (1978b: 95). The capitalist type of state establishes a distinctive national language and forms of writing; it also reproduces the mental–manual division of labour through education and other institutions (1978b: 56).

Although this tends to exclude the popular masses from direct control over state power,

> the State is also the result of the national process of class struggle – that is to say, both the struggle of the bourgeoisie against the working class, and the struggle of the working class against the bourgeoisie. Just like the national culture, history or language, the State is a strategic field ploughed from one end to the other by working-class and popular struggle and resistance; these are inscribed in the State, albeit in a deformed manner, and they always break through the wall of silence with which the State hems in the workers' memory. (1978b: 119)

In particular, this type of state establishes a specific spatio-temporal matrix inside which the territorial identity and socio-cultural tradition of the nation are crystallized. Although Poulantzas grounds modern notions of time and space in the organization of capitalist production, he adds that the modern state systematizes these conceptions and extends them to the political field. Thus he discusses the state's role in demarcating frontiers, integrating the national space within these boundaries, unifying the internal market thus constituted, and homogenizing the 'people' living within the national territory. Poulantzas also notes that, once these frontiers, internal markets, and nations are constituted, they become the nodal points for the transnationalization of production, territorial wars of redivision, and even genocide (1978b: 99–107, 117). He also refers to the state's role in constituting time and historicity. In particular he notes how it establishes temporal norms and standards of measurement, tries to master the different temporalities and rhythms of social development, represses the traditions of subordinate nations, monopolizes the national tradition, charts the nation's future, and so forth (1978b: 107–15, 119).

So we must consider both the *genealogy* of the production of space (and time) and the history of their appropriation (1978b: 100). As Poulantzas puts it:

> In reality, however, transformations of the spatio-temporal matrices [namely in the transition and development of capitalism] refer to the materiality of the social division of labour, of the structure of the State, and of the practices and techniques of capitalist economic, political and ideological power; they are the real substratum of mythical, religious, philosophical or 'experiential' representations of space-time. Just as these changes are not reducible to the representations which they occasion, so they cannot be identified with the scientific concepts of space and time which allow us to grasp them. (1978b: 98)

For both spatial and temporal organization, Poulantzas stresses that the state always modifies the supposedly 'natural' pre-given elements of nationhood. Thus it always integrates elements such as economic unity, territory, language, tradition, and so forth, into the basic spatio-temporal matrix of capitalism. Indeed Poulantzas is careful to contrast the spatial and temporal organization of capitalist societies with those in ancient and feudal systems and to trace its implications for the divisions between nations, between civilized peoples and barbarians, and between believers and infidels, respectively. In this respect he emphasizes that the modern nation is always a product of state intervention and should not be considered as pre-political or primordial (1978b: 94, 96–103, 108–10, 113).

Poulantzas also stresses that conceptions of time, space, and nationhood are overdetermined by class struggle. There are bourgeois and proletarian variants of the capitalist spatio-temporal matrix and also contrasting class versions of the nation. The modern nation is not the creation of the bourgeoisie alone but actually reflects a relationship of forces between the 'modern' social classes. It is still pre-eminently marked, however, by the development of the bourgeoisie. Indeed, even when capitalism is undergoing *trans*nationalization, bourgeois reproduction is still focused on the nation-state. Thus the modern nation, the national state, and the bourgeoisie are intimately connected and all are constituted on the same terrain of capitalist relations. Poulantzas concludes that 'the modern nation is written into the state, and it is this national state which organizes the bourgeoisie as the dominant class' (1978b: 117).

The state's institutional ensemble also privileges the adoption of certain spatial and temporal horizons of action by those trying to access the state, influence it from a distance, or transform its structural selectivities. Drawing on more recent accounts of the strategic-relational approach (Jessop 2001a, 2002d, 2007a), spatio-temporal selectivity refers here to the diverse ways in which spatial and temporal horizons of action in different fields are produced, spatial and temporal rhythms are created, certain practices and strategies are privileged and others hindered according to their 'fit' with the temporal and spatial patterns inscribed in the state's structures. This is reflected not only in the generic forms of spatiality and historicity associated with the capitalist national state, which have their own distinctive implications for forms of economic, political, and ideological struggle as compared to pre-capitalist formations (1978b: 99–106, 116), but also in the specific forms of de- and re-territorialization, time-space distantiation, and time-space compression that are associated with different stages of capitalism and different phases in the class struggle (1978b: 116–20). Many of these ideas are developed in Lefebvre's analysis of the strategic selectivity and power relations inscribed within the abstract space of capitalist societies (Lefebvre 1974: 278–82). The significance of these national spatio-temporal matrices is also reflected in Poulantzas's conclusion that 'only a *national transition to socialism* is possible . . . in the sense of a multiplicity of original roads to socialism, whose general principles, drawn from the theory and experience of the workers' movement, cannot be more than signs on the road' (1978b: 118, italics in original).

Poulantzas admitted that these remarks on spatio-temporality were very preliminary (1978b: 119–20). But he failed to note that they were wedded to the primacy of national formations associated with earlier stages of capitalism (up to and including Atlantic Fordism) and did not anticipate the relativization of scale that is associated with the current stage of globalization-localization. For new forms of time-space distantiation, time-space compression, and the emergence of cyberspace and nano-second temporalities are transforming the national matrices of capital accumulation so that it is no longer so self-evident that the national state is the primary scale of economic, political, and ideological struggles. This does not mean that the national is redundant, that the national state is dead, or that national struggles no longer matter (whether for the bourgeoisie or other classes). Indeed Poulantzas gave compelling reasons in his analysis of internationalization and the nation-state why the national still mattered so much (1975: 70–84; see also Jessop 2002b). But the continuing development of the spatio-temporal matrices of capitalism has altered their role in shaping the forms of struggle (see chapter 8 below).

Conclusions

A theorist's legacy does not consist in his/her literary remains but in how they are taken up and used by contemporaries and successors. Hence a legacy comes to include far more than the original literary archives (and may well, paradoxically, marginalize or exclude some of them). It involves the uses, often unintended or perverse, often synthetic or eclectic, often as controversial or negative reference points, often secondary or marginal, that are made of these remains by subsequent generations. Or, as Prezzolini put it, 'the real life of an author emanates from his readers, disciples, commentators, opponents, critics. An author has no other existence' (1967: 190). In short, the influence of theorists, for good or bad, continues as long as their work leaves identifiable traces on the work of others. In these terms, Poulantzas's legacy is ambivalent. He contributed significantly to the theoretical agenda in state theory in the 1970s and, in particular, its concern with the so-called 'relative autonomy' of the state. He also engaged in debates on the middle classes and productive and unproductive labour, on imperialism and the changing forms of internationalization and fractionation of capital, and, for a time, on the problems of a democratic transition to democratic socialism. In other respects, however, his influence has been limited. Thus his invariably interesting and often incisive remarks on the specificity of capitalist law, the nature and dynamic of exceptional regimes, forms of ideological class struggle, or the difficulties of Foucault's 'micro-physics' of power appear to have fallen largely on deaf ears. Moreover, even where he did help to set the theoretical agenda, it was not his solutions that came to be accepted as the conventional wisdom in state theory or class analysis or that set the terms of debate in political strategy.

A theory is 'classical' when it offers an interconnected set of claims that has been superseded by later developments and is no longer convincing in its original form. Yet it survives as a theoretical challenge, desideratum, or problem because its way of posing problems remains productive. Thus its authority is ambivalent: it indicates *what* must be done but not *how* to achieve it (Luhmann 1982a: 4; cf. Baehr and O'Brien 1994). This distinction enables us to identify problems in Poulantzas's work and to continue to treat it as a productive heuristic about the state, social classes, and political mobilization. In particular, his work is most problematic where it subordinates the development of his emerging relational approach to political prejudices about appropriate revolutionary strategies; and most productive where he used the approach to rethink central issues in the face of apparent anomalies thrown up by actual political events that did not conform to his political expectations. Poulantzas himself was always prepared to rethink crucial assumptions, especially when unconstrained by organizational commitments, but he still retained a residual class reductionism and could not anticipate the significant reorganization of capitalism that would occur following the crisis of Atlantic Fordism. This chapter is a further modest effort (building on Jessop 1985a) to redirect Poulantzas's theoretical legacy and to recover the significance of his strategic-relational approach to the state.

I conclude that Poulantzas's theory is both classical and contemporary. We cannot accept what he wrote in an uncritical, passive manner. This is especially clear in the relative underdevelopment of his approach to issues of political economy (as tackled, for example, in the regulation approach) or issues of ideology (a distinct theoretical object in Althusserian structuralism that has been steadily deconstructed through discourse analysis).

But his work remains a critical source for a continuing critical tradition of state theory and can facilitate advances in conventional 'society-centred' analyses as well as the newer 'state-centred' analyses. There is also enormous value in his strategic-relational approach. At stake here is continuing the unfinished work of a basic theoretical revolution in Marxist analyses of the state. We should approach his work in the same critical spirit as that adopted by Poulantzas in his own studies: to appreciate its significant theoretical ruptures, to fill its gaps, to assess its relevance to new problems and theoretical currents, to develop it in new directions. Fortunately, in recent years there is some evidence for a Poulantzas revival as scholars read his book-length studies and assess their contemporary implications rather than seek short-cuts through the Poulantzas–Miliband debate (for four examples, see Aronowitz and Bratsis 2002; Bretthauer et al. 2006; and Demirović 2007; and, in relation to Miliband too, Wetherly et al. 2007).

6

Foucault on State, State Formation, and Statecraft

This chapter revisits Foucault's analytics of power in the light of his lectures on governmentality and biopolitics in *Society Must be Defended* (1975–6, translated 2003), *Securité, territoire, population* (1977–8, first published 2004a) and *Naissance de la biopolitique* (1978–9. first published 2004b). Foucault is renowned both for his criticisms of state theory and for his own bottom-up approach to power. Yet these lectures, especially that on governmentality, turn decisively to changing forms of statehood and statecraft and their subsequent role in capitalist reproduction. This turn casts new light on Foucault's alleged anti-statism and anti-Marxism and offers new insights into the complex and restless nature of his intellectual development. To show this, I review Foucault's hostility to Marxism and theories of the state, compare the work of Poulantzas and Foucault to assess how far the latter's criticisms of Marxism apply to a strategic-relational theorist of state power, then consider Foucault's apparent turn from the micro-physics and microdiversity of power relations to their macro-physics and strategic codification through the normalizing, governmentalized state, and, finally, suggest how to develop an evolutionary account of state formation on the basis of these new arguments about emerging forms of statecraft. This intervention does not claim to uncover the hidden essence of Foucault's interest in governmentality but aims merely to offer an alternative reading alongside more conventional accounts of this stage in his work.

Foucault and the 'Crisis of Marxism'

After the May events in 1968, many French intellectuals proclaimed a 'crisis of Marxism'. The first such crisis was declared by Masaryk at the end of the nineteenth century, and others have been announced regularly ever since.

This chapter is a revised and expanded version of 'From micro-powers to governmentality: Foucault's work on statehood, state formation, statecraft, and state power', *Political Geography*, 26 (1), 2007, 34–40; and also includes material from *State Theory* (1990b) and 'Pouvoir et stratégies chez Poulantzas et Foucault', *Actuel Marx*, 36, 2004, 89–107.

But the post-'68 crisis appeared more serious and many doubted that it could be resolved simply by reviving or revising traditional Marxism. Indeed, May 1968 triggered a strong theoretical reaction against both orthodox and structural Marxism (Ferry and Renaut 1985). Its most extreme expression was the virulently anti-Marxist, post-gauchiste, post-modern, *nouvelle philosophie* (Dews 1979; Resch 1992). More temperate were attempts to rescue Marxism from its alleged over-identification with orthodox Communism and Stalinism by drawing on other theories. These included existentialism, structuralism, post-structuralism, psychoanalysis, linguistics, and Foucault's work (Poster 1984: 20–40; for Foucault's reflections on May 1968 for the changing intellectual climate, see 1997: 115, 125).

Foucault's work reveals the paradox of an outspoken opposition to official and vulgar Marxist positions and an implicit appropriation and development of Marxian insights.[1] In criticizing Marxism, Foucault rarely identified specific theorists, preferring general problematization to detailed critique (Fontana and Bertani 2003: 287). At different times he rejected vulgar Marxism; Freudo-Marxism; academic (or university) Marxism; para-Marxism; treatments of labour as 'man's [sic] concrete essence' (Foucault 2001: 86); 'endless commentaries on surplus-value'; abstract interest in 'class' rather than detailed studies of the subjects, stakes, and modalities of 'class' struggle; the grounding of power in the economy and/or class relations; the reduction of the state to a set of functions, such as managing productive forces and relations; concern with consciousness and ideology rather than the materiality of the body and anatomo-politics; epiphenomenalist analyses of infrastructure and superstructure relations; the sterility of dialectics and the logic of contradiction; the 'hypermarxification' of social and political analyses; Marxist hagiography; and 'communistology'.[2] He also dismissed Marxian political economy as part of the 'Classical' episteme and attacked Marxist claims to scientificity to the exclusion of other forms of knowledge.

Despite this, 'Foucault maintained a sort of "uninterrupted dialogue" with Marx, [who] was in fact not unaware of the question of power and its disciplines' (Fontana and Bertani 2003: 277). Thus we can find increasingly sympathetic but generally covert references to some core themes in Marx's critique of political economy, some of them deliberately and provocatively undeclared, as well as apparent engagement with some less reductionist contemporary currents outside 'official Marxism' (Balibar 1992; Elden 2008; Kalyvas 2004; Lemke 2003). Thus he began to argue that capitalism has penetrated deeply into our existence, especially because it required diverse techniques of power to enable capital to exploit people's bodies and their time, transforming them into labour power and labour time, respectively, to create surplus profit (Foucault 2003: 32–7; see also Marsden 1999) This prompted Balibar to suggest that Foucault moved from a break to a tactical alliance with Marxism, '[with] the first involving a global critique of Marxism as a "theory"; the second a partial usage of Marxist tenets or affirmations compatible with Marxism. . . .Thus, in contradictory fashion, the opposition to Marxist "theory" grows deeper and deeper whilst the convergence of the analyses and concepts taken from Marx becomes more and more significant' (Balibar 1992: 53).

Poulantzas and Foucault Compared

These apparently contradictory attitudes towards Marxism provide a good basis for comparing Foucault and Poulantzas in regard to the strategic-relational analysis of power and the state. In contrast to Foucault, Poulantzas never abandoned his fundamental commitment to Marxism. Nonetheless, like others in the wake of May 1968, he recommended resort to other disciplines and approaches to reinvigorate Marxism. These included linguistics, psychoanalysis, and Foucault's work (Poulantzas 1979c: 14–15; 1979b; 1979e). But he largely ignored psychoanalysis, paid limited attention to linguistics, and took only Foucault seriously. Even then he distinguished Foucault as an epistemologist and general theorist from Foucault as an analyst of specific techniques of power and aspects of the state form. For, while Poulantzas rejected Foucault's general epistemological and theoretical project, he found his critique of discipline, power, and knowledge useful (citing *Discipline and Punish* and *History of Sexuality, Volume 1*, with qualified approval in his own great work, *State, Power, Socialism* [1978b: 66–9]). This rejection makes sense on both counts. On the one hand, Foucault's epistemology is incompatible with Marxism (Lecourt 1975); and, more particularly, he had dismissed Marxian political economy as part of the 'Classical' episteme and even accorded Ricardo greater weight than Marx in this regard (Foucault 1970: 262–6). Moreover, while Foucault had rejected the temptations of state theory, Poulantzas aimed to develop an autonomous Marxist political science within a broad historical materialist approach and eventually claimed to have completed Marx's unfinished theory of the state. Yet he recognized that this work of completion depended on his development of a more general, and resolutely relational, account of power and drew significantly on Foucault in this regard.

Despite some obvious differences, it is clear that Foucault's criticisms of Marxism hardly apply to the work of Poulantzas. Indeed some fascinating and surprising convergences developed in their work over the course of the

1970s. This seems to be a response to the cathartic impact of May 1968 because both thinkers moved beyond their earlier theoretical approaches and focused increasingly, each in his own way, on the complexities of power, resistance, and their strategic codification. Indeed, the confused political and theoretical conjuncture of 1972–7 was an especially creative period for both thinkers (on Foucault, see Gordon 1980: ix). It is particularly interesting to note how they both developed relational approaches to the state, with Poulantzas putting more emphasis on strategy in his later work compared with the earlier period and Foucault becoming more interested in the institutional codification of power relations in the state compared with his earlier emphasis on the micro-physics of power. Indeed, Poulantzas was far less of an orthodox 'Marxist' and far more 'Foucauldian' than many critics suggest. Conversely, while Foucault was a vehement critic of Marxism as distorted by communist party apparatchiks and lazy or self-serving theoreticism, he was by no means hostile to concepts and arguments drawn from the Marxian critique of political economy.

There are eight main areas of theoretical convergence between the contemporaries. In listing these, I will sometimes focus on the figure whose position is more surprising in terms of conventional wisdom about the two thinkers.

1 Each denied the existence of subjects endowed with free will and both examined the mechanisms in and through which acting and knowing subjects were constituted. Whereas Poulantzas explored this in terms of the 'isolation effect' produced by juridico-political institutions in capitalist societies, Foucault explored the mechanisms of individualization and normalization and their role in shaping bodies as well as minds in different historical periods and sites of power. Poulantzas would later acknowledge the superiority of Foucault's analyses of normalization and the state's role in shaping corporality compared to his own account of the 'isolation effect' (1978b: 70).

2 Each explored the relations between sovereignty and individual citizenship and its impact on political relations. As I have already shown this for Poulantzas in chapter 5, I will now cite Foucault. The latter argued that

> modern society, then, from the nineteenth century up to our own day, has been characterized both by a legislation, a discourse, an organization based on public right, whose principle of articulation is the social body and the delegative status of each citizen; and by a closely linked grid of disciplinary coercions whose purpose is in fact to assure the cohesion of this same social body. (1980b: 106)

3 Each adopted a relational approach to power and explored the links between power and strategies. Indeed, while Poulantzas (1973) anticipated Foucault in this respect in treating power as the capacity to realize interests in a specific conjuncture, he went on to integrate Foucauldian ideas into his emerging strategic-relational approach to the state. Later he examined the complex links among class interests, class power, and class strategies and eventually concluded that state power is the material condensation of the balance of class forces in struggle. Foucault developed his relational analytics of power during the same period and, having initially emphasized the micro-physics of power, soon turned to the role of the state in the strategic codification of power relations.

4 Each insisted that power is always correlated with resistance. Poulantzas initially based this on the antagonistic character of the social relations of production in class-divided societies and its repercussions in the political and ideological field. He later flirted with Foucauldian language to extend this claim, noting that 'there are no social classes prior to their opposition in struggle' and that class struggle is never in a position of exteriority to class relations: they are coeval (1978b: 27, cf. 45, 141, 145; compare with Foucault 1980a: 95).

5 They agreed in treating power as productive and positive rather than simply repressive and negative. Already in the mid-1970s Poulantzas had implicitly rejected the 'Nietzschean hypothesis' that power is repressive, censorious, and negative; and accepted that it could have productive, normalizing, and positive functions in regard to the relations of production, the organization of material concessions, unification of the power bloc, producing knowledge, shaping the spatio-temporal matrix of capitalist societies, and so forth (1975, 1976a, 1978b). And, while Foucault initially rejected power in Nietzschean fashion as a repressive mechanism, he went on to develop a more positive, productive reading (see below).

6 While Foucault is widely and rightly celebrated for his analyses of the mutual implication of power and knowledge, Poulantzas noted how political and ideological class domination was reproduced in part through the mental–manual division of labour and its consequences for the exclusion of the working class and other subaltern elements from the 'secrecy or knowledge' (1975: 31, 180, 233, 237–40, 249, 255, 274–5, 322–3). Poulantzas also suggested that basic research, technology, management, and bureaucratic organization are always closely interwoven with the dominant ideology, and added that this involves specific material practices of ideological domination as well as ideas (1975: 181, 236–8, 240, 255).

7 Both were staunch critics of fascism and Stalinism but also noted the continuities between liberal democracy and fascist and Stalinist forms of totalitarianism grounded in the matrix of statehood, with its social construction of a variable public–private distinction, the individualization of political subjects, and the role of nationalism in the modern state (Poulantzas 1974: 320–4; 1978b: 72–4; Foucault 1995). In the late 1970s, both thinkers turned to the restructuring of the post-war welfare state, new authoritarian tendencies, and the rise of neo-liberalism (Foucault 2004b; Poulantzas 1978b).

8 Following May 1968 and the development of new forms of struggle, both thinkers became interested in 'micro-revolts', rank-and-file movements, and what Poulantzas termed 'struggles at a distance from the state'. Moreover, while Poulantzas criticized Foucault for insisting that micro-revolts could only succeed if they remained dispersed and uncoordinated, Foucault later accepted that different forms of resistance would need to be readjusted, reinforced, and transformed by global strategies of societal transformation (1980a: 96; 1980b: 159, 203; 1979b: 60).

Despite these convergences (or, perhaps, because of them) Poulantzas criticized Foucault on several occasions, especially in areas where they had occurred. Foucault did not single out his antagonist for special attention in his frequent criticisms of various contemporary Marxist positions. Nonetheless his later work does show some interesting, if generally unacknowledged and perhaps unintentional, convergences toward more sophisticated Marxist positions, including those of Gramsci and Poulantzas. Before I summarize Poulantzas's criticisms, it should be noted that they were directed against the analytics of power in *Discipline and Punish* (1975/1979a) and *History of Sexuality, Volume 1* (1976/1980a). Poulantzas did not (or could not) take account of the lectures at the Collège de France (1976–9) when Foucault turned his attention to governmentality. These are especially interesting because they contain Foucault's self-criticism for committing some of the errors criticized by Poulantzas as well as others that he had not identified. Noting these self-criticisms and corrections occurred does not imply that he was responding directly to Poulantzas's criticisms. I present them below in the form of a Poulantzasian criticism followed by a possible response from Foucault.

First, concern with anatomo- and bio-politics ignores the state's real foundations in capitalist relations of production and class struggle (Poulantzas 1978b: 75). This might be true of the early work on the disciplinary normalization of conduct regarding persons who were not directly involved in capitalist production (e.g., asylums, prisons, schools, barracks); but Foucault's lectures at the Collège de France did consider how these practices came to serve capital and the modern state.

Second, in arguing that power has no bases beyond the power relation itself, Foucault implies that it consists purely in the modalities of its exercise across many dispersed sites (Poulantzas 1978b: 70). While this may hold for the early analytics of power in *Discipline and Punish*, Foucault later insisted that his work on technologies of power was not 'a metaphysics of Power with a capital P'. Indeed, in a possibly indirect reference to Poulantzas, Foucault criticized 'some French "Marxists" [who] maintain that power for me is "endogenous" and that I would like to construct a real and true onto-logical circle, deducing power from power'. On the contrary, he 'always tried to do just the opposite' (1978: 185). Thus power always operates on pre-existing differentiations and can involve different media and mechanisms, different objectives, different forms of institutionalization, different ratio-nalizations (Foucault 2001: 337, 344–5; 1980b: 164). Foucault also argued that relations of power are interwoven with other kinds of relations (pro-duction, kinship, family, sexuality) for which they play at once a condition-ing and a conditioned role (2001: 425). And he suggested that types of power vary according to how these different aspects are articulated. For example, the monastery and penitentiary illustrated an emphasis on power and obe-dience; goal-directedness was exemplified in the workshop or hospital; apprenticeship was based on communication; and military discipline was saturated by all three mechanisms of power (2001: 83, 338–9). Foucault also argued that the state, for all its omnipotence, does not occupy the whole field of power relations, and that it can only operate on the basis of other, already existing power relations, which it invests and colonizes in a condi-tioning–conditioned relationship to generate a kind of 'meta-power' that makes its own functioning possible (1980a: 122–3). Indeed, as we shall see below, he argued that 'power relations have been progressively governmen-talized, that is to say, elaborated, rationalized, and centralized in the form of, or under the auspices of, state institutions' (2001: 345). This explains why Barret-Kriegel could later note that 'Foucault's thought opened the way to a return to the study of the State and the law' (1992: 192).

Third, Foucault privileges 'power' over resistance and, at best, explained the latter in terms of a natural, primordial plebeian spirit of resistance. In contrast, for Poulantzas, the limits to power are inherent in the way in which its mechanisms incorporate and condense the struggles of the dom-inated classes without being able to fully integrate and absorb them (1978b: 149–52). Foucault might well have responded that he had begun to explain resistance in terms of how *assujettissement* and technologies of the self created independent bases from which to resist the exercise of power (1982).

Fourth, Foucault stressed only the repressive, prohibitive side of law and only the positive, productive side of disciplinary (state) power. He therefore exaggerated the general significance of disciplinary techniques in the modern state and their particular role as a productive and positive force in securing compliance (Poulantzas 1978b: 77–8). However, while these criticisms were well directed at Foucault's earlier analytics of power, they could not take account of his later rejection of such positions in the unpublished lectures at the Collège de France. Thus Foucault conceded that he had overemphasized disciplinary power in adopting Nietzsche's repressive hypothesis and so began to focus on the 'art of government' (the conduct of conduct) as a means of securing the active complicity of the subjects of power in their own self-regulation. Foucault's later analyses of liberalism, the Ordo-liberals, and the Chicago School show that he recognized the complex articulation and mutual implications of direct repression, constitutional law, police measures, and self-regulation (see especially 2004a).

Fifth, Foucault's analyses are ultimately descriptive and, worse still, as in the study of the Panopticon, functionalist (Poulantzas 1978b: 67–8). Foucault denied describing Bentham's Panopticon as a practical model for the exercise of power and claimed to have treated it instead as an ideal-typical construction that was never implemented (Foucault 1978: 183). But it should be admitted that Foucault certainly did offer a genealogy of 'panopticism' as a distinctive technique, technology, or diagram of power that could be found in many different institutional sites, that came to characterize the nineteenth-century disciplinary society, and that, whatever its complex genealogy, was subsequently mobilized in the service of industrial capitalism (see below).

The Analytics of Power versus State Theory

Whereas Poulantzas devoted his life to a critique of the capitalist state, Foucault had an antipathy to state theory. Indeed, he once claimed that 'I do, I want to, and I must pass up on state theory – just as one would with an indigestible meal' (2004b: 78, my translation). This is reflected in his well-known hostility to general theorizations about the state – whether juridico-political, Marxist, or realist – and his grounding of power and control in the modern state, to the extent that it exists, in social norms and institutions rather than in sovereign authority. Foucault stressed three themes in his 'nominalist' analytics of power: it is immanent in all social relations, articulated with discourses as well as institutions, and necessarily polyvalent because its impact and significance vary with how social relations, discourses, and institutions are integrated into different strategies. He also focused on technologies of power, power-knowledge relations, and changing strategies for structuring and deploying power relations. In developing this analytics of power, Foucault rejected attempts to develop any general theory about state power or about power more generally that were based on *a priori* assumptions about its essential unity, its pre-given functions, its inherent tendency to expand through its own power dynamics, or its global strategic deployment by a master subject (see especially Foucault 1979b, 1980b: *passim*; cf. 2003: 27–31; 2004b: 79, 193–4).

Based on his early comments, which were largely recapitulated in his courses at the Collège de France on biopolitics and governmentality from 1975 to 1979, Foucault's analytics of power can be summarized as follows. The study of power should begin from below, in the heterogeneous and dispersed micro-physics of power, explore specific forms of its exercise in different institutional sites, and consider how, if at all, these were articulated to produce broader and more persistent societal configurations. One should study power where it is exercised over individuals rather than legitimated at the centre; explore the actual practices of subjugation rather than the intentions that guide attempts at domination; and recognize that power circulates through networks rather than being applied at particular points. However, following this initial move, Foucault began increasingly to emphasize that, whilst starting at the bottom with the micro-diversity of power relations across a multiplicity of dispersed sites, it was necessary to consider two further interrelated issues: first, how do diverse power relations come to be colonized and articulated into more general mechanisms that sustain more encompassing forms of domination, and, second, how are they linked to specific forms and means of producing knowledge?

Foucault developed the problematic of government here to explore the historical constitution and periodization of the state and the important strategic and tactical dimensions of power relations and their associated discourses. For, in rejecting various essentialist, transhistorical, universal, and deductive analyses of the state and state power, he created a space for exploring its 'polymorphous crystallization' (cf. Mann 1986) in and through interrelated changes in technologies of power, objects of governance, governmental projects, and modes of political calculation. Indeed, he argued that 'the state is nothing more than the mobile effect of a regime of multiple governmentalities' (2004b: 79). For Foucault, this does not mean that one needs a universal notion of the state before one can interrogate and deconstruct it through historically specific, concrete practices. He avoids this paradox by asking how one might explore history if the state did not always already exist (2004b: 4–5). For example, *Society Must be Defended* shows how the modern idea of the universal state emerged from a complex series of discursive shifts and the eventual combination of disciplinary and bio-political power within a redefined framework of sovereignty (2003: 37–9, 242–50). Now let us see what it means to explore the historical emergence of 'state effects' as revealed in the two texts of interest here.

Foucault as a Genealogist of Statecraft

Although Foucault often refers to the state in his work, he denied that its existence can be taken for granted and so rejected the utility of any state theory that rested on this assumption. The current texts reiterate that the state has no essence, is not a universal, is not an autonomous source of power. Instead it is an emergent and changeable effect of incessant transactions, multiple governmentalities, perpetual statizations (2004b: 79).

> An analysis in terms of power must not assume that state sovereignty, the form of the law, or the overall unity of a domination is given at the outset; rather, these are only the terminal forms power takes. . . . power must be understood in the first instance as the multiplicity of force relations immanent in the sphere in which they operate and that constitute their own organization; as the process which, through ceaseless struggles and confrontations, transforms, strengthens, or reverses them; as the support which these force relations find in one another, thus forming a chain or a system, or, on the contrary, the disjunctions and contradictions that isolate them from each other; and, lastly, as the strategies in which they take effect, whose general design or institutional crystallization is embodied in the state apparatus, in the formulation of the law, in various social hegemonies. Power's condition of possibility [and its] grid of intelligibility of the social order must not be sought in the primary existence of a central point, in a unique source of sovereignty from which secondary and derived forms might emanate; it is the moving substrate of force relations which, by virtue of their inequality, constantly engender states of power, but the latter are always local and unstable. . . . Power is everywhere; not because it embraces everything, but because it comes from everywhere. (2004b: 92–3, my translation)

In this context, the art of government, or governmentality, is said to involve 'the ensemble formed by the institutions, procedures, analyses, and reflections, the calculations and tactics that allow the exercise of this very specific, albeit complex form of power, which has, as its target, population; as its principal form of knowledge, political economy; and, as its essential technical means, apparatuses of security' (2001: 219–20). Thus Foucault regards the state as a relational ensemble and treats governmentality as a set of practices and strategies that operate on the terrain of a non-essentialized set of political relations. This is why he criticized analyses of the state (or states in the plural) as a juridico-political instance, a calculating subject, an instrument of class rule, or an epiphenomenon of production relations.

In later work, however, Foucault began to analyse state(s) as a crucial site for the strategic (re-)codification of power relations linked to new governmental projects and modes of calculation. These operate on something called the state; but the latter is something that is not only pre-given as an object of governance but is also being (re)constructed through changing practices of government (2004b: 5–6). In short, to study governmentality is to study the historical constitution of different state forms in and through practices of government without assuming that the state has a universal or general essence. Thus, whilst eschewing any attempt to develop a general theory of the state, Foucault certainly investigated emergent strategies (state projects, governmentalizing projects) that identified the nature and purposes of government (hence alternative forms of *raison d'état*) in different contexts and periods. In particular, his lectures at the Collège de France from 1975 to 1979 argued that disciplinary power was later supplemented by the emergence of biopolitics and security as new forms of *ratio gouvernmentale*. While the former could compensate for the failure of sovereign power at the level of individual bodies, the harder task of controlling the population was only resolved through the development of biopolitics.

This was a core theme of the two sets of lectures considered here. For they studied changing theories and practices about the art of government as well as the changing institutions and institutional ensembles with which such practices were linked. Thus Foucault identified three forms of government: sovereignty, disciplinarity, and governmentality. The first is associated with the medieval state based on customary law, written law, and litigation and concerned with control over land and wealth; the second with the rise of the administrative state of the fifteenth and sixteenth centuries based on the disciplinary regulation of individual bodies in different institutional contexts; and the third with the increasingly governmentalized state, which dates from the late sixteenth century and came to fruition in the nineteenth century, when state concern was henceforth focused on controlling the mass of the population on its territory rather than controlling territoriality as such (2004a: 221; cf., with the same sequence but different dates, 2003: 37–9, 249–50). Further, expanding this account, Foucault traced governmental concerns back to the sixteenth-century interest in the administration of territorial monarchies; to the sixteenth- and seventeenth-century development of new analyses and forms of 'statistical' knowledge, that is, knowledge of the state, in all its elements, dimensions, and factors of power; and, finally, to the rise of mercantilism and cameralistic police science (or *Polizeiwissenschaft*) (Foucault 2004a: 212). In this sense, the rise of the governmental state involved the governmentalization of the state rather than the statization of society, based on a continual definition and redefinition of state competences and the division between public and private (2004a: 220–1).

With Foucault beyond Foucault

Some of the ambiguities and confusions surrounding Foucault's analyses of power and its significance in social life can be resolved if we distinguish three moments in the development of power relations. These are *variation* in the objects, subjects, purposes, and technologies of power; *selection* of some technologies and practices rather than others; and *retention* of some of these in turn as they are integrated into broader and more stable strategies of state and/or class (or national or racial) power. These three moments overlap and interact in actual social relations, but Foucault tended to come to them (or, at least, elaborate them) separately in his work, focusing first on genealogical variation, then on the emergent convergence and selection of various technologies of power to delineate general conditions of domination as they are seen to have economic or political utility for an emerging bourgeoisie, and finally on the strategic codification and retention of these practices of government to produce a global strategy oriented to a more or less unified objective. The first step introduces the familiar notion of genealogy, the importance of which is what many commentators take away from these and earlier texts. Far more interesting in this trajectory, however, is that its second and, even more, its third step re-introduce state power as a crucial emergent field of strategic action and link state power to issues of capitalist political economy and to the interests of an emerging bourgeois class without ever treating the state, capital, or the bourgeoisie as taken-for-granted, pre-given social forces. This is sometimes included in commentaries, but its significance for an anti-essentialist, non-teleological, and *ex post* functionalist explanation of capitalist development and state formation is rarely remarked.

First, following his more general rejection of attempts to provide a totalizing account of social events, Foucault typically rejected any *a priori* assumption that different forms of power were connected to produce an overall pattern of class domination. He noted that the modern state's disciplinary techniques originated in dispersed local sites well away from the centres of state power in the *Ancien Régime* and well away from emerging sites of capitalist production. Thus disciplinary normalization focused on the conduct of persons who were not directly involved in capitalist production (e.g., in asylums, prisons, schools, barracks). Second, Foucault recognized that some technologies and practices were selected and integrated into other sites of power. So, while *Discipline and Punish* emphasized the dispersion of power mechanisms, the *History of Sexuality* began to explore how different mechanisms were combined to produce social order through a strategic codification that made them more coherent and complementary. In this and a contemporary work, *Society Must be Defended*, Foucault links this explicitly to bourgeois recognition of their economic profitability and political utility (1979a: 114, 125, 141; 2003: 30–3). Third, he explored how existing power relations were not only codified but also consolidated and institutionalized. The state is crucial here in combining, arranging, and fixing the micro-relations of power, a process expressed in diverse metaphors: the immanent multiplicity of relations and techniques of power are ' "colonized", "utilized", "displaced", "extended", "altered", "reinforced", "transformed", "strengthened", "reversed", and so forth, in their relations with one another, and within more "global phenomena" and "more general powers" ' (Dean 1994: 157; Foucault 2003: 30–1).

This codification and consolidation occurred in quite specific historical conditions that, according to Foucault, cannot be derived from the functional needs of the economy but have their own pre-history and developmental dynamic. For example, Foucault argues that only a post-sovereign state could consolidate the new forms of government insofar as the emergence of the problem of population enabled power to be refocused on the economy rather than the family writ large (2004a: 214–15). The articulation of the economic and political should not be explained in terms of functional subordination or formal isomorphism but in terms of functional overdetermination and a perpetual process of strategic elaboration or completion (1979b: 89, 219; 1980b: 195f.). The former occurs when 'each effect – positive or negative, intentional or unintentional – enters into resonance or contradiction with the others and thereby calls for a readjustment or a re-working of the heterogeneous elements that surface at various points' (1980b: 195). In describing this general line, Foucault invoked concepts such as 'social hegemonies', 'hegemonic effects', 'hegemony of the bourgeoisie', 'meta-power', 'class domination', 'sur-pouvoir' (or a 'surplus-power' analogous to surplus-value), 'global strategy', and so forth (e.g., 1980a: 92–3, 94; 1982: 156, 122, 188). He also gave a privileged role to the state as the point of strategic codification of the multitude of power relations and the apparatus in which hegemony, meta-power, class domination, or 'sur-pouvoir' are crystallized (e.g., 1980: 92, 141; 1982: 101, 122, 199–200). For example, it was the rise of the population–territory–wealth nexus in political economy and police that created the space for the revalorization and re-articulation of disciplines that had emerged in the seventeenth and eighteenth centuries, that is, schools, manufactories, armies, and so forth (2004a: 217–19).

In approaching Foucault's work in these terms, we can escape the dichotomy of micro- and macro-power, the antinomy of an analytics of micro-powers and a theory of sovereignty, and the problematic relation between micro-diversity and macro-necessity in power relations (cf. Jessop 1990b; Kerr 1999: 176). The idea of government as a strategic codification of power relations provides a bridge between micro-diversity and macro-necessity, and, as Foucault argues, a focus on micro-powers is determined by scale but applies across all scales. It is a perspective, not a reality delimited to one scale (2004b: 193; cf. 2003: 244). Introducing the concept of biopolitics requires Foucault to say more about the global strategies of the state and the 'general line of force that traverses local oppositions and links them together' (1980a: 94). In this way we can move from the analysis of variation to the crucial issues of selection and retention that produce a distinctive articulation of the economic and political in particular historical contexts.

Conclusions

Foucault always rejected attempts to develop a general theory and changed direction and argument according to his changing interests and the changing political conjuncture. This is why we should not seek an 'essential Foucault'. Nonetheless the three lecture courses on governmentality (2003, 2004a, 2004b) do indicate an increasing interest in complex and contingent problems of political economy and statecraft. Foucault certainly rejected crude 'capital-logic' arguments about socio-economic development and state-centric accounts of the state. But his 'critical and effective histories' were increasingly brought to bear in the mid- to late 1970s on questions of political economy and the historical constitution of the state from the sixteenth to twentieth centuries. His novel and highly productive approach also showed how the economy and the state were increasingly organized in conformity with key features of capitalist political economy without ever being reducible thereto and without these features in turn being fully pre-given. In this sense, generalizing from Marsden's re-reading of Marx and Foucault on capitalism (1999), it seems that, while Marx seeks to explain the *why* of capital accumulation and state power, Foucault's analyses of disciplinarity and governmentality try to explain the *how* of economic exploitation and political domination. There is far more, of course, to Foucault's work in this period, but this re-reading shows that there is more scope than many believe for dialogue between critical Marxist and Foucauldian analyses.

Part III

Applying the Strategic-Relational Approach

7

The Gender Selectivities of the State

This chapter draws freely from feminist theorists, recent work on masculinity, and some insights from 'queer theory'. It aims to show the contingently necessary nature of the gender biases in the state's institutional architecture and operation and suggest ways to explain this from a critical realist, strategic-relational perspective. The chapter has three main parts. These deal with (a) the implications of the SRA for analysing gender selectivities; (b) the gender selectivities of advanced capitalist democratic states; and (c) some implications of strategic selectivity for feminist action. The chapter ends with general observations on problems in describing and explaining gender selectivities within an anti-essentialist framework.

Analysing Gender Selectivities

A strategic-relational approach to the state's gender selectivities should examine how the state transforms, maintains, and reproduces modes of domination (or institutionally and discursively materialized, asymmetrically structured power relations) between men and women. The SRA is premised on the contingent, relational nature of all identities, interests, strategies, and spatio-temporal horizons; and it allows for, without taking for granted, their reflexive transformation. These premises problematize the state's gender selectivities by highlighting the contingency and the variety of gender identities and interests that might serve as reference points for assessing these selectivities. As Scott notes, one cannot assume 'the abiding existence of a homogeneous collectivity called "women" upon which measurable experiences are visited' (1999: 78). The same premises suggest a broad range of explanatory factors. For an adequate strategic-relational analysis of gender relations would refer to the constitution of

This is a shortened and updated version of 'Die geschlechtsspezifische Selektivität des Staates', in E. Kreisky, S. Lang, and B. Sauer, eds, *EU, Geschlecht, Staat*, Vienna: Wien Universitätsverlag, 2001, 55–85.

competing, inconsistent, and even contradictory identities for both males and females, their grounding in discourses and fantasies about masculinity and/or femininity,[1] their explicit and/or implicit embedding in various institutions and material practices,[2] and their physico-cultural materialization in human bodies. It is especially important how specific constructions of masculinity and femininity, their associated gender identities, interests, roles, and bodily forms come to be privileged in the state's own discourses, institutions, and material practices.

Such an approach is very useful in contesting the recurrent tendency to 'naturalize' gender and gender relations rather than to analyse them as social and/or discursive constructs. This tendency is not confined to 'malestream' analyses – it also occurs in much feminist work – especially in first- and second-wave feminisms (for good critiques, see Fraser 1997; Scott 1999). Several theoretical and political strategies have been suggested to overcome this tendency. Two are worth noting here. First, according to 'queer theory', sexual or gender identities (and, by analogy, all other identities) tend to be ambivalent and unstable and sexual orientations and practices are 'polymorphous'. (On the state, see, e.g., Duggan 1994; and for a critique of some political implications of queer theory, see Walters 1996.) Second, whether or not they share this rejection of 'heteronormative' analyses, many other approaches emphasize the differential articulation (or intersection) of gender with class, ethnicity, 'race', disability, and so on (see below). Such radical deconstructions of gender and sexuality reveal the complex overdetermination of the state's gender selectivities, their inherently relational – including spatio-temporal – nature, and their variable impact on political strategies and practice. This approach denies that the state is a simple expression of patriarchal domination and even questions the utility of 'patriarchy' as an analytical category. It takes us beyond the recognition that there are multiple structures of patriarchy, that these are liable to transformation, and that any changes within and across interlocking forms of patriarchy are contingent and overdetermined. It suggests that the significance of such patriarchal structures and their articulation to produce specific 'gender regimes' can be adequately grasped only through a further round of deconstruction inspired by third-wave feminism, 'queer theory', and similar modes of analysis of other sites and forms of domination.

These assertions can be fruitfully developed in relation to what MacInnes (1998) calls the 'post-patriarchal' modern period. His work enables me to pose two sets of questions about the institutional materiality of domination that sometimes get neglected in second- and third-wave feminist concern with the politics of identity (Fraser 1997). These are: (a) the implications of capitalist societalization for the survival and transformation of patriarchy in what some Marxists regard as the 'unity-in-separation' of the economic and political systems; and (b) the complex articulation of the system- and life-worlds as more complex sites of domination and resistance.

MacInnes claims that the modern period is a transitional one between a (moribund) traditional patriarchal and a (potential) non-patriarchal future. It is marked by various structural and discursive contradictions insofar as important institutional and ideological legacies dating from the era of open private and public patriarchal domination have come to be threatened and, indeed, despite occasional significant temporary reversals, increasingly undermined by the more universalist logics of the market and liberal democracy. He writes: 'The history of the last 300 years has been the history of the erosion of patriarchy by possessive individualism' (1998: 130). This erosion has developed unevenly, of course, and is still far from complete. Nor is the extension of possessive individualism an unqualified good.[3] MacInnes recognizes that a sexual division of labour survives in which 'males and females routinely perform different activities or occupy different social roles, receive different material rewards and have access to contrasting amounts of power and status because of their sex' (1998: 1). But these enduring inequalities cannot be explained in terms of (naturalized) gender differences because, for him, these are 'the ideological result of a material struggle over the sexual division of labour' as well as social constructions of masculinity and femininity based on alleged differences between males and females (1982: 2; cf. Scott 1999; Weeks 1996). Such fetishism can best be understood in turn as an unstable expression of efforts to re-assert the legitimacy of the sexual division of labour after the 'naturalness' of patriarchy had been challenged by commitments to formal[4] equality in market relations and liberal democratic politics. MacInnes concludes there is 'a real contradiction in modernity at both the ideological and material levels between the legacy of patriarchy and its historical defeat – between the sexual contract and the social contract' (1998: 131).

MacInnes's approach implies that there will be significant structural and discursive contradictions between the gender selectivities and operational logics of different functional orders of modern society – the capitalist economy, the formally democratic state, the family,[5] and so forth. Each of these embeds the historical contradiction between the *substantive* institutional and discursive legacies of patriarchy and the – at least – *formally* gender-neutral potential of modern institutions. However, drawing on third-wave feminism and queer theory, MacInnes's account can be criticized on three grounds. First, his distinction between patriarchal, transitional, and post-patriarchal periods inclines to a progressive, liberal, and possibly teleological reading of history. It tends to ignore the scope for transformations in patriarchy, for example from private patriarchy to public patriarchy, as well as the scope for reversals. It also tends to subscribe to the individualist, universalist values of the capitalist market, liberal democracy, and so forth, as well as the various discursive, institutional, and systemic boundaries and/or exclusion–inclusion mechanisms with which these systems are associated. And it tends to imply that patriarchy will be eroded when these individualist, universalist values have been achieved – even though a rich feminist (and, indeed, other radical) critique identifies biases in such 'gender-blind' discourses and institutions. This leaves little space for considering the arguments and strategies of third-wave feminism and 'queer theory', which criticize and oppose the liberal strategies implicit in MacInnes's analysis. Second, perhaps because it is so strongly grounded in a critique of Western political theory and radical first-wave feminism, his arguments tend to be Eurocentric or, at least, to be grounded in Enlightenment thought. They therefore ignore problems posed by imperialism, colonialism, and post-colonialism and the 'peculiarities' (from a Eurocentric viewpoint) of patriarchy outside the European and North American heartlands. Thus his analysis risks reproducing an implicit modernization thesis in which all societies face a putative post-patriarchal future similar to that in the allegedly most progressive Western societies. And, third, MacInnes's analysis focuses more or less exclusively on the antagonisms rooted in the 'sex–gender' nexus and thereby ignores the lessons of third-wave feminist analyses of the intersection of gender, class, 'race', ethnicity, nation, and other identities. Taking account of these issues poses quite different problems about identities, interests, alliances, political strategies and tactics, spatial and temporal horizons of action, respect for boundaries and borders, and so forth.

This argument is reinforced when one considers the complexities of the 'lifeworld'. This comprises social identities, values, discourses, and practices that are largely located beyond the system world.[6] It is a complex, heterogeneous space in which different modes of domination (as defined above) can, and certainly do, exist. Gender relations are just one, albeit a very important, locus of domination within the lifeworld; others include (likewise socially constructed) social relations such as ethnicity, 'race', nations, generation, and lifestyle. It follows that the lifeworld cannot be properly contrasted, as it sometimes is in idealized Habermasian terms, as a sphere of freedom opposed to a sphere of domination confined to the system world. Both the system world and lifeworld, in their respective but often overlapping pluralities, are sites of struggle. In strategic-relational terms, they constitute strategic terrains for attempts to resolve the general contradiction between pre-modern patriarchal legacies and the logics of modern functional systems as these are overdetermined in particular social formations; and for challenges to prevailing discourses of masculinity and femininity as these are expressed in and across these two disparate worlds. The temporary, partial, and unstable compromises that tend to emerge in these fields of gender struggle will be codified in different discourses, institutions, and practices. At least some fields will institutionalize the prevailing hegemonic or dominant images of masculinity and femininity – even as others, perhaps, provide bases of strategic resistance or tactical opposition thereto.

These ideas are consistent with the rejection of two basic assumptions once implicit in much feminist argument: first, there is a single, well-defined, and strongly institutionalized form of patriarchy with its own distinctive logic that is expressed in different fields; and, second, there is a sharp division, if not antagonism, between all men and all women. It is now widely recognized that there are different forms of patriarchy (e.g., Walby 1990), that there is wide variation in both masculinities and femininities and therefore in possible 'gender regimes' (e.g., Connell 1990, 1995), and that gender regimes are always and everywhere overdetermined by at least class, nation, ethnicity, and 'race' (e.g., Boris 1995; Callaway 1987; Canning 1992; Collins 1998; Fraser 1997; Jenson 1986; Mohanty et al. 1991; Yuval-Davis 1996, 1997). The debate has moved well beyond the stage when the state could be defined as the 'patriarch general' (Mies 1986), or its policies towards women could be derived from the logic(s) of production and/or reproduction in capitalist societies (Barrett and McIntosh 1985). Instead the current theoretical and analytical agenda concerns how best to analyse the contingent co-evolution, structural coupling, and discursive articulation of various state structures, discourses, and practices with equally various patriarchal structures, discourses, and practices – whilst paying due regard to the structural contradictions, strategic dilemmas, and discursive paradoxes that are typically associated with these processes. The following remarks pose three closely interrelated sets of questions in this emerging strategic-relational research agenda.

First, to what extent do the various orders in the 'system world' consistently tend to select and thereby reinforce some gender-coded differences and/or some sexual orientations rather than others in terms of their own particular operational codes and programmes? Even if the general codes of functional systems are gender-neutral, particular programmes applied by specific organizations and actors may well be gender-biased. Thus one could ask how far, in what respects, and under what conditions it is in the interests of 'particular capitals' or, indeed, 'capital in general' to exploit gender differences to enhance opportunities for profit? Moreover, given that the interests of different capitals may be opposed in this regard, can the resulting contradictions, dilemmas, and paradoxes be managed through specific institutional and/or spatio-temporal fixes? Making due allowances for different operational codes and programmes, similar questions can be posed about other functional systems, such as politics, law, education, art, science, war, religion, or medicine. In all cases, I suggest, there are advantages as well as disadvantages *from a given system perspective* in exploiting or otherwise reinforcing gender differences.

Second, how far, in what respects, and under what conditions do hegemonic and/or dominant concepts of masculinity and femininity (or maleness and femaleness) serve to organize men's and women's differential participation in the system world? While the first set of questions concerns the general interest, if any, of functional systems in gender discrimination, this set concerns possible discursive, institutional, and material obstacles to 'gender blindness' where such neutrality might otherwise be favoured by the general code or specific programmes of a given functional system.

The third set, although analytically distinct from the second, shares its concerns. It asks how far, in what respects, and under what conditions do concepts of masculinity and femininity (or maleness and femaleness) organize social identities, interests, values, discourses, and practices that are external to, or cut across, the system world? Concepts of masculinity and femininity as well as of maleness and femaleness should be studied in terms of their discursive constitution, institutional embeddednesss, and personal embodiment. Masculine and feminine (or male and female) stereotypes may be more or less sharply differentiated in terms of their substantive and/or evaluative content in regard to both systems and the 'lifeworld'. They may also be more or less tightly (or loosely) coupled to a wider (or narrower) range of activities in both regards. The less substantive and evaluative differentiation there is between the concepts of masculinity–femininity and/or maleness–femaleness, the less tightly coupled are these two conceptual couplets, and the narrower is the scope of their institutionally and discursively constituted relevance, then the less likely it is that we will find well-established gender selectivities. Studying these concepts offers us one way to explore the differential impact and decline of the legacies of private and/or patriarchy considered as sites or mechanisms of gender domination.

These three sets of questions provide a useful way to analyse and explain not only the gender selectivities of the state and the overall political system but also their contradictions, dilemmas, and paradoxes. For there are various forms of gender regime and gender selectivity and these can have markedly differential effects on different social categories or social forces according to their identities, interests, and strategic orientations to maleness–femaleness, masculinity–femininity, or sexual orientation. The specific configuration of selectivities associated with a specific gender regime in particular conjunctures is a product of a complex set of path-dependent interactions. Among the factors involved are the operational logics of modern functional systems, the legacies of pre-modern patriarchy, current modes of domination in the lifeworld and the struggles around them, attempts to colonize the lifeworld by specific systems and resistance thereto, and the hegemonic struggles to secure an overall balance between system integration and social cohesion. If one accepts this strategic-relational approach, there is no transhistorical inevitability about patriarchy. For the SRA challenges accounts of patriarchy that treat it as monolithic and / or inertial and highlights, instead, the polymorphy and contingency of gender regimes. It also suggests that any impression that patriarchy (whether seen as monolithic or polymorphous) is necessarily inscribed into capitalism and / or the state probably results from the structural coupling and contingent co-evolution of the system world (especially the market economy and the liberal democratic state) with modes of domination rooted in the lifeworld. Any such inscription is 'contingently necessary' (Jessop 1982: 212–19). This does not mean, of course, that gender domination is less real because it is far from transhistorical. But social forces might be better placed to challenge, modify, and eliminate gender domination if they recognize its contingency and search for its vulnerabilities as well as its strengths.

Gender Selectivities in the State

There can be no final judgement about the state's gender selectivities. First, there are many forms of state and political regime with different structures of political opportunity. Second, there are different forms of gender-conditioned, gender-conscious, and gender-relevant mobilization, different identities and interests around which such mobilization occurs, different standpoints and horizons of action with which it is associated, and different strategies and tactics that are pursued. And, third, since gender selectivities are the product of structures *and* strategies, any blanket claim risks being tautological, trivial, or overly abstract. Nonetheless, certain broad principles can be established. I will identify these primarily from first- and second-wave feminist perspectives that tend to work within some of the key institutional features of the modern state and its environing political system.[7]

Historical and Formal Constitution of the Modern State

We can refine MacInnes's analysis by distinguishing between the historical and formal constitution of the modern state. The former concerns the complex, path-dependent, historical emergence of a modern state with a legitimate monopoly of organized coercion *vis-à-vis* its political subjects within a given territorial area; and the latter refers to the state's acquisition, if at all, of a formal structure adequate to the expanded reproduction of rational capitalism (Jessop 1982, 2007c; Weber 1978). This distinction has two key implications. On the one hand, modern states were not constructed on a political *tabula rasa* on the basis of first principles but on the historically variable foundations of past social forms and discourses. The path-dependent structural coupling of old and new helps explain the contradiction between the pre-modern era's substantive patriarchal legacies and the emergent, formally rational form of the modern state. The uneven survival of such patriarchal legacies affected the efforts to establish the formally rational (and at least potentially gender-blind) features of the modern state. On the other hand, since its formal constitution develops in an inherited patriarchal context, the modern state also displays a substantive, path-dependent structured coherence with patriarchy. This involves: (a) the reproduction of a *de facto* patriarchal modern state through the recursive selection and reinforcement of 'appropriate' political practices that tend to reproduce the disempowerment of women; and (b) the self-limiting nature of attempts to change this state form with the result that its gender selectivities are maintained. An exemplary study of such structural coupling (although not presented as such) is Vogel's account (1999) of how the contradiction between private possessive individualism and patriarchal state control over marriage was entrenched in the 1804 French *Code civil*. Periods when these selectivities are significantly altered are of special interest for revealing which identities, strategies, and tactics were effective and the exceptional conjunctures in which they made a difference.

Formal Features of the Modern State

I now explore three key features of the formally rational modern state. These are its constitutionalized monopoly of organized violence *vis-à-vis* the economy and civil society and its territorialized sovereignty *vis-à-vis* other states; its nature as a state based on the rule of law, with its clear demarcation between public and private; and the nature of statecraft, statistics, and other aspects of official discourse as forms of power / knowledge.

The modern state's *Gewaltmonopol* has two interesting features: first, it excludes direct coercion from the organization of production for the market; and, second, from a police-military rather than economic perspective, it promotes the pacification of civil society and allows the centralization of military force to defend the state's territorial integrity. These features are often considered hallmarks of modernity. However, although formally 'gender-neutral', they are actually quite consistent with continuing patriarchal practices. The absence of direct coercion by no means rules out gendered divisions in the labour process. Moreover, insofar as the modern state is also a *Steuerstaat* (i.e., a state that depends for its revenues on monetary taxation of the market economy), attempts to challenge such divisions could prompt a fiscal crisis or capital strike. The absence of direct coercion from production is also quite consistent with state indifference – official or unofficial – to abuse and violence in the 'private' sphere directed against women and children.[8] Nor does the pacification of civil society exclude other forms of domination. Indeed continuing gender bias has provoked attempts to politicize the personal, to open public space to women's interests, and to establish children's rights. Likewise the state's control of police-military functions does not as such prevent hegemonic masculinity influencing their exercise. This is reflected in the historical link between citizenship and military service obligations, in institutionalized gender and 'heteronormative' bias(es) in the organization and operations of the police and military, in state- or military-sponsored prostitution, and, too often, in practices such as martial rape or torture. Indeed, insofar as police-military functions are still central to the state's overall operation, they may spread masculinist or patriarchal influence throughout the state system. Institutionalized racism and nationalism are also, of course, central features of the organization of police-military functions.

Territorialized sovereignty is another important feature of the modern state. It has been the historical basis of inter-state relations, military-police organization, nation-statehood, and the national demarcation of legal and civil rights (Behnke 1997). A growing body of feminist criticism has shown that international relations (especially in their realist or neo-realist geopolitical and geo-economic versions) are premised on a view of the state and inter-state relations as thoroughly infused with dominant masculinities (e.g., Enloe 1989; Grant and Newland 1991; Locher-Dodge 1997; Peterson

1992; Pettman 1996; Sylvester 1994). I have already commented on the gender selectivities of the military-police organization. The nation-state also tends to be strongly gendered. Indeed, '[t]he control of territory (by each state) is entwined with a definable gender contract that is a result of social struggle and is linked to a wider gender order in society' (Cravey 1998: 538). The sovereign state functions as a 'power container' that institutionalizes gender and gender relations as well as classes and class compromises. It does this in three ways: its construction and consolidation of particular masculinities and femininities; its role in defining and monitoring the boundaries between different masculinities and femininities, classifying and sanctioning 'deviant' behaviours; and selecting only some identities as the basis for integrating individuals into the state apparatus as state managers, representatives, or dialogue partners (Radcliffe 1993: 201). Similar points hold for citizenship rights, which are also far more differentiated *de jure* and/or *de facto* than the liberal rhetoric of universal citizenship rights might suggest.

Globalization, the expansion of cyberspace, and the extension of universal human rights are now challenging these associations. Although human rights tend to generalize liberal assumptions of (Western male) citizenship so that they are limited in intent and practice to men, they can serve as important strategic resources in gender and/or sexual preference struggles (Okin, 1979; Reynolds 1986). They may also underpin transnational movements based on solidarity in difference, a particularization of rights, and a differentiated universalism (Lister 1996: 11); and, linked to citizenship, they can provide the basis for multi-tiered and pluralist struggles amenable to the pursuit of a broad spectrum of feminist concerns (Nash 1998).

Much has been written on women and the modern *Rechtsstaat*. Its emergence did not immediately or directly challenge patriarchal forms of property *in general* as opposed to *particular* pre-capitalist instantiations thereof. Nor did it challenge the sexual contract implicit in the family as an organizational form. Moreover, even where formal equality was instituted in the public sphere, it still co-existed with substantive inequalities. These issues can be explored in terms of three interrelated aspects of citizenship: (a) the 'isolation effect' and its implications for political struggles; (b) the relationship between the 'sexual contract' and social contract; and (c) the role of gender relations in reproducing the nation during the period of national states and in a possible future post-national era.

First, the grounding of political representation in individualized forms of national citizenship associated with the abstract individual rather than class position creates an 'isolation effect' (Poulantzas 1973). This encourages the organization of political space(s) around issues of formal equality, negotiated difference, or contested identities. In addition, macro-politics tends to take the form of hegemonic struggles to define the 'national-popular' interest in a sovereign state (Gramsci 1971). Second, even if citizenship is formally gender-neutral under universal suffrage (a right typically conceded quite late during modern state formation), it is historically and substantively based on a model of male citizenship (Lloyd 1984). The reasons for this include stereotypical contrasts between male rationality and female emotion, men's military and fiscal duties as opposed to women's reproductive duties, and the perceived (male?) need to preserve domestic peace in the patriarchal family by depoliticizing gender relations (on the third reason, see MacInnes 1998; Pateman 1988). Unsurprisingly, therefore, contradictions arose between the abstract right to citizenship and the particularities of gender. The resulting conflicts have led to an uneven development and expansion of rights as well as to corresponding changes in the state (Wiener 1996). The development of human rights in three successive waves or generations (negative liberal individualist freedoms, positive rights based on state intervention, and solidarity rights) has also failed to address the specifically patriarchal bases of women's oppression. This is reflected in the fact that the Convention on the Elimination of all Forms of Discrimination against Women (1979) is the UN convention that has been ratified with the largest number of reservations by the largest number of signatory states (James 1994: 568–9). Thus, '[d]espite the protection of women's rights incorporated into the language of the Universal Declaration, the Covenants, and the various human rights conventions, normative systems of gender-based oppression continue to be operational across time and space, spanning all levels from the familial to the international' (James 1994: 569). Interestingly, this observation illustrates the complexities of contemporary feminism. For other feminists have criticized human rights discourse and practices not for their disregard of the specificities of women's oppression but for their cultural blindness – for imposing a universalizing approach to women's rights without regard to legitimate cultural differences (Brems 1997: 149–50). However, as Fraser notes in the context of her critique of third-wave feminism, neither universalism nor multiculturalism provides a basis for distinguishing just, democratic, and emancipatory identity claims from unjust, anti-democratic, oppressive identity claims (1997: 103–4).

Third, the national state has taken three main forms: *Volksnation, Kulturnation*, and *Staatsnation*. Gender is most important in the ethnic nation because membership of the 'imagined community' of the nation is derived from descent and is inherited through the family. This gives women a key role as maternal 'bearers' of the nation but also leads to stricter control over their reproductive role in the 'national' interest (Yuval-Davis 1996). Membership of a cultural nation is more dependent on acculturation or assimilation. Women still have a key role as socializers, however, along with state and non-state ideological apparatuses.[9] The state nation is yet more open because inclusion depends on loyalty to the constitution and patriotism. The decomposition of each of these forms of national state is putting a general strain on the role of gender in their reproduction. At the same time it creates opportunities to rethink what it might mean to belong to a state (*Staatszugehörigkeit*) in a post-national era when the ethnic and/or cultural bases of *Staatsangehörigkeit* (nationality) are being dissolved through trends towards more multi-ethnic or 'melting pot' and/or towards multicultural or fragmented, 'hybridic' post-modern societies. These trends undermine the status of women as 'bearers' of the nation and/or national identity and have opened political spaces to redefine citizenship, to multiply the spheres of legitimate political action both within and across national borders, and to develop multiple political loyalties or even cosmopolitan patriotism (Habermas 1992; Held 1992; Nash 1998; Wiener 1996).

Strategic Selectivity and Strategic Action

The general features of the modern state need to be re-specified at more concrete and complex levels of analysis and related to strategic alternatives to begin to reveal more fully their strategically selective implications. There is now a vast historical and/or comparative literature on the gendering of particular state formations, welfare regimes, and policy domains; the specificities of different feminist movements and currents, successive 'waves' of feminism, and the impact of lesbian, gay, and 'queer' struggles; the intersection of different types of struggle (class, gender, ethnic, generational, anti-imperial, third-world, post-colonial, post-socialist, etc.); and different strategies, alliances, tactics, spatial and temporal horizons. It is impossible to address even a small fraction of these studies here. Instead I want to highlight a few relevant issues around some basic dimensions of the state and political system.

Political Representation

Forms of political representation are gender-biased. This is seen in legal definitions of individual citizenship, the mode of separation between the private and public spheres, the nature of the public sphere as a site of political deliberation, the relative importance of territorial and functional bases of political decision-making, individual and/or collective mechanisms of decision-making, and electoral rules such as proportional representation, majority voting, or simple plurality. More substantive differences in representation also make a difference. Included here are the social, ideological, and organizational aspects of political representation in the party system, interest groups, or social movements; varying capacities to access the public sphere and mass media; and differential capacities to access or intervene in the state.

The private–public separation also has specific effects. These are stronger, of course, the more this distinction is fetishized. Not only do women tend to be confined to the private sphere, but the public sphere is also said to favour appeals to rational and 'universal' rather than emotional and/or 'particular' interests (Calhoun 1994; Cohen and Arato, 1992; Landes 1998; Rosenberger 1997). Together these tendencies are said to marginalize women's issues and interests. In first- and second-wave feminisms this has been associated with attempts to move into the public sphere and to emphasize either the value of 'maternal' or other feminine values to political life and/or the capacity of women to engage in rational argument. Moreover, where women do enter the formal public sphere, advocates of women's 'natural' roles find it easier than advocates of lesbian, gay, or 'queer' movements and/or other challenges to these roles. It is also easier for liberal feminists to access the public sphere than radical, socialist, or anarchist feminists. Focusing on the public sphere also produces neglect of areas where women are politically active outside the formal party and parliamentary political arenas – such as informal neighbourhood politics, local social movements, or client–state negotiations in the welfare regimes (O'Connor 1993). This does not mean, of course, that the private–public distinction should be wholly rejected as opposed to being demystified; that it is useless to engage in struggles to draw the distinction in other ways or to exploit its ambiguities or, indeed, to note the irrationality of certain masculine forms of politics; that new networking forms of politics or governance may well be challenging the apparent clarity of the private–public distinction; or even that ideas and strategies grounded in the third-wave feminist concept of cyborg politics might not better correspond to women's experience of the private–public distinction and exploit more effectively the energy of 'borderlands' (Haraway 1991).

Regarding territorial representation, the more local the level of political organization, the easier is women's access to political power. Different biases occur in corporatist or functional forms of representation. Estate-like corporatism is more patriarchal than social democratic forms (Neyer 1996). Even the latter privilege the male-dominated world of business organizations, trade unions, and other producer interests at the expense of those without gainful employment and consumers. Unsurprisingly, the greater the political influence of corporatist compared to parliamentary institutions, the greater the social and economic gap between men and women and the harder it is to realize gender equality policies (Neyer 1996: 84).[10]

The marginalization of women candidates and women's issues as well as the de-thematization of the private sphere have long shaped electoral politics – especially in majoritarian rather than proportional representation systems. The former encourage catchall parties that are less inclined to allow serious space for feminist concerns. But women can have more impact on formal politics where the nature of any compact between feminists and a party (or parties) allows women's policy activists to access state institutions (Threlfall 1998: 71). Types of issue also shape women's unity and influence. Thus they are strongest for issues around sexual politics – abortion, violence against women, incest, pornography – or daily life – work hours, child care, pay and employment equity (O'Connor 1993: 506). Social movements may take up women's issues but they have less privileged access to the state or face the dilemmas of being in and against the state (on femocracy see Franzway et al. 1980; Stetson and Mazur 1995; Threlfall 1998; Watson 1992). Moreover, as the suffrage expanded to include workers and women, significant areas of political power were displaced from elected legislatures to the executive, quangos, and functional representation (Dahlerup 1994; Hernes 1987; Siim 1991).

The Architecture of the State

Gender effects are found in the formal and material distribution of powers in and/or among parts of the state apparatus. As well as the relative separation of executive, legislative, and judicial powers, there is also a hierarchy of departments within the state system and a relative distribution of powers across its different tiers. It is well known that the closer a department is to the core of the repressive state apparatus (military, police, security, foreign policy, and treasury), the fewer women are present. Likewise, the higher the tier of government, the fewer women are involved. These trends are related, of course, since the state's 'softer' functions tend to be located at the local level. We also need to consider the informal 'parallel power networks' that help to unify formal hierarchies. Some feminist research indicates that these parallel power networks are often more male-dominated than are formal bureaucratic bodies (Ferguson 1984). For such networks tend to display the atmosphere and mores of a men's club. Some gay theorists also suggest that the military is more heterosexist than civilian state apparatuses (Greenberg and Bystryn 1996). A related concern is the continual redefinition of the state's boundaries of action to re- or de-politicize certain issues. Overall, one must examine how the state's precarious unity is created and how this, in turn, creates various gender selectivities.

State feminism provides an interesting test case here as it promotes policy-making bodies led by women and/or dedicated to women's issues. These are a response to pressures from below as well as an attempt to co-opt feminism. They can empower women to pursue their own interests but can also generate public forms of patriarchy whereby women come to depend collectively on 'father state' rather than individually on fathers, husbands, or sons (Hatem 1992; Walby 1990). Threlfall (1998) identifies several forms of state feminism – ranging from social democratic femocracies to patriarchal-authoritarian forms of national mobilization – with a correspondingly wide range of effects. There is a similarly broad range of dilemmas and contradictions in women's involvement in and against the state (Findlay 1988; Stetson and Mazur 1995; Threlfall 1996).

The Primary 'Media' of State Intervention and Forms of Intervention

The state deploys various means of intervention, each of which has its own forms of gender bias. Here I consider force, law, money, and knowledge. The masculine and military values linked to the state's monopoly of force were noted above. The formality of *positive law* tends to abstract not only from substantive class differences but also from those based on gender. Moreover, even where the latter are recognized (if not also, indeed, actually constituted) in some branches of the law, their recognition may serve to create and/or re-impose forms of public and private patriarchy (MacKinnon 1988). Thus law may offer women special treatment by virtue of their gender (e.g., maternalist or natalist policies) or protect them only if they accept their subordinate status in the private sphere. Law also gives the state rights to intervene in women's lives – especially if they present themselves and/or are presented as victims (Brown 1995). More generally, 'in accepting law's terms in order to challenge law, feminism always concedes too much' (Smart 1989: 5). For this concedes the hegemony of law and its androcentric standards, fetishizes legal categories and methods, and marginalizes non-legal knowledge and experiences as well as extra-legal strategies (Smart 1989: 5). The shift from formal procedural to reflexive law might make a difference here by opening legislation and adjudication to debate over substantive inequalities. There is some progress in this regard through the work of feminist legal theorists as well as of legal practitioners on behalf of their clients (Farganis 1994).

Money is the basis of formally rational calculation on capitalist markets, and in ideal market conditions such calculation would ignore differences that do not affect profit-and-loss or purchasing power.[11] In the real world, of course, this disadvantages most women, who are typically poorer than men. Nonetheless the emergence of the 'pink pound' or pornography targeted at women rather than men suggests that markets will exploit profitable new niches. The state reproduces the same utilitarian calculus whenever it adopts cost-benefit analysis (with women's costs-benefits having a lower value than those of men) or confirms differentials rooted in the division of labour or differences in income or wealth. This is especially evident in the ways in which the state reproduces the relation between capital and wage labour – including a politics of *workers-men* (Kuwalik 1996: 52); in the gender-specific impact of structural adjustment policies (Connelly 1996); and in the sphere of welfare policies (e.g., pensions or social security benefits). Knowledge has become more and more important for the state's operations. However, not only are there frequently substantive biases in bodies of knowledge (linked as they are to power), but there is also a sense in which the very formal, systematic, rational, and scientized form of knowledge embodies masculine perspectives. In addition, insofar as statecraft is intrinsically connected to the concepts of sovereignty, *Realpolitik*, and hegemonic masculinity, then political knowledge reproduces gender differences (see Grant and Newland 1991).

These media can be combined to support specific forms of state intervention. Welfare regimes illustrate this well because they are located at the intersection of state, market, and family-gender relations and thereby embody many of the contradictions between women and the state. Maintaining the traditional family was an important object as well as presumption in the initial design of welfare states; for the state organized welfare 'not around a biological core, but a state-sanctioned, heterosexual marriage that confers legitimacy not only on the family structure itself but on children born into it' (Collins 1998: 63). Yet variations occur in welfare regimes not only concerning de-commodification (reducing workers' dependence on the labour market) but also regarding a person's insulation from involuntary economic dependence on other family members and/or state agencies (O'Connor 1993: 512). In the latter respect women rely disproportionately on dependence-enhancing income and/or means-tested benefits rather than on universal citizenship rights. Thus they can be regarded as second-class citizens or welfare claimants.

The women-friendliness of welfare regimes varies greatly (see O'Connor 1996). Skocpol (1992) notes how a maternalist welfare regime developed at the states level in the USA ahead of Europe's more paternalist, male breadwinner model at the national level. Yet, as Kuwalik (1996) notes, although the maternalist regime was based on women's political mobilization at decentralized states level, this actually served to ensure the secondary status of American welfare compared to rights-based European regimes. There are variations within Europe too. The more estate-like (*ständischer*) corporatist welfare regimes found in Austria and Switzerland are less women-friendly than social democratic welfare regimes in Scandinavia (Neyer 1996: 82–104). Even the latter, whilst more advanced in integrating women into the labour market, de-familializing care work, and enabling women to share in welfare policy-making, have actually seen little real increase in women's social and political power or development of an autonomous collective identity as feminists (Kuwalik 1996: 86).

Gender-Specific Inequalities within the Social Bases of State Power

The social bases of state power are linked to hegemonic masculinities and femininities as well as to the material foundations of state power. These affect the formation of a relatively stable social compromise and loyalty to the state form or regime. They also shape the compatibility between the demands of political legitimacy (electoral success) and those of real politics (including both accumulation and geo-politics). These features must be elaborated for individual state forms. In this context one can consider not only institutionalized class compromises but also specific forms of gender contract. Duncan has defined the latter as 'the balance of power that is worked out between men and women in particular places' (1994: 1186; also Connell 1996; Naples, 1997). A key question here is whether the social basis is also the principal beneficiary of state power. It is a well-known psephological fact, for example, that women tend to vote for conservative parties; but it does not follow that they benefit therefrom. Patriarchal, maternalist, and nationalist discourses all have key mystificatory roles in this regard. For these shape the identities and interests that provide the material and symbolic substratum for gender contracts, for the recruitment and stabilization of supporting classes, for the stakes to be negotiated in temporary alliances, and for the roles of different sex/gender categories in private and public life. Together with material structures of power, they also shape the forms of social inclusion and exclusion. In all cases there are clear links to the structural aspects of the gendered selectivity of the state.

Accumulation Strategies and Economic Projects

Accumulation strategies and economic projects should be understood in a broad sense and include, alongside techno-economic conditions for economic growth, their multifarious extra-economic conditions. Expanding the analysis of economic strategies to include their social conditions of existence opens a broad field for the analysis of gender-specific inequalities (see also Gibson-Graham 1995).

State Hegemonic Projects

Hegemonic projects define the nature and purposes of the state and are typically gender-biased. This is a vast field of research and space limits preclude giving more than one example. Thus Brodie (1997) explores this in the successive meso-narratives that have structured the state as a form of political domination. She argues that liberal citizenship was oriented to universalism over particularism – with women regarded as particularist and unable to transcend this to achieve universalism. Next, the 'laissez-faire state was extremely active in ensuring the autonomy of the market and the domestic sphere and the power relations exercised within them. It pronounced its "others" (sc. market, home) as apolitical and self-regulating and, thus, not subject to public intervention' (Brodie 1997: 230). Later, the Keynesian welfare national state 'realized a radical expansion of the public through direct intervention in the economy, and by subjecting the family, and other aspects of private life, to new forms of state scrutiny and assistance. . . . The family wage and the dependent homemaker/mother were cultural forms that were cultivated by the welfare state' (Brodie 1997: 232, 233). This state form advances the claims of the white middle class. Finally, the neo-liberal meso-narrative emphasizes performativity. In its fatalism in the face of market forces, its emphasis on the positive effects of globalization, and its gender-neutral approach to restructuring, it can be regarded as a phallocentric discourse (Brodie 1997: 238).

Conclusions

Although 'there is no patriarchy in general', particular forms of patriarchy do exist. Indeed they are institutionalized in, and reproduced by, the modern state. But we should distinguish the gender-conditioned aspects of the state, its substantively gendered nature, and its gender-relevance beyond the state. Each aspect needs to be explored, not in terms of fetishized, naturalized sex or gender distinctions, but in terms of the multifarious forms in which sex and/or gender are constructed, selected, and reproduced. This complicates analyses of the state's gender selectivity.

First, gender regimes condition the state insofar as they shape political opportunities and constraints. Just as capitalist forces and male-dominated unions sometimes find it 'profitable' to exploit existing gender differences to segment the labour force structurally and divide it organizationally, so state managers and politicians may exploit gender divisions by fashioning political appeals, building social bases, and so forth, on gender lines. Moreover, even when women win formal equality as citizens, gender regimes may prevent its realization. For example, while state action may compensate for private patriarchy or the gendered division of labour, it may also create forms of public patriarchy that bind women to men via the welfare state (Hernes 1987; Kuwalik 1997; Walby 1990). (For the counterargument that women need the welfare state to advance some of their interests, see Hernes 1987.) In short, insofar as the modern state's operations are gender-conditioned (because they are structurally coupled to and co-evolve with patriarchal relations), its own gender-neutrality must be limited. Second, insofar as the modern state reproduces patriarchy and patriarchal ideology in its own organization, it is itself gendered. This occurs through a myriad contingent practices and, following Butler (1990), one could say that states *perform* gender. Finally, third, state activities are *gender-relevant* insofar as they reproduce institutionalized contexts and discourses in which patriarchy appears natural – for example, the role of social policy in reproducing the patriarchal family or gender-specific differences on the labour market.

Nonetheless, since the modern state's patriarchal features derive from a contingent co-evolution with patriarchal relations beyond the state, feminist strategies that make it 'bad for government' to pursue patriarchy-friendly policies may be effective. This has occurred in the last two decades or so in advanced capitalist democracies. There is still far to go, however, and many achievements may prove reversible. Yet the lines of conflict have become harder to decipher due to the proliferation of femininities/masculinities and/or the growing recognition of the problems of heteronormativity. This makes it even more imperative to distinguish among the naturally necessary aspects of the state as a patriarchal institution; contingent structural features of the state in a patriarchal society; and random features that are more readily modifiable.

The implications of the contingently necessary nature of the state's selectivities are complex. It is far easier to note what they exclude than work out what they entail. A critical realist SRA to this question excludes naturalizing, universalizing essentialisms based on simple oppositions such as male/female and masculine/feminine. For the state's structurally inscribed strategic selectivities do not operate in the sort of binary fashion that would justify its description as the 'patriarch general' or as necessarily heteronormative. Strategic selectivities are real causal mechanisms that operate tendentially, are subject to counter-tendencies, and are actualized through specific social practices and actions. But even those who reject such essentialist claims sometimes deploy 'strategic essentialism' and/or 'asymmetrical anti-essentialism' in political struggles. In this regard, whereas strategic essentialism involves a self-conscious, provisional, and even ironical deployment of essentialist arguments for strategic purposes in specific contexts, asymmetrical anti-essentialism only tolerates such arguments when voiced by subaltern groups to contest their stereotypical 'otherization', to resist their inclusion within Enlightenment time and space, and to assert the authenticity of their cultures (on strategic essentialism, see Spivak 1988 and, critically, Duggan 1994 and Sum 2000; on asymmetrical anti-essentialism, see Bunting 1993). But, however self-conscious and self-limiting, both strategies are problematic insofar as they privilege an identitarian approach to political mobilization, that is, an essentializing politics of identity. This reifies boundaries between groups and, by homogenizing and collapsing individual into collective identities, also tends to be undemocratic within groups (Yuval-Davis 1996: 94). At most these strategies can provide the basis for political mobilization resting on an aggregative, serialized but still essentializing concept of identity that ignores 'the complex interweaving and continual re-embedding of identities and subjectivities' (Sum 2000: 137). Such effects are opposed in the emerging third-wave feminist emphasis on intersectionality (and the parallel critique of essentialism from queer theorists) and on the benefits of dialogue between different standpoints or positions (cf. feminist standpoint epistemologies).

Thus the emphasis should be on possible, negotiable, and partial collaborations between feminists and other social categories around specific projects; and on how different projects can be unified into broader, more general struggles. This approach has been described as 'transversal politics' and, according to Yuval-Davis, it stops 'where the proposed aims of the struggle are aimed at conserving or promoting unequal relations of power, and where essentialized notions of identity and difference naturalize forms of social, political and economic exclusion' (1996: 97). This approach fits feminist ideas about contextual ethics, and the need for situated, local under-standing rather than universal, codified knowledge. In adopting this approach, one moves beyond the old feminist question – 'can we achieve feminist goals directly through the agencies of the state?' – to a new ques-tion: 'what kind of state should we be attempting to construct?' (Curthoys 1993: 36). A provisional answer is that this should be a state form that insti-tutionalizes a mode of political engagement that sustains conflict in polit-ically productive ways (Butler 1997: 269). This works against both universalist feminisms and multicultural rainbow coalitions that operate in a mechani-cally aggregative manner. Thus we need 'to find a way to combine the strug-gle for an anti-essentialist multiculturalism with the struggle for social equality and democracy' (Fraser 1997: 108). But this in turn requires atten-tion to the politics of complexity as well as the politics of identity (Sum 2000). In short, it requires attention to the complex strategic-relational inter-action between state structures and individual and collective identities and interests in specific conjunctures (see also Demirović and Pühl 1997). The preceding remarks provide some preliminary theoretical indications on how to proceed in this regard, but they cannot substitute for practical interven-tions to test the nature and limits of the state's selectivities and the merits of different strategies.

8

Spatio-Temporal Dynamics and
Temporal Sovereignty

This chapter adopts a strategic-relational approach to globalization. It argues, only partly in a wilfully contrarian spirit, that the spatial turn in studies of globalization has been overdone and that a temporal (re)turn is overdue. For time and temporality are as important as, if not more important than, space and spatiality in the unfolding logic (and illogic) of economic globalization. I ground this claim in the capital relation and its contradictions and explore its implications for national states as they seek to defend their temporal as well as territorial sovereignty and guide globalization.

Globalization Defined

'Globalization' is a polyvalent, promiscuous, controversial word that often obscures more than it reveals about recent economic, political, social, and cultural changes. It is best used to denote a multicentric, multiscalar, multitemporal, multiform, and multicausal process. It is *multicentric* because it emerges from activities in many places rather than from a single centre. It is *multiscalar* because it emerges from actions on many scales – which are no longer seen as nested in a neat hierarchy but seem to co-exist and interpenetrate in a tangled and confused manner – and because it develops and deepens the scalar as well as the spatial division of labour. Thus what could be described from one viewpoint as globalization might appear quite differently (and perhaps more accurately) from other scalar viewpoints: for example, as internationalization, triadization, regional bloc formation, global city network-building, cross-border cooperation, international localization, glocalization, glurbanization, or transnationalization (on the last three see, respectively, Brenner 1999, 2004, and Swyngedouw 1997; Jessop and Sum 2000; and M.P. Smith 2000). It is *multitemporal* because it involves

This is a new contribution based in part on 'Time and space in the globalization of capital and their implications for state power', *Rethinking Marxism*, 14 (1), 2002, 97–116, and *The Future of the Capitalist State*, Cambridge: Polity, 2002.

ever more complex restructuring and re-articulation of temporalities and time horizons. This aspect is captured in the notions of time-space distantiation and time-space compression. The former process involves the stretching of social relations over time and space so that relations can be controlled or coordinated over longer periods of time (including into the ever more distant future) and longer distances, greater areas, or more scales of activity. Time-space compression involves the intensification of 'discrete' events in real time and/or the increased velocity of material and immaterial flows over a given distance.[1] Globalization is clearly *multicausal* because it results from the complex, contingent interaction of many different causal processes. It is also *multiform*. It assumes different forms in different contexts and can be realized through different strategies – neo-liberal globalization is only one and, indeed, requires complementary and flanking strategies even where it does take root. Taken together, these features mean that globalization is the complex, emergent product of many different forces operating on many scales. Hence nothing can be explained in terms of the causal powers of globalization – let alone inevitable, irreversible powers that are actualized on some intangible stage behind our backs or on some intangible plane above our heads. Instead it is globalization*s* (in the plural) that need explaining in all their manifold spatio-temporal complexity.

From a strategic-relational perspective, globalization has both structural and strategic moments. Structurally, it involves the objective processes whereby increasing global interdependence is created among actions, organizations, and institutions within (but not necessarily across) different functional systems (economy, law, politics, education, science, sport, etc.) and the lifeworld that lies beyond them. These processes occur on various spatial scales, operate differently in each functional subsystem, involve complex and tangled causal hierarchies rather than a simple, unilinear, bottom-up or top-down movement, and often display an eccentric 'nesting' of the different scales of social organization. They also develop unevenly in space-time. Nonetheless, globalization can be said to increase insofar as the co-variation of actions, events, and institutional orders involves more (and more important) relevant activities, is spatially more extensive, and occurs more rapidly. Strategically, globalization refers to conscious attempts to promote global coordination of activities in (but not necessarily across) different functional subsystems and/or in the lifeworld. This does not require that the actors involved are physically present at all points in the planet but only requires them to monitor relevant activities, communicate about these, and try to coordinate their activities with others to produce global effects. Such coordination efforts range from generalized meta-steering (constitutional or institutional design) intended to produce a more or less comprehensive global order through creation of international regimes to particularistic pursuit of specific economic-corporate interests within such (meta-)frameworks. Not all actors are (or could hope to be) major global players, but many more have to monitor the global as a horizon of action, the implications of changing scalar divisions, and the impact of time-space distantiation and compression on their identities, interests, and strategies. The overall course of globalization will be the largely unintended, relatively chaotic outcome of interaction among various strategies to shape or resist globalization in a complex, path-dependent world society.

Globalization is part of a proliferation of scales and temporalities as narrated, institutionalized objects of action, regularization, and governance. The number of scales and temporalities of action that can be distinguished is immense,[2] but far fewer ever get explicitly institutionalized. The degree to which this happens depends on the prevailing technologies of power – material, social, and spatio-temporal – that enable the identification and institutionalization of specific scales of action and temporalities. It is the development of new logistical means (of distantiation, compression, communication), organizational technologies, institutions with new spatio-temporal horizons of action, broader institutional architectures, new global standards (including world time), and modes of governance that helps to explain this growing proliferation of economically and politically significant institutionalized scales and temporalities. Moreover, as new scales and temporalities emerge and/or existing ones gain in institutional thickness, social forces also tend to develop new mechanisms to link or coordinate them. This in turn often prompts efforts to coordinate these new coordination mechanisms. Thus, as the triad regions have begun to acquire institutional form and identity, new forums have developed to coordinate their bi- and trilateral relations. Analogous processes occur on other scales. The overall result is growing scalar complexity, greater scope for deliberate interscalar articulation, and more problems in making such interscalar articulation work. Similar issues are occurring around time and its governance. This can be seen in the rise of both nano-temporalities and long-term action oriented to environmental sustainability and in more general problems of intertemporal governance.

Globalization and the Spatial Turn

Social theorists often suggest that globalization is a key factor behind the 'spatial turn'. For example, noting a major paradigm shift from concern with modernization to interest in globalization, Dirlik links this 'to the spatial turn or, more accurately, the ascendancy of the spatial over the temporal' (2001: 6). Further, insofar as globalization is inherently spatial, many social scientists agree on the need for sensitivity to issues of space, place, and scale. Thus Harvey presents the spatial turn as an important reaction against the privileging, in conventional dialectics, of time over space (1996a: 4). Theoretically this involves an '[e]scape from the teleologies of Hegel and Marx [that] can . . . most readily be achieved by appeal to the particularities of spatiality (network, levels, connections)' (Harvey 1996b: 109). And, practically, it involves encouragement to 'militant particularism' based *in the first instance* on local mobilization (Harvey 1996b: 191–3; 2002: 41–4).

Such arguments can give rise to a paradox. Some writers link globalization to the spatial turn and condemn the overly temporal and teleological nature of the dialectic at the same time as they cite Marx, himself a major dialectical thinker, as a far-sighted analyst of globalization. It is a commonplace that *The Communist Manifesto* anticipated many aspects of contemporary globalization (e.g., Dirlik 2001; Harvey 1998). However, although the *Manifesto* identified important spatial moments of capitalism and presented the world market as the ultimate horizon of capital accumulation, it does not follow that its analysis was essentially spatial. Indeed, as Neil Smith notes about Marx's work as a whole, 'the lively spatial implications of Marx's analyses were rarely developed' (1984: 81). This is especially clear in the *Manifesto*. For, if it has a grand narrative, this is essentially temporal. It describes a history of class struggles that must end in the victory of the proletariat as the universal class. When dealing specifically with capitalism, of course, it also presents a spatial narrative. The *Manifesto* argues that capitalism is inherently global in its scope and dynamic, involving cosmopolitan production, the world market, the rise of world literature, and so forth. But this spatialization is subordinate to a revolutionary telos: its primary task is to universalize the capital relation and thereby prepare the conditions for a worldwide revolution. Likewise, as capitalism develops, workers are concentrated in factories and cities and power is centralized in the hands of a few large capitalists. This also stimulates revolutionary consciousness and politically isolates the exploiting class before, finally, the world's workers unite to overthrow it.

A similar subordination of space to time, albeit one that endows capitalism with a broad direction rather than a specific telos, occurs in *Capital* (Postone 1993). This offers a spatialized account of primitive accumulation, the industrial revolution (including the transition from 'putting out' to the factory system), and, indeed, England's pioneering, prefigurative role in industrial capitalism (*de te fabula narratur*) (Marx 1867: 19). It also offers many incidental comments on space and place, town and countryside, the social division of labour, changes in means of transportation and communication, colonialism and the world market, and other spatial themes. When Marx unfolds the basic logic of the fully constituted capitalist mode of production, however, he systematically privileges time over space.[3] In this respect, place and space appear as both the material support (Graham 2002) and material effect of the logic of capitalism considered as an economy of time. Thus Marx explains capital's self-expansion in terms of the complex articulation between multiple concrete temporalities and the singular abstract time of exchange-value (Postone 1993: 292–3 and *passim*). He was a pioneer in both respects and, given the absence of relevant concepts in classical political economy, he had to develop an appropriate language for addressing the dialectic between the concrete and abstract moments of the time factor. Among his key concepts were labour time, absolute surplus-value, socially necessary labour time, relative surplus-value, machine time, circulation time, turnover time, turnover cycle, socially necessary turnover time, interest-bearing capital, and expanded reproduction (cf. Grossman 1977a, 1977b).

The key point to make here is that the spatial *dynamic* of capitalism (as opposed to its spatial conditions of existence) can be derived in the first instance[4] from the competition among capitalists to gain competitive advantages by reducing labour time below what is currently socially necessary and/or to reduce the total time involved in the production and circulation of their commodities below the prevailing socially necessary turnover time (Bensaïd 2002; Harvey 1982; Postone 1993). In this sense the overall dynamic of capitalism derives from the interaction of socially necessary labour and turnover times as mediated through class struggle and capitalist competition. One result is that the repeated circular motion of self-valorization is linked to the increasing speed of the capitalist treadmill (Kittsteiner 1991: 59). Thus Marx's analysis 'seeks to justify the temporal determination of both production and the dynamic of the whole, and not – as it might seem at first – simply as one of the regulation of exchange' (Postone 1993: 190, cf. 269). This emerges most clearly when Marx moves from the generalization of the commodity form to labour power as the distinctive feature of capital accumulation, to the roles of machinofacture and relative surplus-value as the most adequate technological form and social form of the capital relation, respectively (Beamish 1992; Postone 1993).

Capitalists also face pressure to innovate in other ways that may affect the spatial and scalar divisions of labour. In this sense, although place and space are certainly regarded as a basic presupposition of all social activities, they enter Marx's analysis as major variables relatively late. They are first seriously introduced in terms of particular capitals rather than capital in general; in terms of relative surplus-value as opposed to absolute surplus-value; in terms of turnover time rather than production time; and in the context of use-value (e.g., transportation) rather than that of value or exchange-value (de la Haye 1988). Such spatial reorganization was as prone to contradictions, however, as other aspects of capital as a social relation.

These points are worth making because Marx's commentators disagree about the relative weight of time and space in capitalist dynamics. We can explore this in relation to exchange-value, surplus-value, use-value, and class struggle. It has been suggested, first, that capital's concern with *exchange-value* leads to the dominance of temporal over spatial concerns (Wilson 1999: 161).[5] This is because exchange-value depends on the socially necessary labour time embodied in commodities. Matters become more complex, however, when socially necessary turnover time is introduced. For the competition to reduce turnover time involves fixed capital and the reorganization of the spatial and scalar divisions of labour. Thus Harvey notes that money 'measure[s] socially necessary labour *time* through coordinating the trading of values over *space*' (1996b: 238, original italics). Second, other commentators suggest that capital's concern with extracting *surplus-value* prioritizes control over space and the importance of constructing and reconstructing space relations and the global space economy (Brennan 1997: 34; Lefebvre 1974). This is reflected in Marx's analyses of factory despotism and colonialism and of the reserve army of labour and surplus population. Yet surplus-value depends on speed as well as space (Harvey 1996b: 241). Third, a concern with *use-value* could highlight the extent to which spatial relations determine the usefulness of particular goods and services. Thus Smith notes that, 'where Marx does refer to space, this tends to be at precisely the points in his arguments where he reincorporates use-value into the analysis' (1984: 81). But time and/or timing also determine use-value. Fourth, those who start from *class struggle* (especially that of subordinate classes) are also strongly interested in place and space (cf. Harvey 1996a). This is especially clear in Lefebvre's work. For, as Soja notes, class struggle 'must encompass and focus on the vulnerable point: the production of space, the territorial structure of exploitation and domination, the spatially controlled reproduction of the system as a whole' (Soja 1989: 82).

Such contrasting opinions may sometimes be due to intellectual incoherence. But they can also be fruitfully interpreted as expressions of basic contradictions in the capital relation and/or reflections of the movement from abstract-simple to concrete-complex analyses in Marx's own work. There is not time here to dwell on methodological aspects. Suffice to say that, as Marx moves from the analysis of capital in general through the analysis of the different circuits of capital towards his (never completed) analysis of the overall movement of capital within the framework of the world market, he pays increasing attention to the complex articulation of concrete time and place with the more fundamental dynamic of socially necessary labour time in the form of both absolute and relative surplus-value (for a brief summary of some basic dimensions of this in *Capital*, see Table 8.1).

Turning to ontological aspects of the capital relation, the time of abstract (or general) labour central to exchange-value exists only in and through concrete, particular labours performed in specific times and places. In other words, value as a measure of abstract time is indissolubly linked to activities that occur in concrete times and places and, indeed, actually depends on *current* rather than historical levels of productivity – a criterion that is often linked to uneven development and the displacement of the cutting-edge centres of innovation and productivity. This said, 'exchange values tend to prioritize time over space while use-values tend to prioritize space over time' (Wilson 1999: 162). Interestingly, even this contrast is transcended through the money form because the circulation of commodities overcomes the temporal, spatial, and personal barriers that are associated with direct exchange of products (Postone 1993: 264). This is reflected in the contrast between the mobility of abstract money capital in a space of flows and the consumption of specific use-values in specific times and places. Yet even this prioritization is tendential and relative, for 'in every instance when we accentuate space or time, the other aspect is still present, although hidden' (Czarniawska and Sevón 1996: 21). Harvey echoes this point in citing Rescher's view that 'space and time are "mutually coordinate in such a way that neither is more fundamental than the other"' (1996b: 252). There are also 'contradictory movements in which time is simultaneously compressed and expanded, depending on which part of the system one examines, so that the general progression is uneven and punctuated by more or less significant reverses' (Schoenberger 1997: 19). This suggests the need to make a thematic and methodological *temporal* (re)turn to redress one-sided concern with space in studies of globalization. Interestingly, such a temporal (re)turn can be seen in growing recognition of the need to bring time (back) into the analysis of globalization among those who had previously privileged the spatial (for a discussion of three representative cases, see Jessop 2002d). It is this primacy of the political economy of time in capitalist dynamics that led Harvey, a leading theorist of capital's spatiality,

Table 8.1 Marx's *Capital*, time, and space

Vol.	Successive concepts of capital	How time enters the analysis	How space enters the analysis	Premature closure of analysis of this concept of capital
I	Class relations involved in the appropriation of surplus-value	Linear production time: class struggle over necessary and surplus labour time	Extension of primitive accumulation to non-capitalist social formations	Based on a quasi-embodied labour theory of value, not on an abstract social labour theory of value. Thus the worker becomes an exploited object, not an active subject
II	Value in motion (unity of circuits of productive, commodity, and money capital)	Syllogisms of time: metamorphoses and circulation of capital	International mobility of money and commodities	Continuity of the circuit of capital is emphasized at the expense of possible ruptures
III	Transformation of values into prices: value as the price of production	Reproduction as a whole: living time of conflicts and crises rooted in competition and transformation of surplus-value into profit	Internationalized prices of production. World market and the audit of economic practices through global competition	Eruptions in the circuit of capital are introduced in an *ad hoc* manner, as digressions, with the result that no unified theory of crisis is presented

Sources:
Column 2: Bensaïd 2002.
Column 3: Bryan 1995.
Column 4: Shortall 1994.

to argue that '[u]nder capitalism, therefore, the meaning of space and the impulse to create new spatial configurations of human affairs can be understood only in relation to such temporal requirements' (1985: 37).

Some Spatio-Temporal Contradictions of Globalizing Capitalism

A globalizing capitalism typically intensifies the spatio-temporal contradictions and tensions inherent in the capital relation and/or the articulation and co-evolution of that relation with the more general spatialities and temporalities of the natural and social world. The increasing emphasis on speed and the growing acceleration of social life have many disruptive and disorienting effects on modern societies (see Armitage and Graham 2001; Virilio 1994, 1998). Here I note five tensions they introduce into the world market: the first is ecological, the second is existential, the third concerns the relation between the economic and extra-economic moments of capital accumulation, and the fourth and fifth are mainly internal to the value-driven logic of capitalism. These are not tensions of globalization as such but they do become more severe with the increasing complexity and flexibility in the circuits of capital associated with globalization.

First, there is a tension between the complex, reciprocally interdependent substantive reproduction requirements of real natural, social, and cultural processes and the simplified, one-sided, monetized temporalities involved in capital's emphasis on exchange-value (Altvater 1993: Altvater and Mahnkopf 1999; Crocker 1998; Lipietz 1997; O'Connor 1998; Stahel 1999). Globalization reinforces this tension by making it easier for capital to appropriate the local bounties of first and second nature without regard to their long-term reproduction and to move on whenever it becomes expedient to do so. Indeed, the growing emphasis on artificial short-term profit means that, 'as capital speeds up, it diminishes or degrades the conditions of the natural reproduction of natural things' (Brennan 1997: 31).

Second, there is a tension among the many and varied substantive temporalities of human existence (biological, sentient, socio-cultural, self-reflexive) and the abstract time inherent in the commodification of labour power and the dominance of formal market rationality (Polanyi 1957; Stahel 1999). This is reflected in the stresses of everyday life and in a growing sense of time-space compression (Eriksen 2001).

Third, contemporary capitalism involves a paradox that '[t]he most advanced economies function more and more in terms of the extra-economic' (Veltz 1996: 12). Among the factors behind this development are the increasing interdependence between the economic and extra-economic factors making for structural competitiveness. This is linked to the growth of new technologies based on more complex transnational, national, and regional systems of innovation, to the paradigm shift from Fordism, with its emphasis on productivity growth rooted in economies of scale, to post-Fordism, with its emphasis on mobilizing social as well as economic sources of flexibility and entrepreneurialism, and to the more general attempts to penetrate micro-social relations in the interests of valorization. It is reflected in the emphasis now given to social capital, trust, and communities of learning as well as to the competitive role of entrepreneurial cities, enterprise culture, and enterprising subjects (cf. Jessop 1997c, 1998a). This paradox generates major contradictions in both temporal and spatial terms. Thus, temporally, short-term economic calculation (especially in financial flows) comes into increasing conflict with the long-term dynamic of 'real competition'. For the latter is rooted in resources (skills, trust, heightened reflexivity, collective mastery of techniques, economies of agglomeration and size) that may take years to create, stabilize, and reproduce. Likewise, spatially, there is a basic contradiction between the economy seen as a de-territorialized, socially disembedded space of flows and as a territorially rooted, socially embedded system of extra-economic as well as economic resources, competencies, and activities (Storper 1997). The latter moment is reflected in a wide range of emerging concepts to describe the knowl-edge-driven economy – national, regional, and local systems of innovation, innovative milieus, systemic or structural competitiveness, learning regions, social capital, trust, learning-by-doing, speed-based competition, and so forth. The growing complexity of time-space-scale relations aggra-vates issues concerning the improbability of capital accumulation in terms of the compossibility and cogredience of its economic and extra-economic conditions of existence. For, if the capital relation is to be stabilized across more places, spaces, and scales and over increasingly compressed as well as extended temporal horizons of action, then partial fixes must be found to the problems of the co-existence of quite different ensembles of social rela-tions with different conditions of existence and dynamics (*compossibility*) and of the interweaving of their different temporal and spatial rhythms and horizons within a given set of spatio-temporal matrices (what one might term, extending Whitehead's analysis beyond its original meaning, issues of *cogredience*).[6]

Fourth, temporally, there is a tension between, on the one hand, the drive to accelerate the circulation of capital by shortening the production cycle between design and final consumption and, on the other, the long-term infrastructural development on which this depends. Harvey is especially incisive here. He notes that

> it takes a specific organization of space to try and annihilate space and it takes capital of long turnover time to facilitate the more rapid turnover of the rest. But the reduction of spatial barriers has an equally powerful opposite effect; small-scale and finely graded differences between the qualities of places (their labour supply, their infrastructures, and political receptivity, their resource mixes, their market niches, etc.) become even more important because multinational capital is better able to exploit them. (Harvey 1996b: 246–7)

This set of contradictions is aggravated by the increasing capacity for temporal compression permitted by the latest developments in information and communication technologies. In general, the scope that time-space compression opens for disjunction between the short-term interests of hypermobile capital and the interests of other social agents often causes distress to other fractions of capital and also puts pressure on inherited state forms and less mobile social forces.

Fifth, spatially, there is a tension between extending the scope of markets through the annihilation of space by time and the need for fixed infrastructure to enable rapid movement through space (which must be destroyed in turn as the next round of accumulation develops) (Harvey 1996a: 6). This contradiction may be aggravated by the expansion of production through mechanization and scale economies. Because this requires larger markets, it extends the time of commodity circulation and may also extend the overall turnover time due to the higher proportion of fixed to total capital. It can also lead to a dialectic of spatial concentration (agglomeration economies) and dispersal (congestion, land prices, unionization, etc.) (Schoenberger 1997: 19–21).

There are spiral processes at work in the last two contradictions that tend to increase the spatio-temporal complexities of regularizing and governing capital accumulation. 'Every local decentralization presupposes a renewed form of centralization at a higher level. Every temporal flexibilization requires, with increasing complexity, new mechanisms in order to hold the seemingly loosening temporal connections together. Flexibility becomes possible against the background of a previously unattained degree of constant temporal availability, as the prerequisite and consequence of which it functions' (Nowotny 1994: 99). There are also oscillations in the relative importance of time and space. Thus, whereas mass production compressed time in production, it extended it in product life cycles to valorize dedicated fixed capital and allow for the unmanageability of time required for product development. Now the situation is reversed. The current emphasis is on speeding up product development times and the order-to-delivery cycle. This also involves maximum flexibility in organization of production, economies of scope, and so forth (Schoenberger 1997: 45).

The Implications of Globalization for (National) States

Much has been written on the competing claims that globalization under-mines the national state and/or that the national state has a key role in sus-taining globalization. Such writings have been plagued by false oppositions and assumptions. One such opposition is that between the state as a 'power container' that operates exclusively within defined territorial frontiers and the economy as a borderless exchange mechanism with no important ter-ritorial anchoring. This opposition illustrates four errors. First, there is no reason to assume the fixity of its frontiers or temporal horizons. For states (and the social forces they represent) are actively involved in constituting and reconstituting the spatio-temporal matrices that organize politics, including its inter-state and international moments (Gross 1985; Poulantzas 1978b). Second, as form-determined condensations of a changing balance of social forces, state apparatuses and state power reflect the manifold processes involved in globalization. Thus the state apparatus may interior-ize the interests of foreign capital as well as project the interests of national capital abroad (Poulantzas 1975, 1978b). Third, the economy should not be reduced to a market-mediated space of flows operating in timeless time: markets also operate in accordance with other spatio-temporalities, and the economy more generally involves various non-market governance mecha-nisms with yet other spatio-temporal dynamics. So the regularization and governance of globalization is bound to involve many different scales and temporal horizons. And, fourth, the specificity of many economic assets and their embedding in extra-economic institutions mean that much eco-nomic activity remains place- and time-bound (Polanyi 1957; Storper 1997; Storper and Scott 1995). Combining these objections, one could conclude that the state operates as a *power connector*, that is, as a nodal or network state within a broader political system (Brunn 1999: 114), as well as a *power container*; and, likewise, that the economy has important territorial dimen-sions (reflected in concepts such as industrial districts, agglomeration economies, global cities, and regional or national capitalisms). Thus we should focus on the changing organization of politics and economics and their respective institutional embodiments and see frontiers and borders as actively reproduced and contingent rather than as pre-given and fixed.

Another false opposition involves treating the state as a political force and globalization as an economic process, with the corollary that their relationship is zero-sum in nature. This ignores how states help to constitute the economy as an object of regulation and how far economic globalization continues to depend on politics. For the capital relation is constitutively incomplete and needs extra-economic supplementation if the inherently improbable process of accumulation is to continue. States are heavily involved in this supplementation both directly and through their modulation of other extra-economic modes of regulation; and their equally improbable capacity to achieve this depends in part on revenues and resources derived from the accumulation process. In short, state–economy relations inevitably involve reciprocal interdependence, prompt attempts at strategic coordination, and produce structural coupling. They cannot be understood in zero-sum terms. Attempts to do so also ignore the complexities of globalization. Not only are many states actively involved in constituting the conditions for globalization, which is multiform and hence contested, but globalization is also linked to processes on other scales, such as regionalization, triadization, international localization, and cross-borderization, and states engage in promoting/resisting these processes too. Finally, zero-sum analyses ignore the extent to which the unfolding economic logic (and illogic) of globalization can constrain firms as well as political actors.

This leads us to a third area of conceptual confusion: the claim that globalization puts pressure on the sovereign state. This is misleading for four reasons. First, sovereignty is only one aspect of the form of the modern state. As a specific juridico-political form, sovereignty certainly organizes key features of state power; but it is struggles over state power(s) that are ultimately primary, not the particular forms in which it is (they are) exercised. Forms of sovereignty have been reorganized in the past and a post-sovereign international system is imaginable. Second, it is not the state as such (sovereign or otherwise) that is pressured by globalization. The processes that generate globalization can only put pressure on particular forms of state with particular state capacities and liabilities, such as the Keynesian Welfare National State in Atlantic Fordism or the Listian Workfare National State in East Asian Exportism (Jessop and Sum 2006). In so doing, globalization also modifies the balance of forces within states. For any differential loss of capacities will favour some fractions, classes, and social forces over others; it also creates space for, and prompts, struggles to reorganize state forms and capacities.

Important aspects of such pressures are the acceleration of economic decision-making and temporal compression of significant economic events relative to the time required for considered political decision-making. This weakens what one might call the 'time sovereignty' of the state in its current form (Scheuerman 2004). Third, since globalization is not a single causal mechanism with a universal, unitary logic but is multicentric, multiscalar, multitemporal, and multiform, it does not generate a single, uniform set of pressures. All states and state capacities will be pressured by globalization but each will be affected in different ways. Indeed, while some states actively promote globalization, others can be seen as its victims. Thus, even if one agreed that globalization mainly means Americanization (and I do not), the 'Great Satan' would still experience pressures emanating from other centres and forms of globalization as well as from the internal impact of its own neoliberal form and the resistance it inevitably generates at home and abroad. Similar arguments hold for the differential impact of the multiscalar nature of globalization, with states being differentially involved in various scalar projects and processes; and for that of its multitemporal nature, with some states more actively involved in and/or more vulnerable to time-space distantiation and compression. Finally, fourth, some aspects of globalization might actually enhance rather than diminish state capacities.

Having clarified possible misconceptions, we can now consider how (national) states are involved in, and affected by, globalization (see also Jessop 2002b, 2002d). In broad terms, states are actively engaged in redrawing the spatio-temporal matrices within which capital operates. In doing so, they are trying to manage the tension between potentially mobile capital's interests in reducing its place-dependency and/or liberating itself from temporal constraints, on the one hand, and, on the other hand, their own interest in fixing (allegedly beneficial)[7] capital within their own territories and rendering capital's temporal horizons and rhythms compatible with their statal and/or political routines, temporalities, and crisis-tendencies. For, as globalization increases, national states in the advanced capitalist economies can no longer presume, as they did in the heyday of Atlantic Fordism, that their primary economic task is to govern a relatively closed national economy – instead they are increasingly involved in managing a range of transnational processes and creating the spatial and temporal fixes appropriate thereto. Particularly important here are the changing relations between the economic and the extra-economic factors bearing on competitiveness and state roles in redefining the boundaries between the economic and extra-economic and/or reorganizing the latter and subordinating them to the perceived demands and pressures of globalization. Thus, to take a paradoxical example, even as neo-liberal states seem to disengage from the market economy, they intervene more in the extra-economic field and subordinate it to the demands of valorization (cf. Jessop 2002d).

More generally, the activities of capitalist states, almost regardless of their specific form and projects, have been reshaping the spatio-temporal matrices of globalization. Their roles here reflect the balance of internal and external forces, with some states more willing and active participants in these processes than others. Nonetheless, among many relevant activities, we can mention:

- deregulating, liberalizing, and shaping the institutional architecture of finance, facilitating thereby its accelerating internationalization and its global acceleration;[8]
- modifying institutional frameworks for international trade and foreign direct investment;
- planning and subsidizing the spatial fixes that support the activities of financial, industrial, and commercial capital within and across borders;
- promoting uneven development through policies for inter-urban and inter-regional as well as international competition;
- cooperating in the rebordering and re-scaling of state functions – including decentralization and cross-border region formation, regional bloc formation, and participating in forums for inter-triad negotiation;
- de-statizing current state functions by transferring them to private–public partnerships or place-bound market forces and thereby linking them to market-oriented temporalities;[9]
- de-territorializing some state functions by transferring them to private forms of functional authority (including international regimes) and/or to mobile market forces;
- attempting, conversely, to fit some non-territorial problems into an areal structure (e.g., making national states responsible for enforcing international agreements on global warming);
- and, finally, addressing the multiformity of globalization processes by engaging in the struggle to define the rules for harmonizing or standardizing a wide range of technological, economic, juridico-political, socio-cultural, and environmental issues (see also Jessop 2002d: 133–9).

More specifically, given the multicentric and multiform nature of globalization, some states are committed to promoting their own national or regional capitalisms, and the appropriate conditions for the expanded reproduction of these forms of capitalism on a global scale. The neo-liberal project has, of course, been most successful in this regard in the past two decades; but it has not gone uncontested, and the European model in particular may regain ground in the coming decade. They are also establishing new scales of activity (and dismantling others) and thereby rescaling and re-articulating various state powers, institutional forms, and regulatory capacities and creating the possibility for themselves and other actors to 'jump scales' in response to specific problems. They are promoting the space of flows by organizing conditions favourable to the international mobility of technologies, industrial and commercial capital, intellectual property, and at least some types of labour power. And, conversely, they are engaged in complementary forms of *Standortpolitik* and other forms of place-based competition in the attempt to fix mobile capital in their own economic spaces and to enhance the inter-urban, inter-regional, or international competitiveness of their own place-bound capitals.

An important source of pressure on states comes from the growing complexity of the political economy of time and its implications for politics as the 'art of the possible'. States increasingly face temporal pressures in their policy-making and implementation due to new forms of time-space distantiation, compression, and differentiation. For, as the temporalities of the economy accelerate relative to those of the state, the time to determine and coordinate political responses to economic events shrinks – especially in relation to superfast and/or hypermobile capital. This reinforces conflicts between the time(s) of the state and the time(s) of the market. One solution to the state's loss of time sovereignty is *laissez-faire*. This approach reinforces the temporality of deregulated exchange-value, however, which becomes problematic when market forces provoke economic crises and states are expected to respond. Two other options are for states to try to compress their own decision-making cycles so that they can make more timely and appropriate interventions and/or to attempt to decelerate the activities of 'fast capitalism' to match existing political routines.

A strategy of temporal compression increases pressures to make decisions on the basis of unreliable information, insufficient consultation, lack of participation, and so forth, even as state managers believe that policy is still taking too long to negotiate, formulate, enact, adjudicate, determine, and implement. The commitment to 'fast policy' is reflected in the shortening of policy development cycles, fast-tracking decision-making, rapid programme rollout, continuing policy experimentation, institutional and policy Darwinism, and relentless revision of guidelines and benchmarks. Scheuerman has summarized some of these trends in the general claim that there has been a shift to 'economic states of emergency' characterized by executive dominance and constant legal change and dynamism. It is particularly associated with a decline in the power of the judiciary (which looks to past precedent) and the legislature (which legislates for the future) and with an enhanced power for the executive (which has the power to take fast decisions) (Scheuerman 2000, 2004).

More generally this privileges those who can operate within compressed time scales, narrows the range of participants in the policy process, and limits the scope for deliberation, consultation, and negotiation. This can significantly affect the choice of policies, the initial targets of policy, the sites where policy is implemented, and the criteria adopted to demonstrate success. For example, as Wilson notes, an emphasis on rapid policy formulation and neglect of implementation serves the interests of efficiency criteria and productivity at the expense of concern with effectiveness and thereby reinforces instrumental rationality and exchange-value over deliberation and use-value (Wilson 1999: 175). An emphasis on speed also affects whether any lessons learnt are relevant to other targets, sites, or criteria; and it discourages proper evaluation of a policy's impact over different spatio-temporal horizons, including delayed and/or unintended consequences and feedback effects. In such situations, 'spin' trumps substance and modifies the nature of politics and policy-making. It may also help to accelerate policy-making and implementation cycles so that different approaches are tried in rapid succession as each is seen to fail. One symptom of this is the shortening 'half life' of legislation and other policies (Scheuerman 2001: 91–2). And it produces the dilemma that unchanged policies become irrelevant or even counterproductive whilst constant changes in policies risk being seen as opportunistic or illegitimate (de Sousa Santos 1995: 79–118).

Even if fast policy appears irrational from a purely *policy-making* perspective, it may still be rational for some interests in *politics-* or *polity-making* terms. For fast policy is antagonistic to corporatism, stakeholding, the rule of law, formal bureaucracy, and, indeed, to the routines and cycles of democratic politics more generally. It privileges the executive over the legislature and the judiciary, finance over industrial capital, consumption over long-term investment. In general, resort to fast policy undermines the power of decision-makers who have long decision-taking cycles – because they lose the capacity to make decisions in terms of their own routines and procedures, having to adapt to the speed of fast thinkers and fast policy-makers. It also tends to destroy institutional memory, on the grounds that new circumstances require new approaches, and to block efforts to anticipate future difficulties and policy failures. Hence the present is extended at the expense of both past and future and politics is lived in the mediatized world of spin and presentation, the quick fix, rapid churning of policies, and plebiscitarian democracy (Chesneaux 2000; Hoogerwerf 1990; Santiso and Schedler 1998; for a counterargument, see Grande 2000).

An alternative strategy is not to compress absolute political time but to create relative political time by slowing the circuits of capital. Perhaps the most celebrated, if not yet implemented, example of this strategy is the Tobin tax, which would decelerate the flow of superfast and hypermobile financial capital and limit its distorting impact on the real economy (Jetin and de Brunhoff 2000). Other examples include an energy tax on fossil fuels and nuclear power, consistent introduction of the polluter-pays principle on a global scale, resort to a worldwide prudential principle in the introduction of new technologies, and inclusion of recycling and disposal costs in pricing goods (Altvater and Mahnkopf 1999). For these could tilt the balance away from globalization in favour of regional and local economies, slow the rate of environmental destruction, and allow proper evaluation of the likely consequences of technological innovation. This could be supplemented by a fourth political time-management option. This is to establish the institutional framework for subsiditarian guided self-regulation on various scales as well as for continuous monitoring of how well such self-regulation is operating in the light of agreed criteria (Scheuerman 2004). This strategy of reflexive metagovernance would enable the state to retain the capacity to coordinate activities across different time zones and temporalities without the risk of overload (Hoogerwerf 1990).

More generally, on the temporal front, states are getting involved in promoting new temporal horizons of action and new forms of temporal flexibility, in coping with the increased salience of multiple time zones (in commerce, diplomacy, security, etc.), in recalibrating and managing the intersection of temporalities (e.g., regulating computer-programmed trading, promoting the 24-hour city as centre of consumption, managing environmental risk), and socializing long-term conditions of production as short-term calculation becomes more important for marketized economic activities. Of particular importance is the restructuring of welfare regimes to promote flexible economic and social adjustment and socialize its costs as economies become more vulnerable to the cyclical fluctuations and other vagaries of the world market (Jessop 1993, 2002d). A welfare orientation was always a feature of small open economies but is now becoming more general. For, '[t]he more the welfare state is able to guarantee security and a "future" beyond the market place, the more political space there is to relax closure vis-à-vis world markets' (Rieger and Leibfried 1998: 368).

More generally, in the spirit of Marx's analysis of time, wealth should be regarded as free time, not as the accumulation of the products of labour time. In this context a post-capitalist order would be oriented to maximizing free time and production would be subordinated to needs, among which unbound time would be central (Booth 1991).

Conclusions

The national state has long played a key role in establishing and regulating the relation between the spatial and the temporal matrices of social life (Poulantzas 1978b: 114). This remains true in a period of globalization, but the forms of this engagement have been changing. For states are modifying the spatio-temporal matrices of capitalism and the nation; and they have significant roles in managing uneven spatio-temporal development generated by the capital relation. In key respects the processes that produce globalization have undermined the effectiveness of national states as they developed during the post-war period. In particular, some of the distinctive powers and capacities they developed as Keynesian welfare national states have become less relevant to the new spatio-temporal matrices associated with globalization; wages are increasingly regarded as a cost of production rather than a source of demand and it is harder to control the circulation of money as national money with the deregulation of international currency markets; and forms of competition and the state have become much more critical sites of contradictions and dilemmas in a globalizing, knowledge-driven economy. Nonetheless a restructured national state remains central to the effective management of the emerging spatio-temporal matrices of capitalism and the emerging forms of post- or transnational citizenship to be seen in multi-ethnic, multicultural, melting-pot, tribal, cosmopolitan, 'playful' postmodern, and other identities. National states have become even more important arbiters of the movement of state powers upwards, downwards, and sideways; they have become even more important meta-governors of the increasingly complex multicentric, multiscalar, multitemporal, and multiform world of governance; and they are actively involved in shaping the forms of international policy regimes. They are also responding to the crisis in traditional forms and bases of national citizenship. Their activities in these respects have far less to do with globalization in the strongest sense of this polyvalent, promiscuous, and controversial word (i.e., the emergence of a borderless planetary economy – an entity widely and rightly regarded as mythical) than they do with the more general spatio-temporal restructuring of contemporary capitalism. This is why I have focused above on the complex spatio-temporal logics of globalization and their implications for state power. In doing so I hope to have contributed in some small measure to demystifying globalization and suggesting how its associated spatio-temporal transformations can be modified and controlled.

9

Multiscalar Metagovernance in the European Union

This chapter develops a strategic-relational perspective on the European Union as a nodal point in the transformation of statehood. It first reviews state- and governance-centric accounts of the EU as an emerging state form or political regime, considering two variants of each and offering three criticisms of both accounts. The two variants of statism are liberal intergovernmentalism and supranationalism; and the two variants of the governance account are multilevel governance and the 'network polity' (or, sometimes, network state). The chapter then develops a strategic-relational account of the emergence, restructuring, and strategic reorientation of the EU and the development of new forms of metagovernance such as the open method of coordination. A key element of this new account is a distinctive, ironic approach to market, state, and governance failures and the correlative need for sophisticated forms of reflexive meta-steering of state development. This is discussed in section three.

State-Centric Perspectives

State-centred approaches take the late nineteenth-century sovereign national state as their reference point and examine the EU in one of two ways. First, liberal intergovernmentalists note the emergence of an increasingly important new supranational arena in which sovereign national states attempt to pursue their own national interests. This new arena involves intergovernmental (here, international) relations rather than a site to which important sovereign powers have been transferred and so, however important it has

This chapter draws freely from 'Multi-level governance and multi-level meta-governance', in I. Bache and M. Flinders, eds, *Multi-Level Governance*, Oxford: Oxford University Press, 2004, 49–74; 'The European Union and recent transformations in statehood', in S. Puntscher Riekmann, M. Mokre, and M. Latzer, eds, *The State of Europe: Transformations of Statehood from a European Perspective*, Frankfurt: Campus, 2004, 75–94; and 'Avoiding traps, rescaling the state, governing Europe', in R. Keil and R. Mahon, eds, *Leviathan Undone? Towards a Political Economy of Scale*, Vancouver: University of British Columbia Press, in press.

become for the joint pursuit of intergovernmental interests, it does not culminate in a new state form (see especially Hoffman 1995; Moravcsik 1998). Conversely, supranationalists identify a tendential, emergent, upward re-scaling of the traditional form of the sovereign state from the national to the supranational level that will culminate sooner or later in a new form of statehood. They suggest that the re-allocation of formal decision-making powers is leading to a more or less complex form of multilevel government under the overall authority of a supranational superstate (see Pinder 1991; Taylor 1975; Weiler 1991). Whether the joint decision-making that now characterizes this emerging superstate is purely transitional or will remain once the superstate is consolidated is still uncertain.

For liberal intergovernmentalists, national states are, and will necessarily remain, the key players in the emerging European political space. States abandon little or none of their sovereign authority and retain a comprehensive constitutional mandate in contrast to the limited powers of the European Union. Thus inter-state interactions overwhelmingly take the form of international relations oriented to the pursuit of national interests, involving at best the provisional pooling of sovereignty for the pursuit of joint interests. For some this provides a new means to enhance the power and authority of the national state (e.g., Moravcsik 1998). More generally, rather than leading to the transcendence of the national state, intergovernmental cooperation is said to produce at most a set of interlocking international arrangements among a self-selected group of national states. While this may eventually lead to a *Staatenbund* or confederation (e.g., a United Europe of National States), one or more national states could block this development if it is feared that this process would hurt their respective national interests.

Conversely, supranationalists must posit a paradoxical transitional process in which national states conspire in their own transcendence (*Aufhebung*) as they promote supranational state formation. This involves a re-territorialization of political power as the three key features of the modern sovereign state are re-scaled upwards and re-differentiated vertically: *Staatsgewalt* (organized coercion), *Staatsgebiet* (a clearly demarcated territorial domain of state authority), and *Staatsvolk* (state subjects). This is linked to the re-scaling (and, perhaps, re-organization) of mechanisms for constitutionalizing and legitimating state authority in the expanded territory. Two factors distinguish the emergence of the supranational state from the simple territorial expansion of a single national state that absorbs all (or some) of the territories occupied by other relevant national states. First, it emerges from an agreement among independent national states to surrender their sovereignty and transfer it to a higher authority. Second, each of the affected national states becomes a subordinate unit of the new state whilst keeping the same territorial boundaries. Thus the new superstate is a multi-tiered state apparatus.

What do these two approaches imply for multilevel political relations? First, regarding the upward re-scaling (or re-territorialization) of state sovereignty, the development of multilevel government would seem a transitional effect of the transition. In other words, it would take the form of relations between an emergent, but still incompletely realized, supranational state and existing, not yet transcended, national states. Moreover, if the emergent supranational state were to assume the form of a bi- or multi-tiered federal superstate (*Bundesstaat*), one could also analyse the relations between different tiers of government with the tools previously used for the dynamics of other federal states. Second, regarding international relations, multilevel government could be interpreted in terms of the distinctive intergovernmental institutional arrangements established by national states and/or the specific governance strategies that they pursue from time to time. Using the terminology for analysing the relativization of scale presented in chapter 4 (cf. Collinge 1999), while the EU level becomes an increasingly important *nodal* scale in the overall exercise of state power, national states still provide the *dominant* scale. Given the resulting complexities of state power, it might be more appropriate to call this *multilevel governance in the shadow of national government(s)*.

While liberal intergovernmentalism appears more persuasive than supranationalism, especially for the earlier stages of European economic and political integration, the statist approach as a whole commits three errors: a restricted account of the state as a sovereign territorial apparatus, an anachronistic reference point, and, of course, state-centrism. First, although the essence of the state may well consist in the *territorialization of political power*, political power can be territorialized in different ways. Yet analyses of the EU as an emerging supranational state tend to focus on three features of the state apparatus: (a) its monopoly of organized coercion; (b) the constitutionalization of state power through the rule of law and a clear allocation of authority; and (c) control over its own money, taxes, and state budget. This implies that the key criteria for assessing whether a European superstate has emerged are the development of a European *Kriegs- und Friedensgemeinschaft* (a War- and Peace-Community, complete with a European army subject to supranational control, a European police force for internal security, and a European foreign and security policy that pursues distinctively European interests in the global inter-state system), an explicit European constitution (which locates sovereign power at the apex of a multi-tiered political system, defines the relationship between a jointly sovereign European executive, legislature, and judicial system, and determines the division of powers and competencies between the different tiers of government), and a European monetary system, fisco-financial system, and a large, centralized budget. Anti-federalists already claim that the EU has developed these features or, at least, will soon do so. Liberal intergovernmentalists note the absence of all or most of these same features and conclude that the EU is primarily an arena in which traditional national territorial sovereign states compete to influence European policies, politics, and political regimes. Despite these disagreements, however, both sides fetishize formal constitutional and juridical features and ignore *de facto* state capacities and the modalities of the exercise of state power. They also focus excessively on territoriality at the expense of extra-territorial and non-territorial features.

Second, state-centred theorists overlook the successive historical transformations of the modern territorial state forms from the mid- to late nineteenth century onwards. They therefore adopt an *anachronistic* model of the national territorial state to judge whether and how far a European superstate has emerged. This claim can be illustrated from Willke's fourfold periodization of the modern state: the *Sicherheitsstaat* is concerned to defend its territorial integrity at home and abroad; the *Rechtsstaat* provides legal security for its subjects; the *Sozialstaat* establishes and extends welfare rights to its subjects; and the *Risikostaat* protects its citizens from a wide range of unexpected and uncontrollable risks. The key state resource in each stage is respectively: *Gewalt* (organized coercion), *Recht* (law grounded in a constitution), *Geld* (national money and state budgets), and *Wissen* (organized intelligence) (Willke 1992). Although the 'risk state' is not the most useful concept for the contemporary state, Willke's approach does highlight changes in the relative primacy of state resources. So the absence of a European army-police, constitution, and massive budgets may be less important than the EU's ability to mobilize organized intelligence and other forms of soft intervention that shape how national and regional states deploy their respective capacities (cf. Sbragia 2000). Overall, this suggests, first, that the key resources in today's *Staatenwelt* (world of states) – at least as far as relations among advanced bourgeois democratic states are concerned – are not so much coercion or money as soft law and intelligence; and, second, that the appropriate model for analysing EU state-building is not the late nineteenth-century state but national states in advanced capitalism as they have developed in the last couple of decades – whether this be a competition state, regulatory state, or a Schumpeterian Workfare Postnational Regime (on the SWPR, see Jessop 2002d, and below).

A related aspect of this second problem is the adoption of anachronistic normative assumptions about European political democracy. We should compare the still emergent EU polity with actually existing national democracies rather than earlier democratic systems – whether nineteenth-century liberal nightwatchman states, interwar interventionist states, or the postwar Keynesian Welfare National State with its catchall governing parties (on the KWNS, see Jessop 2002d). Contemporary Western states tend towards authoritarian statism, with strong executives, mass-mediatized plebiscitary democracy, and authoritarian mass parties (cf. Poulantzas 1978b; see chapter 5 above). Thus, if there is a democratic deficit in the EU, it may be linked to the contemporary form of statehood more generally, with deficits on different scales reinforcing each other. This suggests that attempts to develop more democratic forms of representation and greater democratic accountability must be oriented to a different understanding of the nature and feasibility of democracy.

The third problem with state-centric analyses is their tendency to naturalize the state–society distinction rather than treat it as socially constructed, internal to the political system, and liable to change (see general introduction and chapter 2 above). Thus, to interpret changes in the EU as moments in the reorganization and reorientation of contemporary statehood, we must consider how the wider political system is organized and how changes in its territorial boundaries may contribute to the more general reorganization of state power. The latter must also be related to the changing patterns of strategic selectivity linked to a changing institutional architecture and new forms of political mobilization. This implies that the EU is not a fixed form of state but an aspect, a path-shaping as well as path-dependent institutional materialization, of a new balance of forces that is expressed, *inter alia*, in state-building.

Governance-Centric Approaches

Simple governance-centric approaches hold that the constitutionalized monopoly of violence and top-down modes of intervention associated with modern states are irrelevant or even harmful in an increasingly complex global social order. Thus they focus on the tendential *de-statization of politics (or de-hierarchization of the state)* rather than the *de-nationalization of statehood*; and they emphasize the enhanced role of reflexive self-organization in solving complex coordination problems that involve a wide range of partners or stakeholders beyond as well as within the state (Jessop 1997b, 2002d, 2003c). This provides two bases on which to analytically distinguish de-centred forms of governance from the activities of centralized sovereign states. First, the sovereign state can be seen as the quintessential expression of hierarchy (imperative coordination) because it is, by definition, the political unit that governs but is not itself governed. Hence, beyond the sovereign state, we find the anarchy of interstate relations and/or the heterarchy of a self-organizing international society. And, second, it is primarily concerned with governing activities in its own territorial domain and defending its territorial integrity against other states. In contrast, governance is based on reflexive self-organization (networks, negotiation, negative coordination, positive concerted action) rather than imperative coordination. And it is concerned in the first instance with managing functional interdependencies, whatever their scope (and perhaps with variable geometries), rather than with activities occurring in a defined and delimited territory.

In these terms the EU is a major emerging site of governance that involves a plurality of state *and non-state* actors on different levels who attempt to coordinate activities around a series of functional problems. Without reference to non-state as well as state actors and to functional as well as territorial issues, it would be hard to distinguish multilevel governance (hereafter MLG) from intergovernmentalism. Thus the key question becomes how state and non-state actors manage, if at all, to organize their common interests across several territorial levels and/or across a range of functional domains. There are two main approaches to this question: the self-described multilevel governance approach, stressing the vertical dimension of coordination, and a parallel body of work that highlights its horizontal dimension through the notion of the 'network polity' (sometimes called the 'network state').

In the present context, MLG involves the institutionalization of reflexive self-organization among multiple stakeholders across several scales of state territorial organization. This has two implications. First, state actors would cooperate as negotiating partners in a complex network, pooling their sovereign authority and other distinctive capacities to help realize collectively agreed aims and objectives on behalf of the network as a whole. They operate at best as *primus inter pares* in a complex and heterogeneous network rather than as immediate holders of sovereign authority in a single hierarchical command structure. Thus the formal sovereignty of states is better seen as one symbolic and/or material resource among others rather than as the dominant resource. Indeed, from this perspective, sovereignty is better interpreted as a series of specific state capacities (e.g., legislative, fiscal, coercive, or other state powers) rather than as one overarching and defining feature of the state. Thus states will supply other resources, too, that are not directly tied to their sovereign control over a national territory with its monopoly of organized coercion, its control over the national money, and its monopoly over taxation (Krätke 1984; Willke 1992). State involvement would therefore become less hierarchical, less centralized, and less directive. Other stakeholders contribute other symbolic and/or material resources (e.g., private money, legitimacy, information, expertise, organizational capacities, or power of numbers) to advance collectively agreed aims and objectives. Second, in contrast to the clear hierarchy of territorial powers allegedly associated with the sovereign state, MLG typically involves tangled hierarchies and complex interdependence. Thus the EU functions less as a re-scaled, supranational sovereign state apparatus than as a nodal point in an extensive and tangled web of governance operations concerned to orchestrate economic and social policy in and across many scales of action with the participation of a wide range of official, quasi-official, private economic interests, and representatives of civil society.

The network polity (or state) provides a complementary account of the nature of the European state political system. Three variants can be noted: Castells' claims about the European network state; a Foucauldian view that interprets recent patterns of European governance as a shift to an advanced (neo-)liberal form of governmentality; and governance-theoretical accounts of the network polity. The third variant is the most widespread but I will comment briefly on each.

Castells claimed that, rather than involving the transfer of authority up to a European state that thereby supplants existing European nation-states, the European Union *as a whole* tends to operate as a network state. He defines the latter as a state that shares authority (that is, in the last resort, the capacity to impose legitimized violence) along a network. Here Castells retains the conventional Weberian notion of the state as an apparatus possessing a legitimate monopoly of violence over a given territorial area, implying that the EU's authority corresponds to a specific territorial domain. But he adds that, by definition, a network has nodes, not a centre, implying that control over this monopoly is dispersed rather than centralized. This is particularly likely because nodes may vary in size and have asymmetrical ties to the network. Indeed, the nodes formed by member states differ in their respective powers and capacities; and even the three largest member states have different strengths (technological, industrial, financial, military). Castells argues, for example, that Germany is the hegemonic economic power, Britain and France have greater military power, and all three have at least equal technological capacity compared with other member states (2000: 5). This dispersion of authority and influence among nodes in the European 'network state' is reflected in the complex, variable, and changing geometry of European institutions. The endless negotiations in this set of institutions, and among the national actors pursing their strategies, may, argues Castells, look cumbersome and inefficient. But it is exactly this indeterminacy and complexity that enable the EU to muddle through, accommodating various interests and changing policies, not only from different countries, but also from the different political orientations of parties elected to government (2000: 2, 5). Castells' account is clearly imprinted by state-theoretical assumptions and, compared with liberal intergovernmentalism and/or supranationalism, its main innovation is its use of the network metaphor to reveal some (but far from all) of the complexity of the linkages between national states and European institutions.

Larner and Walters (2002) distinguish between imperialism, developmentalism, and the 'new regionalism' as arts of international government. Drawing on Foucauldian theory and actual developments in North America and the Asia Pacific as well as Europe, they also enumerate several key distinguishing features of the liberal art of international governmentality. Two more focused Foucauldian accounts are provided by Barry's analysis of the European Union as a network state, inspired in part by actor-network theory (2001); and Haahr's study (2004) of the emerging 'open method of coordination' (OMC) that was formally announced during the 1999–2000 Portuguese Presidency, but which has a longer pre-history. The OMC is a 'soft' form of governance that differs from traditional top-down 'positive government' and the previous trend towards a European 'regulatory state' based on a neo-liberal *Ordnungspolitik* (on which, see Majone 1997). As such, it involves concerted, centralized formulation of objectives, quantification of indicators for measuring progress towards such objectives, decentralized implementation, and systematic monitoring of different member states' progress. It thereby enables member states to address problems at the European level without ceding new juridical competencies to the European Union. In this sense, argues Haahr, the OMC reflects advanced liberal forms of government. These embody a notion of structured and conditioned freedom: they are 'practices of liberty' that establish and facilitate liberty but also discipline it and constrain its exercise. They govern through the manipulation of techniques and mechanisms rather than more directly through a classical liberal and/or Keynesian welfarist manipulation of processes. Thus, while these new techniques of rule involve contracts, consultation, negotiation, partnerships, empowerment, and activation, they also set norms, standards, benchmarks, performance indicators, quality controls, and best-practice standards. In short, '[a]dvanced liberal rule operates through our freedom, through the way this freedom is structured, shaped, predicted and made calculable' (Haahr 2004: 216). Re-scaled from national states to the European level, this is seen in the declared role of the OMC to help member states evolve their own policies in new and major areas in line with the constitutional principle of subsidiarity and in consultation with relevant regional and local political authorities as well as with the social partners and civil society. By developing strategies, setting and monitoring targets, and forming partnerships, such 'advanced liberal' forms of governmentality can both mobilize and discipline the energies of civil society. In this way, while member states appear as agents capable of devising strategies and achieving objectives without being directly subject to EU diktat, the European Commission can appear as the institution empowered to assess their relative performance in attaining the consensually determined agreed objectives (Haahr 2004).

More conventional governance-theoretical analyses of the emerging European network polity start from the difficulties of relying on rigid hierarchical coordination in contexts characterized by complex reciprocal interdependence among different fields across different scales (Ladeur 1997; Pitschas 1995). Ansell provides a good overview of this approach and summarizes his (and other) findings as follows:

> [T]he networked polity is a structure of governance in which both state and societal organization is vertically and horizontally disaggregated (as in pluralism) but linked together by cooperative exchange (as in corporatism). Organizational structures in the networked polity are organic rather than mechanistic, which means that both knowledge and initiative are decentralized and widely distributed. Horizontal relationships within and across organizations are at least as important as vertical relationships, and organizational relationships in general follow a pattern of many-to-many (heterarchy) rather than many-to-one (hierarchy). Exchange is diffuse and/or social rather [than] discrete and/or impersonal. The logic of governance emphasizes the bringing together of unique configurations of actors around specific projects oriented toward integrative solutions rather than dedicated programs. These project teams will criss-cross organizational turf and the boundary between public and private. State actors with a high degree of centrality in the web of interorganizational linkages will be in a position to provide facilitative leadership in constructing or steering these project teams. (2000: 311)

Three main criticisms can be levelled at the main governance-centred approaches, excluding for now Castells and the Foucauldians. First, reflecting its diverse disciplinary roots and wide scope, work on governance often remains at a largely pre-theoretical stage: it is much clearer what the notion of governance excludes than what it contains. This is reflected in a proliferation of typologies of governance mechanisms constructed for different purposes and a large measure of (often unspoken) disagreement about what the concept includes or excludes. Thus many early analyses established that the EU political system cannot easily be assimilated to, or studied in terms of, a traditional conception of government; but it was unclear exactly how MLG operated to produce the European polity, how objects of governance are defined in this context, and how stakeholders are defined. Later work has begun to address these problems but is often limited to specific policy areas or policy networks, leaving open the issue of how different multilevel governance regimes are connected, let alone how, if at all, they may acquire a relative unity. There are also serious ambiguities in the referents of MLG. For the term is used to capture several trends in the development of the contemporary state – the de-nationalization of statehood, the de-statization of politics, and the re-articulation of territorial and functional powers. The fact that it is used to describe the interaction of three analytically distinct trends (each with its own counter-trend), or, at least, to characterize their combined impact, suggests that the concept may obscure as much as it clarifies about recent changes.

Second, governance theories tend to be closely connected to concerns about problem-solving and crisis-management in a wide range of fields. This has led some governance theorists to focus on specific collective decision-making or goal-attainment issues in relation to specific (socially and discursively constituted) problems and to investigate how governance contributes to problem-solving (for a belated self-criticism on this score, see Mayntz 2001). But this can easily lead to a neglect of problems of governance failure, that is, the tendency for governance to fail to achieve its declared objectives; and, *a fortiori*, neglect of the various responses of different agents or subjects of governance to such failures as they attempt to engage in different forms of metagovernance (cf. Jessop 2000b). Two aspects of metagovernance are relevant here. On the one hand, because many studies focus on specific problem fields or objects of governance, they tend to ignore questions of the relative (in)compatibility of different governance regimes and their implications for the overall unity of the European project and European statehood. And, on the other hand, many empirical studies have overlooked (or, at least, failed to theorize) the existence of metagovernance. This complicated process, which Dunsire (1996) terms 'collibration', involves attempts to modify the relative weight and targets of exchange, hierarchy, networking, and solidarity (or community) in the overall coordination of relations of complex interdependence. Yet such metagovernance is central to many of the disputes over European integration and/or state formation and has long been a key issue on the agenda of the European Union itself, especially regarding the different steps in integration. This is reflected in the increasing resort to partnerships, comitology, social dialogue, and the mobilization of non-governmental organizations and social movements as additional elements in the attempts to guide European integration and to steer EU policy-making and implementation (cf. Scott and Trubek 2002). The 'Lisbon Strategy', with its advocacy of the extension of the OMC, and the recent White Paper on Governance are the latest phases in this search for appropriate mechanisms of metagovernance (see below).

Third, work on MLG and the network polity poses fundamental issues about the primacy of any territorial anchoring of the network polity, despite its highly pluralistic functional concerns and its equally variable geometries. Schmitter raised just such issues when he identified four possible, ideal-typical future scenarios for the emerging Europolity. These scenarios derive from cross-tabulation of two axes of political regime formation: (1) an essentially Westphalian versus 'neo-medieval' form of territorial organization; and (2) heterogeneous and flexible versus tightly ordered and highly stable functional representation. The two most interesting (and, he suggested, plausible) scenarios are the *condominio* (a neo-medieval state system with flexible functional representation and policy-making) and the *consortio* (a largely intergovernmental *Europe des patries* with polycentric, incongruent flexible functional representation and policy-making). A Westphalian state re-scaled to the European level with a well-ordered and congruent European system of functional representation (to produce a *stato*, which could be considered equivalent to a supranational European superstate) was deemed unlikely; and a *confederatio* (a neo-medieval territorial arrangement with tightly organized and stable functional representation) was judged even more implausible (Schmitter 1992).

Viewed as an open-ended thought experiment, Schmitter's typological exercise serves two purposes. It suggests, first, that studies of MLG and/or network forms of political organization should not ignore issues of territorial organization; and, second, once functional and territorial issues are posed together, issues of multilevel metagovernance become central both in practice and in theory. We should also question how far analyses of the political actors in the EU can be confined territorially to its member states (and, perhaps, candidate states) and functionally to organized interests and movements that are anchored primarily in the political space directly organized and controlled by the EU and its member states. For the forms, pace, and extent of European integration are also relevant to other states (notably the USA and Russia) and to diverse non-state forces with strong roots outside the European Union.

Each of these problems challenges the adequacy of the MLG approach. In particular, they have produced a situation described by Weiler and Wessels as comprising 'too many case studies, *ad hoc* lessons from limited experiences and organizational description [and] too little theoretical mediation' (1988: 230n). In part, of course, this *ad hocery* reflects the real complexities of the emerging European polity. Indeed, it would be surprising if no such complexities existed. For national states also involve heterogeneous patterns of government and/or governance, with patterns varying with the objects of state intervention, the nature of policy fields, the changing balance of forces in and beyond the state, and so on. In this sense, perhaps, we may be witnessing a re-scaling of the complexities of government and governance rather than a re-scaling of the sovereign state or the emergence of just one more arena in which national states pursue national interests. These complexities at the national scale may provide some insights into the emerging EU polity.

Changes in Statehood in Advanced Capitalist Societies

Here I identify three trends and counter-trends in contemporary statehood to indicate one approach to the 'theoretical mediation' called for by Weiler and Wessels. These three trends are derived from theoretically informed observation of developments in developed capitalist economies in all triad regions (North America, East Asia, and Western Europe) rather than just the last of these. In this sense, their generality across these regions (and, hence, their occurrence elsewhere) suggests they are not generated by processes peculiar to the European region. For this reason they can help to contextualize and interpret recent trends in the development of European statehood (Ziltener 1999). But these trends also have many different causes. They should not be treated as singular causal mechanisms in their own right, which would mean neglecting their essentially descriptive, synthetic, and generalized nature. Nor should they be thought to entail unidirectional movement or multilateral convergence across all national or triadic regimes. Instead, they can, and do, take different empirical forms (for example, on the differing dynamics of cross-border regions in North America and Europe, see Blatter 2001). In addition, each trend can be correlated with a set of counter-trends that necessarily qualify any one-sided claims about a fundamental transformation of territorial statehood. These counter-trends also originate in diverse processes and practices (for more details, see Jessop 2002d: 193–204; for a summary, see Box 9.1).

These three trends and counter-trends matter here for one major reason. If the national state is no longer intelligible in terms of the received notion of the sovereign national state, then perhaps this notion is also inadequate for studying the evolving EU as a state form. Indeed, we can go further: if the national state is changing in the ways suggested above, the EU's future position and activities in a re-territorialized, de-statized, and international-ized *Staatenwelt* must be very carefully reconsidered. What we are witness-ing is the re-scaling of the complexities of government *and governance* rather than the re-scaling of the sovereign state or the emergence of just one more arena in which national states pursue national interests.

Much the same point can be made through changes in the state's form and functions regarding capital accumulation. These can be studied along four key dimensions of economic policy, social policy, scale, and the primary mechanism for compensating for market failure. Referring to these four dimensions, the post-war state in northwestern Europe can be described ideal-typically as a Keynesian Welfare National State (or KWNS). For reasons explored elsewhere (Jessop 2002d), the KWNS experienced a major and multiple crisis in the late 1970s and early 1980s. It has since been ten-dentially replaced by a new form of state with new functions on each dimen-sion. I have termed this the Schumpeterian Workfare Post-national Regime (or SWPR) (2002d) and I now consider its relevance to the European Union.

TRENDS

- De-nationalization of the state (hollowing out of the state)
- De-statization of politics (from government to governance)
- Internationalization of policy regimes (foreign sources of domestic policy)

COUNTER-TRENDS

- Increased scope for states in interscalar articulation
- Increased role for states in metagovernance
- States contest the forms and implementation of international regimes

---

Box 9.1 Trends and counter-trends in state restructuring

The emerging Europolity is an integral moment in the de-nationalization of the state, the de-statization of politics, and the internationalization of regimes – without being the highest level to which national state powers are shifted upwards, at which new forms of partnership are being organized, or on which the internationalization of policy regimes is occurring. Likewise, the changes in the dominant strategies used to build the Europolity, however ineffective, the forms it assumes, however impure, the functions that it exercises, however imperfectly, and the theoretical paradigms used to interpret it, however flawed, are all related to the periodization of the state in the advanced capitalist economies. Thus, to narrate rather breathlessly the phases of Europolity development detailed at length by Ziltener (1999):

1 The initial steps towards Western European integration were initiated through a transatlantic coalition aiming to promote a post-war reconstruction that would integrate Western Europe into the economic and political circuits of Atlantic Fordism (cf. van der Pijl 1984).
2 During the boom years of Atlantic Fordism, the 'Monnet mode of integration' was concerned to create a 'Keynesian-corporatist' (*sic*) form of statehood on the European level that could secure the conditions for different national Fordist modes of development (cf. Ruigrok and van Tulder 1996) but developed crisis symptoms as the member states pursued divergent strategies in response to the interconnected economic and political crises in/of Fordism.
3 The resulting crisis in European integration prompted the search for a new mode of integration and led to the internal market project – with important conflicts between neo-liberal, neo-corporatist, and neo-statist currents – and the development of new modes of economic and political coordination (cf. van Apeldoorn 2002).
4 After a period of experimentation with new modes of coordination, the provisional outcome of these conflicts can be discerned in a new 'Schumpeterian workfare' mode of integration and coordination concerned to promote the structural competitiveness of Europe in a globalizing knowledge-based economy (cf. Telò 2002).

Ziltener also suggests that the dominant line of conflict regarding Europolity construction in the Monnet period of Keynesian-corporatism was supranationalism versus intergovernmentalism and that the Delors project could be seen as a failed supranational attempt to re-scale the Keynesian welfare state (or KWNS) to the European level (1999: 129–30,

180–4). To this we might add that the shift towards a European SWPR is clearly associated with a shift in the dominant line of conflict around appropriate forms of multilevel governance and the 'network polity'. This story is too brief, of course, to do justice to the complexities of European integration, the complexities of modes of coordination, their intended functions, and their variation with the objects of coordination, and the complexities of competing paradigms and paradigm shifts within and across different disciplines. But it does illustrate the need to periodize the Europolity and, indeed, to locate it in a broader context concerned with the reorganization of statehood on a still more global scale.

The EU as a Schumpeterian Workfare Post-National Regime

To clarify what is at stake in these changes and to introduce some order into the discussion of otherwise confusing trends and counter-trends, we can examine recent changes in the EU in terms of the four interrelated shifts involved in the transition from KWNS to SWPR. Each of these four shifts can be found in the European Union. This is hardly surprising because the hypothesized transition from the KWNS to the SWPR derives from theoretical analysis of developmental tendencies in capitalism combined with careful empirical observation of national economies within the circuits of Atlantic Fordism. But, since the preceding account derives from the North American and Antipodean cases as well as from Northwestern Europe and also took the national economy and national state in Atlantic Fordism as its theoretical and historical starting point, it is worth asking whether these national tendencies are also found at the European level.

A complicating factor in assessing the case for such a transition is that the six initial members of the EEC had modes of growth and modes of regulation belonging to one or other of the regulated varieties of capitalism and either had one or other form of conservative-corporativist welfare regime or, in Italy's case, a clientelist Mediterranean welfare regime (cf. Hantrais 2000; Ruigrok and van Tulder 1996). The varieties of state within the European Community increased, however, as new members with different modes of growth, modes of regulation, and welfare regimes joined it. This introduced greater economic and social heterogeneity into the European economy and helped to shift the balance of forces in a neo-liberal direction. The Eastwards expansion of the European Union has had a key role here – and one that is by no means accidental. It has been correspondingly more difficult to establish the conditions for re-scaling state planning from the national to the

European level or to establish Euro-corporatism (on Euro-corporatism, see Falkner 1998 and Vobruba 1995; and on its limits, Streeck 1994).

These difficulties have been reinforced through the manner in which monetary union and the Euro have been instituted. The Maastricht convergence criteria make it harder for member states to break out of the neo-liberal framework and the limited EU budget prevents it from financing a major expansion of a European welfare regime. In addition, the Growth and Stability Pact has served as a new 'gold standard', requiring conformity to relatively rigid norms of economic and political conduct favourable to a liberal (money) conception of economic stability and growth. In particular, the Maastricht criteria and the Growth and Stability Pact together require public spending cuts or constraints, social security and welfare reforms, and more or less significant privatization of state-owned enterprises and commercialization of public services. Nonetheless, we can observe growing concern with active involvement in promoting competitiveness, innovation, and enterprise in line with Schumpeterian perspectives. Although the main thrust of this involvement accords well with neo-liberal strategy, it is nonetheless flanked by neo-statist and neo-corporatist strategies, illustrated by key features of EU technology policies and social policy, respectively (for a brief summary of the distinctions between neo-liberal, neo-statist, neo-corporatist, and neo-communitarian variants of the SWPR, see Gottfried 1995; Jessop 2002d). A major development in this area is the resurgence of corporatism in a new guise – social pacts oriented to wage restraint, social security reform, supply-side competitiveness, and general conformity to the logic of the new monetary system (see Grote and Schmitter 1999; Regini 2000; Rhodes 1998).

Turning now to the case for the SWPR in Europe, we can note, first, that the EU's overall economic policy has been reoriented in the direction of a Schumpeterian strategy from an earlier period when it was more suited to Atlantic Fordism. The origins of European integration can be found in postwar reconstruction that prepared the ground for Atlantic Fordism in Europe (for details, see van der Pijl 1984; Ziltener 2001). Thus, in addition to their initial post-war role in restructuring iron, steel, and coal in this context, the European communities also emphasized the creation of an integrated market so that industrial enterprises could realize optimal economies of scale. This involved an essentially liberal *Ordnungspolitik* to create a single market and was an important supplement to the pursuit of national Keynesian policies – especially as the Treaty of Rome left official responsibility for employment policy at the national level. Indeed, as Sbragia notes, the EU's basic constitutional framework structurally privileges liberal economic strategies: 'the norm of economic liberalization, embedded in the Treaty of Rome, was reinforced and elaborated in the Single European Act and the Treaty of Maastricht' (Sbragia 2000: 224). Thus even when the EU, under Delors' presidency (1985–95), began to develop a more active employment policy and to plan for a Social Europe and then attempted to institutionalize these twin responsibilities for the first time in the Maastricht Treaty (1991), this occurred in an institutional context that was already biased in favour of liberalism and in an ideological climate that was dominated by neo-liberalism. Whether this would lead only to neo-liberal policy adjustments or to a more radical neo-liberal regime shift, however, would depend on the struggles between economic, political, and social forces rather than having been pre-scripted by the logic of the post-Fordist knowledge-based economy.

Second, on the welfare–workfare shift, welfare and social policy was retained as a national competence in the founding treaties of the European Community, and policy-making at the European level in these fields has systematically lagged behind macro-economic, industrial, and technology policies. Thus, as Kuhnle and Alestalo note, '[t]here exists as of today no European social law on the basis of which individual citizens can claim benefits from Brussels; no direct taxation or social contributions to EU which can finance social welfare; and there hardly exists any welfare bureaucracy in the EU' (2000: 6). Moreover, rather than seeing a re-scaling of the KWNS upwards to the European Union, EU social policy largely takes the form of social regulation. For, as Majone notes,

> measures proposed by the Commission in the social field must be compatible with the 'economic constitution' of the Community, that is, with the principle of a liberal economic order. This requirement creates an ideological climate quite unlike that which made possible the development of the welfare state in the Member States . . . The economic liberalism that pervades the Founding Treaty and its subsequent revisions gives priority to the allocation of public policy over distributional objectives. Hence the best rationale for social initiatives at Community level is one which stresses the efficiency-improving aspects of the proposed measures. (1993: 156)

Nonetheless there is increasing evidence of a complex and complicated reorientation of welfare policy at the European level. This involves two apparently contradictory tendencies. On the one hand, some welfare policies (such as equal pay, equal opportunities, portable welfare benefits, minimum standards for health and security at work, and rules on working hours) have been gradually re-scaled to the EU level to supplement the more traditional nationally scaled welfare measures; and some structural policies have also been re-scaled at a European level to facilitate industrial restructuring, compensate for uneven regional development, support agriculture, and help to regenerate declining communities. On the other hand, the emergence of social policy at the European level tends to assume a workfare rather than welfare orientation. Thus 'the political point of reference [of such economic and social policy initiatives] is not so much social integration but rather the instrumentalization of policy as a resource for competition oriented structural change' (Deppe et al. 2000: 20). This is reflected in a tendential Europeanization of labour market policies, the transformation of national corporatist and bargaining arrangements, and the development of 'social pacts'. In short, there is a growing mix of welfare and workfare strategies at the European level; but they are unified around concern to create the conditions for an effective single market in post-Fordist rather than Fordist conditions.

One of the earliest signs of this reorientation was the European Commission's White Paper on *Growth, Competitiveness, Employment* (1993). This reviewed a wide range of factors affecting the competitiveness of the European economy and its capacity to generate good jobs and sustainable economic growth; and it recommended an equally wide range of trans-European macro-economic, environmental, infrastructural, technological, educational, vocational, and social policy initiatives that might address – rhetorically at least – the challenges of the coming century. In the field of labour market policy, for example, the Commission called for a broad 'advanced training offensive' and other measures to enhance labour market flexibility. This reorientation was taken further at the 1994 EU summit in Essen, when it was finally recognized that effective employment policies conducted exclusively at the national level can no longer be successfully managed under the conditions of globalization and European integration (Hoffman and Hoffman 1998: 124). The Treaty of Amsterdam, which was signed on 2 October 1997 and entered into force on 1 May 1999, finally embedded a commitment to full employment as a 'matter of common concern' for the EU, translated this into the goal of reaching a 'high level of employment' without undermining competitiveness, and established an Employment Committee to discuss appropriate policy in this area and to monitor progress. In line with the European Union penchant for 'metagovernance' rather than direct top-down intervention, however, the Community's responsibility in this area is to complement the activities of member states by developing a 'coordinated strategy', to formulate common guidelines, to establish benchmarks and 'best practice', and to monitor the pursuit of national action plans for employment. This penetration of the workfarist reorientation of social policy to the EU level is also linked to the expansion of the directly 'economic' into areas previously regarded as non-economic. An aspect of this, noted by Deppe et al. (2000: 15–16), is that, for the first time, the breadth of the EU labour market guidelines has forced the ministries of economy, culture, finance, welfare and labour to present a joint plan and interweave separate policies. This approach was consolidated at the Lisbon Summit in 2000, when the European Union committed itself to becoming the most competitive knowledge-based economy in the world whilst maintaining the European social model.

Third, almost by definition, European economic and social policy illustrates the post-nationality of the emerging welfare regimes. Before reviewing the EU's role, however, we should note that it is part of a wider, more complex internationalization of economic and social policy. EU policies are evolving in a larger framework of agenda-setting and policy-making by international institutions, supranational apparatuses, intergovernmental organizations and forums, transnational think tanks, and transnational interest groups and social movements (cf. Deacon and Hulse 1997; on policy transfer, see Dolowitz and Marsh 1996; Peck and Theodore 2001; and Stella 2000). It is important to recognize, with Deacon and Hulse (1997), that there is some real disagreement among these different bodies on policy recommendations; but this should not be exaggerated since the bodies aligned with the 'Washington Consensus' tend to be the most influential in the internationalization of economic and social policy. In particular, they note some convergence between EU and OECD policies as the EU has discovered the adverse impact on competitiveness of KWNS social policy and the OECD's Directorate of Education, Employment, Labour and Social Affairs has come to recognize the economic benefits of expanded income support programmes (Deacon and Hulse 1997: 45–58). This development, mediated through an increasingly dense web of parallel power networks, reflects the increased formation of a transnational capitalist class concerned to secure the conditions for capital accumulation on a global scale. This is linked to a 'new constitutionalism' (Gill 2001), that is, an attempt to establish a new articulation between the economic and the political on a global rather than merely national scale. But it is also associated, as noted above, with attempts to re-articulate the relationship between the economic and the extra-economic conditions for capital accumulation in a globalizing, post-Fordist, knowledge-based economy.

The EU is a key player as well as a key site in the struggles to shape this new constitutional settlement. It acts both as a relay for American neo-liberal pressures to redesign the world order and as an advocate of an alternative European model. Its central role in this regard also makes it a crucial site for contending political forces both within and beyond the EU as they seek to shape its overall strategic direction and/or specific economic and social policies (cf. van Apeldoorn 2002; Ziltener 1999). This can be seen in its general commitment to the reorientation of economic and social policy away from the primacy of the national scale in post-war 'embedded liberalism' towards a post-national 'embedded neo-liberalism' – albeit one inflected differently from the hegemonic American model. At the same time, however, the tendential Europeanization of economic and social policy is closely linked, in accordance with the principle of subsidiarity, to the increased role of subnational and cross-national agencies, territorial and/or functional in form, in its formulation and implementation. In this regard there is an interesting scalar division of labour between the EU, national states, and subnational tiers of government. For, whereas national states retain significant powers in the traditional spheres of the sovereign state (military, police) and in welfare policy (where the limited EU budget blocks a major role in general social redistribution even if it acquired this competence), the EU has acquired increasing influence over economic policy.

Fourth, because the EU has never acquired the characteristics of a supranational sovereign state or even a confederation of states, it cannot be said to have undergone a straightforward shift from supranational govern*ment* to supranational govern*ance*. Nonetheless, it has developed an increasingly wide and deep array of both governance and metagovernance capacities that enable it to influence economic and social policy in most areas and on most scales. In this regard, it is plausible to speak of the growing development of multiscalar metagovernance capacities at the EU level (Jessop 2004f, 2006c; see below). Specific features of the EU give it special capacities to engage in metagovernance across different tiers of government, different functional systems, and different stakeholders: the role of judges and litigation (which enables the EU to override national laws and to 'constitutionalize' the treaties), its location at the heart of information flows (which gives it a relative monopoly in organizational intelligence), its fiscal poverty (which limits its vulnerability to claims on public spending and thereby circumscribes the political agenda) (Sbragia 2000); and the increasing adoption of European projects and guidelines which entitle the EU to monitor national and regional state activities and partnerships across an increasingly interconnected set of policy areas – thereby giving a means to steer national policy and endow it with greater coherence (Deppe et al. 2000; Majone 1993; Telò 2002; Wallace 2000).

The European Union and Multiscalar Metagovernance

I now consider the emergence of metagovernance in the European Union as part of the more general change in the forms of statehood. Metagovernance is a response to governance failure. The latter occurs on two levels: the failure of particular attempts at governance using a particular governance mechanism and the more general failure of a mode of governance. Thus, corresponding to the three basic modes of governance, namely, the anarchy of the market, the hierarchy of command, and the heterarchy of networks, we can distinguish three basic modes of metagovernance and one overarching mode. First, there is the reflexive redesign of individual markets and/or the reflexive reordering of relations among two or more markets by modifying their operation, nesting, articulation, embedding, disembedding, or re-embedding. There are also 'markets in markets'. This can lead to 'regime shopping', competitive 'races to the bottom', or, in certain conditions, 'races to the top'. Moreover, because markets function in the shadow of hierarchy and/or heterarchy, attempts are also made by non-market agents to modify markets, their institutional supports, and their agents to improve their efficiency and/or compensate for market failures and inadequacies. Second, there is the reflexive redesign of organizations, the creation of intermediating organizations, the reordering of inter-organizational relations, and the management of organizational ecologies (i.e., the organization of the conditions of organizational evolution in conditions where many organizations co-exist, compete, cooperate, and co-evolve). This is reflected in the continuing redesign, re-scaling, and adaptation of the state apparatus, sometimes more ruptural, sometimes more continuous, and the manner in which it is embedded within the wider political system. And, third, there is the reflexive organization of the conditions of self-organization through dialogue and deliberation. There are many activities involved here, from organizing opportunities for spontaneous sociability, through various measures to promote networking and negotiation, to the facilitation of 'institutional thickness'. Fourth, and finally, there is collibration or 'metagovernance' proper. This involves managing the complexity, plurality, and tangled hierarchies found in prevailing modes of coordination. It is the organization of the conditions for governance and involves the judicious mixing of market, hierarchy, and networks to achieve the best possible outcomes from the viewpoint of those engaged in metagovernance. In this sense it also means the organization of the conditions of governance in terms of their structurally inscribed strategic selectivity, that is, in terms of their asymmetrical privileging of some outcomes over others. However, since every practice is prone to failure, metagovernance and collibration are also likely to fail. So there is no Archimedean point from which governance or collibration can be guaranteed to succeed, and an element of irony is required in attempts to engage in collibration in the face of likely failure.

Governments play a major and increasing role in all aspects of metagovernance: they get involved in redesigning markets, in constitutional change and the juridical re-regulation of organizational forms and objectives, in organizing the conditions for self-organization, and, most importantly, in collibration. Thus metagovernance does not eliminate other modes of coordination. Markets, hierarchies, and heterarchies still exist; but they operate in a context of 'negotiated decision-making'. On the one hand, market competition will be balanced by cooperation; the invisible hand will be combined with a visible handshake. On the other hand, the state is no longer the sovereign authority. It becomes just one participant among others in the pluralistic guidance system and contributes its own distinctive resources to the negotiation process. As the range of networks, partnerships, and other models of economic and political governance expand, official apparatuses remain at best first among equals.

It is in this context that we can best interpret the continuities and discontinuities in the development of the European Union as a moment in the structural transformation and strategic reorientation of statehood in a world of states that is not limited to Europe but extends to the global polity (cf. Hettne 1997; Shaw 2000; Sørensen 2001). For the EU can be seen as a major and, indeed, increasingly important, supranational instance of *multiscalar metagovernance* in relation to a wide range of complex and interrelated problems. While the sources and reach of these problems go well beyond the territorial space occupied by its member states, the EU is an important, if complex, point of intersection (or node) in the emerging, hypercomplex, and chaotic system of global governance (or, better, metagovernance) and is seeking to develop its own long-term 'Grand Strategy' for Europe (Telò 2002: 266). But it is still one node among several within this emerging system of global metagovernance and cannot be fully understood without taking account of its complex relations with other nodes located above, below, and transversal to the European Union.

The perceptive reader will have noticed by now that I am using the notion of multiscalar metagovernance rather than multilevel metagovernance. This is because of difficulties in the notion of multilevel governance itself. The latter was introduced to identify a 'third way' between supranational imperative coordination and standardization, on the one hand, and, on the other hand, a relatively anarchic, negatively coordinated, and fragmented pursuit of common economic, social, and political objectives. Its full significance becomes even more evident, however, if this phenomenon is termed multiscalar metagovernance. The notion of MLG could prove misleading on four grounds: (a) it focuses on levels of political organization in a nested territorial hierarchy and, in this sense, reflects the period when the main axis of theoretical and political debate concerned the respective merits of supranationalism and intergovernmentalism; (b) it directs attention to relations of vertical interdependence, communication, and joint decision-making without emphasizing the tangled and shifting nature of dominant, nodal, and marginal levels of government in different areas; (c) it tends to focus on specific policy and issue areas rather than coordination problems across different areas; and (d) despite reference to governance, it is often more concerned with government and, when it does deal with governance, it neglects problems of 'metagovernance'. In practice, however, many studies of MLG have escaped these potential traps in their theoretical and/or empirical analyses.

It would nonetheless be more precise and productive to discuss such institutional patterns, political practices, and policy processes in terms of *multiscalar metagovernance*. This alternative concept highlights: (a) the irreducible plurality of levels, scales, areas, and sites that are involved in, affected by, and/or mobilized in these institutions, practices, and processes; (b) the complex, tangled, and interwoven nature of the relevant political relations, which include important horizontal and transversal linkages – indicated in notions such as 'network state' or 'network polity' – as well as the vertical linkages implied in multilevel governance; (c) the importance of metagovernance as the reflexive art of balancing government and other forms of governance to create requisite variety, flexibility, and adaptability in coordinated policy-formulation, policy-making, and implementation; and (d) the plurality and, indeed, heterogeneity of actors potentially involved in such institutions and practices, which stretch well beyond different tiers of government and well beyond the confines of the European Union as an administrative, political, or economic space. This is quite explicit in the Lisbon European Council statement itself, which recommends not only that the European Union pursue a more coherent and systematic approach to governance to be guided by the European Council, but also that this should involve a 'fully decentralized approach . . . applied in line with the principle of subsidiarity in which the Union, the Member States, the regional and local levels, as well as the social partners and civil society, will be actively involved, using variable forms of partnership' (Lisbon European Council 2000: paragraphs 37–8).

It is clearly premature at a time when the European Union is conducting yet another debate on its future governance to predict the eventual shape of what is bound to be a complex and compromise-based form of multiscalar metagovernance in the shadow of a post-national form of statehood. This underlines that the development of multilevel metagovernance is a reflexive process, involving intergovernmental conferences and other modes of meta-constitutional conversation (Walker 2000). But there can be little doubt that the overall movement is towards metagovernance rather than a re-scaling of the traditional form of sovereign statehood or a revamped form of intergovernmentalism inherited from earlier rounds of European integration. As an institutionalized form of metagovernance, emphasis falls on efforts at collibration in an unstable equilibrium of compromise rather than on a systematic, consistent resort to one dominant method of coordination of complex interdependence. Apparent inconsistencies may be part of an overall self-organizing, self-adjusting practice of metagovernance within a complex division of government and governance powers. Seen as a form of metagovernance, the emphasis is on a combination of 'super-vision' and 'supervision', that is, a relative monopoly of organized intelligence and overall monitoring of adherence to benchmarks. But in this evolving framework, there is also a synergetic division of metagovernance labour between the European Council, the specialized Councils, and the European Commission. The European Council is the political metagovernance network of prime ministers that decides on the overall political dynamic around economic and social objectives, providing a 'centripetal orientation of subsidiarity' (Telò 2002: 253), acting by qualified majority, and playing a key intergovernmental and monitoring role. The European Commission plays a key metagovernance role in organizing parallel power networks, providing expertise and recommendations, developing benchmarks, monitoring progress, exchanging best practice, promoting mutual learning, and ensuring continuity and coherence across Presidencies. This is associated with increasing networking across old and new policy fields at the European level as well as with a widening range of economic, political, and social forces that are being drawn into multilevel consultation, policy formulation, and policy implementation.

New methods of multiscalar metagovernance are being developed and combined in a complex system of metagovernance (cf. Scott and Trubek 2002) that is 'being made more precise and applied (with adaptations as for its intensity) to other fundamental policy fields, traditionally under the competence of national and subnational authorities: education, structural reform and internal market, technological innovation and knowledge-based society, research and social protection' (Telò 2002: 253).[1] From a strategic-relational perspective, this clearly implies a shift in the strategic selectivities of the modes of governance and metagovernance in the European Union. For, while it builds on past patterns of liberal intergovernmentalism and neo-functionalist spillover, it has its own distinctive momentum and will weaken – without fully replacing – more hierarchical forms of coordination (whether intergovernmental or supranational). It also entails complementary changes in the strategic selectivities of national states and subordinate levels of government and governance, calling for new forms of strategic coordination and new forms of (meta)governance in and across a wide range of policy fields. Nonetheless, statehood in the European Union is still evolving and, given the tendencies towards failure inherent in all major forms of governance (market, hierarchy, network, etc.) as well as metagovernance, continuing experimentation, improvisation, and adaptation are highly probable (cf. Dehousse 2002; Radaelli 2003).

The pattern of multiscalar metagovernance in the European Union is still evolving and, given the inherent tendencies towards failure typical of metagovernance as well as of all major forms of governance (market, hierarchy, network, etc), continuing experimentation, improvisation, and adaptation is only to be expected. Nonetheless,

> the perspective would be that of a new system of democratic legitimacy and governance: multilevel (international, national, supranational, transnational), multifaced (territorial, functional, modern and post-modern) and with a multitude of actors (social, economic, political and cultural; institutional and extra-institutional), rather than that of a classical democratic normative model – federal/constitutional or democrat/republican. (Telò 2002: 266; cf. Schmitter 1992)

Thus the key issue for a research agenda into this new form of statehood becomes the manner and extent to which the multiplying levels, arenas, and regimes of politics, policy-making, and policy implementation can be endowed with a certain apparatus and operational unity horizontally and vertically; and how this affects the overall operation of politics and the legitimacy of the new political arrangements.

Conclusions

I have argued that neither the state- nor the governance-centric perspective is adequate for analysing the complexities of multiscalar metagovernance in Europe. Each approach is flawed theoretically in its own distinctive ways;

nor can their respective deficits be overcome by combining them to produce a more coherent account. Each approach is also plagued to different degrees by anachronistic views about the contemporary world – whether about the state or about the objects and subjects of governance. This means that neither approach can capture the novelty of the emerging European polity as a 'political machine' for multiscalar metagovernance (cf. Barry 2001). The alternative approach offered here draws on the SRA and its application to the more general transformation of contemporary political economy as a means to contextualize and 'theoretically mediate' recent changes in statehood. This has two sets of implications for future research.

First, regarding the more immediate questions of governance and metagovernance, the SRA emphasizes the strategic selectivity of institutional arrangements. Multilevel government, multilevel governance, and multiscalar metagovernance arrangements will all have their own distinctive strategic selectivities: that is, they are never neutral among actors, interests, spatio-temporal horizons, alliances, strategies, tactics, and so on. They also have their own distinctive modalities of success, failure, tension, crisis, reflexivity, and crisis-management. These selectivities and modalities depend on specific institutional, organizational, and practical contexts and few generalizations are possible about them (for further discussion, including some possibly hubristic generalizations, see Jessop 2003c). Nonetheless, one generalization that can safely be hazarded is that the belief that multilevel governance can solve old problems without creating new ones is wishful thinking (cf. Mayntz 2001). In turn this implies the need for an ironic, experimental approach to multiscalar metagovernance that is concerned to ensure requisite variety in available modes of coordination as well as appropriate levels of reflexivity, super-vision, and supervision in their combination and implementation (cf. Jessop 1997b).

Second, and perhaps more importantly, it is only by situating the changing political forms of the European Union as part of the ongoing transformation and attempted re-regulation of global capitalism as well as part of the more general transformation of statehood in response to major sociocultural as well as politico-economic changes that one can adequately understand what is at stake in these changes. Among other interesting results, this approach reinforces the importance of examining not only *multilevel (or, better, multiscalar) governance* but also *multiscalar metagovernance*. For the development of the European Union can be seen as part of continuing efforts (often at cross-purposes) by key economic and political actors to produce an appropriate balance between different modes of economic and political coordination across functional and territorial divides and to ensure, under the primacy of the political, a measure of apparatus unity and political legitimacy for the European Union. This has taken different forms at different periods in the pursuit of the European project, especially as this has been shaped at different times by shifts in the relative weight of Atlanticist and European economic and political strategies, by shifts in the relative weight of liberal and neo-liberal *échangiste* (money capital) perspectives and neo-corporatist and neo-mercantilist productivist projects, and by the tendential shift from a KWNS approach, concerned to create a single market to realize economies of scale, to a SWPR approach, concerned to transform the European Union into the most competitive and dynamic knowledge-based economy and to 'modernize' the European social model. In addition, of course, this European-wide multiscalar metagovernance project is being conducted in conditions of successive rounds of expansion (which have increased the heterogeneity of the growth dynamics and modes of regulation of different regional and national economies as well as the forms and extent of uneven development and inequalities) and in conditions where national economies and national states have been subject to their own individual structural problems and crises as well as the shared crisis-tendencies derived from their integration into the circuits of Atlantic Fordism and into the emerging globalizing knowledge-based economy. And, finally, this multiscalar metagovernance project is part of a broader post-Westphalian 'meta-constitutional conversation' that is occurring between non-state and state actors (including meta-states such as the EU) as they struggle to develop and institutionalize a new political order (Walker 2000). While it has been impossible here to develop the analysis that this approach demands, enough should have been said to show the promise of the SRA as one among several options to be explored in future work on the European Union.

10

Complexity, Contingent Necessity, Semiosis, and the SRA

[A]ll science would be superfluous if the outward appearances and essence of things directly coincided.

(Marx 1894: 817)

Do not multiply complications beyond what is necessary but do introduce as many as are necessary.

(cf. Jessop 1982: 214–17)[1]

This chapter presents a preliminary account of the mutual implications of complexity and critical realism and indicates how to apply this account by moving towards a cultural political economy of contemporary capitalism. In this way I hope to avoid complexity becoming a 'chaotic conception' (Marx 1857: 100; cf. Sayer 2000) that can provide neither a coherent research object nor a coherent explanatory principle. Thus I distinguish between complexity in general and specific modes of complexity and argue against using complexity as a metaphor without regard to its modalities in particular contexts. The four main sections of the chapter address the following problems: (a) the complexity of complexity and the implications of contingent necessity for research strategy; (b) complexity reduction and the strategic-relational approach; (c) the role of semiosis in complexity reduction and its implications for cultural political economy; and (d) some key features of a fourth-generation strategic-relational agenda.

Complexity and Contingent Necessity

Complexity is complex. There are many ways to define complexity and not all are relevant to critical realism and the strategic-relational approach. Thus my first task is to reduce the complexity of complexity in order to connect it to critical realism and the SRA rather than to another topic. Indeed such an act of simplification is an inevitable task for any agent (or operating system) in the face of complexity (cf. Luhmann 1989, 1995). Focusing on the nature of complexity in the natural *and social* worlds would enable us to understand the distinctive contribution of the strategic-relational approach, critical semiosis, and, for some purposes, cultural political economy to social description and explanation. Thus I now identify different forms of complexity, assess their implications for the possibility of knowledge, and suggest that the social world, whilst inevitably socially constructed, has emergent properties that can also be seen as mind-independent – especially from the viewpoint of non-participant observers. I begin with descriptive complexity and then turn to the more fundamental question of ontological complexity.

Rescher argues that

> the number of true descriptive remarks that can be made about a thing – about any concrete element of existence and, in specific, any particular physical object – is theoretically inexhaustible. . . . there is no inherent limit to the number of distinct descriptive kinds or categories to which the things of this world can belong. As best we can possibly tell, natural reality has an infinite descriptive depth. It confronts us with a law of natural complexity: *There is no limit to the number of natural kinds to which any concrete particular belongs.* (1998: 28, italics in original; cf. Baecker 2001: 63)

Marx had developed a similar, critical realist argument in his distinction between the real-concrete as the complex synthesis of multiple determinations and the real-concrete as the reproduction of the real-concrete in thought (Marx 1857: 101). He missed the ontological, epistemological, and methodological impossibility of ever exhausting the real-concrete through its reproduction in thought. Yet he was well aware that '[e]very beginning is difficult, holds in all sciences' (Marx 1867: 18).

In this sense, as I suggested in the general introduction, to start an analysis of the complexities of the social world from the viewpoint of capital accumulation may not prove the best entry point for any and all investigations. While it might be suitable for cases where the logic of capital accumulation is the dominant mode of societalization (*Vergesellschaftungsmodus*) and/or the theoretical object under investigation is heavily influenced by this logic, it may be less appropriate for cases where other modes of societalization are dominant and/or have the strongest influence on the relevant theoretical object. This is reflected in what Mann (1986) has called, in connection with the state, the polymorphous crystallization of state power; and is used to justify his emphasis on other organizing logics in his organizational materialism (Mann 1986). From a very different philosophical viewpoint, Rickert (1902/1986) developed a similar argument at the turn of the nineteenth century and extended it to the social world (as had Windelband and, no doubt, others before him). He too argued that the world is an infinitely extensive set of objects, each of which is infinitely subdivisible, so that we confront an 'extensively' as well as 'intensively' infinite 'manifold' of particulars. It follows, Rickert continued, that our knowledge cannot be anything like a copy or a reproduction of reality; indeed, we cannot know any object or event in all of its aspects. From this, he drew significant implications for the social as well as natural sciences (on which, see Rickert 1986: 61–137, and below).

More generally, Rescher states:

> It is the very limitation of our knowledge of things – our recognition that reality extends beyond the horizons of what we can possibly know or even conjecture about – that most effectively betokens the mind-independence of the real. A world that is inexhaustible by our minds cannot easily be seen to be a product of their operations. (1998: 52)

Such arguments clearly derive from the *descriptive* complexity of entities and their relations with other entities in the real world. Thus they could perhaps be dismissed as concerned more with epistemic than ontological complexity. But there is a strong connection between epistemic and ontological complexity that bears directly on the relevance of critical realism and the strategic-relational approach in the social sciences. So let me now turn to ontological complexity.

Rescher distinguishes three modes of ontological complexity (each with two or more subtypes): compositional, structural, and operational. The precise details are irrelevant for present purposes. For each mode of complexity poses the same cognitive problem noted above, namely, that the world is too complex ever to be fully grasped by the human mind (or, indeed, any mind). But here the problem is not so much one of the cognitive capacities of the mind (or, better, of science in its transitive dimension) as the ontological (or intransitive) features of complex entities that are at stake.

Two such ontological features are worth noting here. First, there is the question of possibility and compossibility, which is closely related to strategic-relational issues such as path-shaping and path-dependency, operational autonomy and material interdependence, and strategic coordination and structural coupling (see below):

> [E]ntities and their relations in the real world not only have more properties than they ever will overtly manifest, but they have more than they possibly can ever manifest. This is so because the dispositional properties

of things always involve what might be characterized as *mutually pre-emptive* conditions of realization. . . . The perfectly possible realization of various dispositions may fail to be mutually *compossible*, and so the dispositional properties of a thing cannot ever be manifested completely – not just in practice, but in principle. Our objective claims about real things always commit us to more than we can actually ever determine about them. (Rescher 1998: 38; cf. the comments on compossibility and cogredience in chapter 8 above, p. [187])

This point is closely linked to the critical realist distinction between the real and the actual and so, *pace* Rescher,[2] should not be tied too tightly to experience or even experientiability at the cost of careful consideration of the nature of the actual.

Second, the scope for interaction among complex entities, the emergence of new entities and processes therefrom, the simplifications that are introduced by operating agents or systems to reduce complexity to manageable limits, and the emergent effects of such simplifications all tend to mean that complexity becomes self-potentiating. In short, as Luhmann was also wont to emphasize, complexity *breeds complexity*. Or, as Rescher puts it in a remarkably anthropic statement:

Complex systems generally function so as to engender further principles of order that possibilize additional complexities. Complex organisms militate towards complex societies, complex machines towards complex industries, complex armaments towards complex armies. And the world's complexity means that there is, now and always, more to reality than our science – or for that matter our speculation and our philosophy – is able to dream of. (1998: 28)

What do complexity and its self-potentiation imply for analyses of the real world? It is worth distinguishing three sets of implications here: ontological, epistemological, and methodological.

Ontologically, complexity refers to the compositional, structural, or operational nature of events, phenomena, or other relational objects in the real world. Such complexity applies to the natural and social worlds. Social as well as natural events, phenomena, or relational objects can have the naturally necessary features that characterize (one or more of) compositional, structural, or operational complexity. Since complex entities and their interactions have many naturally necessary potentialities that may not be realized and/or cannot be co-realized, there is a necessary impredictability and indeterminacy about their operation. I have tried to capture this with the concept of 'contingent necessity'. The seeming *contradictio in adjecto* in this concept disappears if one recognizes that contingency and necessity have different referents. For 'contingent necessity' indicates both the *de facto* causal determination (necessity) of events and phenomena and their *ex ante* indeterminability (contingency). In other words, events and phenomena are the product of the non-necessary interaction among different causal chains to produce a definite outcome that first became necessary through the contingent articulation of various causal chains (Jessop 1982: 212–14, 218–19, 252, 254; 1985a: 136, 138–144, 188, 216, 343–5; 1990b: 4, 11–13; 1996; and 2002a).

As a feature of the real world, contingent necessity both presupposes and reinforces that world's ontological complexity. Indeed, if the development of the real world involves an infinite succession of contingently interdependent as well as contingently necessary 'contingent necessities', then that world is an infinitely complex open system. This poses a series of questions about how one can best grasp the 'complexity of complexity' in the real world. *Inter alia*, this means that: '(a) the same causes can lead to different and/or divergent effects; (b) different causes can produce the same effects; (c) small causes can entrain very big effects; (d) big causes can produce quite small effects; (e) causes are followed by contrary effects; (f) the effects of antagonistic causes are uncertain' (Schriewer 1999: 91, citing Morin 1980). This excludes any simple algorithm to generate explanations of complex phenomena. Contingent necessity implies the infinite complexity of the real world, and the infinite complexity of the real world implies contingent necessity. This requires us to pursue complexity reduction (i.e., to engage in methodological simplificationism) as well as to adopt methodological relationalism (on the former, see Rescher 1998; on the latter, see Bourdieu and Wacquant 1992; and chapter 1 above). To comprehend reality is thus to simplify and to transform it in the light of a cognitive strategy, and it is in this context that critical semiotic analysis and, especially from a strategic-relational viewpoint, the concept of the 'imaginary' are especially important.

Epistemologically, if the real world is infinitely complex, it cannot be exhausted analytically. This excludes any copy theory of knowledge such that the result of an inquiry involves no more (but no less) than the reproduction of the real world in all its complexity (this is the hubristic error of Marx in his 1857 Introduction). Instead it requires that we select simplifying entry points into that complexity and recognize that all knowledge is partial, provisional, and incompletable. One of the differences among disciplines is the ways in which they set about dividing the real world into manageable sets of theoretical objects (which in turn they may help to constitute in the real world), adopt entry points into their investigation, and explore the interrelations among different aspects of reality, either as divided up by different disciplines or as they emerge from the process of investigation. However, as objects change, specific disciplinary boundaries, divisions of labour, and entry points may become less relevant. This could lead either to further disciplinary subdivisions, transdisciplinarity, or post-disciplinarity (see Jessop and Sum 2001).

In addition, if 'contingent necessities' exist, adequately to explain them requires one to combine concepts, assumptions, and principles of analysis from different theoretical domains and to link them to a given, theoretically defined explanandum. Thus an explanation is only more or less satisfactory relative to a given explanandum that has been isolated (and thus 'constructed') by an observer out of that infinite complexity (cf. Jessop 1982: 213–20). Weber spoke of the practical impossibility (and, in many cases, theoretical redundancy) of following causal relationships down to the microscopic level of necessary connections among the elementary constituents of reality (Ringer 2000: 71–2). This applies regardless of the relatively macro–micro nature of the problem[3] and/or the generality of the historical developments and outcomes to be explained. The key issue is to explain specific explananda in terms of specific causal antecedents, suggesting how specific causal processes or causal intersections from among many possible intersections intervened to produce something that would not otherwise have happened. As noted in chapter 1, this involves a process of attribution, that is, the selection from among many possible causal linkages of those that are regarded as causally effective for this particular explanandum. Redefining the explanandum, extending its spatio-temporal context, or identifying a wider range of relevant causal factors would change the attribution. In this regard, from a strategic-relational perspective, causal explanation, whether by observers or participants, always involves simplification and is, *a fortiori*, contingently necessary and potentially contestable. This is especially important when it comes to explaining events, processes, and outcomes where relations of power and domination are involved and/or where the nature, causes, and solutions to crises are at issue.

More generally, this suggests that we should combine concepts, explanatory principles, and so on, from different disciplines and overcome the distinction between *Gesetzes-* and *Wirklichkeitswissenschaften*. While the former (i.e., the nomological sciences) abstract from the real world to discover general laws and law-like regularities that have limited substantive content, the latter (i.e., disciplines concerned with reality)[4] are concerned with the singularity of specific events and processes, whether these be relatively micro- or macro- in nature. From a critical realist, strategic-relational viewpoint, laws and tendencies are doubly tendential: that is, these tendencies exist to the extent that the mechanisms that generate them are themselves tendentially reproduced. This is particularly important in the social world, where the tendencies associated with specific sets of social relations are themselves only tendentially reproduced in and through social action. And, in turn, the singularities investigated in the *Wirklichkeitswissenschaften* can be understood in terms of contingent necessities that are the product of interaction among the material, discursive, and strategic mechanisms of the natural and social worlds.

Moreover, since explanations cannot fully explain a specific event or process in all its complexity, the investigator must consider 'the degree of generalization and abstraction necessary – and defensible – in the "comparison" between imagined and actual antecedents, causal sequences, and outcomes', or, again, think about 'how best to conceptually isolate the set of antecedent conditions that more or less strongly "favor" the result to be explained' (Ringer 2000: 66 and 67). This implies that 'causal "moments" are not simply given in immediate experience' (Ringer 2000: 71), and this, in turn, explains 'the inescapably "abstract" character of causal analysis' (Weber 1949:113–81). This means in turn that knowledge of a complex world can at best only achieve something akin to 'reasonable approximation'. Another implication is that '[o]ur conceptions of things always present a *moving* rather than a *fixed* object of consideration, and this historical dimension must also be reckoned with. It is thus not only instructive but ultimately essential to view our knowledge of the properties of things in a temporal perspective' (Rescher 1998: 33–4). In other words, 'we expect to have to change our minds about their nature and modes of comportment' (Rescher 1998: 34, italics in original). Similar arguments were presented, of course, in Marx's 1857 Introduction on the movement from abstract-simple to concrete-complex objects (1857: 99–103).

Methodologically, a method is required that respects complexity and contingent necessity. The method of articulation is appropriate here. This involves the dual movement from abstract to concrete along one plane of analysis and from simple to complex as more analytical planes are introduced in order to produce increasingly adequate explanations (Jessop 1982: 213–19; 2001a). This will often involve serious forensic problems of causal attribution in the face of many competing explanations, and resolving these problems could well involve a resort to counterfactual and / or comparative reasoning (Luhmann 1970, 1995; Ringer 2000: 169). Ragin is one of several methodologists who have attempted to specify case- and variable-oriented methods of comparative analysis in order to provide more substantive bases for such counterfactual reasoning (Ragin 1987, 2000). There is a major role for counterfactual reasoning in causal analysis in identifying the relative significance or rank order of different causes in producing a given effect. As the preceding paragraphs have suggested, these ontological, epistemological, and methodological aspects of complexity are closely related. But we must still take care to distinguish them – both to avoid possible misunderstandings and to exploit their connections in developing a critical realist philosophy of the social sciences.

Complexity reinforces the case for critical realism and strategic-relational analysis. For critical realism distinguishes between the real, the actual, and the empirical and thereby allows for the differential realization of possibilities and/or compossibilities, can distinguish between ontological complexity, epistemic complexity, and descriptive complexity, is premised on the distinction between the intransitive nature of the natural and social world and the transitive nature of its machinic or living observation (through, in the case of social observation, non-scientific as well as scientific categories and methods), and insists upon the fallibility and corrigibility of knowledge in line with the prevailing protocols associated with different observational paradigms (including those of scientific investigation). Complexity also highlights the relevance of the concept of *contingent necessity* to the investigation of complex entities, processes, and events. Thus, whereas ontological complexity is especially relevant to the first two levels of a critical realist ontology (the real and the actual), formulaic complexity is especially relevant to its second and third levels (actual and empirical).

'Contingent necessity' indicates certain properties of 'real-concrete' phenomena and explores their ontological, epistemological, methodological, and substantive implications. It assumes that everything that happens in the real world must happen, that is, is in some sense 'necessary'. Rejecting this assumption would render much scientific inquiry pointless. It is the precise meaning of necessity, however, that is at stake in 'contingent necessity'. For it need not, does not, and cannot mean that whatever happens in the real world is due to a *single* causal mechanism. Instead the concrete actualization of events results from the *interaction* of diverse causal tendencies and counter-tendencies. Now, whilst it may be tempting to argue that this interaction itself can serve as the single causal mechanism that necessarily generates the necessary happening, this is invalid because the nature and outcome of this interaction cannot be attributed to the operation of a single causal mechanism. For such interactions result from interactions among diverse causal tendencies and counter-tendencies: they are the result of interactions among interactions.

This opens the route to an infinite explanatory regress into the path-dependent past, but, as Rescher notes in his rendering of Occam's razor, complications should not be multiplied beyond what is necessary (1998: 62; see also note 1). Thus, to avoid infinite regress, it is essential to define the material, social, and spatio-temporal limits of any explanandum. This lends itself to more extensive genealogical analysis and/or a selective focus on the current conjuncture. Nonetheless, from a strategic-relational view-point, even the current conjuncture cannot be analysed as an abstract 'point' without spatio-temporal depth and extent. Instead it demands a strategic-relational conjunctural analysis relevant to particular actors, identities, interests, spatio-temporal horizons, and strategic objectives. From a genealogical viewpoint, the current conjuncture is the *necessary* product of *contingent* interactions among different sets of causal mechanisms in the past and present. From the viewpoint of strategic-relational context analysis, the current conjuncture is an asymmetrical strategic terrain that offers differential material, spatio-temporal, and social opportunities for different actors to pursue different objectives in a heterogeneous set of time-space geometries ranging from the immediate 'here-now' to world society in an indeterminate future. Seen in these terms, of course, contingent necessity also implies an unbounded surplus of (unmanageable, often mutually exclusive) future possibilities such that the social world has an 'open' structure (cf. Luhmann 1979: 6, 13). From a strategic-relational viewpoint, then, even before we introduce issues such as contradictions, dilemmas, paradoxes, and undecidability, it entails the necessity of choice and the contingency of what gets chosen (cf. Scherrer 1995).

Complexity and the Strategic-Relational Approach

I now address the conventional distinction between the natural and social sciences and their implications for a strategic-relational analysis of the social world. In his treatment of the possibility of naturalism, that is, similarity between the methods of both the natural and social sciences, Bhaskar rejects both the reductionist view that the phenomena of the social world can be reduced to those of the natural world and the scientistic view that there is no difference in the methods of the natural and social sciences. Instead he argues that the natural and social sciences share certain ontological, epistemological, and relational considerations but that there are also significant differences between them due to the importance of meaning in action (Bhaskar 1989: 44–55, 80–90). However, if we reconsider the distinction between the natural and social sciences from a complexity perspective, Bhaskar's argument requires redefinition. For the operation of all living systems could be said to involve meaning, that is, the drawing of system–environment boundaries, selective attention to events within the system and its environment, and capacities for selective learning. Thus it may be more useful, at the risk of falling into the trap of a radical constructivism that privileges subjective construal over material construction, to distinguish between two modes of observing natural and social systems rather than between natural and social systems as such. This is also reflected in the development of cognitive or information approaches to the natural world; and attempts to build a natural science of society alongside interpretive, hermeneutic, and phenomenological approaches to social action.

The two modes of observing complex natural and social systems examine the complexity of operations and the complexity of meaning, respectively. In the first case, the scientist seeks to describe and explain the structuring of specific complex systems, i.e., the disjunction between the full set of all logically possible relations among the elements of a system and the relative probability or improbability of the actual realization of such logically possible relations. A related question is why certain possible properties of the system rather than others come to be realized in specific circumstances. This first mode of observation directs attention towards the selective bias (or limited selective capacity) in a given system's operation(s). In this sense, the structure of a system characterized by 'organized complexity' would consist in the rules governing the selection of possible configurations of its elements. In the second case, what is at stake is the complexity of observation, i.e., the fact that the world is pregnant with many possibilities for action (or inaction). This problem concerns uncertainty about the conclusions to be drawn from actual observations in a situation where one cannot observe everything (Luhmann 1990a: 81–2). It follows that

> [m]eaning always involves focusing attention on one possibility among many. . . . There is always a core that is given and taken for granted which is surrounded by references to other possibilities that cannot be pursued at the same time. Meaning, then, is actuality surrounded by possibilities. The structure of meaning is the structure of this difference between actuality and potentiality. Meaning is the link between the actual and the possible; it is not one or the other. (Luhmann 1990a: 83)

This emphasis on selectivity is quite consistent with the notion of complexity. Luhmann expresses this well in the following statement:

> Complexity thus means that every operation is a selection, whether intentional or not, whether controlled or not, whether observed or not.

Being an element of a system, an operation cannot avoid bypassing other possibilities. Only because this is the case can we observe an operation selecting a particular course to the exclusion of others. And only because operations can be observed, self-observation becomes possible (be it necessary or not as a requirement of the operation itself). Enforced selectivity is the condition of the possibility for both operation and observation. Further, enforced selectivity is the core problem that defines complexity as a problem for both operations and observations. The latter statement is at the basis of my contention that *meaning is nothing but a way to experience and to handle enforced selectivity*. (1990a: 82, italics in original)

Meaning provides a way to cope with complexity under the unavoidable condition of enforced selectivity, that is, the inability to observe everything in a complex world, let alone to do so contemporaneously and then to act on those observations in real time. Since observation takes time, rules tend to evolve for selecting what to select for observation; and, where action is required, for selecting which causal mechanisms to attempt to activate or, at least, to control, in order to produce specific effects. Here again, then, we encounter the question of enforced selectivity as a condition of 'going on' in the world. This also applies to 'observation' of the world. For, since observation occurs in the world, it is open to (self-)observation. By observing their own observations, observers can reflect on the contingent necessity (situatedness) of their own concepts, categories, and conduct. This is an important source of self-reflexivity and can lead to the redefinition of identities, interests, and objectives and hence to the re-evaluation of strategic contexts, strategies, and projects (see chapter 1). Such processes of (self-)observation and (self-)reflection generate in turn the paradox that complexity reduction mechanisms and practices add to the complexity of the real world (cf. Poggi 1979; Luhmann 1982a, 1989).[5] This is yet another example of the self-potentiation of complexity and relates to what critical semiosis and its elaboration in the form of cultural political economy refer to as the 'imaginary' (see Jessop 2004d; Jessop and Sum 2001).

This distinction between two modes of observing complex systems provides one way to resolve the 'structure–agency' problem in the social sciences. For, if the complexity of their operations and their meaning systems can be seen as complementary foci in observing social systems rather than as opposed claims about their essence, one can relate structure to action, action to structure. This has been noted by Hay: *'[S]tructure–agency is not so much a problem as a language by which ontological differences between contending narratives might be registered'* (2001: 3, italics in original). Structuration theory proposes to do this by bracketing either structure or action and focusing on the other term of the structure–agency duality. The SRA provides a means to escape duality without resort to bracketing. Thus structures are treated analytically as strategic in their form, content, and operation; and actions are treated analytically as structured, more or less context-sensitive, and structuring. Applying this approach involves examining how a given structure may privilege some actors, some identities, some strategies, some spatial and temporal horizons, some actions, over others; and the ways, if any, in which actors (individual and/or collective) take account of this differential privileging through 'strategic-context' analysis when choosing a course of action.[6] In other words it involves studying structures in terms of their structurally inscribed strategic selectivities and actions in terms of (differentially reflexive) structurally oriented strategic calculation (see chapter 1; and Jessop 1996).

Complexity Reduction and Cultural Political Economy

Until now I have been concerned to relate the SRA to issues of ontological and epistemic complexity and to explore the relevance of critical realism as a general meta-theoretical framework for strategic-relational analysis. This indicates why the latest phase in the development of the SRA has combined evolutionary and cultural turns to produce what, in the context of historical materialism, Sum has proposed to call 'cultural political economy' (or CPE). The same general propositions and heuristic can also be applied in contexts outside political economy, so that, like the SRA, it may illuminate any substantive issue in social analysis. The evolutionary turn is concerned with the role of the general evolutionary mechanisms of variation, selection, and retention in the strategic-relational dialectic of path-shaping in the context of path-dependency (Hausner et al. 1995: 5–8). And the cultural turn, which includes approaches oriented to argumentation, narrativity, rhetoric, hermeneutics, identity, reflexivity, historicity, and discourse, is concerned with the crucial role of semiosis in simplifying meaning in the face of complexity and, indeed, in contributing to the social construction as well as the social construal of the social world (on the distinction between construction and construal, see Sayer 2000: 90–3). An appropriate catchall term for all these approaches is *semiosis*, that is, the intersubjective production of meaning (for a good survey of forms of the cultural turn, see Bachmann-Medick 2006). For each assumes that semiosis is causally efficacious as well as meaningful and that semiosis can provide not only a means to *interpret* actual events and processes and their emergent effects but also a means, at least in part, to *explain* them.

The SRA in cultural political economy has three defining features. First, like other currents in evolutionary and institutional political economy and unlike the more usual generic studies of semiosis, CPE opposes transhistorical analyses, insisting that both history and institutions matter. This is where the strategic-relational dialectic of path-dependency and path-shaping and its associated emphasis on the evolutionary mechanisms of variation, selection, and retention (Campbell 1969) have a key role in shaping the dynamics of semiosis. In developing CPE we have called for serious analysis of variation, selection, and retention in terms of semiotic and extra-semiotic mechanisms. Indeed, CPE is especially concerned with the semiotic and extra-semiotic mechanisms that determine the co-evolution of semiotic and extra-semiotic aspects of political economy (and, by extension, of other types of social relation). And, *a fortiori*, it is especially concerned with the structural properties and dynamics that result from such material interactions. It also stresses the materiality of social relations and highlights the constraints involved in processes that operate 'behind the backs' of the relevant agents. This enables us to distinguish cultural political economy from critical discourse analysis in terms of its 'value-added'. For, whereas critical discourse analysis tends to focus on specific texts, to undertake static comparative analyses of selected texts at different times, or to study linguistic corpora over time, CPE is also interested in the variation, selection, and retention of different discourses and, in this regard, is also concerned with their extra-semiotic as well as semiotic features.

Second, unlike many currents in evolutionary and institutional political economy but like other variants of cultural materialism, CPE takes the cultural turn seriously, highlighting the complex relations between meanings and practices (see above). For the production of intersubjective meaning is crucial to the description, understanding, and explanation of economic and political conduct just as it is for other types of behaviour and their emergent properties. It also recognizes that, while semiosis initially refers to the inter-subjective production of meaning, it is also an important element/moment of 'the social' more generally. Indeed, the semiotic turn in the SRA (and its reflection in cultural political economy) refuses any ontological distinction between the social and cultural. Like structure and agency (and other strategic-relational dualities), the social and cultural are dialectically related moments of the social world. Thus the SRA distinguishes between the social moment of social relations in terms of the emergent properties of social interaction that are irreducible to the qualities of the individual parties to the interaction (or individual components or modules of social structures or social ecologies) and their cultural moment in terms of intersubjective meaning, the properties of semiotic systems (such as discourses, genres, genre chains, styles, or inter-textuality), and any subsequent attempts to construe or interpret emergent social properties (for a handbook of critical discourse analysis and introduction to key semiotic concepts, see Fairclough 2003; see also Lakoff and Johnson 1980; van Dijk 1997; Wodak and Meyer 2001).

In stressing the semiotic moment of social relations and of the construal of relations among social relations as well as their material moment as expressed in the emergent patterns and properties of social interaction in different contexts and on different scales, CPE aims to avoid two complementary temptations in social analysis. The first is the temptation of radical social constructivism, according to which social reality is reducible to participants' meanings and understandings of their social world. This sort of reductionism generates an arbitrary account of the social world that ignores the unacknowledged conditions of action as well as the many and varied emergent properties of action that go un- or mis-recognized by the relevant actors. It also ignores the many and varied struggles to transform the conditions of action, actors' meanings and understandings, and to modify emergent properties. In this sense a strategic-relational approach to cultural political economy rejects both the sociological imperialism of pure social constructionism and the voluntarist vacuity of certain lines of discourse analysis, which seem to imply that agents can will anything into existence in and through an appropriately articulated discourse. The second temptation is that of different forms of structuralism and social determinism, which reduce agents and actions to passive bearers of self-reproducing, self-transforming social structures. This is a constant *bête noire* of the strategic-relational approach and does not warrant further discussion here. In short, CPE notes both the constitutive role of semiosis and the emergent extra-semiotic features of social relations and their impact on capacities for action and transformation.

Thus CPE is not only concerned with how texts produce meaning and thereby help to generate social structure but also how such production is constrained by emergent, non-semiotic features of social structure as well as by inherently semiotic factors. Although every social practice is semiotic (insofar as practices entail meaning), no social practice is reducible to semiosis. Semiosis is never a purely intra-semiotic matter without external reference and involves more than the play of differences among networks of signs. It cannot be understood without identifying and exploring the extra-semiotic conditions that make semiosis possible and secure its effectivity – this includes both the overall configuration of specific semiotic action contexts and the complexities of the natural and social world in which any and all semiosis occurs.

In short, accepting the complexity of the natural and social world and the cognate importance of complexity reduction as a condition of social action, the semiotic turn in the strategic-relational approach assumes that complexity reduction involves discursively selective 'imaginaries' and structurally selective institutions. Whereas the 'imaginary' is a general term for semiotic systems that provide the basis for the lived experience of an inordinately complex world, 'institutions' is one of a family of terms that identify different mechanisms of embedding lived experience in broader social relations and, perhaps, rendering it consistent across different social spheres. Previous work in the SRA has highlighted the significance of accumulation strategies, state projects, and hegemonic visions. These can now be seen as specific instances of the more general phenomenon of semiosis and its role in simplifying-construing-constructing-contesting the natural and social world. Indeed, drawing on previous SRA language, we can argue that semiosis contributes to the overall constitution of specific social objects and social subjects and, *a fortiori*, to their co-constitution and co-evolution in wider ensembles of social relations. Semiosis has a key role in the overall constitution of specific social objects and social subjects and, *a fortiori*, in their co-constitution and co-evolution in wider ensembles of social relations.

The 'play of difference' among signifiers could not be sustained without extensive embedding of semiosis in material practice, in the constraints and affordances of the material world. Although individual words or phrases do not have a one-to-one relation to the objects to which they refer, the world does still constrain language and ways of thinking. This occurs over time, if not at every point in time. Not all possible discursive construals can be durably constructed materially, and attempts to realize them materially may have unintended effects (Sayer 2000).[7] The relative success or failure of construals depends on how both they and any attempts at construction correspond to the properties of the materials (including social phenomena such as actors and institutions) used to construct social reality. This reinforces my earlier arguments about the dialectic of discursivity and materiality and the importance of both to an adequate account of the reproduction of political economies. It also provides the basis for thinking about semiosis in terms of variation, selection, and retention – since there is far greater scope for random variation in one-off construals than there is in construals that may facilitate enduring constructions. It is to the conditions shaping the selection and retention of construals that we now turn.

The third defining feature of CPE, building on previous arguments, is its focus on the co-evolution of semiotic and extra-semiotic processes and their conjoint impact on the constitution and dynamic of capitalist formations. This implies that actual events and processes and their emergent effects can be *explained*, at least in part, as well as *interpreted* in terms of semiosis. Thus CPE studies the role of semiotic practices not only in the continual (re)making of social relations but also in the contingent emergence (variation), privileging (selection), ongoing realization (retention), subsequent reinforcement through structural coupling (consolidation) of their extra-semiotic properties, or their weakening through contestation. It is the continuing interaction between the semiotic and extra-semiotic in a complex co-evolutionary process of variation, selection, and retention that gives relatively successful economic and political imaginaries their performative, constitutive force in the material world.

Towards a New Strategic-Relational Agenda

Each of the previous four texts in my series of strategic-relational monographs concluded with a restatement of the strategic-relational research agenda. Chapter 1 of the present work summarized some key themes from each of the successive sets of strategic-relational conclusions and also indicated how the agenda had been moved forward since the last major theoretical text was being written. Later chapters have been concerned in different ways to apply the research agenda as it had developed through to the 1990s and to draw additional strategic-relational lessons relevant to future work. The present chapter has not departed from this tradition. It has attempted to push the SRA agenda forward in ways consistent with the third phase in its development identified in chapter 1. The first phase began with a critique of specific positions in Marxist state theory and then sought to generalize the strategic-theoretical alternative to the more general critique of political economy. A second, partly overlapping phase sought to transform the SRA into a general heuristic for the analysis of the dialectic of structure and agency and related dualities, such as path-dependency and path-shaping, the material and discursive, and spatiality and temporality. A third phase was initiated with the cultural turn and has been continued in joint work with Ngai-Ling Sum, the fruits of which build on our co-authored work, *Beyond the Regulation Approach* (Jessop and Sum 2006), and will appear as *Towards Cultural Political Economy* (Sum and Jessop

2008). Without seeking to pre-empt or undercut the arguments of this forthcoming study, I have here simply indicated some foundational assumptions of a strategic-relational approach to cultural political economy (see also Fairclough et al. 2004; Jessop 2004d; Jessop and Sum 2001; and Sum 2006a, 2006b).[8]

The present chapter builds on previous work in four main ways. First, it introduces into the SRA the notions of complexity, complexity reduction, and the self-potentiating nature of complexity as complementary moments of the natural and social world. This is the area where the influence of autopoietic theory has become more evident in the current phase of development – another area is my renewed interest in the nature of 'ecological dominance' as an alternative explanation for the increasing dominance of the logic of capital accumulation in an increasingly complex world society (see Jessop 1990b, 2000b, 2002d, and 2007a).

Second, it integrates a concern with semiosis as a foundational moment of the strategic-relational approach, grounding this in the significance of meaning in complexity reduction and relating it to the role of the 'imaginary' as the basis for lived experience, social construal, and social construction. Thus, from being significant only in relation to specific classes of imaginary (such as accumulation strategies, state projects, or hegemonic visions), semiosis has now been put in its rightful place in the strategic-relational approach as a foundational moment alongside that of the social (in the form of the always relational emergent structural-conjunctural properties of social interaction). This second innovation has been crucial for the development of cultural political economy and it also appears, albeit in different forms and with different knowledge interests, in a broad range of post-modern and post-structural approaches to the state that emphasize the role of different types of political imaginary, governmentality, and spatial imaginary in the organization and operations of the state.

The third new element is a more explicit institutional and evolutionary turn. The institutional turn was concerned to demonstrate the relevance of general strategic-relational principles to institutional analysis and to show how institutions could be better described, interpreted, and explained if they were put into their broader strategic-relational place (Jessop 2001a). Likewise, the evolutionary turn was initially concerned to explore more explicitly the mechanisms of selection, variation, and retention that could help to explain the recursive selection and reproduction of an otherwise improbable 'structured coherence' of social relations within specific spatial-temporal fixes (or time-space envelopes) associated with zones of relative stability at the expense of the deferral and/or displacement of contradictions, dilemmas, crisis-tendencies, and conflictuality into the future and/or elsewhere (see Jessop 2001a, 2001d, 2002a, 2002d, 2004g, and 2006b). As such, the evolutionary turn should not be confused with a commitment to evolutionism, that is, the view that there is a pre-determined course of development. On the contrary, an evolutionary turn highlights the contingencies of evolution generated by the contingently necessary development of semiosis and social relations such that, even if there is a particular directionality to social development during some periods, this is doubly tendential and involves no final destination (cf. Postone 1993). Indeed the strategic-relational approach to periodization is particularly concerned with discontinuity in continuity and continuity in discontinuity and the problems of identifying different types of conjuncture where strategic interventions could make a decisive contribution to path-shaping in spite of path-dependent legacies (see Hausner et al. 1995; Jessop 2001d). In this sense, the role of the evolutionary turn is to direct attention more explicitly to the mechanisms of variation, selection, and retention that generate the contingently necessary development of social practices, organizations, organizational ecologies, institutions, institutional orders, and patterns of societalization.

The fourth and potentially most significant shift in the strategic-relational research agenda is the semiotic turn and its articulation with the evolutionary turn. This has transformed the typical concerns of discourse analysis in the field of state theory from individual texts or discursive genres to a more explicit concern with the semiotic and extra-semiotic mechanisms that shape the variation, selection, and retention of particular imaginaries in a continuing dialectic of path-dependent path-shaping. This brings the strategic-relational approach much closer to established fields of inquiry and historical approaches such as historical semantics, conceptual history, and Foucauldian genealogies of power-knowledge (on the last of these, see chapter 6). In particular, it opens a space for examining the long-run correlation between the introduction of new social imaginaries (such as the emergence and consolidation of concepts such as the 'state' or 'sovereignty') and processes of structural transformation that provoke the search for new meanings and help to select some social imaginaries rather than others, which, in turn, may play a constitutive role in the consolidation-contestation of still emerging institutions and structures (cf. Bartelson 1995; Brunner et al. 1990; Luhmann 1990d; Skinner 1989; and the ongoing work of the *Historisch-Kritisches Wörterbuch des Marxismus*). This could mark a further step in the development of the strategic-relational approach insofar as it provides means to link the genealogy of imaginaries with their role in the consolidation of distinct patterns of structured coherence, historical blocs, and spatio-temporal fixes. It also opens the space for a more nuanced analysis of the relative weight of semiotic and extra-semiotic mechanisms in the different phases of evolution, with the working hypothesis that semiotic mechanisms have greater weight in the stage of variation and that extra-semiotic mechanisms are more important in the phase of retention. But this should be combined with the second working hypothesis that the relative weight of semiotic and extra-semiotic mechanisms will also vary with the type of social field, organizational ecology, or institutional order in which the new imaginaries emerge. Indeed, it requires no great leap of imagination to suggest that extra-semiotic mechanisms will play a smaller role in the fields of theology and philosophy than they will in those of technology and natural science and that semiotic mechanisms will be more significant in the former than the latter. Nonetheless, given the importance of imaginaries in each field to the reproduction of systems of domination, we will find both semiotic and extra-semiotic mechanisms at play in them all.

Conclusions

> Complexity theory is . . . a scientific amalgam. It is an accretion of ideas, a rhetorical hybrid. . . . [T]he chief impulse behind complexity theory is an anti-reductionist one, representing a shift towards understanding the properties of interaction of systems as more than the sum of their parts. This is, then, the idea of a science of holistic *emergent* order; a science of qualities as much as of quantities, a science of 'the potential for emergent order in complex and unpredictable phenomena' (Goodwin, 1997: 112), a more open science which asserts 'the primacy of processes over events, of relationships over entities and of development over structure' (Ingol, 1990: 209).
>
> (Thrift 1999: 33)

I have no quarrel with Thrift's remarks, but they do hint that complexity theory risks becoming 'chaotic' insofar as it is an eclectic amalgam of ideas and metaphors. It follows that we need not only to develop a more rigorous account of complexity in general terms but also to explore both the specificities of different complex systems and the specificities of paradigms for identifying/observing complexity. Accordingly I have connected complexity, critical realism, and ideas about autopoietic systems with a view to introducing some rigour into the discussion of the significance of complexity in the natural and social worlds for the strategic-relational approach. Thus my remarks on complexity were supplemented by reflections on the dialectic between the complexity of operations and the complexity of meaning and the implications of this dialectic for the structure–agency problem. In particular I have argued that ontological complexity enforces selection on natural and social systems and that one among many options is to interpret such systems in terms of how selections are selected. This leads to a concern with the selectivity of systems and the reflexivity of agents. It also raises the issue of the dialectic between the complexity of the real world and the manner in which the real world comes to be interpreted as complex. All of these are essential basic questions for any strategic-relational approach.

Nonetheless, this takes us so far and no further. For it is one thing to develop a general account of complexity, to justify the superiority of critical realism in general over other ontological, epistemological, and methodological positions in the philosophy of science, or to promote the advantages of a strategic-relational approach over alternative accounts of structure and agency in the social sciences. It is quite another thing to identify the most appropriate particular theory of complexity, particular version of critical realism, or particular specification of the SRA within these broad parameters. In this sense, one is tempted to paraphrase Marx to the effect that there is no such thing as complexity, critical realism, or the SRA in general; there are only particular accounts of complexity, particular versions of critical realism, and particular specifications of the strategic-relational approach. This entails that further development of the SRA depends, as it has done in the past, on a spiral movement between general reflections on the overall approach and the specification and application of particular variants of the SRA. My chosen field of specification and application has been historical-materialist analyses of the capitalist state, the profit-oriented, market-mediated dynamics of capital accumulation, and the structural coupling and co-evolution of the economic and political in capitalist social formations. But this does not exclude other ways of developing the approach in regard to these or other fields. Indeed, I have indicated elsewhere the extent to which conclusions very similar to the SRA have emerged from historical and sociological institutionalism (see Jessop 2001a). This is why three of my previous strategic-relational monographs (1982, 1985a, and 1990b) have ended with general guidelines and recommendations rather than a specific set of prescriptions that might preclude other sorts of application. The exception was, of course, the monograph that applied the strategic-relational approach to the problem of *The Future of the Capitalist State* (2002d) with its quite specific, if not idiosyncratic, foundations in a critical realist, strategic-relational, form-analytical account of the contradictions and dilemmas that shaped the rise and fall of the

Keynesian Welfare National State and its tendential replacement by the Schumpeterian Workfare Post-national Regime. In contrast, this work has reverted to type in its concern to develop the SRA in more general terms and to provide some general indications and particular illustrations of how it might be developed further. And, at this point, therefore, the manuscript breaks off. . . (to be resumed by those who take up the challenge to develop the strategic-relational approach in their own fashion and their own fields).

Notes

General Introduction

1 The arguments in this and the next paragraph are drawn largely verbatim from Jessop (1990b: 341–3).
2 Types of state are theoretical constructs that define which forms of political organization might correspond to the basic elements of different modes of production: they facilitate the analysis of states in specific social formations. Engaging in this sort of theoretical exercise does not imply that every state in a capitalist society will correspond to the capitalist type of state (cf. Poulantzas 1973: 147–67). On the capitalist type of state, see also Jessop (2002d: esp. 36–45).
3 The regional theory was concerned to develop an account of the political region within the overall configuration of economic, political, and ideological regions of a given mode of production, and, as such, the nature and dynamic of the political region was seen as heavily constrained by the overall reproduction requirements of the mode of production (see Jessop 1985a: 53–114; and chapter 5).

Chapter 1 The Development of the Strategic-Relational Approach

1 This is definitely *not* to suggest that the only significant changes in the state system stem from strategic interventions and/or their unintended consequences. Other sources of change also exist but must at some stage be approached strategically within the state system and/or beyond it.
2 For example, Nonhoff (2006) analyses the hegemony of the social market economy in Germany and its neo-liberal re-invention. Our approach differs strongly from the post-Marxist discourse analysis advocated by Laclau and Mouffe (1985), which one-sidedly valorizes discourse without regard to extra-discursive mechanisms of selection and retention. The lack of recognition of the CPE approach in any of its manifestations is illustrated by Grossberg's critique of the cultural turn in political economy: he argues that cultural studies cannot take 'the path of political economy, even when it tries to take the cultural turn seriously, which is rare enough. In the end, it sees culture as a medium into which the economy is translated and through which it moves, but which has no real effects of its own' (2006: 19). For a rebuttal see Jessop and Oosterlynck (2007) and Sum and Jessop (2008).

Chapter 2 Bringing the State Back in (Yet Again)

1 On critical theory and the state, see Horkheimer (1942); Kirchheimer (1969); Neumann (1964). Held (1980) is an accessible introduction to the Frankfurt School.
2 It is no accident that these are all male thinkers.

3 Even Weber's work can be interpreted differently: it has been invoked, for example, to show that the state does not exist but is a reflexive use of ideas to enhance the legitimacy of a ruling elite (Melossi 1990: 63–5).

4 There are four such faces: (a) juridical-legislative or liberal (a proper focus for feminist jurisprudence); (b) capitalist – property rights and capitalism; (c) prerogative – legitimate arbitrary power marking the state as a state (police, military, security); and (d) bureaucratic (Brown 1992: 13–14).

5 MacKinnon (1988) is ambivalent here: she treats law as patriarchal because it is gender-blind and gender interests themselves are pre-given.

6 Feminists usually criticize the oppressive effects of the public–private split; but Elshtain (1981) argues that women who go public must sacrifice the maternal values that are rooted in family life.

7 Thus states have been described as strong because they have a large public sector, authoritarian rule, strong societal support, a weak and gelatinous civil society, cohesive bureaucracies, an interventionist policy, or the power to limit external interference (cf. Lauridsen 1991: 117).

Chapter 3 Marx on Political Representation and the State

1 The term 'expanded reproduction' (Poulantzas 1975) refers to the economic and extra-economic conditions involved in the reproduction of class relations *qua* economic, political, and ideological relations. This notion is well expressed by Marx when he shows how the Orléanist faction of the bourgeoisie, which was 'the most viable faction of the French bourgeoisie', was seriously weakened when 'a blow was struck at its parliament, its legal chambers, its commercial courts, its provincial representatives, its notaries, its universities, its spokesmen and their platforms, its press and its literature, its administrative income and its court fees, its army salaries and its state pensions, its mind and its body' (*18B*: 113).

2 Carver's translation uses periods for both; here I follow Poulantzas's terminology in *Fascism and Dictatorship* in distinguishing periods, phases, and steps (1974).

3 This also explains many of the repetitions in this text on repetition as well as changes in argument over different instalments.

4 Gramsci also argued that the rise of mass politics required a shift from the Forty-Eightist theory of permanent revolution to the importance of a war of position (1971: 179–80, 220–1, 241, 243).

Chapter 4 Gramsci on the Geography of State Power

1 For Said, Gramsci offered 'an essentially geographical, territorial apprehension of human history and society . . . far more than Lukács he was political in the practical sense, conceiving of politics as a contest over territory, both actual and historical, to be won, fought over, controlled, held, lost, gained' (2001: 464).

2 Cf. Gramsci's argument that one can describe Italy's 'Jacobin' intellectuals as ' "Italian" only because culture for many centuries was the only Italian "national" manifestation; this is simply a verbal illusion. Where was the basis for this Italian culture? It was not in Italy; this "Italian" culture is the continuation of the medieval cosmopolitanism linked to the tradition of the Empire and the Church. Universal concepts with "geographical" seats in Italy' (1971: 117).

3 While Gramsci argues that natural resources and landscapes constrain as well as facilitate social practice, this does not involve monocausal determinism. Indeed, as Pandolfi notes, his 'vision of territory differed from the dangerous and arrogant categorizations of some proponents of the Southern Question, and he was careful to dissociate himself

from their essentialism. Such geographical determinisms . . . only legitimated the authoritarian and imperialistic stances of the North. Rather, territoriality was a political perimeter; it referred to a peripheral place subject to imperial and strategic domination by the center' (1998: 286).

4 Gramsci examined imperialism and imperialist rivalries in the context of a hierarchy of advanced capitalist, semi-advanced, and peripheral capitalist states (e.g., England and Germany, France and Czechoslovakia, and Italy, respectively [Ghosh 2001: 3–4]).

5 Gramsci notes how Kjellén, a Swedish sociologist, sought to 'construct a science of the state and of politics on a new basis, taking as his starting point the territorial unit as organized politically (development of the geographical sciences – physical geography, anthropography, geo-politics) and the mass of human beings living in society on that territory (geo-politics and demopolitics)' (1995: 325).

6 Gramsci writes that 'a particular ideology, for instance, born in a highly developed country, is disseminated in less developed countries, impinging on the local interplay of combinations. This relation between international forces and national forces is further complicated by the existence within every state of several structurally diverse territorial sectors, with diverse relations of force at all levels' (1971: 182).

Chapter 5 Poulantzas on the State as a Social Relation

1 This phrase derives from Gramsci's integral analysis of the state as 'political society + civil society'. Poulantzas analysed classes in terms of their expanded reproduction (1975, 1978b). Indeed, apart from his overly politicized and ideologistic view of the petty bourgeoisie in *Fascism and Dictatorship* (1974), he always defined classes in terms of the social relations of economic exploitation, ownership, and control. He also stressed that other institutional orders (notably the state) were deeply involved in reproducing the social relations of production.

2 It is worth noting that 'global' in this context implies relatively comprehensive rather than worldwide; this reflects the French distinction between '*global*' and '*mondial*'.

Chapter 6 Foucault on State, State Formation, and Statecraft

1 Indeed, Foucault can be too keen to link Marx to some of his own ideas. His own editors refute a claim that Marx acknowledged that his views on class struggle derive from the work of French historians on race struggle (2003: 83).

2 See Foucault's many comments on Marxism in *Dits et écrits* (1995).

Chapter 7 The Gender Selectivities of the State

1 Issues about the state's selectivity also arise regarding different biological sexes (including 'awkward' cases, whether due to genetic endowment or surgical intervention), sexual identities (with growing recognition of transgender identities), and sexual preferences (through the rise of the gay, lesbian, and bisexual movements and through debate over issues such as bestiality, incest, paedophilia, pornography, and sado-masochism).

2 In distinguishing discourses, institutions, and material practices, I am not denying the materiality of discourses or suggesting that institutions or material practices are non-discursive. I am simply noting that not all discourses are translated into institutions and material practices with emergent properties that are irreducible to the content of these discourses.

3 This is indicated by the fact that neo-liberal theorists such as Hayek and Friedman believe that, because gender discrimination blocks the efficient allocation of resources

in the interests of profit maximization, it will disappear as rational market calculation comes to dominate a widening range of social relations.

4 Formal equality in market relations and liberal democratic politics is, of course, compatible with substantive inequalities – whether generated by the very logic of the wage relation and social relations of production in capitalism, by the contingent articulation between exchange relations and pre-existing substantive inequalities (as exemplified in segmented labour or product markets), by the contradictions in capitalist societies between the state's democratic public form and its substantive dependence for resources (and, often, legitimacy) on the performance of the capitalist economy, and by the contradictions between the formal equality of citizens and their differential access to public will formation, policy-making, and policy implementation.

5 At least when examined as an Ideological State Apparatus, that is, as a complex institutional ensemble subject to juridico-political control, rather than as the sum of actually existing families.

6 My use of system world and lifeworld here differs from that of Habermas insofar as I distinguish more systems than the economic and juridico-political and regard the lifeworld as more than a sphere of communication.

7 For an earlier strategic-relational deconstruction of the state's 'gender blindness', see Sauer (1997); Cooper (1995) provides an analogous 'queer-theoretical' analysis of the local state.

8 For a feminist critique of Elias's arguments about the origins of civilization as pacification of society, see Bennholdt-Thomsen (1985).

9 Martial rape can be used as a weapon against ethnic and cultural nationhood, destroying families and cultures.

10 On the double gender marginalization produced by the parliamentary *Fraktionsstaat* and corporatism in Germany, see Young (1996: 159–84).

11 On efforts to re-entangle money into gendered social relations, see Zelizer (1998).

Chapter 8 Spatio-Temporal Dynamics and Temporal Sovereignty

1 Time-space compression refers here to actual processes rather than a sense of disorientation produced by the complex spatio-temporal changes associated with globalization.

2 A.N. Whitehead (1922) argues that 'there are an indefinite number of discordant time-series and an indefinite number of distinct spaces'. Hence it is important to examine how 'multiple processes flow together to construct a single consistent, coherent, though multifaceted, time-space system' (cited in Harvey 1996b: 259).

3 Booth suggests that, for Marx, '(a) all economic formations can be grasped as ways in which persons produce and distribute free time (or surplus time . . .); (b) the distinctions between these formations can be expressed as differences in the use and distribution of time; and (c) the idea of time as the realm of freedom and as the scope or space for human development leads to the embedding of the economic conception of time (and so, indirectly, the idea of the economic sphere itself) in an overarching normative inquiry' (1991: 9).

4 This derivation is first established in relatively abstract-simple terms and must be respecified as the analysis gets more concrete and complex.

5 One should add, of course, that capital's concern with exchange-value favours the dominance of short-term concerns at the expense of the long-term reproducibility of the capital relation – and to the general detriment of the natural and social world.

6 On cogredience, see especially Whitehead (1920, 1922). The immediate inspiration for this use of the term, although it is redefined here, is Harvey (1996b: 256–64).

7 Excluded here, for example, might be heavily polluting industries that may be encouraged to relocate – with their products being imported – rather than to undertake expensive environmental protection measures.

8 Measures range from creating and protecting its off-shore bases to bailing out bad loans.
9 Santiso (2000) discusses the temporal implications of privatization for social security and pension funds.

Chapter 9 Multiscalar Metagovernance in the European Union

1 Telò is commenting on the OMC, but his comment can be generalized to other forms of metagovernance, including partnership, comitology, social dialogue, and so forth.

Chapter 10 Complexity, Contingent Necessity, Semiosis, and the SRA

1 William of Occam's razor was probably formulated as follows: '*Numquam ponenda est pluralitas sine necessitate*', that is, plurality should never be posited without necessity. By analogy, Rescher has argued that '[c]*omplicationes non sunt multiplicanda praeter necessitatem*' (1998: 62), that is, complications should not be multiplied beyond what is necessary. For an early attempt to dispel the myth that it was Occam who formulated this rule, see Thorburn (1918), and, for a series of 'anti-razors' akin to that formulated in my own epigram, see the Wikipedia entry: *http://en.wikipedia.org/wiki/Occam's_Razor*, last accessed 18.05.2007.
2 For example: 'the preceding considerations show that real things always have more experientially manifestable properties than they can ever actually manifest in experience. . . . All real things are necessarily thought of as having hidden depths that extend beyond the limits, not only of experience, but also of experientiability' (Rescher 1998: 39).
3 'Micro–macro' is a relative rather than absolute distinction. The meaning of the 'microscopic' varies by context (Jessop 1990a: 191–4; 1990b: 241–5; Wickham 1983).
4 Simmel (1892) introduced this distinction. It differs from that between the natural sciences (*Naturwissenschaften*) and the cultural sciences (*Geisteswissenschaften*).
5 Thus 'the reduction of complexity through the formation of ever more numerous, differentiated, and sophisticated systems [is] a phenomenon which necessarily generates ever new complexity, and thus feeds upon itself' (Poggi 1979: xii).
6 On strategic-context analysis, see Stones (1991, 2005).
7 On the pre-linguistic and material bases of logic, see Archer (2000).
8 The Lancaster School has also produced a series of more substantive analyses from a 'cultural political economy' perspective. Ngai-Ling Sum initiated these studies *avant le concept* in the early 1990s and outside an explicitly strategic-relational framework (for a sample of these studies, see the bibliography). Through our continuing joint discussions and collaborative research, a bilateral convergence has occurred as she has integrated strategic-relational concepts and I have given more – and more explicit – weight to semiosis. As chapter 1 indicates, the roots of this interest go back many years, but it took second place to my interest in state theory and the regulation approach.

Bibliography

Abrams, P. 1988: Notes on the difficulty of studying the state (1977). *Journal of Historical Sociology*, 1 (1), 58–89.

Agamben, G. 2004: *State of Exception*. Chicago: University of Chicago Press.

Agrawal, A. 2006: *Environmentality: Technologies of Government and the Making of Subjects*. New Delhi: Oxford University Press.

Allen, J. 1990: Does feminism need a theory of 'The State'? In S. Watson, ed., *Playing the State*. London: Verso, 21–38.

Almond, G. 1988: Return to the state. *American Political Science Review*, 82 (3), 853–74.

Althusser, L. 1976: *Essays in Self-Criticism*. London: New Left Books.

Althusser, L. 2006: Marx in his limits. In idem, *The Philosophy of the Encounter*. London: Verso, 7–162 (originally written 1978–80).

Altvater, E. 1993: *The Future of the Market: on the Regulation of Money and Nature after the Collapse of 'Real Socialism'*. London: Verso.

Altvater, E., and Hoffman, J. 1990: The West German state derivation debate. *Social Text*, 8 (2), 134–55.

Altvater, E. and Mahnkopf, B. 1999: *Die Grenzen der Globalisierung*. Münster: Westfälisches Dampfboot.

Anderson, P. 1978: The antinomies of Antonio Gramsci. *New Left Review*, 100, 5–78.

Ansell, C. 2000: The networked polity: regional development in Western Europe. *Governance*, 13 (2), 303–33.

Anthias, F. and Yuval-Davis, N. 1989: *Women–Nation–State*. Basingstoke: Macmillan.

Archer, M.S. 1995: *Realist Social Theory: the Morphogenetic Approach*. Cambridge: Cambridge University Press.

Archer, M.S. 2000: *Being Human: The Problem of Agency*. Cambridge: Cambridge University Press.

Archer, M.S., Bhaskar, R., Collier, A., Lawson, T., and Norrie, A., eds, 1998: *Critical Realism: Essential Readings*. London: Routledge.

Armitage, J. and Graham, P. 2001: Dromoeconomics: towards a political economy of speed. *Parallax*, 7 (1), 111–23.

Aronowitz, S. and Bratsis, P., eds, 2002: *Paradigm Lost, State Theory Reconsidered*. Minneapolis: University of Minnesota Press.

Artous, A. 1999: *Marx, l'État et la politique*. Paris: Syllepse.

Atkinson, M.M. and Coleman, W.D. 1989: Strong states and weak states: sectoral policy networks in advanced capitalist economies. *British Journal of Political Science*, 12 (1), 47–67.

Atkinson, M.M. and Coleman, W.D. 1992: Policy networks, policy communities and the problems of governance. *Governance*, 5 (2), 154–80.

Bachmann-Medick, D. 2006: *Cultural Turns. Neuorientierungen in den Kulturwissenschaften*. Reinbeck-bei-Hamburg: Rohwolt.

Badie, B. and Birnbaum, P. 1983: *The Sociology of the State*. Chicago: University of Chicago Press.

Baecker, D. 2001: Why systems? *Theory, Culture, and Society*, 18 (1), 59–74.

Baehr, P. and O'Brien, M. 1994: Founders, classics and the concept of a canon. *Current Sociology*, 42 (1), 1–151.

Balibar, E. 1978: Marx, Engels and the revolutionary party. *Marxist Perspectives*, 2, 124–43.

Balibar, E. 1992: Foucault and Marx: the question of nominalism. In T.J. Armstrong, ed., *Michel Foucault, Philosopher*. London: Routledge, 38–56.

Baratta, G. 1997: Lotte di egemonia nell'epoca di 'Americanismo e postfordismo'. *Critica Marxista* (N.S.), 4, 47–58.

Barret-Kriegel, B. 1992: Michel Foucault and the police state. In T.J. Armstrong, ed., *Michel Foucault, Philosopher*. London: Routledge, 192–7.

Barrett, M. and McIntosh, M. 1985: *The Anti-Social Family*. London: Verso.

Barrow, C.W. 1993: *Critical Theories of the State: Marxist, Neo-Marxist, Post-Marxist*. Madison: University of Wisconsin Press.

Barry, A. 2001: *Political Machines: Governing a Technological Society*. London: Athlone.

Barry, A., Osborne, T., and Rose, N., eds, 1996: *Foucault and Political Reason*. London: UCL Press.

Bartelson, J. 1995: *A Genealogy of Sovereignty*. Cambridge: Cambridge University Press.

Bartelson, J. 2001: *A Critique of the State*. Cambridge: Cambridge University Press.

Bauer, O. 1924: *The Question of Nationalities and Social Democracy*. Minneapolis: University of Minnesota Press (2004).

Beamish, R. 1992: *Marx, Method, and the Division of Labor*. Urbana: University of Illinois Press.

Beck, U. and Grande, E. 2004: *Das kosmopolitsche Europa. Wege in die Zweite Moderne*. Frankfurt: Suhrkamp.

Behnke, A. 1997: Citizenship, nationhood and the production of political space. *Citizenship Studies*, 1 (2), 243–65.

Bennholdt–Thomsen, V. 1985: Zivilisation, moderner Staat und Gewalt. *Beiträge zur feministischen Theorie und Praxis*, 13, 23–35.

Bensaïd, D. 2002: *Marx for our Times*. London: Verso.

Berberoglu, B. 1986: The Eighteenth Brumaire and the controversy over the theory of the state. *Quarterly Review of Historical Studies*, 25 (2), 36–44.

Bertramsen, R.B. 1991: From the capitalist state to the political economy. In idem, J.-P.F. Thomsen and J. Torfing, *State, Economy and Society*. London: Unwin Hyman, 94–145.

Bertramsen, R.B., Thomsen, J.-P.F. and Torfing, J. 1991: *State, Economy, and Society*. London: Unwin Hyman.

Bevir, M. and Rhodes, R.A.W. 2003: *Interpreting British Governance*. London: Routledge.

Bhaskar, R. 1978: *A Realist Theory of Science*. Hassocks: Harvester.

Bhaskar, R. 1989: *The Possibility of Naturalism*. Hemel Hempstead: Harvester Wheatsheaf.

Binder, L. 1986: The natural history of development theory. *Comparative Studies in Society and History*, 28 (1), 3–33.

Blatter, J. 2001: Debordering the world of states. *European Journal of International Relations*, 7 (2), 175–210.

Bobbitt, P. 2002: *The Shield of Achilles: War, Peace and the Course of History*. London: Allen Lane.

Bologna, S. 1993a: Money and crisis: Marx as correspondent of the *New York Daily Tribune*, 1856–57 (Part I). *Common Sense*, 13, 29–53.

Bologna, S. 1993b: Money and crisis: Marx as correspondent of the *New York Daily Tribune*, 1856–57 (Part 2). *Common Sense*, 14, 63–88.

Bonefeld, W. 1987: Reformulation of state theory. *Capital and Class*, 33, 96–127.

Bonefeld, W. 1994: Aglietta in England: Bob Jessop's contribution to the regulation approach. *Futur antérieur*, 28, 299–330.

Booth, W.J. 1991: Economies of time: on the idea of time in Marx's political economy. *Political Theory*, 19 (1), 7–27.

Boris, E. 1995: The racialized gendered state: constructions of citizenship in the United States. *Social Politics*, 2 (2), 160–80.

Bourdieu, P. 1981: Men and machines. In K. Knorr-Cetina and A.V. Cicourel, eds, *Advances in Social Theory and Methodology*. London: Routledge, 304–17.

Bourdieu, P. and Wacquant, L. 1992: *An Invitation to Reflexive Sociology*. Cambridge: Polity.

Boyer, R. and Saillard, Y., eds, 2002: *Régulation Theory: The State of the Art*. London: Routledge.

Boyne, R. 1991: Power-knowledge and social theory: the systematic misrepresentation of contemporary French social theory in the work of Anthony Giddens. In G. Bryant and D. Jary, eds, *Giddens's Theory of Structuration: A Critical Appreciation*. London: Routledge, 52–73.

Brandist, C. 1996: Gramsci, Bakhtin, and the semiotics of hegemony. *New Left Review*, 216, 94–110.

Bratsis, P. 2006: *Everyday Life and the State*. London: Paradigm.

Brems, E. 1997: Enemies or allies? Feminism and cultural relativism as dissident voices in human rights discourse. *Human Rights Quarterly*, 19, 136–64.

Brennan, T. 1997: Why the time is out of joint: Marx's political economy without the subject, Part I. *Strategies*, 9/10, 18–37.

Brenner, J. and Laslett, B. 1991: Gender, social reproduction and women's self-organization: considering the U.S. welfare state. *Gender and Society*, 5 (3), 311–32.

Brenner, N. 1999: Beyond state-centrism? Space, territoriality, and geographical scale in globalization studies. *Theory and Society*, 28 (1), 39–78.

Brenner, N. 2004: *New State Spaces: Urban Restructuring and State Rescaling in Western Europe*. Oxford: Oxford University Press.

Bretthauer, L., Gallas, A., Kannankulam, J., and Stützle, I., eds, 2006: *Poulantzas Lesen. Zur Aktualität marxistischer Staatstheorie*. Hamburg: VSA.

Brodie, J. 1997: Meso-discourses, state forms and the gendering of liberal-democratic citizenship. *Citizenship Studies*, 1 (2), 222–42.

Brødsgaard, K.E. and Young, S., eds, 2000: *State Capacity in East Asia: Japan, Taiwan, China and Vietnam*. Oxford: Oxford University Press.

Brown, W. 1992: Finding the man in the state. *Feminist Studies*, 18 (1), 7–34.

Brown, W. 1995: *States of Injury: Power and Freedom in Late Modernity*. Princeton: Princeton University Press.

Brunn, S.D. 1999: A Treaty of Silicon for the Treaty of Westphalia? New territorial dimensions of modern statehood. In D. Newman, ed., *Boundaries, Territory and Postmodernity*. London: Cass, 106–31.

Brunner, O., Conze, W., and Koselleck, R. 1990: Staat und Souveränität. In *Geschichtliche Grundbegriffe. Historisches Lexikon zur politisch-sozialen Sprache in Deutschland. Band 6*. Stuttgart: Klett–Cotta, 1–153.

Bunting, A. 1993: Theorizing women's cultural diversity in feminist international human rights strategies. *Journal of Law and Society*, 20 (1), 6–22.

Bryan, D. 1995: The internationalisation of capital and Marxian value theory. *Cambridge Journal of Economics*, 19 (3), 421–40.

Burchell, G., Gordon, C., and Miller, P., eds, 1991: *The Foucault Effect: Studies in Governmental Rationality*. Hemel Hempstead: Harvester Wheatsheaf.

Burstyn, V. 1982: Economy, sexuality, and politics: Engels and the sexual division of labour. *Socialist Studies*, 3, 19–39.

Butler, J. 1990: *Gender Trouble: Feminism and the Subversion of Identity*. London: Routledge.

Butler, J. 1997: Merely cultural. *Social Text*, 52/3, 265–77.

Calhoun, C., ed., 1994: *Habermas and the Public Sphere*. Cambridge, MA: MIT Press.

Callaway, H. 1987: *Gender, Culture and Empire: European Women in Colonial Nigeria*. Urbana: University of Illinois Press.

Callon, M., ed., 1998a: *The Laws of the Markets*. Oxford: Blackwell.

Callon, M. 1998b: An essay on framing and overflowing: economic externalities revisited by sociology. In idem, ed., *Laws of the Markets*, 244–69.

Callon, M. 1999: Actor–network theory: the market test. In J. Hassard and J. Law, eds, *Actor Network and After.* Oxford: Blackwell, 181–95.

Callon, M. and Latour, B. 1981: Unscrewing the big Leviathan: how actors macro-structure reality and how sociologists help them to do so. In K. Knorr-Cetina and A.V. Cicourel, eds, *Advances in Social Theory and Methodology.* London: Routledge, 278–303.

Cammack, P. 1980: Review article: bringing the state back in? *British Journal of Political Science,* 19 (2), 261–90.

Cammack, P. 1990: Statism, new institutionalism and Marxism. *Socialist Register 1990,* 147–70.

Campbell, D. 1992: *Writing Security: US Foreign Policy and the Politics of Identity.* Manchester: Manchester University Press.

Campbell, D.T. 1969: Variation and selective retention in socio-cultural evolution. *General Systems,* 14, 69–86.

Candeias, M. 2005: *Neoliberalismus, Hochtechnologie, Hegemonie. Grundrisse einer transnationalen kapitalistischen Produktions- und Lebensweise. Eine Kritik.* Hamburg: Argument Verlag.

Canning, K. 1992: Gender and the politics of class formation: rethinking German labor history. *American Historical Review,* 2, 736–68.

Caporaso, J.A. 1996: The European Union and forms of state: Westphalian, regulatory or post-modern? *Journal of Common Market Studies,* 34 (1), 28–52.

Carnoy, M. 1984: *The State and Political Theory.* Princeton: Princeton University Press.

Castells, M. 1992: Four Asian tigers with a dragon head. In J. Henderson and R.P. Appelbaum, eds, *States and Development in the Pacific Rim.* London: Sage, 33–70.

Castells, M. 2000: Materials for an explanatory theory of the network society. *British Journal of Sociology,* 51 (1), 5–24.

Chandhoke, N. 1995: *State and Civil Society.* New Delhi: Sage.

Chatterjee, P. 2004: *The Politics of the Governed: Reflections on Popular Politics in Most of the World.* New Delhi: Permanent Black.

Chesneaux, J. 2000: Speed and democracy: an uneasy dialogue. *Social Science Information,* 39 (3), 407–20.

Clark, C. and Lemco, J. 1988: The strong state and development: a growing list of caveats. *Journal of Developing Societies,* 4 (1), 1–8.

Clarke, S. 1977: Marxism, sociology, and Poulantzas's theory of the state. *Capital and Class,* 2, 1–31.

Clarke, S., ed., 1990: *The State Debate.* Basingstoke: Macmillan.

Cohen, J.L. and Arato, A., eds, 1992: *Civil Society and Social Theory.* Cambridge, MA: MIT Press.

Collinge, C. 1999: Self-organization of society by scale: a spatial reworking of regulation theory. *Environment and Planning D: Society and Space,* 17 (5), 557–74.

Collins, P.H. 1998: It's all in the family: intersections of gender, race, and nation. *Hypatia,* 13 (3), 62–82.

Connell, R.W. 1987: *Gender and Power*. Cambridge: Polity.

Connell, R.W. 1990: The state, gender, and sexual politics: theory and appraisal. *Theory and Society*, 19 (5), 507–44.

Connell, R.W. 1995: *Masculinities*. Cambridge: Polity.

Connell, R.W. 1996: New directions in gender theory, masculinity research, and gender politics. *Ethnos*, 61 (3–4), 157–76.

Connelly, M.P. 1996: Gender matters: global restructuring and adjustment. *Social Politics*, 3 (1), 12–31.

Cook, D.J. 1982: Marx's critique of philosophical language. *Philosophy and Phenomenological Research*, 42 (4), 530–54.

Cooper, D. 1995: *Sexing the City: Lesbian and Gay Politics within the Activist State*. London: Rivers Oram Press.

Cooper, D. 1998: *Governing Out of Order: Space, Law and the Politics of Belonging*. London: Rivers Oram Press.

Corbridge, S., Williams, G., Srivastava, M., and Veron, R. 2005: *Seeing the State: Governance and Governmentality in India*. Cambridge: Cambridge University Press.

Corrigan, P. and Sayer, D. 1985: *The Great Arch: English State Formation as Cultural Revolution*. London: Quartet.

Cravey, A.J. 1998: Engendering the Latin American state. *Progress in Human Geography*, 22 (4), 523–42.

Crocker, S. 1998: Prolepsis: on speed and time's interval. *Cultural Values*, 2 (4), 485–98.

Cunliffe, J. 1981: Marx, Engels and the party. *History of Political Thought*, 2 (2), 349–67.

Curthoys, A. 1993: Feminism, citizenship and national identity. *Feminist Review*, 44, 19–38.

Czarniawska, B. and Sevón, G. 1996: Travels of ideas. In idem, eds, *Translating Organizational Change*. Berlin: De Gruyter, 13–48.

Dahlerup, D. 1994: Learning to live with the state. State, market, and civil society: Women's need for state intervention in East and West. *Women's Studies International Forum*, 17 (2–3), 117–27.

Daly, M. 1984: *Pure Lust: Elemental Feminist Philosophy*. Boston: Beacon Press.

Dandeker, C. 1990: *Surveillance, Power and Modernity: Bureaucracy and Discipline from 1700 to the Present Day*. Cambridge: Polity.

Davis, J.A., ed., 1970: *Gramsci and Italy's Passive Revolution*. London: Croom Helm.

Deacon, B. and Hulse, M. 1997: The making of post-communist social policy: The role of international agencies. *Journal of Social Policy*, 26 (1), 43–62.

Dean, M. 1994: *Critical and Effective Histories: Foucault's Methods and Historical Sociology*. London: Routledge.

Dean, M. and Hindess, B., eds, 1998: *Governing Australia: Studies in Contemporary Rationalities of Government*. Cambridge: Cambridge University Press.

Debrizzi, J.A. 1982: Marx and Lenin: class, party and democracy. *Studies in Soviet Thought*, 24 (2), 95–116.

Dehousse, R. 2002: Les l'États et l'Union européenne: les effets de l'intégration. In V. Wright and S. Cassese, eds, *La recomposition de l'État en Europe*. Paris: Éditions la Découverte, 55–70.

de la Haye, Y. 1988: *Marx and Engels on the Means of Communication (the Movement of Commodities, People, Information, and Capital)*. New York: International General.

Demirović, A. 2007: *Nicos Poulantzas*. Münster: Westfälisches Dampfboot.

Demirović, A. and Pühl, K. 1997: Identitätspolitik und die Transformation von Staatlichkeit. In E. Kreisky and B. Sauer, eds, *Geschlechtverhältnisse im Kontext politischer Transformation*. Opladen: Westdeutscher Verlag, 220–40.

Deppe, F., Felder, M., and Tidow, S. 2000: Structuring the state – the case of European employment policy. Marburg: Philipps-Universität Marburg.

de Sousa Santos, B. 1995: The postmodern transition: law and politics. In A. Sarat and T.R. Kearns, eds, *The Fate of Law*. Ann Arbor: University of Michigan Press, 79–118.

Dews, P. 1979: The *Nouvelle Philosophie* and Foucault. *Economy and Society*, 8 (2), 127–71.

Dillon, M. and Reid, J. 2001: Global liberal governance: biopolitics, security and war, *Millennium*, 30 (1), 41–66.

Dirlik, A. 2001: Globalization as the end and the beginning of history: the contradictory implications of a new paradigm. *Rethinking Marxism*, 12 (4), 4–22.

Dolowitz, D.P. and Marsh, D. 1996: Who learns what from whom? A review of the policy transfer literature. *Political Studies*, 44 (2), 343–57.

Domhoff, G.W. 1987: The Wagner Act and theories of the state: a new analysis based on class–segment theory. *Political Power and Social Theory*, 6, 159–85.

Domhoff, G.W. 1996: *State Autonomy or Class Dominance?* Hawthorne, NY: Aldine de Gruyter.

Doveton, D. 1994: Marx and Engels on democracy. *History of Political Thought*, 15 (4), 555–92.

Draper, H. 1977: *Karl Marx's Theory of Revolution. Vol. I: State and Bureaucracy*. New York: Monthly Review Press.

Draper, H. 1978: *Karl Marx's Theory of Revolution. Vol. II: The Politics of Social Classes*. New York: Monthly Review Press.

du Gay, P. and Pryke, M. eds, 2002: *Cultural Economy: Cultural Analysis and Commercial Life*. London: Sage.

Duggan, L. 1994: Queering the state. *Social Text*, 39, 1–14.

Duncan, S. 1994: Theorising differences in patriarchy. *Environment and Planning A*, 26, 1177–94.

Dunsire, A. 1996: Tipping the balance: autopoiesis and governance. *Administration & Society*, 28 (3), 299–334.

Dyson, K.H. 1980: *The State Tradition in Western Europe*. Oxford: Martin Robertson.

Easton, D. 1981: The political system besieged by the state. *Political Theory*, 9 (3), 303–25.

Ebert, T.L. 1996: *Ludic Feminism and After: Postmodernism, Desire, and Labor in Late Capitalism*. Detroit: University of Michigan Press.

Ebert, T.L. 2005: Rematerializing feminism. *Science & Society*, 69 (1), 38–55.

Eisenstein, Z. 1981: *The Radical Future of Liberal Feminism*. Harlow: Longman.

Elden, S. 2008: Strategies for waging peace: Foucault as *collaborateur*. In M. Dillon and A. Neal, eds, *Foucault: Politics, Society, and War*. Basingstoke: Palgrave, in press.

Elshtain, J.B. 1981: *Public Man – Private Women. Women in Social and Political Thought*. Princeton: Princeton University Press.

Elshtain, J.B. 1987: *Women and War*. New York: Basic Books.

Engels, F. 1850: The Peasant War in Germany. *Marx–Engels Collected Works* 10. Lawrence & Wishart (1978), 397–482.

Engels, F. 1886: Lawyers' socialism. *Marx–Engels Collected Works* 28, London: Lawrence & Wishart (1990), 597–616.

Enloe, C. 1983: *Does Khaki become You? The Militarisation of Women's Lives*. London: Pluto.

Enloe, C. 1989: *Bananas, Beaches and Bases: Making Feminist Sense of International Politics*. London: Pandora.

Enloe, C. 2000: *Maneuvers: The International Political Economy of Militarizing Women's Lives*. Berkeley: University of California Press.

Erckebrecht, U. 1972: *Marx' materialistische Sprachtheorie*. Krönberg/Taunus: Skriptor Verlag.

Eriksen, T. 2001: *Tyranny of the Moment: Fast and Slow Time in the Information Age*. London: Pluto.

European Commission. 1993: *Growth, Competitiveness, Employment: The Challenges and Ways Forward into the 21st century*. COM(93)700 final. Brussels: Commission of the European Communities.

Evans, P.B. 1989: Predatory, developmental, and other apparatuses: a comparative political economy perspective on the Third World state. *Sociological Forum*, 4 (4), 561–87.

Evans, P.B. 1995: *Embedded Autonomy: States and Industrial Transformation*. Princeton: Princeton University Press.

Evans, P.B., Rueschemeyer, D., and Skocpol, T. 1985: On the road toward a more adequate understanding of the state. In idem, eds, *Bringing the State Back In*. Cambridge: Cambridge University Press, 347–66.

Evers, T. 1994: Supranationale Staatlichkeit am Beispiel der Europäischen Union: Civitas civitatum oder Monstrum? *Leviathan*, 22 (1), 115–34.

Fairclough, N. 1992: *Discourse and Social Change*. Cambridge: Polity.

Fairclough, N. 2003: *Analysing Discourse: Textual Analysis for Social Research.* London: Routledge.

Fairclough, N. and Graham, P. 2002: Marx as a critical discourse analyst. *Journal Estudios de Sociolinguistica,* 3 (1), 185–229.

Fairclough, N., Jessop, B., and Sayer, A. 2004: Critical realism and semiosis. In J. Joseph and J.M. Roberts, eds, *Realism, Discourse and Deconstruction.* London: Routledge, 23–42.

Falkner, G. 1998: *EU Social Policy in the 1990s: Towards a Corporatist Policy Community.* London: Routledge.

Farganis, S. 1994: *Situating Feminism: From Thought to Action.* London: Sage.

Feldman, A. 2004: Securocratic wars of public safety: globalized policing as scopic regime. *Interventions,* 6 (3), 330–50.

Ferguson, J. and Gupta, A. 2005: Spatializing states: toward an ethnography of neoliberal governmentality. In J.X. Inda, ed., *Anthropologies of Modernity: Foucault, Governmentality, and Life Politics.* Oxford: Blackwell, 105–31.

Ferguson, K.E. 1984: *The Feminist Case against Bureaucracy.* Philadelphia: Temple University Press.

Ferguson, Y.H. and Mansbach, R.W. 1989: *The State, Conceptual Chaos, and the Future of International Relations Theory.* Boulder, CO: Lynne Rienner.

Fernbach, D. 1973: Introduction. In *Karl Marx: Surveys from Exile.* Harmondsworth: Penguin, 7–34.

Fernbach, D. 1981: *The Spiral Path.* London: Gay Men's Press.

Ferree, M.M., Lorber, J., and Hess, B.B., eds, 1999: *Revisioning Gender.* London: Sage.

Ferry, L. and Renaut, A. 1985: *La pensée 68: essai sur l'anti-humanisme contemporain.* Paris: Gallimard.

Findlay, S. 1988: Feminist struggles with the Canadian state: 1966–1988. *Resources for Feminist Research,* 17 (3), 5–9.

Fine, B. 1984: *Democracy and the Rule of Law.* London: Pluto.

Fischer, F. and Forester, J., eds, 1993: *The Argumentative Turn in Policy Analysis and Planning.* Durham, NC: Duke University Press.

Fontana, A. and Bertani, M. 2003: Situating the lectures. In M. Foucault, *'Society Must be Defended.' Lectures at the Collège de France 1975–1976.* New York: Picador, 273–93.

Forgacs, D. and Nowell-Smith, G. 1985: Introduction to language, linguistics, and folklore. In A. Gramsci, *Selections from Cultural Writings.* London: Lawrence & Wishart, 164–7.

Foucault, M. 1970: *The Order of Things: An Archaeology of the Human Sciences,* London: Tavistock.

Foucault, M. 1978. Clarifications on the question of power. In S. Lotringer, ed., *Foucault Live: Interviews 1966–84.* New York: Semiotext(e), 1989, 179–92.

Foucault, M. 1979a: *Discipline and Punish.* Harmondsworth: Penguin.

Foucault, M. 1979b: Power and norm: notes. In idem, *Power, Truth, Strategy*. Brisbane: Feral Books, 59–67.

Foucault, M. 1980a. *The History of Sexuality, Vol. 1: An Introduction*. Harmondsworth: Penguin.

Foucault, M. 1980b. *Power/Knowledge: Selected Interviews and Other Writings 1972–1977*. New York: Pantheon.

Foucault, M. 1982: The subject of power. In H. Dreyfus and P. Rabinow, eds, *Michel Foucault: Beyond Structuralism and Hermeneutics*. Hemel Hempstead: Harvester Wheatsheaf, 208–26.

Foucault, M. 1995: *Dits et écrits*. Tumes I–IV. Paris: L'Harmattan.

Foucault, M. 1997: *Ethics: The Essential Works*. London: Allen Lane.

Foucault, M. 2001: *Power. The Essential Works*. London: Allen Lane.

Foucault, M. 2003: *'Society Must be Defended.' Lectures at the Collège de France 1975–1976*. New York: Picador.

Foucault, M. 2004a: *Naissance de la biopolitique. Cours au Collège de France, 1978–1979*. Paris: Seuil/Gallimard.

Foucault, M. 2004b: *Sécurité, territoire, population. Cours au Collège de France, 1977–1978*. Paris: Seuil/Gallimard.

Franzway, S., Court, D. and Connell, R. 1989: *Staking a Claim: Feminism, Bureaucracy and the State*. Cambridge: Polity.

Fraser, N. 1988: *Unruly Practices. Power and Discourse in Contemporary Social Theory*. Cambridge: Polity.

Fraser, N. 1997: Equality, difference and democracy: recent feminist debates in the United States. In J. Dean, ed., *Feminism and the New Democracy*. London: Sage, 98–109.

Frerichs, J. and Kraiker, G. 1975: *Konstitutionsbedingungen des bürgerlichen Staats und der sozialen Revolution bei Marx and Engels*. Frankfurt: Suhrkamp.

Friedland, P. 1999: Métissage. The merging of theater and politics in revolutionary France. Princeton: Institute of Advanced Studies.

Friedland, P. 2002: *Political Actors: Representative Bodies and Theatricality in the Age of the French Revolution*. Ithaca: Cornell University Press.

Fukuyama, F. 2005: *State Building. Governance and World Order in the Twenty-First Century*. London: Profile Books.

Genetti, E. 2003: Das Geschlecht des modernen Staates: Überlegungen zur neueren Staatstheorie. In M. Hierlmeier, M. Wissen, and I. Stützle, eds, *Staatstheorie und Globalisierungskritik. Reader*. Hamburg: Buko-Geschäftsstelle, 20–3.

Ghosh, P. 2001: Gramscian hegemony: an absolutely historicist approach. *History of European Ideas*, 27 (1), 1–43.

Gibson-Graham, J.-K. 1995: Beyond patriarchy and capitalism: reflections on political subjectivity. In B. Caine and R. Pringle, eds, *Transitions*. St Leonards: Allen & Unwin, 172–83.

Giddens, A. 1984: *The Constitution of Society: Outline of the Theory of Structuration.* Berkeley: University of California Press.

Giddens, A. 1989: *The Nation State and Violence.* Cambridge: Polity.

Gill, S.S. 2001: Constitutionalising capital: EMU and disciplinary neo-liberalism. In A. Bieler and A.D. Morton, eds, *Social Forces in the Making of the New Europe.* Basingstoke: Palgrave, 47–69.

Golding, S. 1992: *Gramsci: Contributions to a Theory of Post-Liberal Democracy.* Toronto: Toronto University Press.

Goodwin, B.C. 1997: Community, creativity and society. *Soundings,* 5, 111–23.

Gordon, C. 1980: Preface. In M. Foucault, *Power/Knowledge.* New York: Pantheon, vii–ix.

Gordon, C. 1992: Governmental rationality: An introduction. In G. Burchell, C. Gordon, and P. Miller, eds, *The Foucault Effect.* Brighton: Harvester-Wheatsheaf, 1–51.

Gordon, L. 1990: The welfare state: Towards a socialist-feminist perspective. *Socialist Register 1990,* 171–200.

Goswani, M. 2004: *Producing India: From Colonial Economy to National Space.* Chicago: University of Chicago Press.

Gottfried, H. 1995: Developing neo-Fordism: a comparative perspective. *Critical Sociology,* 21 (3), 39–70.

Graham, P. 2002: Space and cyberspace. On the enclosure of consciousness. In J. Armitage and J. Roberts, eds, *Living with Cyberspace: Technology and Society in the 21st century.* London: Continuum, 156–64.

Gramsci, A. 1971: *Selections from the Prison Notebooks.* London: Lawrence & Wishart.

Gramsci, A. 1978: *Selections from Political Writings (1921–1926).* London: Lawrence & Wishart.

Gramsci, A. 1985: *Selections from Cultural Writings.* London: Lawrence & Wishart.

Gramsci, A. 1995: *Further Selections from the Prison Notebooks.* London: Lawrence & Wishart.

Gramsci, A. and Togliatti, P. 1978: The Italian situation and the tasks of the PCI ('Lyons Theses'). In A. Gramsci, *Selections from Political Writings (1921–1926).* London: Lawrence & Wishart, 340–78.

Grande, E. 2000: Charisma und Komplexität: Verhandlungsdemokratie, Medien-demokratie und der Funktionswandel politischer Eliten. *Leviathan,* 38 (1), 122–41.

Grant, R. and Newland, K., eds, 1991: *Gender and International Relations.* Milton Keynes: Open University Press.

Greenberg, D.F. and Bystryn, M.H. 1996: Capitalism, bureaucracy, and male homosexuality. In S. Seidman, ed., *Queer Theory/Sociology.* Oxford: Blackwell, 83–110.

Gross, D. 1985: Temporality and the modern state. *Theory and Society,* 14 (1), 53–81.

Grossman, H. 1977a: Marx, classical political economy, and the problem of dynamics. Part one. *Capital and Class*, 2, 32–55.

Grossman, H. 1977b: Marx, classical political economy, and the problem of dynamics. Part two. *Capital and Class*, 3, 67–99.

Grote, J.R. and Schmitter, P.C. 1999: The renaissance of national corporatism. *Transfer: Quarterly of the European Trade Union Institute*, 5 (1–2), 34–63.

Haahr, J.H. 2004: Open Coordination as advanced liberal government. *Journal of European Public Policy*, 11 (2), 209–30.

Habermas, J. 1987: *Knowledge and Human Interests*. London: Heinemann.

Habermas, J. 1992: Citizenship and national identity: some reflections on the future of Europe. *Praxis International*, 12 (1), 1–19.

Hajer, M. and Wagenaar, H., eds, 2003: *Deliberative Policy Analysis: Understanding Governance in the Network Society*. Cambridge: Cambridge University Press.

Hall, J.A. and Schroeder, R., eds, 2006: *An Anatomy of Power: The Social Theory of Michael Mann*. Cambridge: Cambridge University Press.

Hall, S. 1985: Authoritarian populism: a reply. *New Left Review*, 151, 115–24.

Hall, S., Critcher, C., Jefferson, T., Clarke, J. and Roberts, B. 1978: *Policing the Crisis: 'Mugging', the State, and Law and Order*. Basingstoke: Macmillan.

Handel, M. 1990: *Weak States in the International System*. London: Cass.

Haney, L.A. 2000: Feminist state theory: applications to jurisprudence, criminology, and the welfare state. *Annual Review of Sociology*, 26, 641–66.

Hannah, M. 2000: *Governmentality and the Mastery of Territory in Nineteenth-Century America*. Cambridge: Cambridge University Press.

Hantrais, L. 2000: *Social Policy in the European Union*. Basingstoke: Macmillan.

Haraway, D. J. 1991: *Simians, Cyborgs, and Women: The Reinvention of Nature*. London: Routledge.

Harvey, D. 1982: *The Limits to Capital*. Oxford: Blackwell.

Harvey, D. 1985: *The Condition of Post-Modernity*. Oxford: Blackwell.

Harvey, D. 1996a: Globalization in question. *Rethinking Marxism*, 8 (4), 1–17.

Harvey, D. 1996b: *Justice, Nature and the Geography of Difference*. Oxford: Blackwell.

Harvey, D. 1998: The geography of class power. In L. Panitch and C. Leys, eds, *Socialist Register 1998: 'The Communist Manifesto' Now*, London: Merlin, 49–74.

Harvey, D. 2002: *Spaces of Capital*. Edinburgh: Edinburgh University Press.

Hatem, M. 1992: Economic and political liberalisation in Egypt and the demise of state feminism. *International Journal of Middle East Studies*, 24, 231–51.

Häusler, J. and Hirsch, J. 1989: Political regulation: The crisis of Fordism and the transformation of the party system in West Germany. In M. Gottdiener and N. Komninos, eds, *Capitalist Development and Crisis Theory*. New York: St Martin's Press, 300–27.

Hausner, J., Jessop B., and Nielsen, K. 1995: Institutional change in post-socialism. In idem, eds, *Strategic Choice and Path-Dependency in Post-Socialism*. Aldershot: Edward Elgar, 3–45.

Hay, C. 1995a: Mobilization through interpellation: James Bulger, juvenile crime and the construction of a moral panic. *Social and Legal Studies*, 4, 197–223.

Hay, C. 1995b: *Re-Stating Social and Political Change*. Milton Keynes: Open University Press.

Hay, C. 1995c: Structure and agency. In D. Marsh and G. Stoker, eds, *Theory and Methods in Political Science*. Basingstoke: Macmillan, 189–208.

Hay, C. 1996: Narrating crisis: the discursive construction of the 'Winter of Discontent'. *Sociology*, 30 (2), 253–77.

Hay, C. 1998: The tangled webs we weave: the discourse, strategy and practice of networking. In D. Marsh, ed., *Comparing Policy Networks*. Buckingham: Open University Press, 33–51.

Hay, C. 2001: What place for ideas in the structure–agency debate? Globalisation as 'process without a subject'. *http://www.theglobalsite. ac.uk/press/109hay.htm*, last accessed 23.05.07.

Hay, C. 2002: *Political Analysis: A Critical Introduction*. Basingstoke: Palgrave.

Hay, C. 2005: (What's Marxist about) Marxist state theory? In idem, M. Lister, and D. Marsh, eds, *The State: Theories and Issues*. Basingstoke: Palgrave, 59–78.

Hay, C. and Jessop, C. 1995: The governance of local economic development and the development of local economic governance: a strategic-relational approach. Paper for American Political Science Association Annual Conference, Chicago.

Hay, C. and Wincott, D. 1998: Structure, agency and historical institutionalism. *Political Studies*, 46 (4), 951–7.

Hay, C., Lister, M., and Marsh, D., eds, 2005: *The State: Theories and Issues*. Basingstoke: Palgrave.

Hegel, G.W.F. 1821: *Hegel's Philosophy of Right*. Cambridge: Cambridge University Press (1975).

Held, D. 1980: *Introduction to Critical Theory: Horkheimer to Habermas*. Berkeley: University of California Press.

Held, D. 1992: Democracy: from city-states to a cosmopolitan order? *Political Studies*, 40 (Special issue), 10–39.

Heller, H. 1992: *Staatslehre*. Tübingen: Mohr.

Helsloot, N. 1980: Linguists of all countries, unite! On Gramsci's premise of coherence. *Journal of Pragmatics*, 13 (4), 547–66.

Hennessy, R. 2000: *Profit and Pleasure: Sexual Identities in Late Capitalism*. London: Routledge.

Hennig, E. 1974: Lesehinweise für die Lektüre der 'politischen Schriften' von Marx und Engels. In idem, J. Hirsch, H. Reichelt, and G. Schäfer, eds, *Karl*

Marx/Friedrich Engels: Staatstheorie. Materialien zur Rekonstruktion der marxistischen Staatstheorie. Frankfurt: Ullstein, lix–xcii.

Hernes, H.M. 1987: Women and the welfare state: the transition from private to public dependence. In A.S. Sassoon, ed., *Women and the State.* London: Hutchinson, 72–92.

Hettne, B. 1997: Europe in a world of regions. In R. Falk and T. Szentes, eds, *A New Europe in the Changing Global System.* Tokyo: United Nations University Press, 16–40.

Hindess, B. 1978: Classes and politics in Marxist theory. In G. Littlejohn, B. Smart, J. Wakeford and N. Yuval-Davis, eds, *Power and the State.* London: Croom Helm, 72–97.

Hirsch, J. 1976: Bemerkungen zum theoretischen Ansatz einer Analyse des bürgerlichen Staates. In *Gesellschaft 8–9.* Frankfurt: Suhrkamp, 99–149.

Hirsch, J. 2005: *Die materialistische Staatstheorie.* Hamburg: VSA.

Hirst, P.Q. 1977: Economic classes and politics. In A. Hunt, ed., *Class and Class Structure.* London: Lawrence & Wishart, 125–54.

Hirst, P.Q. 2001: *War and Power in the 21st Century.* Cambridge: Polity.

Hirst, P.Q. and Thompson, G. 1995: Globalization and the future of the nation-state. *Economy and Society,* 24 (3), 408–42.

Hoare, Q. and Nowell-Smith, G. 1971: Introduction. In A. Gramsci, *Selections from the Prison Notebooks.* London: Lawrence & Wishart, xvii–xcvi.

Hoffman, J. and Hoffman, R. 1998: Globalization – risks and opportunities for European labor policy. In D. Dettke, ed., *The Challenge of Globalization for Germany's Social Democracy. A Policy Agenda for the 21st Century,* Oxford: Berghahn, 113–35.

Hoffman, S. 1995: *The European Sisyphus. Essays on Europe 1964–1994.* Boulder, CO: Westview Press.

Holloway, J. 1988: The Great Bear, post-Fordism and class struggle: a comment on Bonefeld and Jessop. *Capital and Class,* 36, 93–104.

Holmwood, J. and Stewart, A. 1991: *Explanation and Social Theory.* Basingstoke: Macmillan.

Holub, R. 1992: *Antonio Gramsci: Beyond Marxism and Post-modernism.* London: Routledge.

Hood, C. 1998: *The Art of the State: Culture, Rhetoric and Public Management.* Oxford: Oxford University Press.

Hoogerwerf, A. 1990: Policy and time: consequences of time perspectives for the contents, processes and effects of public policies. *International Review of Administrative Sciences,* 56 (4), 671–92.

Horkheimer, M. 1942: The authoritarian state. *Telos,* 15 (1973), 3–20.

Hunt, R.N. 1974: *The Political Ideas of Marx and Engels: Vol. 1. Classical Marxism, 1850–1895.* Pittsburgh: University of Pittsburgh Press.

Ingold, T. 1990: An anthropologist looks at biology. *Man* (N.S.), 25, 208–29.

Isaac, J.C. 1987: *Power: A Realist Analysis.* Ithaca: Cornell University Press.

Isaac, J.C. 1990: The lion's skin of politics: Marx on republicanism. *Polity*, 22 (3), 461–88.

Ives, P. 2004a: *Gramsci's Politics of Language: Engaging the Bakhtin Circle and the Frankfurt School*. Toronto: University of Toronto Press.

Ives, P. 2004b: *Language and Hegemony in Gramsci*. London: Pluto Press.

James, S.M. 1994: Challenging patriarchal privilege through the development of international human rights. *Women's Studies International Forum*, 17 (6), 563–78.

Jellinek, Georg 1921. *Allgemeiner Staatslehre*. Berlin: Julius Springer (third edition).

Jenson, J. 1986: Gender and reproduction: or, babies and state. *Studies in Political Economy*, 20, 9–46.

Jenson, J. 1995: Mapping, naming and remembering: globalisation at the end of the twentieth century. *Review of International Political Economy*, 2 (1), 91–116.

Jessop, B. 1977: Recent theories of the capitalist state. *Cambridge Journal of Economics*, 1 (4), 353–73.

Jessop, B. 1978: Capitalism and democracy: the best possible political shell? In G. Littlejohn, B. Smart, J. Wakeford, and N. Yuval-Davis, eds, *Power and the State*. London: Croom Helm, 10–51.

Jessop, B. 1979: Corporatism, parliamentarism, and social democracy. In P.C. Schmitter and G. Lehmbruch, eds, *Trends towards Corporatist Intermediation*. London: Sage, 185–212.

Jessop, B. 1980: The transformation of the state in post-war Britain. In R. Scase, ed., *The State in Western Europe*. London: Croom Helm, 23–93.

Jessop, B. 1982: *The Capitalist State: Marxist Theories and Methods*. Oxford: Blackwell.

Jessop, B. 1983: Accumulation strategies, state forms and hegemonic projects. *Kapitalistate*, 10/11, 89–112.

Jessop, B. 1985a: *Nicos Poulantzas: Marxist Theory and Political Strategy*. New York: St Martin's Press.

Jessop, B. 1985b: Prospects for a corporatist monetarism. In O. Jacobi, B. Jessop, H. Kastendiek, and M. Regini, eds, *Economic Crisis, Trade Unions, and the State*. London: Croom Helm, 105–30.

Jessop, B. 1986: Corporatism, post-Fordism, and labour exclusion. In G. Brandt, H. Kastendiek, and O. Jacobi, eds, *Labour Exclusion or New Patterns of Cooperation?* Frankfurt: Institut für Sozialforschung.

Jessop, B. 1989a: Neo-conservative regimes and the transition to post-fordism. In M. Gottdiener and N. Komninos, eds, *Capitalist Development and Crisis Theory*. Basingstoke: Macmillan, 261–99.

Jessop, B. 1989b: The nation-state, surveillance, and violence. In D. Held and J.B. Thompson, eds, *Social Theory of Modern Societies: Anthony Giddens and his Critics*. Cambridge: Cambridge University Press, 103–28.

Jessop, B. 1990a: Regulation theories in retrospect and prospect. *Economy and Society*, 19 (2), 154–216.

Jessop, B. 1990b: *State Theory: Putting the Capitalist State in Its Place*. Cambridge: Polity.

Jessop, B. 1991: On the originality, legacy, and actuality of Nicos Poulantzas. *Studies in Political Economy*, 34, 75–108.

Jessop, B. 1992a: From social democracy to Thatcherism: twenty-five years of British politics. In N. Abercrombie and A. Warde, eds, *Social Change in Contemporary Britain*. Cambridge: Polity, 45–68.

Jessop, B. 1992b: Relative autonomy and autopoiesis in law, economy, and state. In G. Teubner and A. Febbrajo, eds, *State, Law, Economy as Autopoietic Systems*. Milan: Giuffrè, 187–265.

Jessop, B. 1992c: Structural competitiveness and strategic capacities: implications for the state and international capital in the 1990s. In P. Kosonen, ed., *Changing Europe and Comparative Research*. Helsinki: VAPK-Publishing, 6–20.

Jessop, B. 1993: Towards a Schumpeterian workfare state? Preliminary remarks on post-Fordist political economy. *Studies in Political Economy*, 40, 7–41.

Jessop, B. 1995: The regulation approach, governance and post-Fordism. *Economy and Society*, 24 (3), 307–33.

Jessop, B. 1996: Interpretive sociology and the dialectic of structure and agency: reflections on Holmwood and Stewart's *Explanation and Social Theory*. *Theory, Culture, & Society*, 13 (1), 119–28.

Jessop, B. 1997a: Nationalstaat, Globalisierung, und Gender. *Politische Vierteljahresschrift, Sonderheft 28*. Opladen: Westdeutsche Verlag, 262–92.

Jessop, B. 1997b: The governance of complexity and the complexity of governance: preliminary remarks on some problems and limits of economic guidance. In A. Amin and J. Hauzner, eds, *Beyond Markets and Hierarchy*. Cheltenham: Edward Elgar, 111–47.

Jessop, B. 1997c: The entrepreneurial city: re-imaging localities, redesigning economic governance, or restructuring capital? In N. Jewson and S. MacGregor, eds, *Realising Cities: New Spatial Divisions and Social Transformation*. London: Routledge, 28–41.

Jessop, B. 1997d: The regulation approach: implications for political theory. *Journal of Political Philosophy*, 5 (3), 287–326.

Jessop, B. 1997e: Twenty years of the regulation approach: the paradox of success and failure at home and abroad. *New Political Economy*, 2 (3), 499–522.

Jessop, B. 1998a: The enterprise of narrative and the narrative of enterprise: place marketing and the entrepreneurial city. In T. Hall and P. Hubbard, eds, *The Entrepreneurial City*. Chichester: Wiley, 77–99.

Jessop, B. 1998b: The rise of governance and the risks of failure: the case of local economic development. *International Social Science Journal*, 155, 29–45.

Jessop, B. 1999: Reflections on the (il)logics of globalization. In K. Olds, P. Dicken, P.F. Kelly, L. Kong, and H.W.-C. Yeung, eds, *Globalization and the Asia Pacific: Contested Territories*. London: Routledge, 19–38.

Jessop, B. 2000a: The crisis of the national spatio-temporal fix and the ecological dominance of globalizing capitalism. *International Journal of Urban and Regional Studies*, 24 (2), 323–60.

Jessop, B. 2000b: Governance failure. In G. Stoker, ed., *The New Politics of Local Governance in Britain*. Basingstoke: Macmillan, 11–32.

Jessop, B. 2001a: Institutional (re)turns and the strategic-relational approach. *Environment and Planning A*, 33 (7), 1213–37.

Jessop, B. 2001b: Regulationist and autopoieticist reflections on Polanyi's account of market economies and the market society. *New Political Economy*, 6 (2), 213–32.

Jessop, B. 2001c: Die geschlechtsspezifische Selektivität des Staates. In E. Kreisky, S. Lang, and B. Sauer, eds, *EU, Geschlecht, Staat*. Vienna: Wien Universitätsverlag, 55–85.

Jessop, B. 2001d: What follows Fordism? On the periodization of capitalism and its regulation. In R. Albritton, M. Itoh, R. Westra, and A. Zuege, eds, *Phases of Capitalist Development: Booms, Crises, and Globalization*. Basingstoke: Palgrave, 282–99.

Jessop, B. 2002a: Capitalism, the regulation approach, and critical realism. In A. Brown, S. Fleetwood, and J. Roberts, eds, *Critical Realism and Marxism*. London: Routledge, 88–115.

Jessop, B. 2002b: Globalization and the National State. In S. Aaronowitz and P. Bratsis, eds, *Paradigm Lost: State Theory Reconsidered*. Minneapolis: University of Minnesota Press, 185–220.

Jessop, B. 2002c: Revisiting Thatcherism and its political economy. In A. Bakkan and E. MacDonald, eds, *Critical Political Studies*. Montreal: McGill University Press, 41–56.

Jessop, B. 2002d: *The Future of the Capitalist State*. Cambridge: Polity.

Jessop, B. 2003a: From Thatcherism to New Labour: neo-liberalism, workfarism, and labour market regulation. In H. Overbeek, ed., *The Political Economy of European Unemployment*. London: Routledge, 137–53.

Jessop, B. 2003b: Informational capitalism and empire: the post-marxist celebration of US hegemony in a new world order. *Studies in Political Economy*, 71/2, 39–58.

Jessop, B. 2003c: Kapitalismus, Steuerung und Staat. In S. Buckel, R.-M. Dackweiler, and R. Noppe, eds, *Formen und Felder politischer Intervention. Zur Relevanz von Staat und Steuereung*. Münster: Westfälisches Dampfboot, 30–49.

Jessop, B. 2003d: The political economy of scale and the construction of microregions. In F. Söderbaum and T. Shaw, eds, *Approaches to the New Regionalism*. Basingstoke: Palgrave, 179–96.

Jessop, B. 2004a: Beyond developmental states: a regulationist and state-theoretical analysis. In R. Boyd and T.-W. Ngo, eds, *Asian States: Beyond the Developmental Perspective*. London: Routledge, 19–42.

Jessop, B. 2004b: Critical semiotic analysis and cultural political economy. *Critical Discourse Studies*, 1 (2), 159–74.

Jessop, B. 2004c: Cultural political economy, the knowledge-based economy, and the state. In A. Barry and D. Slater, eds, *The Technological Economy*. London: Routledge, 144–65.

Jessop, B. 2004d: From localities via the spatial turn to spatio-temporal fixes: a strategic-relational odyssey, *http://www.giub.uni-bonn.de/grabher/downloads/Jessop.pdf*, last accessed 23.05.07.

Jessop, B. 2004e: New Labour's doppelte Kehrtwende. *Das Argument*, 256, 494–504.

Jessop, B. 2004f: Multi-level governance and multi-level meta-governance. In I. Bache and M. Flinders, eds, *Multi-Level Governance*. Oxford: Oxford University Press, 49–74.

Jessop B. 2004g: On the limits of *Limits to Capital. Antipode*, 36 (3), 480–96.

Jessop, B. 2005: Critical realism and the strategic-relational approach. *New Formations*, 56, 40–53.

Jessop, B. 2006a: Der Dritte Weg: Neoliberalismus mit menschlichen Zügen? In S. Berg and A. Kaiser, eds, *New Labour und die Modernisierung Großbritanniens*. Augsberg: Wißner, 338–66.

Jessop, B. 2006b: Spatial fixes, temporal fixes, and spatio-temporal fixes. In N. Castree and D. Gregory, eds, *David Harvey: A Critical Reader*. Oxford: Blackwell, 142–66.

Jessop, B. 2006c: State- and regulation-theoretical perspectives on the European Union and the failure of the Lisbon Agenda. *Competition and Change*, 10 (2), 145–65.

Jessop, B. 2007a: Avoiding traps, rescaling the state, governing Europe. In R. Keil and R. Mahon, eds, *Leviathan Undone? Towards a Political Economy of Scale*. Vancouver: University of British Columbia Press, in press.

Jessop, B. 2007b: Ansätze zu einer Verbindung und theoretischer Vermittlung von Systemtheorie und Marx'scher Staatstheorie sowie die materialistisch orientierte Diskurstheorie (Laclau/Mouffe). In J. Kannankulam and J. Wissel, eds, *Marxistische Staatstheorie*. Baden-Baden: Nomos, in press.

Jessop, B. 2007c: Dialogue of the deaf: some reflections on the Poulantzas–Miliband debate. In P. Wetherly, C.W. Barrow, and P. Burnham, eds, *Class, Power, and the State in Capitalist Society: Essays on Ralph Miliband*. Basingstoke: Palgrave, in press.

Jessop, B. 2007d: Knowledge as a fictitious commodity: insights and limits of a Polanyian analysis. In A. Bugra and K. Aratan, eds, *Market Economy as a Political Project*. Basingstoke: Palgrave, 115–33.

Jessop, B. 2007e: Weiterentwicklung von Gramscis Konzept des integralen Staats: Althusser, Poulantzas, Buci-Glucksmann. In S. Buckel and A. Fischer-Lescano, eds, *Die Organization der Hegemonie: Zum Staatsverständnis Antonio Gramscis*. Baden-Baden, Nomos, 39–61.

Jessop, B. 2007f: What follows neo-liberalism? In R. Albritton, B. Jessop, and R. Westra, eds, *Economy of the Present and Possible Global Future(s)*. New York: Anthem, in press.

Jessop, B. forthcoming: *The State*. Cambridge: Polity.

Jessop, B. and Oosterlynck, S. 2007: Cultural political economy: on making the cultural turn without falling into soft economic sociology. *Geoforum*, in press.

Jessop, B. and Sum, N.-L. 2000: An entrepreneurial city in action: Hong Kong's emerging strategies in and for (inter-)urban competition. *Urban Studies*, 37 (12), 2290–315.

Jessop, B. and Sum, N.-L. 2001: Pre-disciplinary and post-disciplinary perspectives in political economy. *New Political Economy*, 6 (1), 89–101.

Jessop, B. and Sum, N.-L. 2006: *Beyond the Regulation Approach: Putting Capitalist Economies in Their Place*. Cheltenham: Edward Elgar.

Jessop, B., Bonnett, K., Bromley, S. and Ling, T. 1984: Thatcherism, authoritarian populism, and two nations. *New Left Review*, 147, 32–60.

Jessop, B., Bonnett, K., Bromley, S. and Ling, T. 1988: *Thatcherism: A Tale of Two Nations*. Cambridge: Polity.

Jessop, B., Bonnett, K. and Bromley, S. 1990: Farewell to Thatcherism? Neo-Liberalism vs New Times. *New Left Review*, 179, 81–102.

Jessop, B., Kastendiek, H., Nielsen, K., and Pedersen, O.K., eds, 1991: *The Politics of Flexibility: Scandinavia, Great Britain, and West Germany*. Cheltenham: Edward Elgar.

Jessop, B., Nielsen, K. and Pedersen, O.K. 1993: Structural competitiveness and strategic capacities: the cases of Britain, Denmark, and Sweden. In S.E. Sjøstrand, ed., *Institutional Change: Theory and Empirical Findings*. New York: M.E. Sharpe, 227–62.

Jetin, B. and de Brunhoff, S. 2000: The Tobin Tax and the regulation of capital movements. In W. Bello, N. Bullard, and K. Malhotra, eds, *New Thinking on Regulating Speculative Capital Markets*. London: Zed, 195–214.

Johnson, C.J. 1987: Political institutions and economic performance. In F.C. Deyo, ed., *The Political Economy of the New Asian Industrialism*. Ithaca: Cornell University Press, 136–64.

Johnstone, M. 1967: Marx and Engels and the concept of the party. *The Socialist Register 1967*, 121–58.

Kalyvas, A. 2004: The stateless theory. Poulantzas's challenge to postmodernism. In S. Aronowitz and P. Bratsis, eds, *Paradigm Lost: State Theory Reconsidered*. Minnesota: University of Minnesota Press, 105–42.

Katz, C.J. 1992: Marx on the peasantry: class in itself or class in struggle? *Review of Politics*, 54 (1), 50–71.

Kelly, D. 2003: *The State of the Political: Concepts of Politics in the Thought of Max Weber, Carl Schmitt and Franz Neumann*. Oxford: Oxford University Press.

Kerr, D. 1999: Beheading the King and enthroning the market: a critique of Foucauldian governmentality. *Science & Society*, 63 (2), 173–202.

Kirchheimer, O. 1969: *Politics, Law and Social Change.* New York: Columbia University Press.

Kitschelt, H. 1991: Industrial governance structures, innovation strategies, and the case of Japan: sectoral or cross-national comparative analysis? *International Organization,* 45 (4), 453–93.

Kittsteiner, H.D. 1991: Reflections on the construction of historical time in Karl Marx. *History and Memory,* 3 (2) 45–86.

Knuttilla, M. and Kubik, W. 2001: *State Theories: Classical, Global and Feminist Perspectives.* London: Zed.

Kooiman, J., ed., 1993: *Modern Governance: New Government-Society Interactions.* London: Sage.

Krasner, S. D. 1978: *Defending the National Interest.* Princeton: Princeton University Press.

Krätke, M. 1984: *Kritik der Staatsfinanzen. Zur politischen Ökonomie des Steuerstaats.* Hamburg: VSA Verlag.

Krätke, M. 2002: 'Hier bricht das Manuskript ab' (Engels). Hat das Kapital einen Schluss? Teil I. In *Beiträge zur Marx—Engels Forschung. Neue Folge 2001.* Hamburg: Argument Verlag, 7–43.

Krätke, M. 2003: 'Hier bricht das Manuskript ab' (Engels). Hat das Kapital einen Schluss? Teil II. In *Beiträge zur Marx—Engels Forschung. Neue Folge 2002.* Hamburg: Argument Verlag, 211–61.

Kuhnle, S. and Alestalo, M. 2000: Introduction: growth, adjustments and survival of European welfare states. In S. Kuhnle, ed., *The Survival of the European Welfare State.* London: Routledge, 3–18.

Kunz, T. 2005: *Der Sicherheitsdiskurs. Die innere Sicherheitspolitik und ihre Kritik.* Bielefeld: Transkript.

Kuwalik, T. 1996: Modern bis maternalistisch: Theorien des Wohlfahrtsstaates. In idem and Sauer, eds, *Der halbierte Staat.* Frankfurt: Campus, 47–81.

Kuwalik, T. and Sauer, B., eds, 1996: *Der halbierte Staat. Grundlagen feministischer Politikwissenschaft.* Frankfurt: Campus.

LaCapra, D. 1987: Reading Marx: the case of *The Eighteenth Brumaire.* In *Rethinking Intellectual History: Texts, Contexts, Language.* Ithaca: Cornell University Press, 268–90.

Laclau, E. and Mouffe, C. 1985: *Hegemony and Socialist Strategy.* London: New Left Books.

Ladeur, K.-H. 1997: Towards a legal theory of supranationality – the viability of the network concept. *European Law Journal,* 3 (3), 33–54.

Lakatos, I. and Musgrave, A., eds, 1970: *Criticism and the Growth of Knowledge.* Cambridge: Cambridge University Press.

Lakoff, G. and Johnson, M. 1980: *Metaphors We Live By.* Chicago: University of Chicago Press.

Landes, J.B. 1988: *Women and the Public Sphere in the Age of the French Revolution.* Ithaca: Cornell University Press.

Larner, W. and Walters, W. 2002: The political rationality of 'new regionalism': toward a genealogy of the region. *Theory and Society*, 31, 391–432.

Lauridsen, L.S. 1991: The debate on the developmental state. In J. Martinussen, ed., *Development Theory and the Role of the State in Third World Countries*. Roskilde: Roskilde University Centre, 108–33.

Lebowitz, M. 2003: *Beyond Capital: Marx's Political Economy of the Working Class*. Basingstoke: Macmillan.

Lercercle, J.-J. 2004: *Une philosophie marxiste du langage*. Paris: Presses Universitaires de France.

Lecourt, D. 1975: *Marxism and Epistemology*. London: New Left Books.

Lefebvre, H. 1974: *The Production of Space*. Oxford: Blackwell (1991).

Lefort, C. 1978: Marx: from one vision of history to another. *Social Research*, 45 (4), 615–66.

Lemke, T. 2000: Neoliberalismus, Staat und Selbsttechnologien: ein kritischer Überblick über die governmentality studies. *Politische Vierteljahresschrift*, 41 (1), 31–47.

Lemke, T. 2003: Andere Affirmationen. Gesellschaftsanalyse und Kritik im Postfordismus. In A. Honneth and M. Saar, eds, *Zwischenbilanz einer Rezeption. Frankfurter Foucault-Konferenz 2001*. Frankfurt: Suhrkamp, 259–74.

Lenin, V.I. 1913: Three sources and three component parts of Marxism. In *Lenin Collected Works, Volume 1*. Moscow: Progress Publishers (1963), 66–70.

Lester, J. 2000: *Dialogue of Negation: Debates on Hegemony in Russia and the West*. London: Pluto Press.

Levi, M. 1988: *Of Rule and Revenue*. Berkeley: University of California Press.

Lipietz, A. 1997: *Green Hopes*. Cambridge: Polity.

Lisbon European Council 2000. Presidency Conclusions, 23 and 24 March 2000, *http://www.europarl.eu.int/summits/lis1_en.htm*, last accessed 23.05.07.

Lister, R. 1996: Dialectics of citizenship. *Hypatia*, 12 (4), 6–26.

Lloyd, G. 1984: *The Man of Reason: 'Male' and 'Female' in Western Philosophy*. Minneapolis: University of Minnesota Press.

Lloyd, G. 1986: Selfhood, war and masculinity. In C. Pateman and E. Grosz, eds, *Feminist Challenges: Social and Political Theory*. London: Allen & Unwin, 63–76.

Locher-Dodge, B. 1997: Internationale Politik – geschlechtsneutrale Paradigmen? In E. Kreisky and B. Sauer, eds, *Geschlechtverhältnisse im Kontext politischer Transformation*. Opladen: Westdeutscher Verlag, 425–40.

Lo Piparo, F. 1979: *Lingua, intelletuali, egemonia in Gramsci*. Bari: Laterza.

Löwy, M. 1989: The poetry of the past: Marx and the French Revolution. *New Left Review*, 177, 111–24.

Luhmann, N. 1970: Funktion und Kausalität. In idem, *Soziologische Aufklärung 1*. Opladen: Westdeutscher Verlag, 9–30.

Luhmann, N. 1979: *Trust and Power*. Chichester: Wiley.

Luhmann, N. 1982a: *The Differentiation of Society*. New York: Columbia University Press.

Luhmann, N. 1982b: The world society as a social system. *International Journal of General Systems*, 8, 131–8.

Luhmann, N. 1986: The autopoiesis of social systems. In F. Geyer and J. van der Zouwen, eds, *Sociocybernetic Paradoxes: Observation, Control and Evolution in Self-Steering Systems*. London: Sage, 172–92.

Luhmann, N. 1989: *Ecological Communication*. Cambridge: Polity.

Luhmann, N. 1990a: Complexity and meaning. In idem, *Essays in Self-Reference*. New York: Columbia University Press, 80–5.

Luhmann, N. 1990b: *Essays in Self-Reference*. New York: Columbia University Press.

Luhmann, N. 1990c: *Political Theory in the Welfare State*. Berlin: Walter de Gruyter.

Luhmann, N. 1990d: State and politics: towards a semantics of the self-description of political systems. In idem, *Political Theory in the Welfare State*. Berlin: Walter de Gruyter, 117–54.

Luhmann, N. 1990e: The 'State' of the political system. In idem, *Essays in Self-Reference*. New York: Columbia University Press, 165–74.

Luhmann, N. 1995: *Social Systems*. Stanford: Stanford University Press.

Luhmann, N. 1997: Globalization or world society? How to conceive of modern society. *International Review of Sociology*, 7 (1), 67–75.

Luhmann, N. 2000: *Die Politik der Gesellschaft*. Frankfurt: Suhrkamp.

Luke, T.W. 1994: Placing power/siting space: The politics of global and local in the New World Order. *Environment and Planning D: Society and Space*, 12 (4), 613–28.

Lukes, S. 1974: *Power: A Radical Analysis*. Basingstoke: Macmillan.

MacInnes, J. 1998: *The End of Masculinity: The Confusion of Sexual Genesis and Sexual Difference in Modern Society*. Buckingham: Open University Press.

McIntosh, M. 1978: The state and the oppression of women. In A. Kuhn and A. Wolpe, eds, *Feminism and Materialism*. London: Routledge & Kegan Paul, 254–80.

MacKinnon, C.A. 1982: Feminism, Marxism, method, and the sphere of the state: an agenda for theory. *Signs*, 7 (3), 515–44.

MacKinnon, C.A. 1983: Feminism, Marxism, method, and the sphere of the state: towards feminist jurisprudence. *Signs*, 8 (4), 634–58.

MacKinnon, C.A. 1988: *Feminism Unmodified: Discourses on Life and Law*. Cambridge, MA: Harvard University Press.

McLennan, G. 1981: *Marxism and the Methodologies of History*. London: New Left Books.

McNay, L. 1994: *Foucault: A Critical Introduction*. Cambridge: Polity.

Mahon, R. 1991: From 'bringing' to 'putting': the state in late twentieth-century social theory. *Canadian Journal of Sociology*, 16 (2), 119–44.

Majone, G. 1993: The European Community between social policy and social regulation. *Journal of Common Market Studies*, 31 (2), 153–70.

Majone, G. 1997: From the positive to the regulatory state: causes and consequences in the mode of governance. *Journal of Public Policy*, 17 (2), 139–67.

Mann, M. 1984: The autonomous power of the state: its origins, mechanisms and results. *Archives Européennes de Sociologie*, 25, 185–213.

Mann, M. 1986: *The Sources of Social Power: Volume I. A History of Power from the Beginning to A.D. 1760*. Cambridge: Cambridge University Press.

Mann, M. 1987: War and social theory: into battle with classes, nations and states. In C. Creighton and M. Shaw, eds, *The Sociology of War and Peace*. Basingstoke: Macmillan, 54–72.

Mann, M. 1988: *States, War and Capitalism*. Oxford: Blackwell.

Mann, M. 1993: Nation-states in Europe and other continents: diversifying, developing, not dying. *Daedalus*, 122 (3), 115–40.

Mann, S. and Huffman, D.J. 2005: The decentering of second wave feminism and the rise of the third wave. *Science & Society*, 69 (1), 56–91.

Marsden, R. 1999: *The Nature of Capital: Marx after Foucault*. London: Routledge.

Marsh, D., Buller, J., Hay, C., Johnston, J., Kerr, P. and McAnulla, S. 1999: *Postwar British Politics in Perspective*. Cambridge: Polity.

Martin, B. 1982: Feminism, criticism and Foucault. *New German Critique*, 27, 3–30.

Marx, K. 1843: Contribution to a critique of Hegel's *Philosophy of Law*. *Marx–Engels Collected Works 3*. London: Lawrence & Wishart (1975), 3–129.

Marx, K. 1844: Critical marginal notes on the article 'The King of Prussia and Social Reform. By a Prussian'. *Marx–Engels Collected Works 3*. London: Lawrence & Wishart (1975), 189–206.

Marx, K. 1850: *The Class Struggles in France*. *Marx–Engels Collected Works 10*. London: Lawrence & Wishart (1978), 47–145.

Marx, K. 1852: *The Eighteenth Brumaire of Louis Bonaparte* [translated by T. Carver]. In M. Cowling and J. Martin, eds, *The Eighteenth Brumaire Today*. London: Pluto (2002), 19–109.

Marx, K. 1857: Introduction. In idem, *Grundrisse: Foundations of the Critique of Political Economy (Rough Draft)*. Harmondsworth: Penguin (1973), 81–111.

Marx, K. 1858: The rule of the pretorians. *Marx–Engels Collected Works 15*. London: Lawrence & Wishart (1986), 464–7.

Marx, K. 1859: Preface. In *Contribution to the Critique of Political Economy*. *Marx–Engels Collected Works 28*. London: Lawrence & Wishart (1987), 261–5.

Marx, K. 1867: *Capital Vol. I*. London: Lawrence & Wishart (1976).

Marx, K. 1871a: *The Civil War in France*. *Marx–Engels Collected Works 22*. London: Lawrence & Wishart (1986), 307–57.

Marx, K. 1871b: First draft of *The Civil War in France*. *Marx–Engels Collected Works 22*. London: Lawrence & Wishart (1986), 437–514.

Marx, K. 1873: Afterword to the second German edition of *Capital*. In idem, *Capital Vol. I*. London: Lawrence & Wishart (1976), 22–9.

Marx, K. 1894: *Capital Vol. III*. London: Lawrence & Wishart (1976).

Marx, K. and Engels, F. 1848: Manifesto of the Communist Party. *Marx–Engels Collected Works* 6. London: Lawrence & Wishart (1976), 477–519.

Marx, K. and Engels, F. 1850: Address of the Central Authority to the League, March 1850. *Marx–Engels Collected Works* 10. London: Lawrence & Wishart (1978), 277–87.

Massey, D. 1995: Places and their pasts. *History Workshop Journal*, 39, 182–92.

Matzner, E. 1994: Instrument-targeting or context-making? A new look at the theory of economic policy. *Journal of Economic Issues*, 28 (2), 461–76.

Mayntz, R. 2001: *Zur Selektivität der steuerungstheoretischen Perspektive*. Cologne: Max Planck Institut für Gesellschaftsforschung. Working Paper 01/2, *http://www.mpi-fg-koeln.mpg.de/pu/workpap/wp01-2/wp01-2.html*, last accessed 24.05.07.

Mehlman, J. 1977: *Revolution and Repetition: Marx/Hugo/Balzac*. Berkeley: University of California Press.

Melossi, D. 1990: *The State and Social Control*. Cambridge: Polity.

Messner, D. 1998: *The Network Society*. London: Cass.

Meyer, J., Boli, J., Thomas, G.M. and Ramirez, F. 1997: World society and the nation-state. *American Journal of Sociology*, 103 (1), 144–81.

Meyet, S., Naves, M.-C., and Ribmont, T., eds, 2006: *Travailler avec Foucault: retours sur le politique*. Paris: L'Harmattan.

Mies, M. 1986: *Patriarchy and Accumulation on a World Scale*. London: Zed.

Migdal, J. 1988: *Strong States and Weak Societies*. Berkeley: University of California Press.

Miliband, R. 1965: Marx and the state. *Socialist Register 1965*, 278–96.

Miliband, R. 1968: *The State in Capitalist Society*. London: Lawrence & Wishart.

Miliband, R. 1970: The problem of the capitalist state: reply to Poulantzas. *New Left Review*, 59, 43–60.

Miliband, R. 1973: Poulantzas and the capitalist state. *New Left Review*, 82, 83–92.

Miller, P. and Rose, N. 1990: Governing economic life. *Economy and Society*, 19 (1), 1–31.

Mitchell, T.J. 1988: *Colonising Egypt*. Cambridge: Cambridge University Press.

Mitchell, T.J. 1991: The limits of the state: beyond statist approaches and their critics. *American Political Science Review*, 85 (1), 77–96.

Mitchell, T.J. 2001: *Rule of Experts: Egypt, Techno-Politics, Modernity*. Berkeley: University of California Press.

Mohanty, C.T., Russo, A., and Torres, L., eds, 1991: *Third World Women and the Politics of Feminism*. Bloomington: Indiana University Press.

Moore, S.W. 1957: *The Critique of Capitalist Democracy*. New York: Paine Whitman.

Moravcsik, A. 1998: *The Choice for Europe: Social Purpose and State Power from Rome to Maastricht*. Ithaca: Cornell University Press.

Morera, E. 1990: *Gramsci's Historicism: A Realist Interpretation*. London: Routledge.

Morin, E. 1980: *La méthode: la vie de la vie*, Vol 2. Paris: Seuil.

Naples, N.A. 1997: The 'new consensus' on the gendered 'social contract': the 1987–1988 U.S. Congressional hearings on welfare reform. *Signs*, 22 (4), 907–45.

Nash, K. 1998: *Universal Difference: Feminism and the Liberal Undecidability of Women*. Basingstoke: Macmillan.

Neocleous, M. 1996: *Administering Civil Society: Towards a Theory of State Power*. Basingstoke: Macmillan.

Neocleous, M. 2003: *Imagining the State*. Maidenhead: Open University Press.

Nettl, J.P. 1968: The state as a conceptual variable. *World Politics*, 20 (4), 559–92.

Neumann, F. 1964: *The Democratic and the Authoritarian State*. Glencoe, IL: Free Press.

Neyer, G. 1996: Korporatismus und Verbände. Garanten für die Stabilität eines sexistischen Systems. In T. Kuwalik and B. Sauer, eds, *Der halbierte Staat. Grundlagen feministischer Politikwissenschaft*. Frankfurt: Campus, 82–104.

Nimtz, A.H. 1999: Marx and Engels: the unsung heroes of the democratic breakthrough. *Science & Society*, 63 (2), 203–31.

Nimtz, A.H. 2000: *Marx and Engels. Their Contribution to the Democratic Breakthrough*. Albany: State University of New York Press.

Nonhoff, M. 2006. *Politischer Diskurs und Hegemonie. Das Projekt 'Soziale Marktwirtschaft'*. Bielefeld: Transcript.

Nordlinger, E.A. 1981: *The Autonomy of the Democratic State*. Cambridge, MA: Harvard University Press.

Nowotny, H. 1994: *Time*. Cambridge: Polity.

O'Connor, J. 1998: *Natural Causes: Essays in Ecological Marxism*. New York: Guilford.

O'Connor, J.S. 1996: From women in the welfare state to the gendering of welfare state regimes. *Current Sociology*, 44 (2), 1–125.

O'Connor, J.S. 1993: Gender, class and citizenship in comparative analysis of gender relations and welfare states. *British Journal of Sociology*, 44 (4), 501–18.

Offe, C. 1972: *Strukturprobleme des kapitalischen Staates*. Frankfurt: Campus.

Offe, C. 1984: *Contradictions of the Welfare State*. London: Hutchinson.

Okin, S. 1979: *Women in Western Political Thought*. Princeton: Princeton University Press.

Önis, Z. 1991: The logic of the developmental state. *Comparative Politics*, 24 (1), 109–26.

Oppenheimer, F. 1908: *The State*. Indianapolis: Bobbs-Merrill.

O Tuathail, G. 1996: *Critical Geopolitics*. Minneapolis: University of Minnesota Press.

Overbeek, H. 2004: Transnational class formation and concepts of control. *Journal of International Relations and Development*, 7 (2), 113–41.

Painter, J. 2006: Prosaic geographies of stateness. *Political Geography*, 25, 752–74.

Palombarini, S. 1999: Vers une théorie régulationniste de la politique économique. In Association Régulation et Recherche, *L'Année de la régulation 1999*. Paris: La Découverte, 97–126.

Pandolfi, M. 1998: Two Italies: rhetorical figures of failed nationhood. In J. Schneider, ed., *Italy's 'Southern Question': Orientalism in One Country*. Oxford: Berg, 285–9.

Parker, J. 2000: *Structuration*. Buckingham: Open University Press.

Pateman, C. 1988: *The Sexual Contract*. Stanford: Stanford University Press.

Peck, J. and Theodore, N. 2001: Exporting workfare/importing welfare-to-work. *Political Geography*, 20, 427–60.

Peterson, V.S., ed., 1992: *Gendered States: Feminist (Re-)Visions of International Relations Theory*. Boulder, CO: Lynne Rienner.

Petrey, S. 1988: The reality of representation: between Marx and Balzac. *Critical Inquiry*, 14, 448–68.

Pettman, J. J. 1996: *Worlding Women*. London: Routledge.

Pierre, J., ed., 1999: *Debating Governance: Authority, Steering, and Democracy*. Oxford: Oxford University Press.

Pinder, J. 1991: *European Community: The Building of a Union*. Oxford: Oxford University Press.

Pitschas, R. 1995: Europäische Integration als Netzwerkkoordination komplexer Staatsaufgaben. In T. Ellwein, D. Grimm, J.J. Hesse, and G.F. Schuppert, eds, *Jahrbuch zur Staats- und Verwaltungswissehschaft. Band 8*. Baden-Baden: Nomos, 379–416.

Poggi, G. 1979: Introduction. In N. Luhmann, *Trust and Power*. Chichester: Wiley, vii–xii.

Polanyi, K. 1957: *The Great Transformation*. Boston: Beacon.

Portelli, H. 1973: *Gramsci y el bloque histórico*. Mexico: Siglo Veintiuno.

Porter, B. 1994: *War and the Rise of the State*. New York: Free Press.

Poster, M. 1984: *Foucault, Marxism, and History*. Cambridge: Polity.

Postone, M. 1993: *Time, Labor, Social Domination*. Cambridge: Cambridge University Press.

Poulantzas, N. 1967: Marxist political theory in Great Britain. *New Left Review*, 43, 67–78.

Poulantzas, N. 1969: The problem of the capitalist state. *New Left Review*, 58, 67–78.

Poulantzas, N. 1973. *Political Power and Social Classes*. London: New Left Books.

Poulantzas, N. 1974: *Fascism and Dictatorship*. London: New Left Books.

Poulantzas, N. 1975: *Classes in Contemporary Capitalism*. London: Verso.

Poulantzas, N. 1976a: *Crisis of the Dictatorships: Portugal, Greece, Spain*. London: Verso.

Poulantzas, N. 1976b: Les transformations actuelles de l'État, la crise politique et la crise de l'État. In idem, ed., *La Crise de l'État*. Paris: Presses Universitaires de France, 19–58.

Poulantzas, N. 1976c: La crise de l'État. *France Nouvelle*, 1 November.

Poulantzas, N. 1976d: The capitalist state: a reply to Miliband and Laclau. *New Left Review*, 95, 63–83.

Poulantzas, N. 1977: Crise de capitalisme, crise de la société, crise de l'État. *La Nouvelle Critique*, 101, 5–11.

Poulantzas, N. 1978a: L'État, le pouvoir, le socialisme. *Faire*, 29 March.

Poulantzas, N. 1978b: *State, Power, Socialism*. London: Verso.

Poulantzas, N. 1979a: Es geht darum mit der Stalinistischen Tradition zu brechen. *Prokla*, 37, 127–40.

Poulantzas, N. 1979b: Interview with Nicos Poulantzas. *Marxism Today*, July, 198–205.

Poulantzas, N. 1979c: Is there a crisis in Marxism? *Journal of the Hellenic Diaspora*, 6 (3), 7–16.

Poulantzas, N. 1979d: La crise des partis. *Le Monde Diplomatique*, 26, September, 7–16.

Poulantzas, N. 1979e: L'état, les mouvements sociaux, le parti. *Dialectiques*, 28: 7–16.

Poulantzas, N. 1980a: La déplacement des procedures de legitimation. In Université de Vincennes, *Le nouvel ordre intérieur*. Paris: Moreau, 138–43.

Poulantzas, N. 1980b: The ideological fronts must be widened. *Diabazo*, 29 January (in Greek).

Prawer, S.S. 1978: *Karl Marx and World Literature*. Oxford: Oxford University Press.

Prezzolini, C. 1967: *Machiavelli*. London: Robert Hale.

Pringle, R. and Watson, S. 1992: 'Women's interests' and the post-structuralist state. In M. Barrett and A. Phillips, eds, *Destabilizing Theory: Contemporary Feminist Debates*. Cambridge: Polity, 53–73.

Prinz, A.M. 1969: The background and ulterior motive of Marx's Preface of 1859. *Journal of the History of Ideas*, 30 (3), 437–50.

Przeworski, A. 1977: Proletariat into a class: the process of class formation from Karl Kautsky's *The Class Struggle* to recent controversies. *Politics and Society*, 7 (4), 343–402.

Radaelli, C.M. 2003: *The Open Method of Coordination: A New Governance Architecture for Europe?* Swedish Institute of European Policy Studies, *http://www.sieps.se/publ/rapporter/bilagor/20031.pdf*, last accessed 24.05.07.

Radcliffe, S. 1993: 'People have to rise up – like the great women fighters': The state and peasant women in Peru. In S. Radcliffe and S. Westwood, eds, *Viva: Women and Popular Protest in Latin America*. London: Routledge, 197–218.

Ragin, C.C. 1987: *The Comparative Method: Moving beyond Qualitative and Quantitative Strategies*. Berkeley: University of California Press.

Ragin, C.C. 2000: *Fuzzy-Set Social Science*. Chicago: University of Chicago Press.

Ramazanoglu, C., ed., 1993: *Up against Foucault: Explorations of Some Tensions between Foucault and Feminism*. London: Routledge.

Randall, V. and Waylen, G., eds, 1998: *Gender, Politics and the State*. London: Routledge.

Ray, L. and Sayer, A., eds, 1999: *Culture and Economy after the Cultural Turn*. London: Sage.

Regini, M. 2000: Between deregulation and social pacts: the responses of European economies to globalization. *Politics and Society*, 28 (1), 5–33.

Resch, R.P. 1992: *Althusser and the Renewal of Marxist Social Theory*. Berkeley: University of California Press.

Rescher, N. 1998: *Complexity: A Philosophical Overview*. New Brunswick: Transaction Books.

Reuten, G. and Williams, M. 1989: *Value-Form and the State*. London: Routledge.

Reynolds, S., ed., 1986: *Women, State, and Revolution: Essays on Power and Gender in Europe since 1789*. Brighton: Wheatsheaf.

Rhodes, M. 1998: 'Subversive liberalism': market integration, globalization and West European welfare states. In W.D. Coleman and G.R. Underhill, eds, *Regionalism and Global Economic Integration: Europe, Asia and the Americas*. London: Routledge, 99–121.

Richter, D. 1996: *Nation als Form*. Opladen: Westdeutscher Verlag.

Rickert, H. 1902: *Die Grenzen der naturwissenschaftenlichen Begriffsbildung*. Tübingen: J.C.B. Mohr (second edition).

Rickert, H. 1986: *The Limits of Concept Formation in Natural Science: A Logical Introduction to the Historical Sciences*. Cambridge: Cambridge University Press (abridged translation of Rickert 1902).

Rieger, E. and Leibfried, S. 1998: Welfare state limits to globalization. *Politics and Society*, 26 (3), 363–90.

Ringer, F.K. 2000: *Max Weber's Methodology: The Unification of the Cultural and Social Sciences*. Cambridge, MA: Harvard University Press.

Riquelme, J.P. 1980: *The Eighteenth Brumaire* of Karl Marx as symbolic action. *History and Theory*, 19 (1), 58–72.

Roe, E. 1994: *Narrative Policy Analysis: Theory and Practice*. Durham, NC: Duke University Press.

Rose, M.A. 1978: *Reading the Young Marx and Engels*. London: Croom Helm.

Rose, N. 1996: The death of the social? Re-figuring the territory of government. *Economy and Society*, 25 (4), 327–56.

Rose, N. 1999: *Powers of Freedom*. Cambridge: Cambridge University Press.

Rose, N. and Miller, P. 1992: Political power beyond the state: problematics of government. *British Journal of Sociology*, 43 (2), 173–205.

Rosenberg, J. 1994: *The Empire of Civil Society*. London: Verso.

Rosenberger, S.K. 1997: Privatheit und Politik. In E. Kreisky and B. Sauer, eds, *Geschlechtverhältnisse im Kontext politischer Transformation*. Opladen: Westdeutscher Verlag, 129–36.

Ruigrok, W. and van Tulder, R. 1996: The price of diversity: rival concepts of control as a barrier to an EU industrial strategy. In P. Devine, Y. Katsoulacos, and R. Sugden, eds, *Competitiveness, Subsidiarity, and Industrial Policy*. London: Routledge, 79–103.

Ruschinski, H. and Retzleff–Kresse, B., eds, 1974: *Marx–Engels: Über Sprache, Stil und Übersetzung*. Berlin: Dietz Verlag.

Said, E.W. 2001: History, literature and geography. In idem, *Reflections on Exile and Other Literary and Cultural Essays*. London: Granta Books, 453–73.

Sainsbury, D., ed., 1994: *Gendering Welfare States*. London: Sage.

Santiso, J. 2000: Political sluggishness and economic speed: a Latin American perspective. *Social Science Information*, 39 (2), 233–53.

Santiso, J. and Schedler, A. 1998: Democracy and time: an invitation. *International Political Science Review*, 19 (1), 5–18.

Sassoon, A.S. 1987: *Gramsci's Politics*. London: Hutchinson.

Sauer, B. 1997: 'Die Magd der Industriegesellschaft'. Anmerkungen zur Geschlechtsblindheit von Staats- und Institutionentheorie. In B. Kerchner and G. Wilde, eds, *Staat und Privatheit. Aktuelle Studien zu einem schwierigen Verhältnis*. Opladen: Leske & Budrich, 29–54.

Sawacki, J. 1991: Foucault and feminism: towards a politics of difference. In M. Stanley and C. Pateman, eds, *Feminist Interpretations and Political Theory*. Cambridge: Polity, 217–31.

Sayer, A. 2000: *Realism and Social Science*. London: Sage.

Sbragia, A. M. 2000: The European Union as coxswain: governance by steering. In J. Pierre, ed., *Debating Governance: Authority, Steering, and Democracy*. Oxford: Oxford University Press, 219–40.

Scharpf, F.W. 1999: *Governing in Europe: Effective and Democratic?* Oxford: Oxford University Press.

Scherrer, C. 1995: Eine diskursanalytische Kritik der Regulationstheorie. *Prokla*, 100, 457–82.

Scheuerman, W.E. 2000: The economic state of emergency. *Cardozo Law Review*, 21, 1868–94.

Scheuerman, W.E. 2001: Reflexive law and the challenges of globalization. *Journal of Political Philosophy*, 8 (4), 81–102.

Scheuerman, W.E. 2004: *Liberal Democracy and the Social Acceleration of Time*. Baltimore: Johns Hopkins University Press.

Schimank, U. 2005: Funktionale Differenzierung und gesellschaftsweiter Primat von Teilsystemen – offene Fragen bei Parsons und Luhmann. *Soziale Systeme*, 11 (2), 395–414.

Schmitt, C. 1921: *Die Diktatur*. Berlin: Duncker & Humblot.

Schmitt, C. 1928: *Verfassungslehre*. Munich: Duncker & Humblot.

Schmitt, C. 1985: *Political Theology: Four Chapters on the Concept of Sovereignty*. Cambridge, MA: MIT Press.

Schmitt, C. 2001: *State, Movement, People*. Washington, DC: Plutarch Press.

Schmitter, P. C. 1992: Representation and the future Euro-Polity. *Staatswissenschaften und Staatspraxis*, 3 (3), 379–405.

Schoenberger, E.J. 1997: *The Cultural Crisis of the Firm*. Oxford: Blackwell.

Schram, S.F. and Neisser, P.T., eds, 1997: *Tales of the State: Narrative in Contemporary US Politics and Public Policy*. Lanham, MD: Rowman & Littlefield.

Schriewer, J. 1999: Vergleich und Erklärung zwischen Kausalität und Komplexität. In H. Kaelble and J. Schriewer, eds, *Diskurse und Entwicklungspfade: der Gesellschaftsvergleich in den Geschichts- und Sozialwissenschaften*. Frankfurt: Suhrkamp, 53–102.

Scott, J. and Trubek, D. 2002: Mind the gap: law and new approaches to governance in the European Union. *European Law Journal*, 8 (2), 1–18.

Scott, J.C. 1998: *Seeing Like a State: How Certain Schemes to Improve the Human Condition Have Failed*. New Haven: Yale University Press.

Scott, J.W. 1999: Some reflections on gender and politics. In M.M. Ferree, J. Lorder, and B.B. Hess, eds, *Revisioning Gender*. London: Sage, 70–96.

Shaw, M. 1991: *Post-Military Society: Demilitarization, Militarism and War at the End of the Twentieth Century*. Cambridge: Polity.

Shaw, M. 2000: *Theory of the Global State: Globality as an Unfinished Revolution*. Cambridge: Cambridge University Press.

Shortall, F.C. 1994: *The Incomplete Marx*. Aldershot: Ashgate.

Siim, B. 1988: Towards a feminist rethinking of the welfare state. In idem, ed., *The Political Interests of Women*. London: Sage, 160–87.

Siim, B. 1991: Welfare state, gender politics and equality policies: women's citizenship in the Scandinavian welfare states. In K.B. Jones and A.G. Jónasdóttir, eds, *The Political Interests of Gender*. London: Sage, 160–86.

Simmel, G. 1892: *Probleme der Geschichtsphilosophie. Eine erkenntnistheoretische Studie*, Leipzig: Duncker & Humblot. Available at *http://socio.ch/sim/geschichtsphilosophie/index.htm*, last accessed 23.05.07.

Skinner, Q. 1989: The State. In T. Ball, ed., *Political Innovation and Social Change*. Cambridge: Cambridge University Press, 90–131.

Skocpol, T. 1979: *States and Social Revolutions: A Comparative Analysis of France. Russia and China*. Cambridge: Cambridge University Press.

Skocpol, T. 1985: Bringing the state back in: strategies of analysis in current research. In P.B. Evans, D. Rueschemeyer, and T. Skocpol, eds, *Bringing the State Back In*. Cambridge: Cambridge University Press, 3–43.

Skocpol, T. 1992: *Protecting Soldiers and Mothers: The Political Origins of Social Policy in the United States*. Cambridge, MA: Harvard University Press.

Smart, B. 1986: The politics of truth and the power of hegemony. In D. Hoy, ed., *Foucault: A Critical Reader*. Oxford: Blackwell, 157–73.

Smart, C. 1989: *Feminism and the Power of Law.* London: Routledge.

Smend, R. 1955: Verfassung und Verfassungsrecht. In idem, *Staatsrechtliche Abhandlungen und andere Aufsätze.* Berlin: Duncker & Humblot, 119–276 (third edition).

Smith, M.J. 2000: *Rethinking State Theory.* London: Routledge.

Smith, M.P. 2000: *Transnational Urbanism: Locating Globalization,* Oxford: Blackwell.

Smith, N. 1984: *Uneven Development: Nature, Capital and the Production of Space.* Oxford: Blackwell.

Soja, E. 1989: *Post-Modern Geographies: The Reassertion of Space in Critical Social Theory.* Oxford: Blackwell.

Somers, M. 1994: The narrative constitution of identity: a relational and network approach. *Theory and Society,* 23, 605–49.

Sørensen, G. 2001. *Changes in Statehood: The Transformation of International Relations.* Basingstoke: Palgrave.

Spivak, G.C. 1988: Can the subaltern speak? In C. Nelson and L. Grossberg, eds, *Marxism and the Interpretation of Culture.* Urbana: University of Illinois Press, 271–313.

Stahel, A.W. 1999: Time contradictions of capitalism. *Culture, Nature, Society,* 10 (1), 101–32.

Stallybrass, P. 1990: Marx and heterogeneity: thinking the lumpenproletariat. *Representations,* 31, 69–95.

Stallybrass, P. 1998: 'Well grubbed, old mole': Marx, *Hamlet,* and the (un)fixing of representation. *Cultural Studies,* 12 (1), 3–14.

Stella, D. 2000: Globalization, think tanks and policy transfer. In D. Stone, ed., *Banking on Knowledge.* London: Routledge, 203–20.

Stepan, A.D. 1985: State power and the strength of civil society in the Southern Cone of Latin America. In P.B. Evans, D. Rueschemeyer, and T. Skocpol, eds, *Bringing the State Back In.* Cambridge: Cambridge University Press, 317–45.

Stetson, D.M. and Mazur, A.G., eds, 1995: *Comparative State Feminism.* London: Sage.

Stichweh, R. 2000: *Die Weltgesellschaft: Soziologische Analysen.* Frankfurt: Suhrkamp.

Stirk, P.M.R. 2006: The concept of the state in German political thought. *Debatte,* 14 (3), 213–28.

Stones, R. 1991: Strategic context analysis: a new research strategy for structuration theory. *Sociology,* 25 (4), 673–96.

Stones, R. 2005: *Structuration Theory.* Basingstoke: Palgrave.

Storper, M.J. 1997: *The Regional World: Territorial Development in a Global Economy.* New York: Guilford.

Storper, M.J. and Scott, A.J. 1997: The wealth of regions: market forces and policy imperatives in local and global context. *Futures,* 27 (5), 505–26.

Streeck, W. 1994: European social policy after Maastricht: The 'social dialogue' and 'subsidiarity'. *Economic and Industrial Democracy*, 15, 151–77.

Streeck, W. and Schmitter, P.C., eds, 1985: *Private Interest Government: Beyond Market and State*. London: Sage.

Sum, N.-L. 1994: *Reflections on Accumulation, Regulation, the State and Societalization: A Stylized Model of East Asian Capitalism and an Integral Economic Analysis of Hong Kong*, Ph.D. thesis, Department of Sociology, Lancaster University.

Sum, N.-L. 1995: More than a 'war of words': identity politics and the struggle for dominance during the recent 'political reform' period in Hong Kong. *Economy and Society*, 24 (1), 68–99.

Sum, N.-L. 1996: Modified human rights and unmodified liberal feminism: the hegemonic force of Hillary Clinton's 'United Sisterhood'. *New Political Economy*, 1 (2), 278–82.

Sum, N.-L. 1999a: Politics of identities and the making of the 'Greater China' subregion in the post-Cold War era. In G. Hook and I. Kearns, eds, *Subregionalisms and the New World Order*. Basingstoke: Macmillan, 197–222.

Sum, N.-L. 1999b: Rethinking globalization: re-articulating the spatial scale and temporal horizons of trans-border spaces. In K. Olds, P. Dicken, P.F. Kelly, L. Kong, and H.W.-C. Yeung, eds, *Globalization and the Asia-Pacific*. London: Routledge, 129–48.

Sum, N.-L. 2000: From politics of identity to politics of complexity: a research agenda for feminist politics/movements across time. In M. McNeil and S. Ahmed, eds, *Transformations: Thinking through Feminism*. Basingstoke: Macmillan, 131–44.

Sum, N.-L. 2001: A material-discursive approach to the 'Asian Crisis': the roles of the IMF and Japan. In P. Preston and J. Gilson, eds, *The European Union and East Asia: Interregional Linkages in a Changing Global System*. Cheltenham: Edward Elgar, 125–53.

Sum, N.-L. 2002: The material, strategic and discursive dimensions of the Asian crisis. In P. Masina, ed., *Rethinking Development in East Asia: From Illusions Miracle to Economic Crisis*. London: Curzon, 53–78.

Sum, N.-L. 2003: (Re-)Imagining 'Greater China': Silicon Valley and the strategy of siliconization. In C. Hughes and G. Wacker, eds, *China and the Internet: Politics of the Digital Leap Forward*. London: RoutledgeCurzon, 102–26.

Sum, N.-L. 2004: From 'integral state' to 'integral world economic order': towards a neo-Gramscian cultural international political economy. IAS Cultural Political Economy Working Paper Series, No. 7. Lancaster University, *http://www.lancs.ac.uk/ias/polecon/index.htm*, last accessed 25.05.07.

Sum, N.-L. 2005: From 'new constitutionalism' to 'new ethicalism': global business governance and the discourses and practices of corporate social responsibility. Lancaster University, paper prepared for Conference of European Consortium of Political Research, Granada, 14–19 April.

Sum, N.-L. 2006a: From regulation approach to cultural political economy. University of Newcastle, Global Urban Research Unit, *http://demologos.ncl. ac.uk/wp/wp1/disc.php*, last accessed 23.05.07.

Sum, N.-L. 2006b: Culture, ideology, hegemony and discourse model. University of Newcastle, Global Urban Research Unit, *http://www.demologos/ncl.ac.uk/wp/wp2.disc.php*, last accessed 23.05.07.

Sum, N.-L. and Jessop, B. 2006: Towards a cultural international political economy: post-structuralism and the Italian School. In M. de Goede, ed., *International Political Economy and Poststructural Politics*. Basingstoke: Palgrave, 157–76.

Sum, N.-L. and Jessop, B. 2008: *Towards a Cultural Political Economy*. Cheltenham: Edward Elgar, in press.

Sum, N.-L. and Pun, N. 2005: Paradoxes of ethical transnational production: codes of conduct in a Chinese workplace. *Competition and Change*, 9 (2), 181–200.

Swyngedouw, E. A. 1997: Neither global nor local: 'glocalization' and the politics of scale. In K. Cox, ed., *Spaces of Globalization*. New York: Guilford Press, 137–66.

Sylvester, C. 1994: *Feminist Theory and International Relations in a Postmodern Era*. Cambridge: Cambridge University Press.

Sylvester, C. 2002: *Feminist International Relations: An Unfinished Journey*. Cambridge: Cambridge University Press.

Taylor, P. 1975: The politics of the European Communities: the confederal phase. *World Politics*, 27, 336–60.

Taylor, P.J. 1995: Beyond containers, internationality, interstateness, interterritoriality. *Progress in Human Geography*, 19 (1), 1–22.

Taylor, P.J. 1996: Embedded statism and the social sciences: opening up to new spaces. *Environment and Planning A*, 28 (11), 1917–28.

Teeple, G. 1983: *Marx's Critique of Politics, 1842–1847*. Toronto: University of Toronto Press.

Telò, M. 2002: Governance and government in the European Union: the open method of coordination. In M.J. Rodrigues, ed., *The New Knowledge Economy in Europe*. Cheltenham: Edward Elgar, 242–72.

Teschke, B. 2003: *The Myth of 1648: Class, Geopolitics and the Making of Modern International Relations*. London: Verso.

Teschke, B. 2006: Debating 'The Myth of 1648': state formation, the interstate system and the emergence of capitalism in Europe – a rejoinder. *International Politics*, 43 (4), 531–73.

Teubner, G. 1993: *Law as an Autopoietic System*. Oxford: Blackwell.

Théret, B. 1992: *Régimes économiques de l'ordre politique. Ésquisse d'une théorie régulationniste des limites de l'État*, Paris: Presses Universitaires de France.

Théret, B.1994: To have or to be: on the problem of the interaction between state and economy and its 'solidarist' mode of regulation. *Economy and Society*, 23 (1), 1–46.

Thomas, P. 1994: *Alien Politics: Marxist State Theory Revisited*. London: Routledge.

Thorburn, W.M. 1918: The myth of Occam's razor. *Mind*, 27 (107), 345–53.

Threlfall, M. 1998: State feminism or party feminism? *European Journal of Women's Studies*, 5 (1), 69–93.

Threlfall, M., ed., 1996: *Mapping the Women's Movement: Feminist Politics and Social Transformation in the North*. London: Verso.

Thrift, N. 1999: The place of complexity. *Theory, Culture, Society*, 16 (3), 31–69.

Tilly, C. 1973: Reflections on the history of European state-making. In idem, ed., *The Formation of National States in Western Europe*. Princeton: Princeton University Press, 3–83.

Tilly, C. 1992: *Coercion, Capital and European States AD 990–1990*. Oxford: Blackwell.

Vacca, G. 1999: *Appuntamenti con Gramsci. Introduzione allo studio dei 'Quaderni del carcere'*. Rome: Carocci Editore.

van Apeldoorn, B. 2002: *Transnational Capitalism and the Struggle over European Integration*. London: Routledge.

van der Pijl, K. 1984: *The Making of an Atlantic Ruling Class*. London: Verso.

van Dijk, T.A. 1997: *Discourse as Social Interaction*. London: Sage.

Veltz, P. 1996: *Mondialisation, villes et territoires: l'économie archipel*. Paris: Presses Universitaires de France.

Virilio, P. 1994: *The Art of the Motor*. Minnesota: University of Minneapolis Press.

Virilio, P. 1998: *The Virilio Reader* (ed. J. Der Derian). Oxford: Blackwell.

Vobruba, G. 1995: Sozialpolitik im inszenierten Eurokorporatismus. *Zeitschrift für Sozialreform*, 41 (1), 1–17.

Vogel, U. 1999: The state and the making of gender. In V. Randall and G. Waylen, eds, *Gender, Politics and the State*. London: Sage, 29–45.

von Beyme, K. 1985: Karl Marx and party theory. *Government and Opposition*, 20 (1), 70–87.

Wagner, P. 1989: Social science and the state in continental Western Europe: the political structuration of disciplinary discourse. *International Social Science Journal*, 41 (4), 509–28.

Walby, S. 1990: *Theorizing Patriarchy*. Oxford: Basil Blackwell.

Waldner, D. 1999: *State Building and Late Development*. Ithaca: Cornell University Press.

Walker, N. 2000: Flexibility within a metaconstitutional frame: reflexions on the future of legal authority. In G. de Búrca and J. Scott, eds, *Constitutional Change in the EU: From Uniformity to Flexibility?* Oxford: Hart Publishing, 9–30.

Walker, R.B.J. 1993: *Inside/Outside: International Relations as Political Theory.* Cambridge: Cambridge University Press.

Wallace, H. 2000: The institutional setting: five variations on a theme. In H. Wallace and W. Wallace, eds., *Policy-Making in the European Union.* Oxford: Oxford University Press, 3–37.

Walters, S. 1996: From here to queer: radical feminism, postmodernism, and the lesbian menace. *Signs,* 21 (4), 830–69.

Walters, W. and Larner, W., eds, 2004: *Global Governmentality: Governing International Spaces.* London: Routledge.

Watson, S. 1990: The state of play: an introduction. In S. Watson, ed., *Playing the State: Australian Feminist Interventions.* London: Verso, 3–20.

Watson, S. 1992: Femocratic feminisms. In M. Savage and A. Witz, eds, *Gender and Bureaucracy.* Oxford: Blackwell, 186–204.

Weber, M. 1948: Politics as a vocation. In idem, *Essays from Max Weber.* London: Routledge and Kegan Paul, 77–128.

Weber M. 1949: *The Methodology of the Social Sciences.* Glencoe, IL: Free Press.

Weber, M. 1978: *Economy and Society, Vol 1.* Berkeley: University of California Press.

Weeks, J. 1986: *Sexuality.* London: Routledge.

Weiler, J.H. 1991: The transformation of Europe. *Yale Law Journal,* 100, 2403–83.

Weiler, J.H. and Wessels, W. 1988: EPC and the challenge of theory. In A. Pijpers, E. Regelsberger, and W. Wessels, eds, *European Political Cooperation in the 1980s.* Dordrecht: Martinus Nijhoff, 229–58.

Weiss, L. 1998: *The Myth of the Powerless State.* Cambridge: Polity.

Weiss, L. 1999: State power and the Asian crisis. *New Political Economy,* 4 (3), 317–42.

Weiss, L. ed. 2003: *States in the Global Economy.* Cambridge: Cambridge University Press.

Weiss, L. and Hobson, J. 1995: *States and Economic Development.* Cambridge: Polity.

Wetherly, P., Barrow, C.W., and Burnham, P., eds, 2007: *Class, Power, and the State: Essays on Ralph Miliband.* Basingstoke: Palgrave, in press.

White, H. 1973: *Metahistory: The Historical Imagination in Nineteenth-Century Europe.* Baltimore: Johns Hopkins University Press.

Whitehead, A.N. 1920: *The Concept of Nature.* Cambridge: Cambridge University Press.

Whitehead, A.N. 1922: *The Principle of Relativity, with Applications to Physical Science.* Cambridge: Cambridge University Press.

Wickham, G. 1983: Power and power analysis: beyond Foucault? *Economy and Society,* 12 (4), 468–98.

Wiener, A. 1996: StaatsbürgerInnenschaft im Kontext: Staatsangehörigkeit und Zugehörigkeit. In T. Kulawik and B. Sauer, eds, *Der halbierte Staat.* Frankfurt: Campus, 105–33.

Williams, F. 1995: Race/ethnicity, gender, and class in welfare states: a frame-work for comparative analysis. *Social Politics*, 2 (2), 126–59.

Willke, H. 1983: *Entzauberung des Staates. Überlegungen zu einer sozietalen Steuerungstheorie*. Königstein im Taunus: Athenäum.

Willke, H. 1986: The tragedy of the state: prolegomena to a theory of the state in polycentric society. *Archiv für Sozial- und Rechtsphilosophie*, 72 (4), 455–67.

Willke, H. 1992: *Ironie des Staates. Grundlinien einer Staatstheorie polyzentrischer Gesellschaft*. Frankfurt: Suhrkamp.

Willke, H. 1996: *Supervision des Staates*. Frankfurt: Suhrkamp.

Wilson, H.T. 1999: Time, space and value: recovering the public sphere. *Time and Society*, 8 (1), 161–81.

Wittrock, B. 1989: Social science and state development – transformations of the discourse of modernity. *International Social Science Journal*, 41 (4), 497–507.

Wodak, R. and Meyer, M., eds. 2001: *Methods of Critical Discourse Analysis*. London: Sage.

Wood, E.M. 1981: The separation of the economic and the political. *New Left Review*, 127, 66–93.

Young, B. 1996: The German state and feminist politics: a double gender marginalization. *Social Politics*, 3 (2–3), 159–84.

Yuval-Davis, N. 1996: Women and the biological reproduction of 'the nation'. *Women's Studies International Forum*, 19 (1–2), 17–24.

Yuval-Davis, N. 1997: *Gender and Nation*. London: Sage.

Zelizer, V.A. 1998: The proliferation of social currencies. In M. Callon, ed., *The Laws of the Markets*. Oxford: Blackwell, 58–68.

Ziebura, G. 1996: Über den Nationalstaat. *Leviathan*, 15 (4), 467–89.

Ziltener, P. 1999: *Strukturwandel der europäischen Integration*. Münster: Westfälisches Dampfboot.

Zürn, M. 1992: Jenseits der Staatlichkeit. *Leviathan*, 15 (4), 490–513.

Index

Note: The index combines names and subjects. Page numbers printed in **bold** refer to a major discussion of a given topic. Specific page numbers (e.g. 5–8) indicate that the discussion continues over the relevant pages; non-specific page numbers indicate several separate references on two (f.) or more (ff.) pages (5f. or 8ff.). The index is thematic so that entries sometimes refer to a relevant theme rather than an exact use of a given word concept or phrase. Authors are indexed only when they are directly quoted or discussed at length not when they are simply cited in support of one or another argument.

natural governing party 98
state party 131
vanguard party 57, 110
see also party politics
political scene 73, 85, 91, 94, 99
political stage 89–91
politicism, 15, 23, 25, 38, 122f.
polymorphous crystallization 148, 158,
 226
see also Vergesellschaftung
polymorphy of gender regimes 163
popular-democratic struggles 28, 31, 119,
 124
popular masses 122f., 127, 131, 135
population 4, 9, 66, 150ff., 199
Portugal 119, 124, 205
post-disciplinarity 22
post-Fordism 14, 24f., 35, 61, 187, 215
post-patriarchy 158ff.
Poulantzas, Nicos 1, 12, 14, 34, 118–19
 alleged abstractionism of 119
 alleged politicism of 23, 122
 anti-economism of 119–21
 on authoritarian statism 131–3
 on capitalism 119–122, 126
 on class power 122, 124, 127–8
 on class struggle 133–6
 on classes 97, 119, 120, 122ff., 130–1
 on democratic transition 119, 138
 on dictatorships 124, 133–4
 on division of labour 119–26 *passim*, 135
 on exceptional regimes 14, 84f., 126,
  129–31, 139
 on fascism 133–4
 and Foucault 118, 120, 124, 128, 138,
  141–7
 on institutional materiality 120f., 123f.,
  126–7, 135–6
 legacy of 137–9
 on mental–manual division of labour 120,
  122, 124, 126, 134, 144
 and Miliband 32, 119, 139
 on nation 127, 134–6
 on periodization 133–4
 regional theory of 3, 32, 121, 246
 on spatio–temporality 134–5
 on state as a social relation 1, 13f., 31f.,
  34, 56, 59, 118, 120–1, **125–6,** 136
 on state power 121–2
 on strategy, tactics 128–9
 on structural selectivity 59, 98, 125, 129
 on violence and law 67, 130,

power 29, 43, 59, 122, 128, 144, 146–7, 149,
 151
 as explanandum or principle of
  explanation 43–5, 230
 see also agency, analytics of power,
  attribution, conjunctural analysis,
  conjuncture, class domination, class
  powers, class struggle, form-
  determination, institutional
  materiality, interests, micro–macro
  problems, microphysics of power,
  Nietzschean hypothesis, parallel power
  networks, power bloc,
  power/knowledge, power networks,
  resistance, state capacities, state power,
  strategic codification of power
  relations, structure and agency,
  violence
power bloc 25, 35, 114, 122ff., 126f., 131, 133f.
power centres 37, 118, 123, 130
 see also centres of resistance in state
power connector, state as 189
power container, state as 5, 105, 166, 189
power/knowledge 50, 65, 67, 126, 142, 144,
 148, 165, 172, 242
power networks 148
predatory state 77
pre-disciplinarity 22, 101
pre-modern patriarchy 163
pretorian rule 83, 93
Prezzolini, Giuseppe – on intellectual
 legacies 137
primitive accumulation 181, 185
Prinz, Arthur – on misleading nature of
 Marx's 1859 *Preface* 84–5
proletarian revolution 86, 99, 181
proletariat 27, 87, 99, 104, 109f., 123

queer theory 18, 70, 72, 158ff., 176, 249

radical democracy 118ff.
real-concrete 226, 232
reduction of complexity 16, 65, 225–8, **229-
 30**, 234–5, 242, 249
 see also complexity
reductionism 141, 233, 238, 247–8
 class 84, 138
 economic 62
 functionalist 141
 semiotic 52
 see also base–superstructure relations,
  epiphenomenalism, essentialism